THE BEAST & THE SOVEREIGN II

THE SEMINARS OF JACQUES DERRIDA

Edited by Geoffrey Bennington & Peggy Kamuf

The Beast & the Sovereign

VOLUME II

Jacques Derrida

Edited by Michel Lisse, Marie-Louise Mallet,
and Ginette Michaud

Translated by Geoffrey Bennington

The University of Chicago Press ‡ CHICAGO AND LONDON

Originally published as *Séminaire: La bête et le souverain,
Volume II (2002–2003)*. © 2010 Éditions Galilée.

Ouvrage publié avec le soutien du Centre national du
livre—ministère français chargé de la culture / This work
is published with support from the National Center of the
Book—French Ministry of Culture.

The University of Chicago Press, Chicago 60637
The University of Chicago Press, Ltd., London
© 2011 by The University of Chicago
All rights reserved. Published 2011.
Paperback edition 2017
Printed and bound by CPI Group (UK) Ltd, Croydon, CR0 4YY

23 22 21 20 19 18 17   2 3 4 5 6

ISBN-13: 978-0-226-14430-6 (cloth)
ISBN-13: 978-0-226-47853-1 (paper)
ISBN-13: 978-0-226-14440-5 (e-book)
DOI: 10.7208/chicago/9780226144405.001.0001

Library of Congress Cataloging-in-Publication Data
Derrida, Jacques.
[Bête et le souverain. English]
The beast and the sovereign / Jacques Derrida; translated by
Geoffrey Bennington.
    p.   cm. — (Seminars of Jacques Derrida; v. 1)
Translation of: Séminaire: la bête et le souverain.
ISBN-13: 978-0-226-14428-3 (cloth: alk. paper)
1. Sovereignty. 2. Power (Social sciences)—Philosophy.
3. Responsibility. 4. Capital punishment. 5. Perjury.
I. Bennington, Geoffrey. II. Title. III. Series: Derrida,
Jacques. Selections. English. 2009; v. 1.
B2430.D483B4813   2009
194—dc22   2009011389

♾ This paper meets the requirements of ANSI/NISO
z39.48-1992 (Permanence of Paper).

CONTENTS

FOREWORD TO THE ENGLISH EDITION

When the decision was made to edit and publish Jacques Derrida's teaching lectures, there was little question that they would and should be translated into English. From early in his career, in 1968, and annually thereafter until 2003, Derrida regularly taught at U.S. universities. It was his custom to repeat for his American audience the lectures delivered to his students in France the same year. Teaching first at Johns Hopkins and then at Yale, he read the lectures in French as they had been written. But from 1987, when he began teaching at the University of California, Irvine, Derrida undertook to lecture in English, improvising on-the-spot translations of his lectures. Recognizing that the greater part of his audience outside of France depended on translation was easier, however, than providing an *ad libitum* English version of his own elegant, complex, and idiomatic writing. In the circumstance, to his evident joy in teaching was often added a measure of suffering and regret for all that remained behind in the French original. It is to the memory of Derrida the teacher as well as to all his students past and still to come that we offer these English translations of "The Seminars of Jacques Derrida."

The volumes in this series are translations of the original French editions published by Éditions Galilée, Paris, and will in each case follow shortly the publication of the corresponding French volume. The scope of the project, and the basic editorial principles followed in establishing the text, are outlined in the "General Introduction to the French Edition," translated here. Editorial issues and decisions relating more specifically to this volume are addressed in an "Editorial Note." Editors' footnotes and other editorial interventions are all translated without modification, except in the case of footnoted citations of quoted material, which refer to extant English translations of the source as necessary. Additional translators' notes have been kept to a minimum. To facilitate scholarly reference, the page numbers of the French edition are printed in the margin on the line at which the new page begins.

Translating Derrida is a notoriously difficult enterprise, and while the translator of each volume assumes full responsibility for the integrity of the translation, as series editors we have also reviewed the translations and sought to ensure a standard of accuracy and consistency across the volumes. Toward this end, in the first phase of work on the series, we have called upon the advice of other experienced translators of Derrida's work into English and wish to thank them here: Pascale-Anne Brault, Michael Naas, Elizabeth Rottenberg, and David Wills.

Geoffrey Bennington
Peggy Kamuf
OCTOBER 2008

The complete edition of Jacques Derrida's seminars and lectures will give the reader the chance of an unprecedented contact with the philosopher's teaching voice. This edition will constitute a new part of his oeuvre, to be distinguished from the books and other texts published during his lifetime or revised by him before his death, and with a clearly different status. It is not certain that Jacques Derrida would have published the seminars as they stand: probably he would have reorganized or rewritten them. Taken as a whole, but also in their relation to Derrida's philosophical oeuvre, these lectures and seminars will constitute an incomparable research tool and will, we believe, give a different experience of his thinking, here linked to his teaching, which was always, both in France and abroad, a truly vital resource of his writing.

The corpus we are preparing for publication is vast. From the beginning of his teaching career, Derrida was in the habit of completely writing out almost all his lectures and seminars. This means that we have at our disposal the equivalent of some fourteen thousand printed pages, or forty-three volumes, on the basis of one volume per academic year. This material can be classified according to a variety of criteria. First, according to the place where the teaching took place: the Sorbonne from 1960 to 1964; the École normale supérieure in the rue d'Ulm from 1964 to 1984; the École des hautes etudes en sciences sociales (EHESS) from 1984 to 2003.[1] Then

---

1. We need to add the American places too: from fall 1968 to 1974 at the Johns Hopkins University in Baltimore, then as visiting professor in the humanities from 1975 to 1986 at Yale University, where he gave each year, in the fall or spring semester, a regular seminar. From 1987 to 2003, Derrida taught regularly at the University of California (Irvine), and at the New School for Social Research, the Cardozo Law School, and New York University (1992–2003). This American teaching (which, with a few exceptions, repeated the Parisian seminar) was given at first in French, but after 1987 most often in English: Derrida would improvise during the session an English version of his text, which he had previously annotated for this purpose.

10   according to the type of teaching: classes with a very variable number of sessions (from one to fifteen) up until 1964; what he always called "seminars" thereafter. Finally—and no doubt most relevantly for the editorial work—according to the tools used: we have handwritten sessions from 1960 to 1970; typescripts, with manuscript annotations and corrections, from 1970 to 1988; electronic files and printouts from 1988 to 2003.

Derrida's seminars, which already had their own style and already attracted a broad and numerous following at the rue d'Ulm (where the choice of subjects and authors, if not the way they were treated, was constrained by the program of the Agrégation),[2] take on their definitive character at the EHESS where, on Wednesdays from 5 p.m. to 7 p.m., a dozen times a year, Jacques Derrida, sometimes improvising a little, would read before a large audience the text of his seminar, entirely written out for each session as the year proceeded. (Add to that a few improvised sessions, sometimes around a reading, and a few discussion sessions.) Henceforth free in his choice of subjects, Derrida launched research projects over periods of several years, which link together in explicit, coherent, and gripping fashion. The great question of philosophical nationality and nationalism (1984–88) leads to that of the "Politics of Friendship" (1988–91), and then to the long series of "Questions of Responsibility" (1991–2003), focusing successively on the Secret (1991–92), on Testimony (1992–95), Hostility and Hospitality (1995–97), Perjury and Pardon (1997–99), and the Death Penalty (1999–2001), with the final two years devoted to "The Beast and the Sovereign" (2001–3).

Jacques Derrida was in the habit of drawing on the abundant material of these seminars for the very numerous lectures he gave every year throughout the world, and often, via this route, parts of the seminars were reworked and published. Several of his books also find their point of departure in the work of the seminar: *Of Grammatology* (1967), for example, in large part develops sessions of the 1965–66 seminar on "Nature, Culture, Writing"; the seminar on "Hegel's Family" (1971–72) is picked up in *Glas* (1974). *Politics of Friendship* (1994) is explicitly presented as the expansion of the first session of the 1988–89 seminar, and there are traces in it of other sessions too. But in spite of these partial convergences and correspondences, the vast majority of the pages written from week to week for the seminar remain unpublished and will incomparably complement the work already

11

2. [Translator's note:] The Agrégation is the notoriously competitive qualifying examination taken by prospective higher-level teachers in the secondary and university systems.

published. Whenever a session was later published by Jacques Derrida, in modified form or not, we will give the reference. We do not consider it appropriate for the edition of the seminars themselves, as original material, to offer a comparative reading of those versions.

As we have already pointed out, the editorial work varies considerably according to the mode of production of the text. For the typewriter period, many handwritten amendments and annotations require a considerable effort of decipherment; the more so for the seminars entirely written in Jacques Derrida's handsome but difficult handwriting, which require laborious transcription. So we shall begin by publishing the seminars of the last twenty years, while beginning preparation of the rest. In all cases, our primary goal is to present the *text* of the seminar, as *written* by Jacques Derrida, *with a view to* speech, to reading aloud, and thus with some marks of anticipated orality and some familiar turns of phrase. It is not certain that Jacques Derrida would have published these seminars, although he occasionally expressed his intention of doing so,[3] but if he had taken up these texts for publication, he would probably have reworked them, as he always did, in the direction of a more written text. Obviously we have not taken it upon ourselves to do that work in his place. As we mentioned above, the reader may wish to compare the original version presented here with the few sessions published separately by Jacques Derrida himself.

Geoffrey Bennington
Marc Crépon
Marguerite Derrida
Thomas Dutoit
Peggy Kamuf
Michel Lisse
Marie-Louise Mallet
Ginette Michaud

3. See, for example, the foreword to *Politiques de l'amitié* (Paris: Galilée, 1994), p. 11; trans. George Collins as *Politics of Friendship* (London: Verso Books, 1997), p. vii.

The seminar entitled "The Beast and the Sovereign" was the last seminar
given by Jacques Derrida and the École des hautes études en sciences sociales (EHESS) in Paris, from fall 2001 to spring 2003.[1] This second volume corresponds to the year 2002–3 and follows on from the first volume
(2001–2) published (in French) by the Éditions Galilée in 2008 (and in English by the University of Chicago Press in 2009). In his presentation of the
seminar intended for his American audience in spring 2003, Derrida recalls
the outline of his argument and announces the guiding motif of the second
year of the seminar:

> Under this title we are pursuing the research from previous years around
> the sovereignty of the nation-state and its onto-theologico-political founda-
> tion. This research was made necessary for us by the question of *capital
> punishment* which always implies the right, for a sovereign power to have
> the life and death of its subjects at its disposal (the right of pardon for ex-
> ample).
>
>   But this reflection on sovereignty will be inflected this year toward the
> great questions of animal life (that of man, said by Aristotle to be a "politi-
> cal animal," and that of the "beasts") and of the treatment, the subjection,
> of the "beast" by "man."
>
>   We shall ask questions about the literary or rhetorical history of the
> *forms* and *genres* (figures, tropes, metonymies, metaphors, allegories, fa-
> bles, theater, etc.) which propose "animal representations" of the political.
> Hobbes's *Leviathan* or La Fontaine's *Fables* would only give two examples
> among many. The question of gender and sexual difference will cross all
> the others.
>
>   We shall also analyze, through the history of the concept of *sovereignty*

---

1. On March 26, 2003, during the tenth session, Derrida twice implies that it is his
intention to pursue his seminar "next year" (see session 10 below). It is worth noting that
Derrida's seminars at the EHESS were of variable length, from one year to three years.

(Bodin, Hobbes, Rousseau, Schmitt, etc.) what tends to associate and dissociate the figure of the sovereign and the beast (which is not exactly the *animal*). Both indeed seem to stand above or at a distance from the law. Both are, in different ways, of course, but in common, outlaws. What then is the law? And right? The sovereign, says Schmitt, is the one who has the right to suspend right.

Referring frequently to the contemporary situation and to the problems of globalization, that affect the logic of nation-state sovereignty, we shall also address the question of rogue states and their leaders who are often, in the political rhetoric of the most powerful states, compared to "beasts."

At stake here, naturally (long before 9/11 which we shall however discuss), are the concepts of *war*—international or civil—according to European law, of *cruelty*, of *terror* and (national and international) *terrorism*, etc.

What was thus begun last year (2002) will be pursued this year with a different inflexion, especially in the latter weeks of the seminar. We shall begin conjoined readings (sometimes parallel, sometimes intersecting) of Defoe's *Robinson Crusoe* on the one hand, and Heidegger's seminar (1929–30) on the animal on the other (*The Fundamental Concepts of Metaphysics: World, Finitude, Solitude*).

In the EHESS yearbook for 2002–3, Derrida again specifies what is at stake in the reflection carried on in this second year of "The Beast and the Sovereign" seminar:

> Following and developing the premises of the research begun the previous year, we focused all our efforts toward the reading and interpretation of two texts that appear in all respects to be as heterogeneous as possible: *Robinson Crusoe* on the one hand, and a famous seminar of Heidegger's on the other (*The Fundamental Concepts of Metaphysics: World, Finitude, Solitude*), and in it more especially the 1929–30 lecture course, which constitutes Heidegger's most systematic and rich treatise on animality, and more precisely on the world for the animal.
>
> For it is in this seminar that we find the three famous "theses"—problematic theses to our eyes, and extensively questioned in our seminar ("the stone is without world [*weltlos*], the animal is poor in world [*weltarm*], man is world-forming [*weltbildend*]").
>
> Sometimes intersecting, sometimes in parallel, these readings aimed at a common focus: the history (especially the political history) of the concept of sovereignty including, inseparably, the sovereignty of man over animal in the pre-colonial England of Defoe (with its religious background studied in *Robinson Crusoe*) and throughout the many diverse and gripping readings of *Robinson Crusoe* through the centuries (Rousseau especially, Kant, Marx and many nineteenth-century political economists, but also Joyce, Virginia

Woolf, Lacan, Deleuze, etc.) and in Heidegger's modern Germany (the beginning of the 1930s).

These two books are also books on solitude, on the so-called "state of nature," on the history of the concept of Nature (especially in Heidegger) in which we began to study the quite essential lexicon (often associated with *physis*), seldom remarked upon and so difficult to translate, of *Walten* (*Gewalt, Umgewalt, Übergewaltigkeit,* etc.) which will flood Heidegger's texts from 1935 onward, and which designates an archi-originary force or violence, of "sovereignty"—as it is sometimes translated—beyond the onto-theological, i.e. beyond the philosophico-political as such; which is obviously never the case in either Defoe or in the rich philosophical, political and religious context that determines his book.

These, broadly put, are the stakes that guided us in readings that were as minute as possible, sometimes appealing to other works by these two authors.[2]

This edition reproduces the written text of the seminar read by Derrida during the sessions that took place at the EHESS in 2002–3. As always, all the sessions of this seminar are entirely written out on computer.[3] This second volume is made up of ten unpublished sessions, with the exception of a fragment of the seventh session, which was used as a lecture at the conference "Maurice Blanchot, Récits critiques," later reprinted with a few changes in the enlarged edition of *Parages.*[4]

The reference text for this edition, which we shall refer to using the word "typescript," is the printout of this seminar as kept by Derrida in his files. There are two copies deposited in the Jacques Derrida archive at the Institut mémoires de l'édition contemporaine (IMEC, Caen): the first (yellow folder) is comprised of the dated sessions numbered 1, 2, 5, 6, 7, 8, and 9; on the cover of the file one can read the following handwritten annotation: "Missing (SF[5]) 3, 4, 10." The second copy (red folder) that Derrida used for his American seminar[6] is complete and is comprised of ten sessions, continuously numbered.[7] Apart from these ten sessions, Derrida also

16

2. Jacques Derrida, "Questions de responsabilité (X. La bête et le souverain)," in *Annuaire de l'EHESS 2002–2003* (Paris: Editions de l'EHESS, 2003), pp. 587–88.

3. Derrida had entitled each of the files of the seminar "hei/foe," followed by the number of the session. See below, session 2.

4. *Parages,* 2nd augmented ed. (Paris: Galilée, 2003).

5. This abbreviation no doubt corresponds to "Séminaire français."

6. Only a few sessions of the seminar were finally given at UC Irvine in March 2003.

7. On the cover of the folder, along with the abbreviated title, "BS—2002-03 (3)," and an illegible crossed-out word, is this handwritten phrase: "ma peur de la mort, désormais sa souffrance [my fear of death, henceforth his or her suffering]." The word "sa" is circled.

devoted two sessions that year to discussions with the participants of the seminar: these took place on February 19 and March 19, 2003.[8] We have not, any more than for the first volume, and for the same reasons, attempted to transcribe these discussions, following the usage most often adopted for the Cerisy conferences and the major conferences devoted to the work of Jacques Derrida.

In the typescript of the seminar, bibliographical indications were usually clearly marked, in abbreviated form; we have specified them and also completed those that were missing.[9] A certain number of the texts quoted were not copied out in the typescript: they appear in it as photocopied pages of books (French texts, translations and texts in the original language), placed by Derrida between the pages of the typescript where he intended to quote and comment on them. These photocopies comprise numerous traces of reading (underlined passages, circled words, various marginal annotations) used by Derrida during the sessions when he was commenting on or translating these passages; we have chosen not to signal these. As with the edition of the first volume of the seminar, we resorted to the recordings of the sessions, to clarify how these passages were broken up, before reinserting them, because in reading them out Derrida often intercalated passages of the original version and the translation of the texts quoted: because of this interweaving of languages that testifies to a sustained interest brought to bear on the question of translation throughout the seminar (especially as regards the analysis of the Heidegger text), we have decided on several occasions to insert these intercalations on the basis of the recording of the session and signaled each of these additions in a note. Otherwise, we have

8. In this session Derrida, who had just finished writing a text entitled "Justices" (at the end of the typescript he notes "Jacques Derrida, Ris-Orangis, March 16 2003") for a conference he was meant to attend in April 2003, alluded to Gerard Manley Hopkins and the question of "selftaste." This keynote address was given on April 18, 2003, at the conference "'J.' Around the Work of J. Hillis Miller," organized by Dragan Kujundžiç and Barbara Cohen at UC Irvine, April 18–19, 2003. This lecture, still unpublished in French, has appeared in English as "Justices," trans. Peggy Kamuf, *Critical Inquiry* 31, no. 3 (Spring 2005): 689–721, and in *Provocations to Reading,* ed. Barbara Cohen and Dragan Kujundžiç (New York: Fordham University Press, 2005), pp. 228–61.

9. [Translator's note:] In the French edition, the "Editorial Note" adds the following: ". . . completed those that were missing, each time marking that fact by adding '(NdÉ) [*note des éditeurs,* editors' note].' All other editorial interventions are similarly marked." This convention is not followed in the English edition, in which all the notes other than those supplied by the translator, which are marked as such, are either simple references (based by the editors on those given in the body of Derrida's typescript, which contains no footnotes), or editors' notes.

used Derrida's own books whenever it was possible to find them in the library at his home in Ris-Orangis. In cases of uncertainty or where we were unable to track them down, we turned to the editions usually thought to be the most reliable. We have checked and where necessary corrected the quotations given by Derrida, rectifying, without marking the fact, what seemed to us to be obvious errors of transcription. On the other hand, we have systematically pointed out—referring to the pages of the published versions—modifications he made to the translations, as these modifications turn out to be particularly significant in the context of this last seminar where the two principal texts analyzed—Daniel Defoe's *Robinson Crusoe* and Heidegger's 1929–30 seminar—are respectively in English and German: the standard annotation "translation modified by . . ." here covers Derrida's many interventions, be they minor (modification, displacement of a word or punctuation mark, addition or removal of italics, etc.) or more consequential. Finally, to close these remarks on references, throughout the seminar Derrida often refers to his earlier work, whether already published or not: we give references when the citation is explicit, even when it refers to the still unpublished corpus of the seminars themselves.

As for the more technical aspects of our work, they are relatively slight. This edition is of the entire text of Derrida's seminar as it was composed and laid out by him, notably as to its sometimes very long sentences and paragraphs. We have also occasionally corrected typing errors, most often corrected by Derrida during the session. Similarly, at a more micrographic level, the punctuation has been preserved; in particular all the brackets, which are Derrida's own.[10] We have however on a few rare occasions made some corrections or minute alterations when the proliferation of signs such as brackets, parentheses, and dashes (or else their absence) made it difficult to follow the argument.

We have kept all the signs of the seminar's oral quality, and especially some "pickups" Derrida placed in brackets. In the same spirit, we have chosen to leave in parentheses some preparatory notes (e.g., "Photocopy all the texts") and stage directions, such as "(Board)," "(Read and comment)," "(Reread)," "(Develop at length)," which give a sense of the rhythm of the seminar, its accents and intonations. On one occasion, at the beginning of the seventh session, we have inserted in curly brackets, on the basis of the recording, a development improvised by Derrida. The recording also allowed us to signal in the notes a certain number of additions by which Derrida made more explicit for his audience some important aspects of his

19

---

10. [Translator's note:] Except for some translator's glosses.

thinking. Taking account of these additions seemed to be necessary in this second volume of the seminar because, in a way that is more marked than in the first, Derrida had placed references to these complements (which are not however systematic)[11] added during the sessions at many points in the typescript. We wanted to provide these additions every time they noticeably added nuance or precision to the development.

In the case of expressions that sometimes recur in the typescript with slight variations (e.g., variable use of capital letters, quotation marks, italic or roman type, optional elisions, etc.), we did not think it appropriate to undertake a systematic harmonization of these variations, insofar as they do not impede the legibility of the text.[12] Also, in the typescript of this seminar, Derrida often uses abbreviations (RC for *Robinson Crusoe,* H for Heidegger, SZ for *Sein und Zeit,* etc.): we have reestablished titles and names and pointed out in a note the very rare cases in which the context did not permit a decision between two or more alternative expansions of an abbreviation—for example, in the case of RC, between the (English or French) title and the name of the character of Defoe's novel. As for the words in angle brackets (e.g., <word>), they are added by us to fill in certain lacunae in the typescript, most often skipped words.[13] Finally, as Derrida was accustomed to doing, there are sometimes some telegraphic notes at the end of a session as to what was to be discussed in future sessions. These are rarer than in the previous year, do not constitute a continuous text, and have not been retained in this edition.[14]

We thank Timothy Bahti for having communicated to us a letter to Jacques Derrida that allowed us to clarify the beginning of the seventh session. We thank Marie-Joëlle St-Louis Savoie for her help with some bibliographical research and Stéphanie Vanasten for her help in revising some of the German passages. We especially warmly thank Georges Leroux for his careful revision of the transliterations from the Greek. On his suggestion, we decided to follow the code used by Emile Benveniste in *Le Vocabulaire des institutions indo-européennes.* Finally, we thank just as warmly Cécile

11. See session 9, notes 18 and 44, and session 10, notes 31 and 41.

12. [Translator's note:] The editors give the following examples: "Séminaire/séminaire, *Walten/walten,* morts vivants/morts-vivants, funérailles/funéraille, phantasme/fantasme, Robinson Crusoe/Robinson Crusoé, etc.)." Not all of these variations survive the process of translation.

13. [Translator's note:] Not all such cases are marked in the translation.

14. With the exception of two sentences indicated by Derrida to be reinserted at specific places in the third session: see session 3 below, notes 16 and 34.

Bourgignon, our faithful collaborator at the Éditions Galilée, for her assiduous and always thoughtful help, for the constant care and remarkable work she has devoted to the editing of both volumes of this seminar.[15]

Michel Lisse
Marie-Louise Mallet
Ginette Michaud

15. [Translator's note:] The translator would also like to thank Seth Wood for his invaluable editorial and bibliographical assistance in the preparation of the English text.

December 11, 2002

I am alone. Says he or says she. I am alone. Let's hear this sentence all alone, 21
followed by a silence without appeal, or a final period. I am alone. Not: I am
alone in being able to do this or that, to say this or that, to experience this or
that, but "I am alone," absolutely. "I am alone" does moreover mean "I am"
absolute, that is absolved, detached or delivered from all bond, *absolutus,*
safe from any bond, exceptional, even sovereign. Taken on its own, this declaration: "I am alone" can, successively or simultaneously, in a given pragmatic situation, with a given intonation, signify sadness or joy, deploration
or triumph: "I am alone," alas, or "I am alone," thank God, alone at last, etc.

I know a sentence that is still more terrifying, more terribly ambiguous
than "I am alone," and it is, isolated from any other determining context, the
sentence that would say to the other: "I am alone with you." Meditate on the
abyss of such a sentence: I am alone with you, with you I am alone, alone in
all the world. Because we're always talking about the world, when we talk
about solitude. And the relation of the world to solitude will be our subject
this year. I am alone with you in the world. That could be either the most
beautiful declaration of love or the most discouraging despair-inducing testimony, the gravest attestation or protestation of detestation, stifling, suffocation itself: it would be all right to be alone, if at least I could be alone
without you. Being alone with myself.

I am alone with myself. 22

Am I for all that *bored?* What does "I'm bored" mean? The French expression "je m'ennuie" is difficult to translate into many languages, with the
exception of German where one can say *sich langweilen.* And *die Lang(e)
weile* will even, no doubt, be at the center of our seminar this year, especially
das Sichlangweilen that Heidegger talks about in a seminar from 1929–30.[1]

1. Martin Heidegger, *Die Grundbegriffe der Metaphysik: Welt-Endlichkeit-Einsamkeit,*
in *Gesamtausgabe. II. Abteilung: Vorlesungen 1923–1944,* vol. 29/30, ed. Friedrich-Wilhem

But what does "s'ennuyer" mean? What does the relation to self of the "s'ennuyer" signify? To be bored [s'ennuyer] does not necessarily mean to bore oneself [s'ennuyer soi-même]. To bore oneself is something quite different from simply being bored, contrary to what [French] grammar might lead you to believe.

Can beasts be bored?

Can the sovereign be bored? Can he *not* be bored? "The King is amused [le roi s'amuse],"[2] they say sometimes, but also "The King is bored." Is one always bored because one is alone or else can one be bored as a group, with others, intersubjectively, as the other guy would say, or else do people bore each other, which is something else, or again, which is something still quite different and almost the contrary, do people sometimes miss each other [s'ennuie-t-on parfois l'un de l'autre]? Was Robinson Crusoe bored? Was he even alone, this man, because this man is a man, a human and a male human (not a woman), let's never forget it; nothing equivalent or similar, analogous, was ever, to my knowledge (but I may be wrong) written about a woman alone: like an island in an island. Was Robinson Crusoe bored? Was he even alone: when, how, to what extent, up until what moment? For the moment I'll abandon these questions on the high seas, we'll see where they come ashore, but you can sense that they are not simple questions of language or one particular language, of semantics or translation.

And I come back to my first words:

"I am alone." Says he or says she. "I am alone."

Could someone (male or female) be alone who could not say or feel an "I am alone"? Could he be alone? Could she be alone? Could one say of him or her that he or she is alone? And could one say of whomever can neither feel nor speak this solitude that he or she is not alone, meaning—meaning

---

von Herrmann (Frankfurt-am-Main: Vittorio Klostermann, 1992 [1983]). This course was given at the University of Freiburg-im-Breisgau during the 1929–30 winter semester. [Translator's note: Martin Heidegger, *The Fundamental Concepts of Metaphysics: World, Finitude, Solitude,* trans. William McNeill and Nicholas Walker (Bloomington and Indianapolis: Indiana University Press, 1995); references will henceforth be given in the text in the form "(H, German page number/English page number)." I have very occasionally made some slight modifications to the translation for the sake of consistency with the translation Derrida uses or improvises.]

2. [Translator's note:] This common saying in French gives its title to a play by Victor Hugo (*Le roi s'amuse,* 1832), which is the basis for Verdi's opera *Rigoletto.* The play is variously translated into English as *The King's Diversion* or *The King Amuses Himself.*

what? Is not alone in a given social bond or else, which is something quite different, is not alone in the sense that there is not even a social bond yet, no being with the other, no community allowing, precisely, the experience or even the manifestation of solitude? So many formidable questions.

Before even proposing to you a sort of protocol for this year's seminar, let's now, by way of an exergue, try out a few sentences, try them out like warm-up notes for one's voice or vocal chords. You will see that these sentences already have a consonance, a resonance with the first of my sentences today: "I am alone" and if I add the complement that often rounds off the "I am alone," i.e. "I am alone in the world," we'll be even closer to what will be the protocol of this year's seminar. In it we shall be speaking of the world, of world in every sense, of every world, no less.

Three or four sentences, then, to seek a first accord between us.

First, a sentence in question form: "What is an island?" [*Qu'est-ce qu'une île?*]

What is an island? [*Qu'est une île?*]

If you hear [*entendez*] this sentence, or these sentences come to you borne by the wind or an echo: "Qu'est-ce qu'une île? Qu'est une île,"[3] if you hear them in French, if you hear them without reading them, you think you understand them, but you are not sure.

24

So long as you do not read them, so long as you do not have access to how they are spelled (*une île:* how do you write "*il(e)*"?), you cannot be sure, without context, almost totally isolated as you are, as though on an island, or a peninsula [*presqu'île*], you cannot be sure of hearing what you hear, i.e. of understanding what comes to your ears. An "il" [*Une "il"*] can designate that insular thing one calls an island [*une île*], the island of beauty,[4] Treasure Island, Belle-Isle or the Ile de Groix. Or *The Island of Despair,* as Robinson Crusoe nicknames it on the very opening page of his journal. You remember, of course, that first page of *The Journal,* dated September 30, 1659:

> I poor miserable *Robinson Crusoe,* being shipwreck'd during a dreadful Storm, in the offing, came on Shore on the dismal unfortunate Island, which I call'd *the Island of Despair,* all the rest of the Ship's Company being

3. [Translator's note:] Both of these are standard question forms in French (the second a little dated and more formal); both would be translated as "What is an island?"

4. [Translator's note:] "L'île de beauté" is a standard French way of referring to the island of Corsica.

drown'd, and my self almost dead. All the rest of that Day I spent in afflict-ing myself at the dismal Circumstances I was brought to, *viz* I had neither Food, House, Clothes, Weapon, or Place to fly to, and in Despair of any Re-lief, saw nothing but Death before me, either that I should be devoured by wild Beasts, murder'd by Savages, or starv'd to Death for Want of Food. At the Approach of Night, I slept in a Tree for fear of wild Creatures; but slept soundly tho'it rained all Night.[5]

25   You already sense that in this single quotation, in this paragraph that opens Robinson's *Journal,* we have all the material we need for our seminar: the reference to wild beasts, to human "Savages" or "wild Creatures," the reduction of the narrator to a state of savage nature, almost that of a beast, since he has no house, clothes or weapon.[6] And he is scared (he sleeps in a tree, having no house, "for fear of wild Creatures"): he <is> scared, that is his basic feeling, like Hobbes's man for whom fear is the primary passion, the one that originally leads to the foundation of the state and to that alli-ance, that "covenant" that, as we were recalling last year, can be signed only among men, according to Hobbes, and with neither God nor beasts.[7] Daniel Defoe, we know, was a reader of Hobbes, among others.

But "Qu'est-ce qu'une île?" "Qu'est une île ?" can also be a play on words artificially misusing homophony: "une 'il,'" feminine conjoined with masculine, the conjunction of an indefinite feminine article (*une*) and the masculine personal pronoun (*il*), *une* which is *il*. *La bête* and *le souverain,* a beast that is a sovereign, for example. Last year we insisted a good deal on
26   the sexual difference between the beast and the sovereign[8] but also on a cer-tain analogy between the beast and[9] the sovereign, the beast that sometimes seems to be the sovereign, like the beast that is outside or above the law.

5. Daniel Defoe, *Robinson Crusoe,* introduction by Virginia Woolf (New York: Mod-ern Library, 2001), p. 65. [Translator's note: Subsequent references to this edition of *Robinson Crusoe* will be given in the text in the form "(RC, page number)."]

6. During the session, Derrida added, "he has nothing of what is habitually called 'what is proper to man.'"

7. See Jacques Derrida, *La bête et le souverain, I (2001–2),* ed. Michel Lisse, Marie-Louise Mallet, and Ginette Michaud (Paris: Galilée, 2008), session 2, pp. 77–91; trans. Geoffrey Bennington as *The Beast and the Sovereign, I* (Chicago: University of Chicago Press, 2009), pp. 46–57.

8. See *La bête et le souverain, I,* session 1.

9. In the typescript, "La bête est le souverain. [The beast is the sovereign.]" [Transla-tor's note: *The Beast and the Sovereign, I,* plays explicitly on the homophony of "est" and "et" in this phrase.]

Qu'est-ce qu'une île?

Qu'est une île?

Let's leave this question isolated, abandon it for a while, leave it floating in the air that is carrying it: we have heard it borne by the wind but we have not yet read it. And let's continue to stroll on the shore where we have just set foot. We would then stumble, *second,* on another sentence, a second sentence, then, as though written on a pebble. This time the sentence is not only audible, like the others, but appears to be legible in that it is written. It appears to be legible, but perhaps it is not so, in the sense we give to "read" and "legible." That sentence would be:

"The beasts are not alone."

Let's act as though the seminar were now starting this way, on an island, in an island, starting with this sententious aphorism: "The beasts are not alone."

We would encounter this sentence too without a context. As though on an island, isolated as though on an island on which we had just come ashore. It would be preceded or followed by no other sentence. It would have the authority and cutting edge of an aphorism, i.e. a sentence that is separated, dissociated, insularized, a verdict, a judgment in the form *S is P*, subject + predicate, a *sententia* inscribed in stone, given over, entrusted to a stone found on the beach, on an island where we would have just come ashore. And we would keep turning over and over this polished stone and its enig-matic sentence ("The beasts are not alone") in order to find the beginning, the end, its hidden meaning, perhaps the signature. "The beasts are not alone." It would look like an encrypted telegram during wartime, or an encoded signal designed to reassure or worry, and that we would be trying to decipher. We would find nothing and spend an infinite amount of time, or at least a very long time, for example a year's seminar, trying to interpret, translate, i.e. project all the possible meanings of this assertion the form of which is as dogmatic as it is negative, the negative grammar of this asser-tion: "The beasts are not alone."

Start and you'll see that one year might not be enough to make a com-plete inventory of all the meanings and all the possible implications of these five words of everyday language, which are beginning to look like the title

27

of a novel we have not yet opened. You would have to read the novel to find out what the title was announcing. The seminar would be that novel. "The beasts are not alone": *S is P*, proposition, subject, copula and predicate, an assertion, of course, but negative in form: "The beasts are not alone," and we should not forget to emphasize the generic or specific plural: "The beasts *are* not alone," and not "The beast *is* not alone." So let's say that it's engraved on a stone, abandoned or placed deliberately on the shore of an island and that we stumbled upon it, that we tripped over it as though it were a stumbling block. Hang onto the stone, it's the example Heidegger takes when, in a seminar that is nowadays quite well known and to which we shall return, he compares the relations to the world of the inanimate, the animal, and man ("The stone has no world," he says, *der Stein ist weltlos,* "The animal is poor in world," *das Tier ist weltarm,* "Man is world-configuring or world-forming," *der Mensch ist weltbildend* [H, 261/176]). The stone is an example of a lifeless thing, and is the only example Heidegger gives in that

28   series. After which, he gives no further example, he says in a general way, with no examples, "the animal" and "man." Why does he take the example of an inanimate thing, why a stone and not a plank or a piece of iron, or water or fire? One of the reasons, no doubt, is that the generality "inanimate," with no example, would have raised the question of life, which Heidegger does not wish to raise here as such, and which would leave hovering the ambiguity of vegetables and plants, which are more animate and living than the stone, and about which one might wonder what Heidegger would have said (the plant, and therefore wood, for example, living wood if not dead wood—but then what is to be said about the dead animal or the dead man, the cadaver?): would Heidegger have said that the plant is *weltlos* like the stone or *weltarm* like the living animal? Let's leave it there for now: the question will catch up with us later. When he takes up again his three questions, Heidegger says at a given moment that the subject of the comparative examination comprises: material things (*materiellen Dinge (Stein)* [stone]), animal (*Tier*), man (*Mensch*) (H, 263/177).

So we stumble on this stone. That's what it is to stumble, to hit against an obstacle, generally a stone that interrupts one's progress and obliges one to lift one's foot. This stumbling block [*pierre d'achoppement*] that speaks to us as if to say "The beasts are not alone" would also set us going and determine the pace of this seminar that, while trying everything in order to get past it, would find itself constantly going round in circles and winding up having to think that in the dry economy of its five words and three functions (subject, copula, attribute), in its negative and plural form, this stumbling block will have become an unavoidable touchstone.

Take note that the point will not merely be to explore the semantics of a discourse, the meaning of each of these words ("beasts," "are," "alone," etc.), but also all the rhetorics and pragmatics, i.e. all the concrete situations, all the contexts, all the gestures that can determine and transform the sense, meaning, or sought-after effect in the inscription of this sentence that one imagines only a human could have written (for example in French) and that only a human could stumble upon while trying to decipher it, like a Robinson Crusoe setting foot for the first time on his Island of Despair.

29

To give only one example among ten thousand of what I mean here by rhetoric, pragmatics, or discursive gesture, one might imagine (one hypothesis among a thousand) that the unknown and invisible signatory, perhaps never to be identified, perhaps dead for an indeterminate length of time, might have meant, and said: "I am a friend of the beasts, there are all over the world friends of the beasts, the beasts are not alone. The beasts must not be alone, long live the struggle for the beasts, the struggle goes on."

But you can just as well imagine his adversary meaning: "The beasts are not alone, they do not need us, or else they do not need friends, etc.," or else "there are already enough of them, too many, even, and they have too many allies and hidden accomplices in this war we have had to wage on them all this time, our war against bestiality and the axis of evil." Those are one or two hypotheses among a thousand others as to the interpretation of this petrified statement that we are here abandoning to its solitude (for it is, like this stone, isolated, insularized, forlorn, singularly solitary). This statement is itself like an island. It is an island that for its part is both bounded by the sea and infinite. Shores without shores. One never gets to its shore. And among all the things we do not know, is whether the sentence is signed "he" or "she," by a man or a woman, which would not be without some impact on its meaning.

These sentences are exergues: I have not yet reached the protocol of this seminar. But before even introducing more directly and less elliptically this year's seminar, especially for those who are following it for the first time, you can already sense that it will have to do with island, insularity, loneliness (it will, if you like, be a seminar on solitude: what do "being alone" and "I am alone" mean?). But as being alone also means being singular, unique, exceptional, set off, separated, we shall have also to say that if the beasts are not alone, a sovereign is always alone (that is both his absolute power and his vulnerability, or his infinite inconsistency). The sovereign is alone insofar as he is unique, indivisible and exceptional, he is the being of exception who, as Schmitt says — and this is his definition of the sovereign — decides

30

on the exception and has the exceptional right to suspend right, thus standing, in his own way, as we were saying last year, like the beasts or the werewolf, outside the law, above the law.[10] The sovereign is alone in exercising sovereignty. Sovereignty cannot be shared, it is indivisible. The sovereign is alone (sovereign) or is not.

Third. The third sentence will be a question: "What do beasts and men have in common?" Even before attempting to respond to this question, we have to notice that these two plurals (beasts, men) are asymmetrical and problematical. Not only because the questioner (i.e. we ourselves) spontaneously and dogmatically classes him or herself among men who are not beasts, in such a manner that the question is posed only from the point of view and the supposed power, the being-able-to-question of the supposed questioner, so-called man; but above all asymmetrical and problematical in that the two plurals do not correspond to two classes or two species, to two comparable sets. All men are supposed to belong to the same species or the same genus, the human species, the human race, whereas the beasts—even if they belong to the animal realm, the realm of living beings, like man, "the beasts" designates a set with no other unity, any more than that of said animal which has no other supposed unity than a negative one, or one supposed to be negative: namely that of not being a human being. But there is no other positively predicable unity between the ant, the snake, the cat, the dog, the horse, the chimpanzee—or the sperm whale. One can moreover, in all good sense, say at least three different if not incompatible things, according to the chosen angle, about the community or otherwise of the world.
31 1. Incontestably, animals and humans inhabit the same world, the same objective world even if they do not have the same experience of the objectivity of the object. 2. Incontestably, animals and humans do not inhabit the same world, for the human world will never be purely and simply identical to the world of animals. 3. In spite of this identity and this difference, neither animals of different species, nor humans of different cultures, nor any animal or human individual inhabit the same world as another, however close and similar these living individuals may be (be they humans or animals), and the difference between one world and another will remain always unbridgeable, because the community of the world is always constructed, simulated by a set of stabilizing apparatuses, more or less stable, then, and never natural, language in the broad sense, codes of traces being designed, among all living beings, to construct a unity of the world that is always de-

10. See *La bête et le souverain, I,* session 1, pp. 37–38 [pp. 16–17].

constructible, nowhere and never given in nature. Between my world, the "my world," what I call "my world"—and there is no other for me, as any other world is part of it—between my world and any other world there is first the space and the time of an infinite difference, an interruption that is incommensurable with all attempts to make a passage, a bridge, an isthmus, all attempts at communication, translation, trope, and transfer that the desire for a world or the want of a world, the being wanting a world will try to pose, impose, propose, stabilize. There is no world, there are only islands. That is one of the thousand directions in which I would be <tempted> to interpret the last line of a short and great poem by Celan: "Die Welt ist fort, ich muss dich tragen,"[11] a poem of mourning or birth that I do not have time to read with you: the world has gone, the world has gone away, the world is far off, the world is lost, there is no world any more (to sustain us or ground [*fonder*] the two of us like a ground [*sol*]), I must carry you (either in me as in mourning, or else in me as in birth (for *tragen* is also said of the mother carrying a child, in her arms or in her womb). We are *weltlos*, I can only carry you, I am the only one who can and must carry you, etc.; but are we *weltlos*, without world, as Heidegger says of the stone and the material thing that they are *weltlos*?—clearly not. So how are we to think the absence of world, the non-world? A non-world that is not *immonde* [filthy, revolting]? But scarcely have I said that than I must—it is time to do so since we are going to talk a lot about the world this year—call or recall your attention to this anything but insignificant collusion between at least two senses of the Latin *mundus*, between the adjective *mundus* and two nouns *mundus*, from which the French *monde* clearly comes. The adjective *mundus* (*a, um*) means proper, clean, elegant (by opposition with *immundus: immonde*, dirty, impure, foul, abject); and the noun *immundus* means the absence of ornament; the verb *mundo, mundare* means to clean, to purify, as in French *émonder* means to clean, to take away impurities or dead branches, parasites, etc. This, then, in the lineage of the adjective *mundus* (proper). Now there are two masculine nouns, *mundus, mundi*, one of which means

32

11. Paul Celan, "*Grosse, Glühende Wölbung*," in *Atemwende* (Frankfurt-am-Main: Suhrkamp, 1967), p. 93. Derrida commented at length on the import of this line, especially in *Chaque fois unique, la fin du monde* (Paris: Galilée, 2003); *The Work of Mourning*, ed. and trans. by Pascale-Anne Brault and Michael Naas (Chicago: University of Chicago Press, 2003); and in *Béliers: Le dialogue ininterrompu: Entre deux infinis, le poème* (Paris: Galilée, 2003); "Rams: Uninterrupted Dialogue between Two Infinities: The Poem," trans. Thomas Dutoit and Philippe Romanski, in *Sovereignties in Question: The Poetics of Paul Celan*, ed. Thomas Dutoit and Outi Pasanen (New York: Fordham University Press, 2005).

the world, the universal, the globe, or the sky, or the inhabited world, some-times hell, and later, in Christian culture, the created world, the secular world (we shall go back over all this); the other noun *mundus, mundi,* a homonym and quasi-synonym means toiletries (especially women's), orna-ments, finery; but these two apparently different meanings or uses are in-trinsically linked, as in the Greek *cosmos,* which also means the world, but also arrangement, cosmetic decoration. The world as totality of beings is also an order that is appropriate, proper, a good arrangement, a harmony or a beauty. So that the *immonde,* while not being absence of world, in the sense of *Weltlosigkeit,* is nonetheless not totally foreign to this meaning. Of course these semantic data are Greco-Latin, and I do not believe they are to be found in *Welt* or *world.*[12] At least to my knowledge, and even if the idea of order or system, or organized whole, is implicitly present in both words (*Welt* and "world": OED: "organised system of the universe.")

33   Once we have taken this type of precaution, once we have given up on saying anything sensible and acceptable under the general singular con-cept of "the" beast or "the" animal, one can still assert at least that so-called human living beings and so-called animal living beings, men and beasts, have in common the fact of being living beings (whatever the word "life," *bios* or *zoē,* might mean, and supposing one has the right to exclude from it vegetables, plants and flowers); and whatever the difficulty we have in thinking, conceiving life, the limits of life, becoming-alive or dead, we can believe that these living beings have in common the finitude of their life, and therefore, among other features of finitude, their mortality in the place they inhabit, whether one calls that place world or earth (earth including sky and sea) and these places that they inhabit in common, where they co-habit, and *inhabiting* and *co-habiting* meaning things that are perhaps still problematic, and different from one living being to another, taking into ac-count what one understands by world or earth; similarly all these finite, and therefore mortal, living beings have a certain relation to death, whatever the interpretations we give (huge problems) of their respective relations to death, and even if, following Heidegger, we were to say (which I never do) that animals do not die, properly speaking, and have no relation, *properly speaking,* to death *as such*. Without entering again into this zone of question-ing (I have done so elsewhere[13] and will do so again) no one will deny (even

12. [Translator's note:] Here and in the next sentence, the word "world" is in English in Derrida's text.

13. See among other texts, *Apories: Mourir — s'attendre aux "limites de la vérité"* (Paris: Galilée, 1996), p. 132; trans. Thomas Dutoit as *Aporias* (Stanford, Calif.: Stanford Uni-

Heidegger does not deny) that all living beings, humans and animals, have a certain experience of what we call death. Indeed Robinson names death three times on the first page of his journal:

> . . . on the dismal unfortunate Island, which I call'd the *Island of Despair,* all the rest of the Ship's Company being drown'd, and myself almost dead.
>
> All the rest of that Day [. . .], saw nothing but Death before me, either that I should be devour'd by wild Beasts, murther'd by Savages, or starv'd to Death for Want of Food. (RC, 65)

So our seminar will have as its horizon not only the questions of soli-   *34*
tude, loneliness, insularity, isolation and therefore exception, including the sovereign exception. It will have as its horizon the questions of what "in-habit," "cohabit," "inhabit the world" mean—and therefore the question of what *world* means. The world as a great traditional theme of metaphys-ics, and of theology, the world as presupposition of what is today called globalization [*mondialisation*], but also the world of phenomenological and ontological meditations, from Husserl to Heidegger, in the knowledge (I'll come back to this in a moment) that Heidegger, precisely, inscribed his treatment of the animal in an analysis of the *world,* to which we shall be returning as closely as possible (¹⁴this is the famous proposition I was men-tioning a moment ago, that of the 1929–30 seminar entitled *Welt, Endlich-keit, Einsamkeit,* currently translated as *World, Finitude, Solitude,* and the triple proposition, the triple *thesis* (for Heidegger, unusually for him, pres-ents this as theses), the triple thesis around which we shall not cease turning this year ("the stone is without world, the animal is poor in world, man is world-configuring"), this triple "thesis" responds, as it were, to one of the three questions of the book, *world, finitude and loneliness, isolation, solitude (die drei Fragen: Was ist Welt? Was ist Endlichkeit? Was ist Vereinzelung?).*¹⁵
The second chapter of Part II, "The Beginning of Metaphysical Question-   *35*
ing with the Question of World," in §42, which announces the three guid-ing theses ("the stone is without world," "the animal is poor in world," "man is world-configuring"), opens thus: "We begin with the first of our three questions: *What is world?*" (*"Wir beginnen mit der ersten der drei Frage: Was ist Welt?"*) (H, 261/176).

---

versity Press, 1993), p. 75; *L'animal que donc je suis,* ed. Marie-Louise Mallet (Paris: Galilée, 2006), pp. 196ff.; trans. David Wills as *The Animal That Therefore I Am* (New York: Fordham University Press, 2008), pp. 143ff.

14. This parenthesis does not close in the typescript.

15. Heidegger poses these three questions several times in his seminar, especially in Pt. II, chap. 2.

We shall return in detail to the trial or process [*le procès ou le processus*] of this questioning as to the world. Heidegger's solitude. Gadamer notes in one of his essays entitled "Destruction and Deconstruction,"[16] that when he, Gadamer, was himself a student, Heidegger, then a young professor, had burst into the realm of thought by the power of his language; and that, for example, writes Gadamer, "Already in 1920, as I myself can testify, a young thinker—Heidegger to be exact—began to lecture from a German university podium on what it might mean to say '*es weltet*': it worlds [it makes world, it worldifies, becomes world, globalizes itself (in a sense very different from the current usage of the vocabulary of globalization, but perhaps always naively presupposed by it)]," Gadamer adds that this "was an unprecedented break with the solid and dignified, but at the same time scholasticized, language of metaphysics that had become completely alienated from its own origins. What Heidegger was doing signaled a profound linguistic event in its own right, and at the same time the achievement of a deeper understanding of language in general."[17]

Later, as you know, for example in his *Introduction to Metaphysics* (1935), Heidegger will go further—to the point of saying, for example, that *Die Welt weltet,*[18] or, more precisely, that in certain conditions, *keine Welt mehr weltet,* the world no longer worlds, no longer globalizes, etc. He even says that the originary *welten,* the becoming-world, the originary worlding ("le mondant," as G. Kahn translates it) *das ursprüngliche Weltende, die physis,* falls to the rank of a model for imitation, when the being becomes an object. Remember that for Heidegger—because we'll need to think seriously about this—*physis* is not yet objective nature but the whole of the originary world in its appearing and in its originary growing [*poussée originaire*]. It is toward this originary "world," this *physis* older than the objective nature of the natural sciences or of post-Cartesian metaphysics that we must turn our thought in order to speak anew and differently about the being-in-the-world of man or of *Dasein* and animals, of their differential

36

16. Hans-Georg Gadamer, "*Destruktion* and Deconstruction," trans. Geoff Waite and Richard Palmer, in *Dialogue and Deconstruction: The Gadamer-Derrida Encounter,* ed. Diane P. Michelfelder and Richard Palmer (Albany: SUNY Press, 1989), pp. 102–13.

17. Ibid., p. 103.

18. Martin Heidegger, *Einführung in die Metaphysik* (Tübingen: Max Niemeyer Verlag, 1976), p. 48; trans. Gregory Fried and Richard Polt as *Introduction to Metaphysics* (New Haven, Conn., and London: Yale University Press, 2000), p. 66. [Translator's note: In the following sentence Derrida refers to the French translation by Gilbert Kahn (Paris: PUF, 1958), p. 73.]

relation to this world that is supposed to be both common and not common to them.

So much for the exergues and the first accords we are looking for. I move now to the protocol. Given that the title of this seminar, *The Beast and the Sovereign,* has not changed since last year, and that its general perspective and problematic remain the same, I owe you a few, very preliminary explanations as to the new orientation that I nonetheless want to give it, the new rules, methods, techniques, and ways of doing things that I would like to try out.

I shall, of course, have to talk in at least two directions at once: on the one hand, toward those who do me the friendship and honor of having followed this seminar for more than one year and who therefore followed last year's, and on the other, toward those who are here for the first time. And so, on the one hand, what I am going to do will take into account last year's premises, which some of you will recognize. But I shall not go back, I shall not propose any rhetorical transition, and I'll do my best to make the seminar that's starting now intelligible without those premises and thus as independent as possible in its beginning and its developments. On the other hand, instead of having many points of focus and approaching many problematic motifs, many corpuses, as I did last year, I shall do my best to gather our reflection and our readings around two great texts, to isolate like 37 islands two texts that in my view are major texts, which we shall read as closely as possible, as faithfully but, as always, as freely as possible. We shall read them as faithfully and as freely as possible but on the one hand doing our best to keep to our heading [*cap*], if you will, the heading nicknamed by our title, *The Beast and the Sovereign,* if indeed there is a heading, and the point of a heading, for with a problematic sovereignty it is the figure of the heading, the *cap,* the *caput,* the head, the captain of the ship, the chief, the capital that we are questioning, and not only that of another heading but of an other of the heading.[19] But in keeping the heading in view, if not at bay, we shall read these two texts according to an economy that I do not yet see clearly. As one year will not suffice for us to do more, we shall only sketch out a selective reading—and therefore a finite and insufficient reading—of these two texts; and I would be quite unable today to say if one of

19. [Translator's note:] Alluding to a distinction between an "autre cap" and an "autre du cap" first made in *L'autre cap* (Paris: Minuit, 1991), pp. 21–22; trans. Pascale-Anne Brault and Michael Naas as *The Other Heading: Reflections on Today's Europe* (Bloomington: Indiana University Press, 1992), pp. 15–16.

the two will be read in the margins of the other. It is quite possible that both of them, given their difference, the radical heterogeneity of the one to the other, and given that everything separates and isolates them one from the other—their period, their status, their language—it is quite possible that we shall have to read both of them in the margin, the one in the margin of the other and both of them in the margin of the text or the path traced out by this seminar itself.

So as not to make you wait any longer, the two works I isolate thus—you've seen them coming.

First. First corpus. On the one hand we have *Robinson Crusoe,* by Daniel Defoe, which you have all read but that I ask you to reread, as I have, while thinking about the subject of our seminar, *The Beast and the Sovereign.* The idea and the desire to reread this book more than fifty or sixty years after a first childhood reading came to me from one of my American students, John Williams, whom I thank here, who had of his own accord linked his reading of this book to the seminar I gave last April at Irvine, on the beast and the sovereign.[20] Even if I do not reread this book the way he did—very intelligently, moreover—without him I would not have had the desire and the pleasure of rediscovering this book—but as though for the first time, with new eyes—this book and its history, its precursors and its descendants. You know that this book appeared in 1719; Defoe was already fifty-nine and had published a great deal (in particular, in 1710, an *Essay upon Public Credit* that Marx cites several times in *Capital,* once on the law of capitalist accumulation,[21] another time to accuse Malthus of having plagiarized Defoe).[22] This fiction that *Robinson Crusoe* remains had as a referent or real, non-fictional springboard the memoires of Alexander Selkirk, a Scottish seaman. Not a model, but a sort of basic plot or pretext. We'll have a lot to say about its political context and its reception (by Rousseau, Marx, etc.). But today I shall isolate, to give you the measure of its singularity and of the way it has been evaluated in our modernity, two exceptional judgments, those of James Joyce and Virginia Woolf.

20. Derrida gave the seminar *The Beast and the Sovereign, I* at UC Irvine in April 2002.

21. Cf. Karl Marx, *Das Kapital: Kritik der politischen Ökonomie,* vol. 1, book 1, "Der Produktions proceß des Kapitals," in Karl Marx and Friedrich Engels, *Werke* (Berlin: Dietz Verlag, 1972), 23:154, n. 104; trans. Ben Fowkes as *Capital: A Critique of Political Economy* (New York: Random House, 1977), p. 238, n. 55.

22. Ibid., p. 644, n. 75 [p. 766, n. 6].

Both grant an extraordinary and incommensurable place both to Defoe and to the event of this book, which was often held to be the first novel in English.

As to Defoe the novelist, Joyce writes the following, which is very political, very preoccupied with nationality, national independence and primacy in literature—and it looks as though in the lines I am going to read that Joyce was congratulating Defoe for emancipating English literature, for making it accede to a certain national sovereignty. Just before, Joyce had noted that until Defoe, the "great English nation" had been reflected only in variegated, not to say alienated, fashion, for example in Shakespeare whose heroes are "a boorish peasant; a strolling player; a tatterdemalion, half lunatic half fool; a gravedigger." All Shakespeare's heroes are metics [*métèques*], who come "from over the seas and over the mountains": "Othello, a Moorish leader; Shylock, a Venetian Jew; Caesar, a Roman; Hamlet, a prince of Denmark; Macbeth, a Celtic usurper; Juliet and Romeo, residents of Verona." The only true and authentic Englishman is Falstaff, "the fat knight of the monstrous belly."[23] And Joyce continues by denouncing Chaucer, whose *Canterbury Tales* are no more than a version of the *Decameron,* and Milton, whose *Paradise Lost* is supposedly a transposition of the *Divine Comedy.* Finally Defoe came:

> [Defoe was] the first English author to write without imitating or adapting foreign works, to create without literary models and to infuse into the creatures of his pen a truly national spirit, to devise for himself an artistic form which is perhaps without precedent.[24]

So you have noticed Joyce's emphasis on the national character, the nationalist virtue, even, of this work (reread and emphasize "English . . . foreign works, truly national spirit"). Joyce knew all about the history of nations and nationalisms in languages and literature. And this remark puts us on the track of a political or even theologico-political reading of *Robinson Crusoe,* not to mention the problematic of sovereignty that we will systematically select in it. What's more, this is not Joyce's only political judgment on *Robinson Crusoe.* Joyce also reads in *Robinson Crusoe* both the representation of a national type, the national type of a rational animal that an Eng-

39

40

23. James Joyce, "Daniel Defoe," ed. and trans. from the Italian by Joseph Prescott, *Buffalo Studies,* 1, no. 1 (1964): 1–25 (p. 7). [Translator's note: I have made some very slight alterations to Prescott's translation in the light of the original Italian text and the French translation used by Derrida.]
24. Ibid.

lishman is (and Joyce knew what he was talking about when he spoke in English about the English) and the prefiguration of an imperialist, colonialist sovereignty, the first herald of the British empire, the great island setting off to conquer other islands, smaller islands (like Ireland) but above all islands bigger than it, like Africa, New Zealand or Australia (although Joyce does not name them here). Listen to him. (Read and comment on politics <in> Joyce)

> The true symbol of the British conquest is Robinson Crusoe, who, cast away on a desert island, in his pocket a knife and a pipe, becomes an architect, a carpenter, a knifegrinder, an astronomer, a baker, a shipwright, a potter, a saddler, a farmer, a tailor, an umbrella-maker, and a clergyman. He is the true prototype of the British colonist, as Friday (the trusty savage who arrives on an unlucky day) is the symbol of the subject races. The whole Anglo-Saxon spirit is in Crusoe: the manly independence; the unconscious cruelty; the persistence; the slow yet efficient intelligence; the sexual apathy; the practical, well-balanced religiousness; the calculating taciturnity. Whoever rereads this simple, moving book in the light of subsequent history cannot help but fall under its prophetic spell.
>
> Saint John the Evangelist saw on the island of Patmos the apocalyptic ruin of the universe and the building of the walls of the eternal city sparkling with beryl and emerald, with onyx and jasper, with sapphire and ruby. Crusoe saw only one marvel in all the fertile creation around him, the print of a naked foot in the virgin sand. And who knows if the latter is not more significant than the former?[25]

This is taken from a lecture that Joyce never published in his lifetime, the manuscript and typescript of which are preserved in the USA (at Buffalo and Cornell) where they were published in 1964. We know that Joyce was a great admirer of Defoe—he had read all of him and owned his complete works, which was true, he used to say, of only three other authors in the world: Flaubert, Ben Jonson, and Ibsen. And—this is interesting from the national and nationalist point of view—he called Robinson Crusoe the English Ulysses (not Irish but English, the English counterpart to any Ulysses, I suppose his in particular).[26] Moreover *Robinson Crusoe* is very present in Joyce's *Ulysses*. For example in the fourteenth part, during a monologue of Bloom's in which there is much talk of mourning and burial,

41

25. Ibid., pp. 24–25.
26. See Frank Budgen, *James Joyce and the Making of Ulysses* (1934) (Oxford: Oxford University Press, 1972), p. 186. [Translator's note: Quoted by Joseph Prescott in his introduction to Joyce's "Daniel Defoe."]

FIRST SESSION ‡ 17

of gravediggers in *Hamlet*, but also of whoever always digs his own grave, Bloom adds: "We all do [dig our own grave]. Only man buries. No ants do.[27] First thing strikes anybody." [An error by Joyce who thinks like everyone else that beasts do not die in the proper sense, do not wear mourning and do not bury.] Bloom continues: "Bury the dead. Say Robinson Crusoe was true to life. [Another translation, in the Pléiade, has "était un homme de la nature":[28] basically like the beasts . . .]. Well then Friday buried him. Every Friday buries a Thursday if you come to look at it."

> *O, poor Robinson Crusoe*
> *How could you possibly do so?*[29]

Other works of Defoe's are also at work in *Ulysses*, such as *Moll Flanders* behind Molly.

Virginia Woolf, in a long article that serves as an introduction to one of my editions of *Robinson Crusoe* (Modern Library Classics [New York: Random House, 2001])—an Introduction that I cannot quote at length here, as one should—[Virginia Woolf] explains that *Robinson Crusoe* is a "masterpiece" not only because Daniel Defoe was able to maintain and impose his own perspective on us in a consistent way, but because, in doing so, he annoys us, "thwarts us and flouts us at every turn" (RC, xiv). And to show this, she describes the way our expectation is disappointed: we expect an experience of solitude, of isolation far from humans, on a remote island with only sunrises and sunsets. But everything we are shown is anything but states of mind and solitude. There is no sunrise or sunset, no soul or solitude, only "a large earthenware pot" (RC, xiv). And Virginia Woolf tells us in two pages everything there is not, everything that does not exist on this island and in this book: God, nature and death: "God does not exist," and a little later, "Nature does not exist," and further on "Death does not exist. Nothing exists except an earthenware pot. Finally, that is to say, we are forced to drop our own preconceptions and to accept what Defoe himself wishes to give us" (RC, xv).

27. This is a mistaken transcription for "No ants too." Cf. James Joyce, *Ulysses* (Harmondsworth: Penguin Books, 1960), p. 111.

28. [Translator's note:] The translation to which Derrida refers is *Ulysses*, trans. Auguste Morel, assisted by Stuart Gilbert, revised by Valery Larbaud and the author, in *Œuvres. Volume II*, ed. Jacques Aubert, in collaboration with Michel Cusin, Daniel Ferrer, Jean-Michel Rabaté, André Topia, and Marie-Danièle Vors (Paris: Gallimard, 1995), p. 122. The translation of this phrase is in fact: "c'était l'homme de la nature."

29. *Ulysses*, p. 111.

This is false, of course, as we shall see, and it sounds like the (just as false) newspaper descriptions you see of deconstruction today: "Nothing exists, not God, not nature, not death, and we must drop our own preconceptions."[30] It is false but it is interesting to see someone read *Robinson Crusoe* as a sort of "deconstruction" creating a desert, on an island, a desert island, deserted by humans, by the human, creating a desert, then, of all our habits of thought and all our prejudices, all our preconceptions.

Instead of adding a second corpus to this one (I'll specify which one in a moment), we could have been content to read *Robinson Crusoe* (one year would not have sufficed). In doing so, we would have followed Rousseau's advice, the advice given in *Emile*. The first book, "the first that my Emile will read," the "only one" that "for a long time will compose his entire library," will be *Robinson Crusoe*.[31] There too, there's a sort of *tabula rasa,* the island as desert, the phenomenological deconstruction of all prejudices and socio-cultural stratifications, and a naive, native, natural originary return to the things themselves before all the historical perversions of taste, and the social and inegalitarian dissimulations and simulacra, everything Rousseau here calls "prejudices." And it will be, as you'll hear, Robinson before Friday, or more precisely before Friday is no longer sufficient for him. In the long passage I am going to read, the preceptor begins by saying "I hate books," which means that the exception made for *Robinson Crusoe* will consist in holding this book to be *both* the first and only book worthy of the name, *and* a non-book. As, on the other hand, among all the virtues of this book, there will be that of serving for, I quote, "both amusement and instruction," you can always conclude that I have chosen this text for this year because it is the first book and it is not a book, but the world itself, but above all because it amuses me and I hope will amuse us, and I find it even more amusing, even if some may find this in dubious taste, to read it with one hand, with in the other hand a book as different, heterogeneous or even as allergic to it as a particular seminar of Heidegger's on world, finitude, solitude and the animal, about which I shall talk to you in a moment. Here then is one of Rousseau's reverential references to *Robinson Crusoe* in Book III of *Emile:* (Read and comment on pp. 238–40 of *Emile* (photocopy))

30. [Translator's note:] The words "drop our own preconceptions" are in English in the text.

31. Jean-Jacques Rousseau, *Émile ou de l'éducation,* chronology and introduction by Michel Launay (Paris: Garnier-Flammarion, 1966), Book III, p. 239. [Translator's note: my translation of Rousseau here and throughout.]

I hate books: they only teach you how to talk about what you do not know. It is said that Hermes engraved on columns the elements of the sciences, so as to shelter his discoveries from a flood. If he had imprinted them firmly in men's heads, they would have been preserved there by tradition. Well-prepared brains are the monuments in which human knowledge is most securely engraved. Would there not be some means of bringing together all these lessons scattered in all these books, of bringing them under a common object that would be easy to see, interesting to follow, and that could serve as a stimulus, even at this age? If one can invent a situation in which all the natural needs of man are shown to the mind of a child in sensory form, and in which the means of providing for these same needs develop successively with the same facility, it is by the vivid and naïve depiction of this state that one must give his imagination its first exercise.

45

Oh, ardent philosopher, I already see your imagination light up. Do not go to any expense: this situation has already been found, it has been described, and without wishing to wrong you, described much better than you could describe it yourself, or at least with more truth and simplicity. Since we absolutely must have books, there is one that to my mind provides the most felicitous treatise of natural education. This book is the first that my Emile will read; it is the only one that for a long time will compose his entire library, and it will always have a distinguished place in it. It will be the text to which all our conversations on the natural sciences will serve merely as commentary. During our progress it will serve as a test for the state of our judgment; and, so long as our taste is not spoiled, reading it will always please us. What then is this marvelous book? Is it Aristotle? Is it Pliny? Is it Buffon? No: it is *Robinson Crusoe*.

Robinson Crusoe on his island, deprived of the assistance of his fellows and the instruments of all the arts, and nevertheless providing for his subsistence and his preservation, and even procuring for himself a kind of well-being: there is an object that is interesting for all ages, and that there are a thousand ways to make agreeable to children. This is how we make real the desert island that at first served me as a point of comparison. This state is not, I agree, that of social man: most probably it is not to be that of Emile; but it is on the basis of this state that he must appreciate all others. The surest way of rising above prejudices and ordering one's judgments on the true relations of things is to put oneself in the place of a man who is isolated, and judge everything as this man must himself judge everything, with respect to his own utility.

This novel, with all its surplus fat removed, and beginning with Robinson's shipwreck near his island, and ending with the arrival of the vessel that comes to rescue him, will be both Emile's amusement and his instruction during the period of which we are speaking here. I want his head to be turned by it, for him to be constantly occupied with his castle, his goats, his plantings; that he learn in detail, not in books, but with things, all one needs to know in such a case; that he think himself to be Robinson; that he see himself clothed in animal skins, wearing a large bonnet, carrying a big saber, the whole grotesque outfit of the character, except for the parasol, which he will not need. I want him to worry about the measures to be taken, if this or that were to be lacking, to examine the conduct of his hero, to seek to see if he has omitted anything, whether there was not something better he could have done; to mark attentively all his mistakes, and to profit from them so as not to fall into them himself in a similar case; for do not doubt that he has the project of setting up a comparable establishment; this is the true castle in the air of that happy age, in which one knows no happiness other than the necessary, and freedom.

46

What a resource this folly is for a skilful man, who knew how to give rise to it only to turn it to good use! The child, in a hurry to stock up for his island, will be even keener to learn than the master is to teach. He will want to know everything that is useful, and only that; you will no longer need to guide him, you will only have to hold him back. What is more, let us hasten to set him up on this island, while he limits his happiness to it; for the day is approaching when, if he does still want to live there, he will no longer want to live there alone, and when Friday, who now scarcely moves him, will no long be sufficient for him.[32]

But to link firmly our reading to come of *Robinson Crusoe* to our problematic of sovereignty, I shall cite another text of Rousseau's that this time invokes *Robinson Crusoe* not as the experience of an exceptional insular originarity that is freed from all prejudices, but rather <as> sovereign mastery, <as> the monarchy of a Robinson who commands everything on his island, on an island during the time he lives on it alone, the sole inhabitant of his world. This passage is to be found at the end of Chapter II of the first book of the *Social Contract,* just before the chapter on the Right of the Stronger that we read closely last year, just after the critiques of Grotius, Hobbes and Aristotle that we also read last year.[33] What does Rousseau say, not without irony? He says that he has avoided talking about a certain number of natural or mythical sovereigns, as it were: Adam or Noah, King Adam or Emperor Noah, avoided doing so through moderation, for, from filiation to filiation, he could have judged himself to be the natural inheritor of this King and this Emperor and consider himself to be "the legitimate king of the human race." And this is when he mentions *Robinson Crusoe:*

32. Ibid., pp. 238–40.
33. *La bête et le souverain, I,* session 1, pp. 33, 42–43 [pp. 11, 20–21].

I have said nothing of King Adam, nor of Emperor Noah, the father of three great monarchs who divided up the universe, as did the children of Saturn, that people thought they recognized in them. I hope you will appreciate this moderation; for descending directly from one of these princes, and perhaps from the elder branch, what do I know but if, by verification of title, I might not find myself the legitimate king of the human race? However this may be, one cannot disagree that Adam was the sovereign of the world, like Robinson of his island, so long as he was its only inhabitant, and what was convenient in this empire was that the monarch, assured of his throne, need fear neither rebellion, nor war, nor conspirators.[34]

47

This absolute political sovereignty, "Adam sovereign of the world like Robinson of his island," this absolute sovereignty of man over the entire world, i.e. a sovereignty without obstacle and therefore without enemy — and therefore, Schmitt would say, without politics — this sovereignty which is absolute because it is pre-political, the hyperbolical, pre-political or ultra-political sovereignty that is the prize of solitude or isolation, of loneliness or of absolute insularity (all of this before Friday), is sovereignty before the nation-state, the sovereignty of the free and self-determined, self-determining individual, that of the citizen without a state or of the citizen before citizenship, or again of a citizen who is, all alone and immediately, the state itself, the sovereignty of the state-of-citizen, of the citizen-state. Although it corresponds here to a myth or a legend, to a dated literary fiction, the structure that it describes, and that Rousseau describes here, does correspond to what we still think of today when we speak of the absolute freedom of the citizen, who decides sovereignly, for example in a voting booth [isoloir] (the booth is an island), as to his political choice, a freedom and a sovereignty held to be inalienable in democracy, whatever the contradiction or the conflicts between this supposed sovereignty of the citizen subject to the law and the sovereignty of the nation-state.

Now I invite you to reread the whole of Rousseau's *Discourse on the Origin of Inequality* . . . Not only the pages from the first part on the animal and savage man (do read those pages to which we could — though we won't — devote this whole seminar), but especially reread, even before the preface, that sort of initial statement that Rousseau addresses to the Republic of Geneva (Rousseau who was also, as we should not forget, the author, between 1760 and 1769, of a *Project for a Constitution for Corsica,* a work

48

34. Jean-Jacques Rousseau, *Du contrat social ou principes du droit politique* (Paris: Éditions Garnier Frères, 1954), chap. 2, "Des premières sociétés," pp. 237–38.

requested of him by Corsican notables after the praise he had given the
inhabitants of that island in the *Social Contract,* at a time when the whole
of Europe had its eyes turned toward the history of that island, which was
for a long time under the authority of Genoa and traversing war after war
of, let's say, liberation; and this project of Rousseau's starts from the fact
that "the Corsican people are in that happy state that makes a good institution possible," especially by reason of the insularity and the size of the
island, what Rousseau calls "the advantageous situation of the Island of
Corsica and the happy nature of its inhabitants."[35] He recommends democracy for it, an almost closed economy, the quasi-disappearance of imports
and money—all that reduced to a minimum; there too you can reread this
enthralling utopia with an eye turned to *Robinson Crusoe.*) In any case, to
come back to this pre-political sovereignty of the citizen, in the *Discourse on
the Origin of Inequality among Men,* Rousseau describes what was basically
always his political dream, namely a country or a state in which sovereign
and people would be a single person, and he calls this "democracy" (and
this identification of people and sovereign, the sovereignty of the people, is
indeed the very concept of democracy, or at least of what is named by the
name *demokratia*). But what does "person" mean, once the sovereign and
the people are but one? Is it a new definition of person itself, the only political or politico-juridical definition of the person (beyond the individual),
or else is it the insular utopia of an individual alone enough on an island to
be both the sovereign and all the people gathered together, concentrated
or reduced to a single individual, a Robinson on his arrival at the Island of
Despair? In any case, Rousseau presents it as a dream of *failed* origin rather
than one of *lost* origin, a nostalgia for the country that did not see his birth,
a melancholy, rather, the mournful sigh of not having been born where he
would have wished to be born. And right in the middle of a series of paragraphs beginning with "I would have wished," "if I had had to choose my
place of birth, I would have chosen a society limited by the extent of human
faculties"[36] (and so within reach of sight, hearing and grasp), "I would have
wished to live and die free," I would therefore have wished that nobody
in the state," etc., "I would not have wished to live in a recently instituted
republic," etc., and among all these conditionals in "I would have wished,"
<an> "I would have wished to be born" (for this is someone telling us how

49

35. Jean-Jacques Rousseau, *Projet de constitution pour la Corse,* in *Œuvres complètes,* 5
vols., ed. Bernard Gagnebin and Marcel Raymond (Paris: Gallimard, 1959–95), 3:902.
36. Jean-Jacques Rousseau, *Discours sur l'origine et les fondements de l'inégalité parmi
les hommes,* in *Œuvres complètes,* 3:111–13.

and where he would have wished to be born and nothing is more desperate than an "I would have wished to be born," "this is where and how I would have wished to be born if I had been born how I would have wished to be born.") How can one ever think and write, seriously, responsibly, "I would have wished to be born"? What "I" can ever conjugate the verb "to be born" in this tense and mood: "I would have wished"? It cannot be the same I, because an I cannot speak of its birth in this tense and mood. Unless *only* an "I" can do so, say it and think it, however empty and impossible this saying and thinking may seem to remain, this "I" that says and thinks in this way, and signs an "I would have wished to be born." In any case Rousseau knows how to use the rhetoric of this simulacrum to define, in sum, his politics, no less, and his concept of state, sovereign, citizen and person. And this paragraph is not far from what Marx will call a Robinsonade. So Rousseau writes in the *Discourse on the Origin of Inequality among Men,* well before even the preface and before that first part that I am asking you to reread because it is very rich as to the animal, the wolf we talked so much about last year,[37] the bears, the negroes and the savages who "are so little concerned about the fierce beasts they might meet in the woods" (this is where Rousseau defines the man who has left the state of nature, "the man who thinks" as a "depraved animal")—well, long before the preface and the first part, in the *envoi* that dedicates the *Discourse* to the Republic of Geneva, addressing himself to those he calls "Magnificent, highly honored and Sovereign Lords," Rousseau explains where he would have wished to be born, to live and die free:

50

> I would have wished to be born in a country where the sovereign and the people could have but one and the same interest, so that all the movements of the machine could tend only to the common good; which being impossible, unless the people and the sovereign are one and the same person, it follows that I would have wished to be born in a democratic government, sagely tempered.[38]

Which means, among other things, that, given that the Robinsonian dream or ideal—basically that of an absolute identification of the sovereign and the people in a single person, a unique and thus lone person, solitary, exceptional—is inaccessible, what is called "a democratic government, sagely tempered" is the best expedient, the least bad approximation. And the "I would have wished" does not only concern the Robinsonade of a

37. *La bête et le souverain, I,* pp. 19–57 and 139–40 [pp. 1–31 and 95–96].
38. Rousseau, *Discours,* p. 112.

single person, embodying at once, all alone, in solitude, irreplaceable, the sovereign and the people—a hyperbolic and as it were pre-political dream and nostalgia. The "I would have wished" even bespeaks nostalgia, homesickness for the country in which Rousseau was *not* born, i.e. the country of that expedient that would be, in politics this time, a truly democratic government. And Rousseau goes on to speak of a salutary and gentle yoke, which subjects one to the law without alienating one's liberty ("I would have wished to live and die free, i.e. so subject to the laws that neither I nor anyone else could shake their honorable yoke, that salutary, gentle yoke [. . .] I would have wished, then, that no-one in the state be able to declare himself above the law . . ."[39]. What would a sovereign be who was not above the laws, and who would not have the right, as Schmitt would say, to suspend right—that is the question that is posed again and again. Is Rousseau's dream, his "I would have wished," political or pre-political?[40]

This whole historical configuration, this epochal ensemble—I don't know what to call it, let's say this *constructed world,* this *Bildung* of the world, this *Weltbild* or *Weltanschauung*—in which Rousseau recognizes himself in Robinson Crusoe, recognizes in him a brother, and not only the Rousseau of the *Discourse,* of the "I would have wished," but the Rousseau of the *Social Contract* that I was quoting just now, this world or this epoch of the world that goes well beyond the period of the eighteenth century, in that the fascination exercised by *Robinson Crusoe* will survive for a long time; a fascination exercised not only on Joyce or Woolf but on every child and adult the world over—you know that this configuration (I'll content myself with just a reminder) that this configuration, then, this systematic ensemble for which I cannot find a name, was, indeed, treated by Marx as a historical structure, a structure both socio-economical and metaphysico-ideological corresponding, I quote Marx, "to an anticipation of [European] bourgeois society which had been preparing itself since the sixteenth century and which in the eighteenth century was taking giant strides towards maturity."[41] You'll find the most visible and even spectacular expression of Marx's audacity, the interesting temerity that pushes him to recognize in this an epochal structure, a great socio-economico-ideological phase that he calls, precisely, a "Robinsonade," and that he describes, naming in passing

39. Ibid.

40. During the session, Derrida added "or ultra-political."

41. Karl Marx, "Introduction to the Critique of Political Economy," in *Grundrisse, Foundations of the Critique of Political Economy,* trans. Martin Nicolaus (Harmondsworth: Penguin Books, 1973), p. 83.

Rousseau's *Social Contract* — you'll find the most visible and even spectacu-   52
lar expression of this at the beginning of the Introduction to the *Critique of
Political Economy* (1857). Marx's point is serious. It translates an ambition
that is difficult to measure, if not immeasurable, for it consists, among other
things, in trying to refer, or even reduce, no less, what he calls "insipid fictions," here literary fictions (like *Robinson Crusoe,* and Marx's thesis is a
thesis on literature as superstructure) or philosophico-political fictions like
Rousseau's *Discourse* or the *Social Contract,* to aesthetic superstructures at
once significant, symptomatic and dependent on what they signify, namely
merely a phase in the organization of material production and the "anticipation of [European] bourgeois society which had been preparing itself since
the sixteenth and which in the eighteenth century was taking giant strides
towards maturity." Which is not entirely incompatible with—although it
is fundamentally different from—what Joyce says, when he sees in *Robinson Crusoe* a prophetic politico-economical prefiguration of British im-
perialism. I am going to read these few lines from Marx, at the beginning,
then, of this Introduction to the *Critique of Political Economy:* Rousseau and
the Robinsonade, as you will hear, go together in it. Marx announces that
he will treat of production, and primarily of material production. And he
writes:

> The object before us, to begin with, *material production.*
>
> Individuals producing in society—hence socially determined individual
> production—is, of course, the point of departure. The individual and iso-
> lated hunter and fisherman, with whom Smith and Ricardo begin, belongs
> among the unimaginative conceits of the eighteenth-century Robinson-
> ades, which in no way express merely a reaction against over-sophistication
> and a return to a misunderstood natural life, as cultural historians imagine.
> As little as Rousseau's *contrat social,* which brings naturally independent,
> autonomous subjects into relation and connection by contract, rests on such
> naturalism. This is the semblance, the merely aesthetic semblance, of the
> Robinsonades, great and small. It is, rather, the anticipation of "civil soci-
> ety," in preparation since the sixteenth century and making giant strides   53
> towards maturity in the eighteenth.
> [. . .]
> Only in the eighteenth century, in "civil society," do the various forms
> of social connectedness confront the individual as a mere means towards
> his private purposes, as external necessity. But the epoch which produces
> this standpoint, that of the isolated individual, is also precisely that of the
> hitherto most developed social (from this standpoint, general) relations.
> The human being is in the most literal sense a ζῷον πολιτικόν, not merely a
> gregarious animal, but an animal which can individuate itself only in the

midst of society. Production by an isolated individual outside society—a
rare exception which may well occur when a civilized person in whom the
social forces are already dynamically present is cast by accident into the
wilderness—is as much an absurdity as is the development of language
without individuals living *together* and talking to each other.[42]

This is not Marx's only ironic or aggressive reference to Robinsonade and
all the Robinsons. There is at least one other furtive and playful allusion
to Robinson and his Friday in *Capital*. This (reread it) is the extraordinary
Chapter 10 on "The Working Day" in the third section of Book I; a chapter
almost all of the material of which is borrowed from contemporary English
economics. The point for Marx is to denounce *both* the way factory owners
violated or got around an English law regulating the working day of women
and adolescents, or even children (the working day being then limited to ten
hours), *and* the way the judges, the County Magistrates[43] (some of whom
were also factory owners) became their objective accomplices by not pursuing them in law. Marx then cites the case of a certain Robinson, a cotton mill
owner who, although prosecuted, was acquitted thanks to the presence on
the jury of one of his relatives, a man named Eskrigge, himself a cotton mill
owner. Marx then talks of this Eskrigge as the relative, if not the Friday of
this Robinson (*ein Individuum namens Robinson, ebenfalls Baumwollspinner,
und wenn nicht der Freitag, so jedenfalls der Verwandte des Eskrigge*).[44]

Naturally, beyond all the questions it leaves open as to the status of these
fictions (literary or not),[45] and their staying power [*restance*], this Marxist
interpretation of the Robinsonade, this critical interpretation of individual-
ist and asocial isolationism, of insularism as a symptom of the development
of capitalist society, is not homogeneous with, but is not incompatible with
other readings either. I am thinking for example of the way Deleuze, in
the appendix chapter to *Logic of Sense* entitled "Michel Tournier and the
World without Others," which I invite you to reread (it is also published
as the postface to Tournier's book *Vendredi ou les limbes du Pacifique*)–[the
way, then, that Deleuze] wonders "what is the meaning of the fiction 'Robinson'"? The answer comes fast: "A world without others."[46] This direct

42. Ibid., pp. 83–84.
43. [Translator's note:] In English in the text.
44. Marx, *Das Kapital,* p. 306 [pp. 401–2: "an individual named Robinson, also a
cotton-spinner, and if not Eskrigge's Man Friday at least his relative"].
45. In the typescript, this parenthesis closes a few words later, after "restance."
46. Gilles Deleuze, *Logique du sens* (Paris: Minuit, 1969), p. 370; trans. Mark Lester
with Charles Stivale as *Logic of Sense* (London: Athlone Books, 1990; reprinted Con-

reply is then worked out into a theory of perversion that at this point in Deleuze's itinerary owes much to Lacan (and recognizes the fact) and, as he says, Lacan's "school," which, he recalls, insists precisely on the need to "understand perverse behavior on the basis of a *structure*" that displaces desire, makes it detach its cause (the Cause of desire) from its object, disavows sexual difference "in the interests of an androgynous world of doubles," and annuls the other in a "'Beyond the other, or an Other than the other' [*un Autre qu'autrui*]."[47] The sadist does not make the other suffer because he wishes to make the other suffer but because he deprives the other of his alterity, of his "quality of otherness." Against a phenomenology judged to be "hasty" which refers voyeurism or exhibitionism, as perversions, to the presence of the other, in truth, from the point of view of structure, one should say the opposite. It is because the other-structure is lacking that these perversions come about. "The world of the pervert is a world without other, and thereby a world without possibility. The other is what possibilizes [. . .]. All perversion is *autruicide,* altricide, a murder of possibilities. But *altricide* is not committed by perverse behavior, it is presupposed in the perverse structure."[48] A proposition that, if it were followed by effects, would, I believe, upset the whole of penal law. But let's leave that there. Deleuze hurries to add that this perversion is not constitutional but linked to an adventure, to a story that can be both the story of a neurosis and the proximity of a psychosis. Conclusion: "We must imagine Robinson to be perverse; the only Robinsonade is perversion itself."[49]

These are the last words of this chapter, the last sentence that, by associating the adjective "only" to "Robinsonade" ("the only Robinsonade is perversion itself"), leaves open the possibility of not reducing the book *Robinson Crusoe* to a Robinsonade, nor even to Robinson Crusoe himself, in his insular solitude, isolated from his history, his past, his future, the process of his socialization, his relation to many others, including slaves and animals. But that will be *our* story.

Since I am coming to the end of this introductory and scarcely even preliminary session, I'd really like, faced with so many possible readings of *Robinson Crusoe* (and there are certainly more still than those I've just schematically mentioned), [I'd really like] carefully to delimit, and thus also

tinuum Books, 2001), p. 319. [Translator's note: I have occasionally modified the translation slightly in the interests of consistency with Derrida's commentary.]

47. Ibid., p. 371 [p. 319].
48. Ibid., p. 372 [p. 320].
49. Ibid.

55

limit, like an island in an island, the territory of our seminar and the center of gravity that we shall have to constitute as much as to privilege, that is also to restrict—namely, let's say, the beast and the sovereign in *Robinson Crusoe*. As for the beast, it is easy and it goes without saying, even though we have said little about it until now. The book is a long discussion between Robinson and so many beasts. And the theater of that discussion is, indissociably, a theater of solitary sovereignty, of the assertion of mastery (of self, over slaves, over savages and over beasts, without speaking—because the point is precisely not to talk about them—without speaking of women). One archi-preliminary example: even before arriving at the island, and all the stories about the slave trade, there is the episode of the Moor thrown into the sea and of the young boy[50] Xury, also a Muslim, whom Robinson keeps on board and whom Robinson (his master, then), asks to pledge an oath of fidelity, and to do so according to Islamic law, which would bind him the more; an oath to recognize Robinson's sole sovereignty over the swearing subject:

> *Xury,* if you will be faithful to me I'll make you a great Man, but if you will not stroak your Face to be true to me, *that is, swear by* Mahomet *and his Father's Beard,* I must throw you into the Sea too; the Boy smil'd in my Face and spoke so innocently that I could not mistrust him; and swore to be faithful to me, and go all over the World with me. (RC, 21)

This is almost immediately followed—I leave you to go and see—by the episode during which the first proof given by Xury will be to obey Robinson and go kill in dangerous circumstances a terrifying lion whose paw he will offer to Robinson—who skins it and keeps the skin, a huge skin put out to dry in the sun and on which Robinson later sleeps. As for the auto-affirmation of sovereignty by Robinson himself, I'll content myself with reading two other passages to which we shall have to return the better to reinscribe them in the time and consequence of the narrative.

> It would have made a Stoick smile to have seen, me and little Family sit down to Dinner; there was my Majesty the Prince and Lord of the whole Island; I had the Lives of all my Subjects at my absolute Command. I could hang, draw, give Liberty, and take it away, and no Rebels among all my Subjects.
> Then to see how like a King I din'd too all alone, attended by my servants, *Poll,* as if he had been my Favourite, was the only Person permitted to talk to me. My Dog who was now grown very old and crazy, and had

50. [Translator's note:] Derrida adds the English word "boy" in brackets.

found no Species to multiply his Kind upon, sat always, at my Right Hand, and two Cats, one on one Side of the Table, and one on the other, expecting now and then a Bit from my Hand, as a Mark of special Favour.

But these were not the two Cats which I brought on Shore at first, for they were both of them dead, and had been interr'd near my Habitation by my own Hand; but one of them having mutiply'd by I know not what Kind of Creature, these were two which I had preserv'd tame, whereas the rest run wild in the Woods, and became indeed troublesom to me at last; for they would often come into my House, and plunder me too, till at last I was obliged to shoot them, and did kill a great many; at length they left me with this Attendance, and in this plentiful Manner I lived; neither could I be said to want any thing but Society, and of that in some time after this, I was like to have too much. (RC, 137)

My Island was now peopled, and I thought my self very rich in Subjects; and it was a merry Reflection which I frequently made, How like a King I look'd. First of all, the whole country was my own meer Property; so that I had an undoubted Right of Dominion. *2dly,* My People were perfectly subjected: I was absolute Lord and Law-giver; they all owed their Lives to me, and were ready to lay down their Lives, *if there had been Occasion of it,* for me. It was remarkable too, we had but three Subjects, and they were of three different Religions. My Man *Friday* was a Protestant, his Father was a *Pagan* and a *Cannibal,* and the *Spaniard* was a Papist: However, I allow'd Liberty of Conscience throughout my Dominions: But this is by the Way. (RC, 222)[51]

Next time we shall return to the continent, toward the land of continental philosophy, there to open in our own way Heidegger's great and formidable seminar (especially where it concerns poverty of world, the animal), but beginning at the beginning, namely a sentence from Novalis that Heidegger quotes and comments upon. This sentence states that philosophy is really a nostalgia, a homesickness (*Heimweh*), a drive to be everywhere at home, in one's house: "Die Philosophie ist eigentlich Heimweh, ein Trieb überall zu Hause zu sein" (H, 7/5). Heidegger says of this sentence that it is remarkable and clearly romantic, but he also wonders if there is still today something like nostalgia or homesickness. Has this word *Heimweh* not become incomprehensible today, in everyday life? And then here perhaps is a rhetorical prefiguration of the animal that will come on stage only much later in the course of the meditation and of the seminar, Heidegger at this

51. Derrida had planned to read this second passage, of which a photocopy is included with the typescript, but did not do so. He comes back to it at the very beginning of session 2.

58

59

point accusing the city dweller, the man of the town, of being merely the ape of civilization (*Affe der Zivilization*); he wonders whether this ape has not, when all is said and done, long ago rid himself of nostalgia ("Denn hat nicht der heutige städtische Mensch und Affe der Zivilisation das Heimweh längst abgeschafft?") (H, 7/5).

Then we shall link on to this with the three questions Heidegger intends to gather into one: What is world (*Welt*)? What is finitude (*Endlichkeit*)? What is loneliness, isolation or solitude (*Vereinzelung, Einsamkeit*)? This *Vereinzelung* (this loneliness, this isolation, this insularity) is not the stiffening of a little ego puffing itself up before what it takes to be the world. It is rather through loneliness, becoming-alone, the endurance of solitude (*Vereinsamung*) that man comes for the first time into proximity with what is essential in every thing, in proximity to the world (*in die Nähe . . . zur Welt*), *Was ist diese* Einsamkeit, *wo der Mensch je wie ein Einziger sein wird?* [What is this *solitude,* where each human being will be as though alone?] (H, 8/6). Solitude of man, question of man as the only living being capable of being alone and approaching the world as such. The stone is not alone. Will we say of the beast that it is alone (given that it is poor in world)? Or that it is somewhat alone? To relaunch all these questions, and to link them with the question of sovereignty, we shall dwell at the beginning of the next session on the word *walten* (to rule violently) which we can rightly say dominates the beginning of the seminar and everything in it that concerns *physis.*

December 18, 2002

Without wishing to retrace my steps (long pause), without wishing to retrace my steps (long pause) and recall all the readings via which we turned
around, not only the couple, the "odd couple"¹ Heidegger/Robinson Crusoe (I am thinking of the texts—basically all political texts—by Gadamer,
Joyce, Woolf, Rousseau, Marx, Deleuze, etc.) our first incursion in search
of—let's say to stick with the title—the beast and the sovereign in *The
Island of Despair,* and some passages from *Robinson Crusoe* on these two
themes and especially the theater of an autobiography or an Autopresenta-
tion of the sovereign by himself, I must repair an omission. I meant to quote
a passage that, I no longer know why, I omitted.

> My Island was now peopled, and I thought my self very rich in Subjects;
> and it was a merry Reflection which I frequently made, How like a King I
> look'd. First of all, the whole country was my own meer Property; so that I
> had an undoubted Right of Dominion. *2dly,* My People were perfectly sub-
> jected: I was absolute Lord and Law-giver; they all owed their Lives to me,
> and were ready to lay down their Lives, *if there had been Occasion of it,* for
> me. It was remarkable too, we had but three Subjects, and they were of three
> different Religions. My Man *Friday* was a Protestant, his Father was a *Pagan*
> and a *Cannibal,* and the *Spaniard* was a Papist: However, I allow'd Liberty
> of Conscience throughout my Dominions: But this is by the Way. (RC, 222)

What path are we going to privilege today? A path that would avoid, if
that were possible, our having to retrace our steps?

I had announced, in concluding the last session, that to open, at least in a
provisional and preliminary way, Heidegger's Seminar² on *World, Finitude,*
and *Solitude,* and so as to situate in it one of the dimensions of the prob-

---

1. [Translator's note:] In English in the text.
2. Derrida sometimes capitalizes the initial letter of "Seminar," and sometimes not.

lem of sovereignty, before coming to the question of the animal "poor in world [*weltarm*]," we ought to do an initial reconnoiter, at the very beginning of this long seminar of Heidegger's, around one word. This is a recurring word that in my opinion is given too little attention in Heidegger in general, and that the [French] translation most often banalizes, neutralizes and muffles. This word is the German verb *walten*,[3] which means—and which is indeed most often translated as—"to reign, to govern,"[4] but which in French is abandoned to its neutrality, even its non-violence, a certain abstract innocence, as when one speaks of the animal realm, the calm that reigns in a deserted place, the silence that reigns in a room, etc., dissociating what there might be of force and imposed violence (*Gewalt,* precisely), authority, power, reigning and sovereign potency in *Walten* or *Gewalt.* This is a reigning and sovereign potency that is often emphasized in the political order, even though the meaning of *Walten* or *Gewalt* is not limited to that, and finds in that order only one of its figures. But precisely, one of our questions might be how the passage is made from the general and quite indeterminate, in any case quite open sense of *Walten,* to the properly socio-political sense. The neutralization or banalization of the meaning that I've just mentioned for the words "reign, rule, dominate, prevail" in [English] can also happen in German, of course, but my question, precisely, as to the use Heidegger makes of it, everywhere, really everywhere, more insistently than has ever been noticed, to my knowledge—my question here bears on what exactly Heidegger imprints on it, insistently and strangely, but clearly explicitly and deliberately, at the beginning of the seminar.

First of all, let's look at what is happening a little before and a little after the passage that we read last week on Novalis's comment about philosophy as *Heimweh,* on philosophizing as an experience of nostalgia, of philosophy suffering from a constitutional sickness that would be homesickness (and, let it be said in passing, is there a more nostalgic book than *Robinson Crusoe,* whether it be Robinson's nostalgia for the world he has lost (*die Welt ist fort,* as Celan would say), the nostalgia he will feel at the end for the island he has lost after returning to that other island, England, where he will continue to dream of returning to his solitary island—and to which he will indeed return, affected by a real tropism of return to the state of nature, of a nostalgia for a quasi state of natural childhood or native naivety, close to birth; or the affect or phantasm of nostalgia that every reader feels as much

---

3. Derrida sometimes capitalizes the initial letter of "Walten," and sometimes not.

4. [Translator's note:] The English translators of Heidegger's seminar use the verb "prevail" to translate *walten.*

for the state of nature and euphoric childhood which in spite of everything reigns over this island of despair, which reigns over this island and bathes it, surrounding it with all sorts of seas, good and bad),[5] [so, a little before and a little after this passage that we read last week about Novalis's comment and philosophy as *Heimweh*], *Heimweh,* the sickness of returning home, as *Grundstimmung des Philosophierens* (nostalgia as fundamental attunement of philosophizing), at least *two* strange things happen that I'd like to emphasize, even if I do so too rapidly.

The *first thing* to notice is that, suddenly looking like a sort of Robinson, Heidegger isolates himself from the whole tradition, from all traditions, and asks himself, out of nowhere,[6] the question of the path: the question of the <path> to take, the best path for philosophy and for the determination of what metaphysics is, and he poses all these questions according to the turns and tropes of the path, the direct path in the right direction and the byways to avoid, etc. (Not like Descartes, who also, as you know, obsessively asked himself the question of path as method and resembled, in his own way, a first Robinson of philosophy who intended to rely only on his own strength, reconstruct everything himself after having radically doubted every presupposition, as Woolf said of *Robinson Crusoe:* the *cogito ergo sum* is a hyperbolic Robinsonade, particularly at the moment of hyperbolic doubt that absolutely insularizes the self-relation of the *cogito sum,* and we could go a long way analyzing this affinity or this analogy between the Philosopher-voyager Descartes and Robinson Crusoe, even from the Marxist point of view we situated last time); not like Descartes, then, whom Heidegger sends away or recuses in passing. Descartes is for Heidegger someone who wanted to determine philosophy as absolute, indubitable science, which to Heidegger's eyes is a wrong and indirect path to take in determining and thinking philosophy itself. What is more, elsewhere, Heidegger casts doubt on Descartes's determination of the path (*hodos*) as *methodos,* as a calculable and regulated procedure or proceeding (I talked at length about this in a seminar years ago).[7]

5. [Translator's note:] "L'entourant de toutes sortes de mers, bonnes et mauvaises," where the homophony of *mer* (sea) and *mère* (mother) is being exploited by Derrida.

6. During the session, Derrida added: "or he pretends to ask himself out of nowhere."

7. See Jacques Derrida, seminar 1980–81, "La langue et le discours de la méthode," an excerpted lecture from which, with the same title, was delivered in Geneva, and subsequently published in *Recherches sur la philosophie et le langage* (Grenoble, Groupe de recherches sur la philosophie et le langage), "La philosophie dans sa langue," no. 3 (1983), pp. 35–51. The lecture dealt precisely with the relation between Heidegger and Descartes.

In any case, here, after having affirmed that philosophy itself is neither a Science (*Wissenschaft*) nor a vision of the world (*Weltanschauung*), Heidegger wonders how to determine philosophy without going via the byway, the detour (*Umweg*) of a comparison with art and religion. We must find the true and proper path, the authentic *Weg* of philosophy itself, without *Umweg,* without the non-path constituted by a detour or a deferred, diverted path. Philosophy must have its own path determined by itself, a direct and unmediated path, without help or detour via anything other than itself. Heidegger asks himself: will we be able, then, on the diverted path (*auf dem Umweg*), passing through art and religion, to grasp philosophy *in ihrem Wesen,* in its proper essence? Clearly not. Independently of the difficulties presented by "such a path," *ein solcher Weg,* and even if art and religion had the same rank as philosophy, we could not even *compare* if we did not have already in view some essence of philosophizing to distinguish from it art and religion. So we are in a circle which always makes us retrace our steps: in order even to take the *Umweg* of a comparison with art and religion, we must presuppose and give ourselves in advance some comparable determination of philosophy and therefore, through this presupposition or this precomprehension, envelope the defined in the defining or the comparing, and turn in the circle of this presupposition, and thus in advance retrace our steps without advancing. So that, even if, along our way (*auf unserem Wege*), we encounter art and religion, the path of philosophy properly speaking, in its essence, is closed, barred, closed off by this very circle (*So ist auch dieser Weg verschlossen* [H, 3/3]). And thus to accede to the proper essence of philosophy, which is not science, or art, or religion, one goes round in circles, either circularly or specularly, one is sent back to oneself, to one's own point of departure, one steps in one's own footsteps, one goes round in circles as though on an island. And this is indeed what Robinson Heidegger finds: one is always sent back to one's starting point (*züruckgeworfen*) in this attempt to grasp philosophy by comparison. "Alle diese Wege sind in sich selbst unmögliche Umwege [all these paths are in themselves impossible detours, impossible diverted paths]" (H, 4/3).

Faced with the impossible, because of the impossibility of advancing or moving along while turning around, in a detour, an *Umweg,* the question then becomes: how must we experience (*erfahren*) what philosophy itself (*die Philosophie selbst*) *is,* if we must give up on every *Umweg,* every detour (*Umweg*)?

When I say Robinson Heidegger, do not think that I am playing or that I am unfairly using a facile or artificial analogy. I am not unaware of the abyss of differences that separates the two. The two ... what? Well, first, a character on the one hand and a real person on the other, <on the one hand> the fictional character of an English eighteenth-century novel and on the other hand the person of a German philosopher of the twentieth century who claims, precisely, to be talking seriously, in a seminar, in a mode that is anything but imagination and fiction, about the most serious question in the world, namely: "What is philosophy?" and "What is the world?" etc.

But what I am seeking and will be seeking again today to situate, in the analogy between their respective ways of *proceeding* [*démarches*] (and that's the word: *démarche, progress* [*cheminement*], *scene of orientation,* question in view of the best path for the best question, the most appropriate and direct path for the best question, the path that advances, that proceeds in order to accede and does not return to its starting point by going round in circles in its own footsteps), what we'll be seeking to bring out, then, is precisely this common concern with orientation, with "where to go?" "where to head for?" "how to get ahead?" "how to proceed?" "how to progress?" "at what pace?" a concern that, in one place, and from a given place to a non-given place, engages bodily movement in a metaphorical or literal way, and with a metaphor that has one wondering to what proper sense of the body proper it refers, to what time and what space: a concern that thus engages the body proper of a questioner who is walking, of a question on the march that *goes,* that comes and goes, always risks coming back, going around in circles, being sent back over its own steps.

I'll go further in that direction a little later, precisely in the direction of the question of direction, of sense as direction.[8] We shall come back to the sense of orientation and the orientation of a sense that is determined only by orienting itself. Precisely, immediately after the passage that I have just mentioned, and so from the beginning of the seminar (§1, H, 4/3), the word "orientation" [*Orientierung*] provides the title for the first question that follows. Heidegger, as I was just recalling, has just spoken of the closed, barred (*verschlossen*) route, he has just pointed out the illegitimate circularity of all the *Umwege,* and has thus just properly described the *aporia,* i.e. the absence of an open route toward the determination of philosophy itself, and he then asks himself which is the way out, the *Ausweg,* the exit route from this aporia. The point is always to avoid the aporia, i.e. *either/or:* either not get lost, or not allow oneself to be closed in. These are always the two risks of a proceeding [*démarche*]: wander and get lost, or get closed in by retracing one's

8. [Translator's note:] The word *sens* in French can mean both "sense" or "meaning" and "direction."

steps. And that is the Robinsonian trouble with the island. Not get lost and not get closed into the aporia, not get paralyzed. Heidegger may well often make fun of those who seek the security of the safe passage or of the ground, of the grounding ground and the sure route, but he doesn't want to get lost either, he is a thinker of wandering who does not want to wander when he is philosophizing, when he is thinking, writing or above all teaching (for this is a seminar), and he wants not only order and a map, but also the exit route, the way out (*Ausweg*). He wants the right orientation and the right direction to escape from enclosure or circular insularity. The subtitle of this paragraph I was just mentioning aims for the right way out (*Ausweg*), the exit, the right path out of the impasse, avoiding both the detour (*Umweg*) of comparison, and circular closure. Turning to the hypothesis of a historical or historiographical orientation, Heidegger will again show that it leads to an impasse, to a final path that is an impasse ("So führt auch dieser zuletzt noch gebliebene Weg in eine Sackgasse [Thus, this last remaining way also leads to a dead end]" [§1, H, 5/3]).

The subtitle of the paragraph that concludes in this fashion was, then: "Der Ausweg zur Wesensbestimmung der Philosophie über die historische Orientierung als Täuschung [The escape route of determining the essence of philosophy via a historical (historiographical) orientation as an illusion (or mystification)]."

And Heidegger immediately goes on: a final way out, a last escape route (*Ausweg*) remains in order to accede to the essence of philosophy: ask history. And on the path of historical orientation (*Auf dem Wege der historischen Orientierung*), we shall thus try to obtain clarification about metaphysics, which Heidegger notes in passing is, as it were, the other name of philosophy. And he will pass without even giving an explanation from the question: "What is the essence of philosophy?" to the question he holds to be synonymous: "What is the essence of metaphysics? What is metaphysics?" And then, following a tripartite gesture—I dare not say trinitary or triadic, trilobed or triangular—a gesture that we shall see later is recurrent in Heidegger's rhetoric or pedagogy (let us not forget that this is a seminar), Heidegger announces *three* questions or *three* paths in this perspective and this historical orientation.

First path: ask about the noteworthy, curious, strange (*merkwürdige*) history of this noteworthy, curious, strange word "metaphysics."

Second path: through the history of this word or this simple signifier, move on to the signified, the meaning (*Bedeutung*) of the word "metaphysics" as a philosophical discipline.

Third path: through this definition, this signifier/signified, word/meaning couple and disciplinary institution, if you will, go this time right to the thing itself, the thing thus called, metaphysics *itself.*

But there too, we are retracing our steps. We could not undertake this journey, Heidegger makes clear, and this experience, if we did not *already* know, if we were not presupposing *in advance* what metaphysics itself is. Without this circular foreknowledge, all the historical stories in the world would tell us nothing, they would remain mute (*stumm*), we would merely be learning of opinions about metaphysics but would never accede to metaphysics *itself.* This is when Heidegger concludes that there is an impasse: "So führt auch dieser zuletzt noch gebliebene Weg in eine Sackgasse" (H, 4/3).

At this point, I'll leave you to read the following paragraph, paragraph §2 that comprises five or six pages, and which turns, precisely, around Novalis's sentence ("Philosophy is really homesickness, an urge to be at home everywhere").[9] You will again see, at work more than once, that obsession with orientation and direction (*Orientierung* and *Richtung* are recurrent words). Heidegger repeats ten times over that one must avoid *Umwege,* which are so many steps aside to avoid doing what needs to be done, namely look metaphysics in the face without any detour, see it for itself, facing us face on. What the indirect detours have taught us is that we were avoiding looking straight on, *taking sight* of what is proper to metaphysics itself. And so we have acquired, thanks to a detour, a certain important view of what is proper to metaphysics ("eine wichtige und vielleicht wesentliche Einsicht in das Eigentümliche der Metaphysik" [translate]),[10] namely that we turn around, step aside and make detours to dodge it and avoid doing what we ought to do. Then there is no longer a choice, we must get going and look metaphysics in the face ("aber keine Wahl bliebt, als uns selbst aufzumachen und *der Metaphysik ins Gesicht zu sehen,* um sie nicht wieder aus den Augen zu verlieren [no other choice remains than to ready ourselves and to *look metaphysics in the face* (Heidegger's emphasis), so as not to lose sight of it again]").

70

9. Novalis, *Schriften,* ed. Jakob Minor (Iena: Eugen Diederichs, 1923), vol. 2, fragment 21, quoted by Heidegger (H, 7/5).

10. [Translator's note:] Derrida's improvised translation during the session might be in turn translated: "A serious and important and perhaps essential view of what is proper to metaphysics." McNeill and Walker give "an important and perhaps essential insight into what is peculiar about metaphysics" (H, 4).

And everything Heidegger goes on to say is there to affirm that we try to avoid this face to face and this direct path, that we seek the detour and the dodge, that we flee and try to withdraw from this path that leads directly (*direkt* in German) to metaphysics. Metaphysics requires of us that we *avoid avoidance,* that we avoid always avoiding it by means of detours, *Umwege,* and that we not look away from it (*wegsehen* means "to avert one's gaze"). The word that dominates what follows, I leave you to read it, is *Richtung,* direction. What we are showing, what I am showing, says Heidegger, what I am pointing out, is the direction (*Richtung*) in which we have to seek, but also the direction (*Richtung*) in which metaphysics withdraws from us. And in this same movement, Heidegger-Robinson wonders: "Why else would we have come along here [i.e. to the land of philosophy]? (*Denn wozu wären wir sonst hierher gekommen?*). Or have we landed here (*Oder sind wir nur so hierher geraten*) only because others also come along [...]? Why are we here? (*Warum sind wir da?*) Do we know what we are letting ourselves in for? (*Wissen wir, womit wir uns einlassen?*)" (H, 6/4–5).

The already or still Robinsonian landscape of these astonished questions (why have we landed here, why have we wound up in this place, at this place, what are we doing here?)—this already or still Robinsonian landscape becomes even more Robinsonian when, having asked "what is world?" and having insisted on isolation, insularity, loneliness, and solitude, and asked "What is this *solitude* in which each human being will be as though unique—or singularly, uniquely alone (*Was ist diese* Einsamkeit*, wo der Mensch je wie ein Einziger sein wird?*)," after having noted that, along the way, our question, "What is metaphysics?" has become the question, "What is man?" Robinson Heidegger ends up with images of a storm blowing between heaven and earth:

> We ask anew: What is man? A transition (*ein Übergang,* a step beyond, an excess), a direction (*eine Richtung*), a storm (*ein Sturm*) sweeping over our planet (*der über unseren Planeten fegt*), a recurrence (*eine Wiederkehr oder ein Überdruss den Göttern?*), or else a vexation for the gods, an annoyance for the gods? We do not know. But we have seen that in this enigmatic essence, philosophy happens (*geschieht*). (H, 10/7; translation modified)

Perhaps you still remember: this whole detour (*Umweg*) on Heidegger's discourse on the detour to be avoided, on the need to avoid the detour that avoids the direct path and the direction of the face to face—this whole detour was designed to lead us to this vocabulary of *Walten* that I announced at the outset occupies a terrain worthy of our attention, especially at the beginning of the seminar. I'm coming to that now, very fast, too fast, leaving you to read on your own the first two chapters of the seminar. In the third chapter devoted in part to the origin of the word "metaphysics," given that "metaphysics" designates the inclusive or comprehensive interrogation that extends to world, finitude and solitude, Heidegger devotes a first subsection to the clarification of the word "physics," *physika,* and to *physis* "als [das] 'sich bildenden Walten des Seienden im Ganzen,'" "as (I quote first the Gallimard translation, which remains feeble, enfeebling), self-forming[11] realm[12] of beings as a whole."[13] I concede that this is difficult to translate, but the word *walten* deserves a stronger accent, the strongest possible, in fact. *Walten* is dominant, governing power, as self-formed sovereignty, as autonomous, autarcic force, commanding and forming itself,[14] of the totality of beings, beings in their entirety, everything that is. *Physis* is the *Walten* of everything, which depends, as *Walten,* only on itself, which forms itself sovereignly, as power, receiving its form and its image, its figure of domination, from itself. *Walten* as *physis, physis* as *Walten* is everything; *physis* and *Walten* are synonyms of everything, of everything that is, and that is, then, as originarily sovereign power. *Physis,* the *phuein* that thus dominates as totality of beings, is what increases, grows, increases by growing, the growing of blossoming growth. *Physis* means *das Wachsende,* what increases or grows, growing, growth, the very thing that has grown in such a growth, "das Wachsende, das Wachstum, das in solchem Wachstum Gewachsene selbst" (H, 38/25). And there too, the pedagogy whereby Heidegger illustrates what he means by "growing," by growing as nature, as realm or domination of *physis,* takes the form of a Robinsonian landscape: the plants, the animals, the seasons, the day and the night, the stars, the tempest and the storm, the raging elements. Heidegger makes clear that he is taking growing and growth in the broad and elementary sense that they inaugurate in the originary experience (the French translation even says "expérience primitive"[15] for *Urerfahrung*) of man: not merely, Heidegger adds, plants and animals, their arising and passing away as an isolated process (*als bloßer isolierter Vorgang*) but growth as what takes place or comes about (*als dieses Geschehen*), *physis* as history, in short nature as natural history, beyond or

11. During the session, Derrida added: "he'll always say that: *sich bildenden Walten.*"

12. During the session, Derrida added: "*Walten:* reign, potency, force, power, authority, potentiality, etc., power, violence."

13. [Translator's note:] "The 'self-forming prevailing of beings as a whole'" (H, 38–39/25).

14. During the session, Derrida added: "and of course the word *bilden* is very important too."

15. [Translator's note:] "Primal experience" (H, 38/25).

short of the nature/history opposition, for *physis* covers history, natural history in this new extended sense, then, the natural coming about of what is dominated (again, but this time it is *durchherrscht*), of what is under the dominating sovereignty of the changing seasons, the passage from night to day and reciprocally, the movement of the stars, the storms, and weather (*vom Sturm und Wetter*) and the raging of the elements (*und dem Toben der Elemente*).

What justifies my insistence on *Walten,* here, as a figure of absolute power, of sovereignty before even its political determination, is that it seems to me that it answers to Heidegger's most explicit concern. Heidegger who explains to us (H, 38/25) that, if we translate more intelligibly and clearly (*deutlicher*), if we (that is, he) translate *physis* not so much by growth (*Wachstum*) as by *Walten* (by "sich selbst bildenden Walten des Seienden im Ganzen [the self-constituting, self-formed, sovereign predominance of beings in their totality]" [H, 38–39/25]), if, then, we translate *physis* by *Walten* rather than *Wachstum* (as sovereign power rather than growth), this is, as Heidegger expressly says, because it is clearer (*deutlicher*) and closer (note this word, "close," which we shall be seeing again in a decisive strategic place), closer to the originary sense, the intentional sense, the meaning of the originary sense or the originary meaning of the word *physis* ("deutlicher und dem ursprünglich gemeinten Sinn näherkommend φύσις" [H, 38–39/25]).

In other words *physis* is better translated, translated more clearly and closer to its originary sense, as *Walten* than as *Wachstum,* as prevailing violence rather than as increase, growing, growth. And this better translation, this supposedly better translation, closer to the original or the originary, if you will, in both cases concerns *physis* as totality of what is, and not, no longer, nature in the belated and restricted sense of the word, as object of the natural sciences (as opposed to history, society, spirit, liberty, culture, etc.) any more than in the prescientific, romantic, or Goethean sense of nature. No more is it a matter here of the *state of nature* as opposed to the *state of society,* an opposition that has organized so many discourses for so long, in particular discourses of political philosophy on the state of nature or on natural right.

To justify fully this translation of *physis* as *Walten* (*sich bildenden Walten*) and this extension of the sense of the word *physis* toward its originary and pre-oppositional sense, Heidegger insists on this absolute extension, which goes well beyond biological life, biological growth, but includes within itself birth, childhood, maturity, old age, death, human destiny and its his-

"sondern das Waltende in seinem Walten oder das Walten des Waltenden" (translate).[21] Whence a certain subtle indecision, a certain undecidability (*Unentschiedenheit*). Which resembles that of beings and the Being of beings. It is because of this undecidability that *physis* appears both as an excess of power that threatens (*bedroht*) man, which is threatening (*bedrohend*), and on the other hand as a support and a protection.

Let me simply read the translation of these few Robinson-inflected lines and I leave you to study what follows, on the *physei onta* and the *tekhnē onta* (we could easily spend all year on it): "Precisely what prevails as all-powerful (*das übermächtig Waltende*) for immediate experience claims the name φύσις for itself. Yet such is the vault of the heavens, the stars, the ocean, the earth, that which constantly threatens man, yet at the same time protects him too, that which supports, sustains (*trägt*) and nourishes him; that which, in thus threatening and sustaining him, prevails (*waltet*) of its own accord without the assistance of man" (H, 46/30).

3. Finally, this interpretation of both *physis* and *logos* on the basis, let's say, of the hidden or revealed sovereignty of *Walten* is not, to my knowledge (but I have not reread all *Sein und Zeit* recently from this point of view—if someone would like to do so, with a scanner, that would be very useful)—to my knowledge, then, the concept and vocabulary of *Walten* is not at work—at least not centrally—in *Sein und Zeit,* which dates from two years before the Seminar we are reading. Moreover, the lexicon of *Sein und Zeit,* the published glossary of *Sein und Zeit* does not mention *Walten* as an operational or thematic concept. Does not mention it at all. On the other hand, after this Seminar (1929–30), which follows *Sein und Zeit* about two years later, and especially in the *Introduction to Metaphysics,* in 1935 (politically a very marked time, of course), the vocabulary of *Walten* is not only confirmed, but extends, differentiates, grows richer, and becomes invasive, especially around *physis* and *logos* (*walten, das Walten, durchwalten, das Durchwalten, Mitwalten, verwalten, Vorwaltung, überwältigend, Übergewalt, verwaltend, bewaltigen, unbewältigt, Gewalt, Allgewalt, Gewalt-tat, gewalt-tätig, Gewalt-tätigkeit,* etc.) So, reread from this point of view the *Introduction to Metaphysics,* take the book with you, along with RC,[22] to an island over the holidays, you won't be wasting

78

21. During the session, Derrida added: "but the predominant [or *perdominant,* in Gilbert Kahn's translation] in its act of dominating or the act of dominating of the dominant."

22. Thus in the typescript. In this case the abbreviation can designate both the character and the title of Defoe's book.

your time. In the French translation by Gilbert Kahn who took a lot of trouble to translate this whole lexicon of *Walten* into a French that is often laborious and neologizing, there is moreover a glossary and a very useful index.

So much for *Walten,* and for those who are called—we know at least one of them—Walter.[23]

And now, what path are we, ourselves, going to privilege today ? What path that will not oblige us to run the risk of going round in circles and retracing our steps?

On n'en sait trop rien.[24] How do you write: *on en sait trop rien?* Is it "on n'en sait trop rien?" or "on en sait trop rien?" I really don't know too much about it. "Je n'en sais trop rien" or "j'en sais trop rien?"

Too much nothing: it's a whole world.

So what path are we going to privilege today? A decision, any decision, seems—I say *seems*—always to come down to a path to be taken, or a track [*une trace*] to be followed along a path to be determined. To decide is to decide on a direction, on a sense in the topographical sense of orientation. Such at least is the dominant trope or figure. Where to go? Where to take oneself? How to orient one's step? That is the form of every question concerning a decision, a decision to be taken. Where to go? Where to take oneself? Am I going to go there or not, here or there? What is the best path?

79   But there is decision only where, at first, one does not know where to go. When one knows the path in advance, the best path, when one knows the map, when one knows in advance where to take one's steps and toward which destination, there is no reflection, no deliberation, no justification to be given, neither question nor decision, because there is no indecision. It is decided in advance, so there is no decision to be taken. The path is already

23. [Translator's note:] An allusion to Derrida's earlier discussion of *Walten* and *Walter* Benjamin's essay *Zur Kritik der Gewalt* in the second part of *Force de loi* (Paris: Galilée, 1994), entitled "Prénom de Benjamin."

24. [Translator's note:] The French idiom "correctly" written "Je n'en sais trop rien," literally "I don't know too much nothing about it," means "I don't know too much about it," "I really don't know anything about it." Derrida is playing on the tendency in spoken French to drop the initial "ne" in negative formulations (so that the "correct" "Je ne sais pas," for example, is often spoken as "Je sais pas"). Here the paradoxical possibilities are further increased by the fact that "too much nothing" is hard to construe literally, and that, in the French expression "(ne) . . . rien," the *rien* derives from the Latin *res,* thing.

taken, and this is, as they say *tout bête*.[25] What I am saying here is, moreover, *tout bête* but undeniable, which also means that it is so simply and so constrainingly obvious that, if one wants to oppose it, one can *only* deny it.

To decide on the path to take or to privilege today, we must recall the context of the contract or the contract of the context: the beast and the sovereign. The beast and the sovereign are like the coats of arms of the seminar, like the dolphin was on the coat of arms of a certain sovereign realm that became the province of the Dauphiné, as we were saying last year.[26]

The beast and the sovereign resemble each other, as we have been saying insistently since last year. They resemble each other in that they both seem to be outside the law, above or alongside the law. And yet, even if they resemble each other, they are not fellows [*semblables*]. Nor are they, or so we think, our fellows.

Who is that, the beast and the sovereign? Who are the beast and the sovereign? What are they, *elle* and *lui*?[27]

Our suggestion is the following: we are committed to discourse here about the beast and the sovereign, and the contract that is proposed or, if you prefer, the rule of the game that I did more than propose to you, that I imposed on you without discussion (not without some *Gewalt*), that I decided on all alone, the rule of this game that is so improbable or a bit crazy, is to read on this subject Heidegger *with* Defoe: to read the Seminar given in Freiburg im Breisgau in 1929–30, entitled *Die Grundbegriffe der Metaphysik: Welt-Endlichkeit-Einsamkeit, The Fundamental Concepts of Metaphysics: World, Finitude, Solitude* (in which Heidegger addresses as never before, and better than anywhere else or since, the question of the beast or the animal) and on the other hand *Robinson Crusoe*. Heidegger in one hand, then, and Defoe in the other, crossing our eyes or squinting a bit to see what is left standing out in this binocular vision. Heidegger-Defoe.

(On my computer, the title of the document for this seminar is *hei/foe* (board), and you know that *foe* in English means enemy. In fact, Defoe's real name, his family's real name, was Foe: his name was Daniel Foe, Daniel Enemy, Daniel the Enemy. I believe that Schmitt somewhere—I do not remember where—tries laboriously to distinguish the two uses: *foe* for

25. [Translator's note:] "Tout bête," literally "quite stupid," but here in the sense of "it's simple," "it's a no-brainer."

26. *La bête et le souverain, I*, p. 341 [p. 253].

27. [Translator's note:] *La bête et le souverain, I,* makes a good deal of the fact that "souverain" is a masculine noun in French, and "bête" feminine.

inimicus (biblical and not political sense) and *enemy* in the sense of *hostis,* political enemy. Defoe's name is as though it meant enemy; and here I rec- ommend that you read at least two or three magnificent novels by J. M Coetzee, the great South African writer who wrote a novel called *Foe,*[28] which presents itself as an oblique reading-rewriting of *Robinson Crusoe,* with embedded quotations, but also because Coetzee bears in his thought and his *oeuvre* the grave concern of the animal, I advise you to read also *The Lives of Animals* and *Disgrace.*)[29]

In order to bring Robinson Crusoe closer to Heidegger, I will not misuse the fact that if Foe is a real English name, Crusoe, as Robinson explains to us from the very opening lines of his autobiographical self-presentation, from the opening lines of the book that are like the genealogical presenta- tion of an identity card or a family record book, Crusoe is the Anglicization of the German name *Kreutznaer.* Kreutznaer is the name of the father, a foreign trader originally from Bremen, with Robinson being the name of the maternal line.

Now, to begin to cross the paths of Robinson and Heidegger in the most improbable places, you will have noticed (if, as I hope, you have reread *Rob- inson Crusoe*) that he is always looking for, or breaking, paths on his island. He tries to get his bearings [*s'orienter*]. He tries to decide, to come to a deci- sion as to the best path. His island is an isolated world within the world, and we see him, and he constantly shows himself, solitary in this insular- ity, constantly in the process of deciding as to the best path, given that he has no map, neither a map of the world nor above all a map of the island. Refer for example to the moment when, having not yet found any trace of human life on the island, having not yet heard any voice other than that of his parrot Poll who echoes his own voice, Robinson discovers "the Print of a Man's naked Foot on the Shore" (RC, 142). It is as though he had been struck by lightning or thunder ("I stood like one Thunder-struck") and as though he had seen a ghost, the vision of a specter (*an Apparition*): the footprint on the sand of the shore becomes not only a spectral apparition, a "fantôme" says Borel's French translation, but a paralyzing hallucina- tion, a sign come from heaven, a sign that is as menacing as it is promising, uncanny,[30] as diabolical as it is divine: the other man. What terrifies Robin-

28. J. M. Coetzee, *Foe* (London: Secker & Warburg, 1986).

29. J. M. Coetzee, *The Lives of Animals,* edited with an introduction by Amy Gut- mann (Princeton, N.J.: Princeton University Press, 1999); *Disgrace* (London: Secker & Warburg, 1999).

30. [Translator's note:] "Uncanny" is in English in the text.

son is the possible trace of the spectral presence of another, another man on the island.

In a certain way, this is everything he was looking for or dreaming of, but the signal of the arrival of what he was hoping for, a bit like the messiah, suddenly terrifies him. Who is the other? And what if the other were worse than anything, what if he were a bad messiah, an envoy of the devil (and Robinson mentions more than once Satan or the Devil, a Satan or Devil (RC, 143) who has taken on human form or who has sent him another man to be his enemy, another foe, if you like)? As always, he is keen to hope that all this is a good sign of divine providence, but he is afraid that, instead of God, behind the God, the devil or an evil Genius (Robinson Descartes again) might have come to do his work, like a malign substitute for God who, instead of saving him, might have come to destroy him by sending him another man to be his enemy, another foe. He is not confident enough that God will save him. (Tell the joke about "Is anybody else there????")[31]

Now what happens during the feverish reflection that, for many pages, follows this discovery of a footprint? A footprint that basically frightens him rather than giving him hope, which makes him think of the devil as much as of God, which even makes him invoke several times the sovereignty of an omnipotent God:

> I consider'd that this was the Station of Life the infinitely wise and good Providence of God had determin'd for me, that as I could not foresee what the Ends of Divine Wisdom might be in all this, so I was not to dispute his Sovereignty, who, as I was his Creature, had an undoubted Right by Creation to govern and dispose of me absolutely as he thought fit; and who, as I was a Creature who had offended him, had likewise a judicial Right to condemn me to what Punishment he thought fit; and that it was my Part to submit to bear his Indignation, because I had sinn'd against him. / I then reflected that God, who was not only Righteous but Omnipotent, as he had thought fit thus to punish and afflict me, so he was able to deliver me; [. . .] (Read what follows [RC, 145]).

31. Thus in the typescript. During the session, Derrida told this joke: "I saw on television the other day a story that's a bit vulgar but quite funny: someone is all alone on an island, with cliffs, and he stumbles . . . and falls . . . And he grabs onto some branches, you see . . . he grabs onto some vines, some trees . . . hanging, and he calls for help. He calls for help knowing that he is alone, like Robinson . . . He calls for help, and suddenly he hears the voice of God saying to him: 'My child, fear not . . . Fear not . . . Let yourself drop and when you're sixty feet from the ground, I'll catch you in my hands . . .' And you hear the man say, 'Help! Help! Isn't anybody *else* there?' [Laughter] That's a bit like Robinson: he has hope in God, but he's afraid that . . ."

83 Which, be it said in passing, means at least two or three things:

1. *On the one hand,* the world is already determined as the totality of divine creation: I am a creature of God, God is the name of the originary creation of the world (and we shall see later that Heidegger inscribes and interprets this determination of the world, as created world, and as Christian world, in the history of the concept of the world);

2. *On the other hand,* this creation is indeed conceived on the Christian model by Robinson, and when he prays, when he learns how to pray (and the whole of *Robinson Crusoe* can be read as a rhythmic series of attempts to learn how to pray properly, authentically, in the Bible, on the Bible; and one also needs to know, and it is known, concerning the Bible, that Foe, Daniel Foe [Defoe] and some of his friends, around 1678, when people expected a *coup* by Charles II with the help of an Irish papist army — that Foe, then, and his friends, were fearful that their Bibles might be confiscated and learned it by heart; you need to know this context, this and so many other features of the politico-religious context of England at the time, to read *Robinson Crusoe*) — well, having just seen this bare footprint of another man, Robinson Crusoe prays on the Bible that he has taken with him and of which he will have, at a given moment, more than one copy ("which book would you take to a desert island, the Bible or a Heidegger seminar about the concept of world?");

3. *Finally,* having put his Bible down and comforted himself through prayer, he asks where he is, in what place, what his path will have been. He then wonders even more anxiously if this bare footprint is not that of his own foot. His own foot on a path he had already taken. Just as Poll the parrot returns to him only the echo of his voice, so the bare footprint is the more *unheimlich,* uncanny,[32] for being quite possibly his own, on a path already trodden, that he has always described without knowing it, described in the sense that to describe a movement is also to execute it. Fundamentally, he cannot decide if this track is his own or not, a track left on a path

84 that he does not know if he has already trodden, broken or walked — or not. He really does not know [*Il n'en sait trop rien*]. Is it me? Is it my track? Is it my path? Is it the specter of my print, the print of my specter? Am I coming back? Am I or am I not returning? Am I a revenant of myself that I cross on my path like the trace of the other, on a path that is already a return path or a path of revenance, etc? I really don't know [*J'en sais trop rien*], or I really don't know about the possibility of this uncanny, *unheimlich* double. When I discover this path and this track, have I not already been this way,

32. [Translator's note:] The word "uncanny," here and a few lines later, is in English in the text.

already, without knowing or wanting to, decided to go this way? I really don't know. [*Je n'en sais trop rien. J'en sais trop rien.*] Who will have decided what? And to go where? That's the question that this bare footprint is asking me, as the trace of a man. The other man, the step of the other man — is it not me again, me alone who, returning like a revenant on the circular path of the island, become an apparition for myself, a specular phantom, a specular specter (the other man as myself, myself as another, I who am an other), but a specular phantom who cannot, who does not know if he is himself, *ipse,* who really doesn't know [*qui n'en sait trop rien*]–nor whether he can still look at himself in the mirror?

He scares himself [*il se fait peur:* literally "he makes himself fear"]. He becomes the fear that he is and that he makes himself. And all these pages, among the most extraordinary in the book, on which he is shown, in which he shows himself, meditating, in terror, on this bare footprint — these pages should be read step by step, and for example in parallel with Freud's *Gradiva,* with all the *phantasmata,* i.e. the phantasms and phantoms that return on the print of a step, or "the Print of a naked Foot."

> In the middle of these Cogitations, Apprehensions and Reflections, it came into my Thought one Day, that all this might be a meer Chimera of my own; and that this Foot might be the Print of my own Foot, when I came on Shore from my Boat: This chear'd me up a little too, and I began to persuade my self it was all a Delusion; that it was nothing else but my own Foot, and why might not I come that way from the Boat, as well as I was going that way to the Boat; again, I consider'd also that I could by no Means tell for certain where I had trod, and where I had not; and that if at last this was only the Print of my own Foot, I had play'd the Part of those Fools, who strive to make stories of Spectres, and Apparitions; and then are frighted at them more than any body. (RC, 145–46)

85

Note that the Devil and the Good Lord, those two figures of all-powerful sovereignty, specters and ghosts, are not the only figures invoked in the wandering of these paths without path. There is also, in this book which is, as you know, an immense zoology, both a taxonomy of the animals — a Noah's ark, a zoological park, a farm, a slaughterhouse, a hunting ground, a jungle of savage beasts — and, as he says, so often, of beasts that are "ravenous," "furious," "venomous," "poisonous;"[33] it is also a protection society for domestic animals, a stockbreeding center, etc.

33. RC, 122–23: "[. . .] so I found no ravenous Beast, no furious Wolves or Tygers to threaten my Life, no venomous Creatures or poisonous, which I might feed on to my Hurt, no Savages to murther and devour me."

In short, in this bestiary book that forms an island between heaven and hell, there is a moment—which immediately follows the moment of discovery of the bare footprint which could be his or that of the other, on this path that he might have taken or that remains the path of the other—there is a moment when Robinson retreats. He withdraws into what he calls his Castle, he takes off, feeling himself followed by a trace, basically, hunted or tracked by a trace. Or even by his own trace. Perhaps persecuted by himself and by his own revenance. As though he were living everything in the past of his own past as a terrifying future. He believes he is shortly going to die, that he is running after his death or that death is running after him, that life will have been so short, and thus, as though he were already dead, because of this race with his revenance, everything that happens to him happens not as new, fresh, or to come, but as (perhaps, he really does not know [*il n'en sait trop rien*]) already past, already seen, to come as yesterday and not as tomorrow. You know these sublime and infinite lines from John Donne, which come back to my memory from I know not where: (Board)

> I run to Death and Death meets me as fast
> And all my Pleasures are like Yesterday.[34]

I run toward death, I hurry toward death and death comes to meet me just as fast. (I run at death, I run to death and death comes upon me, chance death encounter seizes me, catches me or catches up with me just as fast, as soon.)

And all my pleasures are like yesterday,[35] like the yesterday, as though come from yesterday, my pleasures are already of yesterday, my pleasures are the yesterday itself, in advance they are dated—from yesterday. In advance they have passed, they are past, already past and passed by, overtaken, already memories of bygone enjoyment or returns of pleasure. My present pleasures are in the present yesterday's presents, they are yesterday. Not: they have been or were yesterday, but they are presently yesterday. Their being-present is yesterday, the yesterday. It is as if presently I were already dead, death coming so quickly to meet me and me to meet it, and there is no knowing whether I'm going quicker than it toward it or it quicker than I toward me, we are running at each other, as if in order to find out who

---

34. The lines are from the first of John Donne's *Holy Sonnets*. The following pages were published and commented on by Ginette Michaud in "Courir à toute *vie*tesse: Note télégraphique sur un poème de pensée de J.D.," *Mosaic* 40, no. 2 (June 2007): 56–62.

35. [Translator's note:] Derrida inserts the English words "like yesterday."

will arrive first, and at the moment of a meeting that never keeps one waiting, there is no knowing who will, who will have, yesterday, arrived first,
quicker than life in any case, a life that this accelerated movement takes by
speed, thus taking time by speed, even taking speed by speed, a speed beyond speed, a speed winning out over speed, going quicker than time and
even than speed, taking time by speed, so fast that what I live in the present,
or even what I expect from the future, is already past, already memory and
melancholy, or nostalgia (*Heimweh*). That's what it means whenever I say:
"Life will have been so short." Incalculable, incommensurable precipitation
or acceleration, ahead of itself—and taking time by speed.

So clearly "I run to Death" can mean both "I run toward death, I hurry
toward death, I rush in the direction of death which comes at me just as
fast," but also "I run to death," I run like a madman, out of breath, to flee
death, I run to death to avoid death, I run on ahead of death so as not to
have it surprise me, to take the initiative: but it catches up with me immediately; but "catch up with" won't do here for "meet," one must therefore
suppose that even if I run to death, before death, ahead of death in order
to flee it, death is there before me, it already awaits me, in Samarkand,[36]
both because it goes faster and because, going ahead of me, taking the lead,
it outstrips me, awaits me and comes to meet me at the very moment I am
running to death—both to flee it and to catch up with it. *Both* to flee it *and*
to catch up with it. The more I flee it, the faster I flee it, I chase it, the faster
I approach it, I take it upon me, I take it in the sense that, in chasing it, I
run after it. I learn it, I take it in [*je l'apprends, je la prends*], and it takes me
by surprise. All the *Umwege,* all the detours of the race are outplayed by a
death that precedes me, that is ahead of me, before me—since yesterday.
Always anterior, in its very futurity, like what remains to come, affecting
itself in advance from the nostalgia of its own archive—its very light affecting itself without delay with photography, autobiophotography. Or affecting itself in advance, via what in photography is called a delay mechanism,
with its own photograph, a photograph that is itself not reappropriable.
Everything begins with the archive or with archive fever.

But that is not even everything and it is not even so simple <in> the
thinking, giving [*donnante*] writing and the unheard-of signature of this
metaphysical poem. By making "yesterday" a noun, and not an adverb:

88

36. [Translator's note:] An allusion to the ancient Middle Eastern story often referred to as "Death in Samarkand," whereby a man who attempts to escape death by
fleeing to Samarkand finds that that is precisely where his appointed encounter with
death is to take place.

"And all my Pleasures are like Yesterday," Donne gives us the chance of thinking even more than what I have just been saying. What, then? Well, perhaps that this race to death, this race to death of death, this running out of breath, this being-in-the-race at high speed, a speed that is all-powerful and indifferent, without speed-differentiation, this absolute speed, this speed beyond speed, this speed that is the whole, as infinite speed that takes itself by speed and overtakes itself, passes itself, as they say in [American] English for overtake, when one vehicle overtakes another, this speed that passes itself, this race at full speed, this race of death to death, this race unto death *not only* means that my present pleasures are presently and in advance gone, past, already gone by in their very present, already dated yesterday in their present and their here and now. No: one would have to say and think, to the contrary, taking seriously and taking into account the grammar of a proposition that dares to take "yesterday" as a noun, *the* yesterday, and not an adverb (my pleasures are yesterday, as though yesterday), one would have to emphasize and unsettle the meaning of the *like,* by beginning to understand not only that my pleasures are always affected with expiration and in advance dated, dated from yesterday, past and imprinted with nostalgia, as though one first thought the essence of present pleasure and then noticed, in a second moment, the predicative tense, that what we know and feel under this name pleasure or enjoyment and as present pleasure is *then,* into the bargain and as soon as possible, determined as past, affected with past, with yesterdayness. No, it is the contrary, the other way round,[37] if I can say so, it is yesterday that gives the pleasure, pleasure is yesterday, like yesterday, it begins now by being yesterday, not only in the manner of yesterday but as yesterday. I have pleasure only because there is the past of yesterday, only because pleasure is originarily yesterday, it is in its essence, in its now, in the presence of its essence and in the essence of its presence, a having-been-yesterday, it is (present) in its *Gewesenheit,* it is in its essence (*Wesen*), a *Gewesenheit,* a being-having-been, and that's the nostalgia of yesterday, of a death already come, an originary mourning, this is the nostalgia that does not come after pleasure but which, alone, gives me pleasure and gives it to me *as yesterday.* I do not enjoy a pleasure first present that is immediately past, nostalgic, in mourning: no, the pleasure is born only of the mourning, of enjoyment as mourning. And not any mourning and any memory of death, but the mourning of myself. I am from yesterday, I am no longer, I am no longer present, I am already yesterday, I enjoy from yesterday, not because I have enjoyed or have been, or because I was born

89

---

37. [Translator's note:] "The other way round" is in English in the text.

yesterday, but because only yesterday will have given me, only my death or the feeling of my death, a death that will have taken me by speed, only my death lets me enjoy and take pleasure—in this very moment. Only the absolute yesterday gives me pleasure. The yesterday itself gives enjoyment, makes a present in the present of enjoyment as yesterdaily enjoyment, if I can put it like that. Without mourning, and the mourning of myself, the mourning of my "I am present," there would be no pleasure. There would not even be an "I am," consciousness, *cogito,* I think, or present enjoyment of my Cartesian-Robinsonian existence. Pleasure, my pleasures are yesterday, they are the yesterday, they are like the yesterday. They are neither present nor future, I enjoy them only as a memory; and even then, "memory" and "past" are concepts that are too broad and vague. The yesterday is not only the past the memory of which I keep or lose: yesterday is the day ahead, the day that has just passed, whose phenomenal light has just faded. Yesterday is the past imminence of today itself, the imminence of day's dawning, the dawning that gives light to the day [*donne le jour au jour*]. And that is the first metonymy, the major metonymy of the past in general, as past of the experience of what appears in the light of day, comes to see the light of day. Of what is born but, since we are here dealing with a past like a death already happened, having won the race, faster than speed itself, what is born as though stillborn. My pleasures are stillborn. Another way of saying and thinking the *pas de plaisir,* the step or the not of an enjoyment that is in advance the past of itself, a step [*pas*] as past, as what comes to pass as, and passes on [*se passe de*] present pleasure in pleasure and that I enjoy only in the trace of the *pas de plaisir.* Coming back to haunt all the steps [*pas*]. Pleasure is the revenance of the *pas* — all the *pas,* all the past passages of the *pas.* Terrifying or terrified pleasure, this could be the fright of a Robinson, the pleasure-terror (the one in the other, terror in pleasure and pleasure in terror)—the pleasure-terror that consists in not being able to do anything, not take a step [*pas un pas*], in not being anything other than the return of revenance over the track of its own steps, a revenance thenceforth the more fearful—a little as Robinson is scared by the footprint he is not sure is his own, about which he is not sure if he can recognize himself in it, find himself in it, reappropriate his track—a revenance that is thenceforth the more fearsome or fearful for the fact that one is not sure, in the blazed trace of a pleasure, an enjoyment, a joy, in the trace of this *pas de jouissance,* one is never sure of being able to recognize one's own or that of another. Not only is it that what I enjoy is yesterday but perhaps, it is perhaps *my* yesterday or perhaps the yesterday, already, today, *of an other,* and in any case of another, even it is already, even if it were already another myself. My pleasure is,

90

from yesterday on, by yesterday altered, come from the other, the coming of the other.

And the other would say to me, or else I would say myself to the other: as I run to death always after yesterday, yesterday will always be to come: not tomorrow, in the future, but to come, ahead, there in front, the day before yesterday.

91   And here is Robinson comparing himself to a hunted animal, more than one hunted animal, a hare or a fox, so that—and this makes us think of Kafka from another century—his castle looks like a burrow in which he takes refuge:

> When I came to my Castle, for so I think I call'd it ever after this, I fled into it like one pursued; whether I went over by the Ladder as first contriv'd, or went in at the Hole in the Rock, which I call'd a Door, I cannot remember; no, nor could I remember the next Morning, for never frighted Hare fled to Cover, or Fox to Earth, with more Terror of Mind than I to this Retreat. (RC, 142)

You have already noticed the fact, especially if you have just reread *Robinson Crusoe,* that in Robinson Crusoe's solitude, loneliness, insular isolation, even after the footprint, and even, later, after the meeting with Friday, there are on this island only men and beasts: those are the only living beings. And when I say men, I mean men, not only humans but men without women and without sex. Until the last pages of the book it is a world without women and without sex, or, if you prefer, men without sexual difference and without desire, without obvious sexual concern as such. This is no doubt what explains in part the profound affect that attracts and attaches readers the world over, readers become children again, dreaming of such a paradisiacal place in spite of all the dangers that Robinson Crusoe seems to confront and fear. As if, like in Paradise, sexual difference had not yet taken place or no longer had any reason for being. Later we'll cite the moments of euphoria, Robinson's moments of extreme and declared enjoy-
92   ment, Robinson who declares himself, in spite of all the difficulties, menaces, and privations, the happiest of men. This happy man never thinks, for almost thirty years, for at least twenty-eight years, of the fact that there are women in the world. As he seems never to have thought about it before being cast ashore on the island. In any case he never talks about it, this is the absolute unspoken aspect of these memoires. A little as though there were some secret contract between sovereign euphoria, paradisiacal euphoria, and the absence of women, of the other as woman, even the desire of or for the other woman, the other as woman. There is nobody else,

there is a sort of slave, there are some animals and nobody else. And nobody else, "alone at last," that means: no woman, no more women. No trace of woman. [*Pas trace de femme.*] Because above all he never imagines for a moment that the footprint might be a feminine footprint. *Il,* the *Il,* an *il,* him, an island [*île*] and not them [*elles*], no woman. No trace of woman's step. [*Pas de trace de pas de femme.*] That's sovereignty, that's solitary and exceptional sovereignty: slave, animal, and no woman. No desire to come along and limit sovereignty. In any case no heterosexual desire, and if there were homosexual desire, it would go, symbolically and symptomatically, via the symbolics of young slaves and beasts. Beasts you eat or that constantly threaten to eat you (the great gesture, the great phantasmatic *gesta* of the book, which rules its whole vocabulary, its speech, its mouth, its tongue and its teeth, is that of eating and devouring, eating the other, that's all we ever hear about, the fear of being devoured by wild beasts or by savage canni-bals, and the need to eat beasts, beasts that you hunt, that you raise or that you domesticate. Whose skin you always keep. You will have noticed on a hundred occasions: those beasts, he'll have their hide. He keeps it and uses it to clothe himself, protect himself, to build, but also as an emblem of sov-ereignty, etc. The skin of beasts is like the origin of his technology and su-premacy as a man. So there are all the animals in the world, the most "rav-enous, furious, venomous, poisonous" beasts, but no women. No trace of woman's step.)

Only in the last six pages of the book, and as though in passing, through   93
preterition, does Robinson mention two women.

And in both cases, death is there waiting.

The other woman is always death.

In the first case, it is an old woman to whom he had sent money and who is so grateful that she is ready to do anything for him. Now this woman is a widow, he says, "my good antient Widow" (RC, 279). He sees her again on his return, and she gives him the good advice not to go back to his island as he had wished ("My true Friend, the Widow, earnestly diswaded me from it . . ." [RC, 280]).

Death and the other woman. As for the other woman, his wife, she is not a widow, but he is himself a widower, since he tells us, as though in a post-script and by preterition, in one sentence, in the final pages that describe his return, that, upon his return, precisely, and before setting off again for what he calls his "new Collony in the Island" ("In this Voyage I visited my new Collony in the Island, saw my Successors the *Spaniards* . . ." [RC, 281]), on his return, then, and before setting off again to his "new Collony in the Island," he tells us in passing, in three lines, less than a sentence, he says in passing that in passing, between his two voyages to the island, he got married, had two sons and a daughter, but that his wife died. He says nothing about her but "she died": "My Wife dying . . ."; she doesn't die, she is "dying," or rather, she dies, she is dying:

> In the mean Time, I in Part settled myself here, for first of all I marry'd,
> and that not either to my Disadvantage or Dissatisfaction, and had three
> children, two Sons and one Daughter. But my Wife dying, and my Nephew
> coming Home . . . my Inclination to go Abroad, and his Importunity pre-
> vailed . . . (RC, 281)

94

This does not stop him going on to speak of the five women taken back to the island by his Spanish successors and of the seven women he sent them himself, as though by mail or by cargo boat. A cargo of women like "surface mail."[38] This is the last page: ". . . besides other Supplies, I sent seven Women, being such as I found proper for Service, or for Wives to such as would take them: As to the *English* Men, I promis'd them to send them some Women from *England,* with a good Cargoe of Necessaries, if they would apply themselves to Planting" (RC, 282).

Now: Now, holding [*Maintenant, maintenant*] in one hand [*main*] *Robinson Crusoe,* and keeping it in memory and in sight, we now take in the other hand Heidegger's seminar on World, Finitude and Solitude (*Welt, Endlich-keit, Einsamkeit*), and to make a path for ourselves toward the animal, we open the book right and exactly in its middle (p. 265 out of 532 pages [179 of 366]). Let us not forget the radical differences of status: we have in one hand an English book, a book of fiction that pretends to present itself as realistic and non-fictional memoirs, and in the other a book in German, a written seminar that, in another language and another country, more than two centuries later, in <a> mode as heterogeneous as possible, speaks to us of world, finitude, solitude, and animals.

95   What do we find, in this seminar? Someone, a German, this time, who unlike the Kreutznaers did not emigrate to England, who is seeking his path, the best path (his word, a hundred times, *Weg*) among many others, at least three, in order to ask the question of the world (*Was ist Welt?*), to question after the world, and a world in which there are stones, animals, and men, the stone, the animal, and the man. We are in the second chapter of the second part of the book or the seminar. It is called "The Beginning of Metaphysical Questioning with the Question of World. The Path of the Investigation and Its Difficulties" ["Der Beginn des metaphysischen Fra-

---

38. [Translator's note:] "Surface mail" is in English in the text.

gens mit der Frage nach der Welt. Der Weg der Untersuchung und seine Schwierigkeiten"] (H, 261/176).

The gesture whereby I decide to open the book at its center is neither neutral, nor innocent, nor totally justifiable. I hope to correct that fact with you, either by returning, as I intend to, over what comes earlier, or by inviting you to do it yourselves (we can't do everything in one course).

My strategic justification is a double one: *on the one hand,* it is from this halfway point that Heidegger explicitly and systematically broaches the question of the animal, which is our theme here; *on the other hand,* the figure of the path, the decision to take one path rather than others in order to present theses (and the gesture of presenting theses *as such* is in itself very odd in Heidegger, merits special reflection) interests us, among other things, because of what we have just identified as Robinson's anguish about the path and the cartography to be opened, including that of the risk of a vicious circle as a hermeneutic circle that consists in retracing one's steps, in always presupposing oneself, allowing oneself to be hallucinated by the specter of one's own tracks as tracks of the other man.

If, then, we open this chapter, we find that everything in it goes by *three.* From the title onward, Heidegger announces to us that in this path (*Weg*) we have taken, there are *three* guiding theses: 1. The stone is worldless; 2. The animal is poor in world; 3. Man is world-forming: "Der Weg der vergleichenden Betrachtung von drei leitenden Thesen: der Stein ist weltlos, das Tier ist weltarm, der Mensch ist weltbildend" (H, 261/176). 96

That's the title, a path, and three theses. But when we begin to read the chapter, we are told that to arrive at these three theses, we already had to hesitate and already choose among three paths.

Which paths?

You have noticed that the three theses all concern the world, the question of world (*Welt*), the different modalities of the relation to what one calls the world: *weltlos* for the stone, *weltarm* for the animal, *weltbildend* for man, each time it is an attribute or participle that qualifies the *world,* the presence or absence of *world,* the having or not-having a world, the world, etc. One might say that Heidegger's point is less to say something essential about the stone, the animal or man than to say something essential about differences *as to the world.*

The question is indeed that of the world, and the three theses are theses about the world, *as to the world,* more still than about those entities: stone, animal and man. And it is precisely on the subject of the world, the question "*Was ist Welt?*" that, even before the three theses, Heidegger envisages three paths. Indeed he writes:

We begin with the first of our three questions [it being understood: *world, finitude, and solitude* that form the triple coordinated theme of the seminar]: *What is world?* Even now we tend to take this explicit question as a free-floating question asked along the way just like any other (*Wir nehmen diese ausgesprochene Frage auch jetzt noch leicht als eine freischwebende, so in den Tag hinein gesprochene Frage*). Initially we do not know where we should look for an answer to it. Indeed, if we consider the matter more closely, we do not even know what we are asking about, or in what direction our questioning is moving (*in welcher Richtung des Fragens wir uns bewegen*). (H, 261/176)

97 In other words, and it's a bit like it is for the question of Being, we do not know what it is, world, what being it is and therefore in view of what we are questioning. We think we know what the world is, what we mean when we say "world," and that everything is the world, everything is in the world or of the world, that there is nothing outside the world, and therefore we are unable to specify, to determine a question bearing on the world, as it would bear on this or that, on a determinable being. A question about the world is a question about everything and nothing. About everything, therefore about nothing, it's an empty question that bites the tail of its own presupposition. One knows too much and one knows nothing, of the world. *On en sait trop rien.* One could stop there and thus refuse even the possibility of determining such a question, determining and specifying its meaning. Kant said of the world that it was merely a regulative Idea of Reason.

But what interests me, what seems interesting to me here, and what remains at bottom unreflected by Heidegger, is that instead of getting paralyzed or giving up, faced with the all and nothing, the all or nothing of this empty question, faced with *je n'en sais trop rien,* or *j'en sais trop rien,* Heidegger makes a gesture: he decides, without thematizing the sense and necessity of this decision — he takes, will have taken the decision to make the gesture that consists in determining the difficulty or the aporia as the figure of *direction,* the path to be taken. To pose and determine a question, one apparently needs to know where to go, on what path, in what direction, with what step to move along (*sich bewegen*) a path (*Weg*). That such a question paralyzes us seems to mean in his eyes that, as one must move forward (that is the presupposition), as the discourse must discourse going forward, proceeding, progressing; as one must walk [*marcher*], as it must work [*il faut que ça marche*], as one must go to it, one must go, precisely — the question insists as a question of orientation, of direction (*Richtung*) on the path (*Weg*) of moving along (*sich bewegen*). Where to go? In what direction should one take oneself? We are alone, immobilized on an island and we wonder how to start walking, toward the world, that is, without going around in circles or retracing our steps. In which direction? How to orient oneself in thinking the world? one might say to parody and displace Kant's question in that extraordinary little great text entitled *Was heißt: Sich im Denken orientieren?* (1786). If I had not chosen to read a seminar of Heidegger's at the same time as *Robinson Crusoe,* I would have chosen and perhaps should have chosen to read with you, to reread this text of Kant's, closer in the Age of Enlightenment to Defoe, and the exercise would have been fruitful. From the very start of this text that you no doubt know or else should read and reread, Kant articulates his question as would a Robinson who was at once a seafarer, an astronomer, and a geographer and who, left to himself, wonders how to orient himself, and what "to orient oneself" means. He then sets off from the *etymon,* i.e. the orient, and he specifies that to orient oneself in the proper sense of the word (*in der eigentlichen Bedeutung des Worts*)[39] means—since one always orients oneself in the world, on the basis of a given region of the world (*aus einer gegebenen Weltgegend*), and since there are four of them on the horizon—that the point is to find the orient, the Levant, the sunrise (*Aufgang*). If I see (and I need to see) the sun in the sky and if I know it is noon, I will find the south, east, west and north. But for that to be possible, I must feel, I must have a feeling of difference in my own subject (*an meinen eigenen* Subjekt). And you see that the value of property or propriety is indispensable, along with the value of the proper: to determine the proper sense of the word "orient" (*die eigentliche Bedeutung des Worts*), I have to refer myself to what affects the feeling (*Gefühl*) of my own proper subject (*an meinen eigenen* Subjekt). If Kant speaks of feeling and not of concept or idea, it is because this is about the sensory experience of my own body, namely the difference between right and left. Because this difference—as you know, he shows this elsewhere—is not conceptual but sensible and because between my right hand and my left hand there is no predicable conceptual difference, but only a sensory difference of orientation and place, and thereby of sensory irreplaceability (one cannot put one's right hand in a left-hand glove even though there is no intelligible conceptual difference, nor even an objectively describable difference between the two gloves and the two hands, merely a difference of sensory orientation).[40]

98

99

---

39. Immanuel Kant, *Was heißt: Sich im Denken orientieren?* (1786), in *Kants Werke: Abhandlungen nach 1781* (Berlin: Walter de Gruyter & Co., 1968), 8:134; trans. H. B. Nisbet as "What Is Orientation in Thinking?," in *Kant's Political Writings,* ed. H. S. Reiss, 2nd ed. (Cambridge: Cambridge University Press, 1991), pp. 237–49.

40. [Translator's note:] This sentence is incomplete in the French text.

And this allows Kant to posit that geographical orientation (in the world and on the earth) depends in the last analysis on no objective or objectifiable datum but merely on a principle of subjective differentiation. The major interest of this text (a text that is Robinsonian in its way, since it poses the question and answers the question of orientation in the world on the basis of the situation of a solitary body proper, which at least alleges, claims to be without any objective or intersubjective reference point, deprived of any socialized techno-science, etc., which therefore alleges and claims to come forward as the pure, solitary subjectivity of the naked body proper), the major interest of the text also hangs on the moment when Kant wants to "extend" (*erweitern*), without betraying it, what he calls the sensory and subjective principle of differentiation in orientation, when he extends it, then, to everything, to mathematics, logic, to *thinking* in general, in particular to thinking in the shape of the rationality of reason. It is thus that he accounts for what he calls the "*need* of reason," as elsewhere he talks of the interest of reason, the "feeling of the proper *need* of reason [*Das Gefühl des der Vernunft eigenen* Bedürfnisses]," and Kant underlines the word "need," *Bedürfniss*, then the "*right of the need* of reason [das Recht des Bedürfnisses der Vernunft]" (Kant's emphasis again . . .).[41]

What right, what right of need? The right, I quote, "to suppose and admit (*vorauszusetzen und anzunehmen*) something that it [reason] cannot claim to know by objective principles; and consequently *to orient oneself* in thought (*sich im Denken . . . zu* orientieren) through its own proper need (the need of reason alone: *durch ihr eigenis Bedürfniss*) in the incommensurable space (that is for us full of dense shadows) of the supra-sensible (*für uns mit dicker Nacht erfüllten Raume des Übersinnlichen*)."[42]

The point, then, is to extend the always subjective, but sensory, principle of orientation to the right of reason, the right of the need proper to reason to orient itself in thought on the basis of a principle that is always subjective, of course, but this time carried beyond the sensory field and into the black night of the suprasensible, and thus the invisible, the metempirical. This leap into the night, the leap of right on the basis of need is an infinite leap, an infinite extension. And if you follow the huge consequences of this, the oceanic consequences in what follows in the text that I am leaving you to read, you will see why the need of *practical* reason is absolutely, unconditionally privileged with respect to the need of theoretical reason, for the need of reason in its practical use is, precisely, unconditional (*unbedingt*).

41. Ibid., pp. 136–37 [p. 240].
42. Ibid.

You will also see Kant define and determine what he calls a *belief of reason,* and even a "purely rational belief" (*Ein reiner Vernunftglaube*) and to describe this belief of reason, here too he takes what I shall call a Robinsonian tone, or at least he navigates like a sailor in the Robinsonian ocean. The point is always to orient oneself and trace one's path:

> A purely rational belief is the signpost [*Wegweiser,* what shows the way] or compass (*oder Kompass*) by means of which the speculative thinker can orient himself on his rational wanderings in the field of supra-sensory objects, while the man of ordinary but (morally) healthy (*moralisch gesunder*) reason can use it to plan his course (*seinen Weg vorzeichnen*), for both theoretical and practical purposes, in complete conformity (*Angemessen*) with the whole end of his destiny; and this same rational belief must also be made the basis of every other belief, and indeed of every revelation (*Offenbarung*).[43] (Reread without the German.)

Then he moves on, in the same movement, to the concept of God. You'll read it.

One last return to Heidegger, and I'm done for today.

In what direction? he was asking himself. Toward which path should we orient this question that is so open and indeterminate, namely: "what is world?" In what sense, in the sense of direction, should we orient this question that does not, itself, even indicate the direction in which we can pose it, in which we can organize ourselves and relate to it? The world is an island whose map we do not have. We are in it and we want to go toward it, and we do not know which way to turn to take our first step.

Now here he goes (it looks like a *coup de théâtre* or a *coup de force,* although that is not Heidegger's tone, but I maintain that more than once he is taking decisions that are so many arbitrary *coups de force* or *coups de théâtre,* so many unjustifiable decisions: that would be Heidegger's *Walten*), here he goes starting to name the first path, as the closest path ("*Der nächste Weg zu einer ersten Klärung . . .*" [H, 261/176]).

What does "the closest" mean here? And why begin this way, with the one closest to us, as Heidegger already had done in *Sein und Zeit,* right at the beginning, to take *Dasein* as point of departure and exemplary being as to which to ask the question of the meaning of Being?

Those are questions that will wait for us until 2003: I remind you it'll be the twenty-second of January.

---

43. Ibid., p. 142 [p. 245].

January 22, 2003

103   Does solitude *distance* one from others? What am I saying when I say "I am alone"? Does it distance me or bring me closer to the other or the others? Am I coming closer or distancing myself from the others or a particular other by the simple statement that "I am alone," be it a complaint, a sigh of despair, or on the contrary the sign of a complacent and narcissistic presumptuousness? And what if this statement were a strategy, the misuse of a fiction, a simulacrum, would it be designed to bring the other closer or to distance him or her, to tie or untie what they call the social bond? In any case, I am certainly doing something other than when I say "I am *the* only one." "I am the only one [*je suis le seul*]" means something quite different from "I am alone [*je suis seul*]." And the thing would be still more complicated, to the point of dizziness, if I said "I am alone" and "moreover I'm the only one," in truth, "I am the only one to be alone," "the only one to be so alone."

    Does saying oneself to be "the only one" bring one nearer, or distance one? Does saying oneself to be "the only one to be alone, so alone" bring the other in the world closer or make them more distant? Does it build or destroy the social bond?

    To begin to reply to these questions or even to elaborate them as questions, we would need to begin by agreeing as to what *coming closer* or *distancing* mean.

    What is proximity? The proxim*ity* of the close? The proxim*ity* of the close is not, for its part, necessarily close. Such and such a thing, such and such a country, such and such a person might be close or distant, but the
104   essence or the meaning of the close, the close *as such,* the proximity of the close *as* close, and appearing *as such,* is not necessarily close. At least not in the same sense. It might be distant, even inaccessible. And conversely, the distance of the distant, being-distant can be close and un-distance itself by appearing to us as such. These are, in any case, questions of meaning, of

the essence, of the "as such" of the appearing of meaning that we will come across again during our readings and our discussions of Heidegger's great meditation on the animal said to be "poor in world" (*weltarm*), to the extent that the animal is precisely supposed to be deprived of the "as such" (*als, als solche*)[1] of what, according to Heidegger, can appear to us, us as *Dasein*, "as such," *als*,[2] in a structure of the *as such*, in an experience of the relation to the as such (*das als-Struktur, als-Beziehung*). In what Heidegger calls the *Benommenheit* of the animal (translated—but we shall see that the translation is difficult and carries the whole weight of the reading—as *benumbment* or *captivation*), in its *Benommenheit*, well, the animal defined by this *Benommenheit* has, then, the possibility of relating to the entity *as such* removed from it, the possibility of perceiving as such what it perceives or relating to the entity and to the world *as such*, in its opening and being-manifest, in manifestation or manifestness, in the opening of what is manifest to it.[3]

We parted last time on a question precisely about what Heidegger meant by the closest, in the choice of the closest path, by which he proposed to begin his questioning and his mode of questioning. What does "close" mean? And why this privilege of the close, of the "closer to us" that we were already recognizing in the choice of methodological approach that Heidegger had already made, a few years before this 1929–30 seminar, in *Sein und Zeit* (1927), when he privileged[4] Dasein, the analytic of Dasein as the analytic of the exemplary being for the question of Being because it is closest to *us,* as questioning beings, the closest, the absolutely close to us who are asking the question of Being or are not indifferent to our Being, etc.?

So how is it with this enigmatic proximity that becomes the principle of orientation of thought? That is the question we left suspended at the end of the last session. We are going to approach this question in our turn, but without hesitating[5] to make quite a long detour before returning, taking our distances to retrace our steps. All the while remaining aware of this possibility of taking one's distance in order to retrace one's steps. What kind

1. During the session, Derrida added: "deprived of appearing as such, deprived of the as such of appearing."
2. During the session, Derrida added: "we see the sun, like the animal, but according to Heidegger we see it as such; the animal sees the sun or warms itself in the sun, without seeing it as such."
3. On the *als-Struktur,* see H, 453–56/312–15. On the concept of *Benommenheit,* see §§60–61. Derrida discusses these concepts in more detail in the seventh, eighth, and tenth sessions.
4. During the session, Derrida added: "and felt justified in privileging."
5. In the typescript: "but not without hesitating," corrected during the session.

of space are we dealing with, what figure or structure of space (and time) and what kind of path is it when it turns out that the more one takes one's distance from the starting point, the closer one gets to it, the more distance one takes from the origin the closer <one> gets to it?

So where are we going to start out from again and for what journey?

I propose, so as not to give in too much to boredom, but in order not to flee it either — boredom always running the risk of being fled or being itself a flight — I propose to start out this time from boredom, precisely, which is one of the great themes of the 1929–30 seminar.

What is boredom?

Did Robinson get bored? Was he not too captivated by various urgencies to get bored?

The least one can say is that no, this man did not get bored, he had no time to get bored. And if he never got bored on his island, that is basically — and this is confirmed by many passages we have read and will still read — because he loved his island, he desired the island that he appropriated for *106* himself at any price, over which he declared more and more often that he was reigning as a sovereign, like a sovereign, even if it was full of dangers, or mortal threats, etc.

Why does one love islands? Why does one not love islands? Why do some people love islands while others do not love islands, some people dreaming of them, seeking them out, inhabiting them, taking refuge on them, and others avoiding them, even fleeing them instead of taking refuge on them?

But fleeing them, as much as taking refuge on them, presupposes a movement of flight. One cannot dissociate the figure of the island from the experience of flight. For example, one can long for the island as for a distant refuge to which one could flee humanity for a chosen exile. At the end of the Fifth Walk [in the *Reveries of a Solitary Walker*], Rousseau, that man of the island, admirer of Robinson, author of a *Project for a Constitution for Corsica,* whose situation he emphasizes, the "advantageous situation of the Island of Corsica," Rousseau also longs for the Island of St. Pierre on Lake Bienne:

> Why can I not finish my days on that beloved Island and never leave it, never see any inhabitant of the continent who would remind me of the calamities of all sorts that they have delighted in piling on me for so many years! They would soon be forgotten forever: no doubt they will not forget me the same way: but what matter to me so long as they would have no way to come and trouble my repose?[6]

6. Jean-Jacques Rousseau, "Cinquième promenade," in *Les rêveries du promeneur solitaire,* in *Œuvres complètes,* ed. Marcel Raymond and Bernard Gagnebin, 5 vols. (Paris: Gallimard, 1959–95), 1:1048.

Note first, to remember it later, that at the beginning of this walk, Rousseau uses the word "alone" [*seul*] and the syntagm "the only" [*le seul*] in a way that will not fail to interest us. He doesn't just say that he likes to be alone, that he loves and chooses solitude or loneliness (a theme of Heidegger's seminar: World, Finitude, Solitude: *Einsamkeit*), he does not say only that he loves the solitude or loneliness of the solitary walker who happens to be alone; no, Rousseau also says, and this is something else, that he really is "alone" in this situation, and therefore the one and only, the singular, as singular moreover as the Island of St. Pierre itself, as alone and exceptional as the *situation,* the site of the Island of St. Pierre. Here's what he says, with an extraordinary subtlety, with a non-sophistical sophistication of vocabulary, at the beginning of the same Fifth Walk, at the moment he is singing of his happiness on the island, and of the island's charms: 107

> Yet it is agreeable and *singularly* situated [I emphasize *singularly:* the island itself is isolated; not merely isolated, insularized as an island and like all islands, but isolated and alone of its type among islands by reason of its place, its site, and therefore also its topo-geographical environment: it is singularly situated] for the happiness of a man who likes to circumscribe himself [and thus to isolate himself]; for although I am *the only one* in the world to have a destiny that has made a law of it for him [so the only one for whom the solitude that he loves has also been imposed on him by a law that thus makes him alone twice over: alone not only by taste but alone by sanction], I cannot believe that I am alone in having such a natural taste, although I have so far found it in no one else.[7]

Admire the complexity of this argumentation: not only am I alone, solitary, etc., but I am alone, the only one (therefore unique, irreplaceable, almost the chosen one) for whom this solitude that I love naturally, solitary as I am by nature, has been imposed like a law; and even if I cannot believe that I am alone in having this innate, natural love of solitude, until now I have met no other with whom to share it. So I naturally love solitude but they have also made it, against me, a law imposed, for me alone they have transformed nature into law, *physis* into *nomos,* as it were. But even if I find it hard to believe, I am alone in having this natural taste for solitude since I have met no one to share it with me. So I am alone [*seul*], I naturally love solitude and I am *alone* [*le* seul] in having solitude *both* by nature *and* by law. This solitude is therefore so essential, so profound, so abyssal that it defines me in my absolute ipseity or in the unique destiny of my ipseity. I 108 am alone, I am alone in being so alone, and alone in naturally loving being alone. But you can see that as I was suggesting at the outset, that "being

7. Ibid., p. 1040; Derrida's emphasis on "the only one."

alone" and "being the only one," even "being the only one to be so alone," or "alone in liking being alone," are not exactly the same thing, even if the two meanings and the two syntaxes (*seul* and *le seul*) receive the hospitality of *one* and the same [*seul et même*] word and even if this sameness of the word as a homonym with two meanings does not come about [*only*] by chance *alone*. It is not by chance that two meanings as different as "I am alone" (in the sense of solitude) and "I am alone," in the sense of exception, singularity, unicity, election, and irreplaceability (often, moreover, the features of sovereignty) here lodge in the same word, in the same adjective, in different grammars in which the epithet "alone" seems to begin to substantify itself or nominalize itself as alone, the only one.

What is more, in this same text, in the seventh of the *Rêveries,* Rousseau draws pride from his situation as refugee who, in his very flight, becomes the discoverer, the conqueror and the sovereign of his island, and transforms his exile into an empire. The island of St. Pierre becomes the America colonized by this new Columbus, by what he calls "another Columbus:"[8]

109
> I began to dream more at ease, thinking that I was there in a refuge unknown to the entire universe, from which my persecutors would not dig me up.[9]

[I pause for a moment on this strange figure, for reasons that will become clearer to us later when we come back to Robinson: my persecutors will not dig me up, says Rousseau. So they will not succeed in following me, nor finding me in and on this land, in the hole that is this island where I am, on this land, as if buried alive, where I am lucky enough, and bless the luck I have, to be as though buried alive.]

> . . . I began to dream more at ease, thinking that I was there in a refuge unknown to the entire universe, from which my persecutors would not dig me up. A movement of pride soon became mixed with this reverie. I compared myself to those great voyagers who discover a desert island, and I said to myself complacently: no doubt I am the first mortal who has come this far; I looked upon myself almost as another Columbus.[10]

8. [Translator's note:] Derrida adds, "à prononcer comme vous voudrez, lui, il l'écrit Colomb [pronounce it how you like: [Rousseau] writes 'Colomb']." "Christophe Colomb" is the standard French spelling of the name that in English is rendered "Christopher Columbus": Derrida's point seems to be that "Colomb" is phonetically indistinguishable from the French word "colon," colonist or colonizer.

9. Rousseau, "Septième promenade," p. 1071.

10. Ibid.

Read what follows, when he discovers a stocking factory: it's quite funny.

In the *Rêveries,* Rousseau does not name Robinson, but in the *Confessions,* Book XII, when he recounts at length his exile as a persecuted refugee on the island of St. Pierre, his enjoyments or his ecstasies as a botanist, and when he dreams that the lake is an ocean, he names Robinson and compares himself to "another Robinson." This time it is not Robinson as politico-pedagogical model, praise for which we have seen in *Emile, The Social Contract,* or the second *Discourse,* but another "other Robinson," the imaginary Robinson who builds his dwelling: ". . . and to build like another Robinson an imaginary dwelling on this little island."[11] In the second dialogue of *Rousseau juge de Jean-Jaques,* another Robinson, yet another, a sort of literal reference to Robinson, to the "*Robinson* novel" consists in an interesting upping of the ante that pushes Rousseau to say that Jean-Jacques is at bottom more Robinsonian than Robinson because he loves solitude and living alone so much that he would not even have suffered as did Robinson from his insularity:

> J.-J. has not always fled other men, but he has always loved solitude. He was happy with the friends he *thought* he had [. . .], but he was happier still with himself. He cherished their society; but sometimes he needed to be on his own, and perhaps he would have liked even better *always living alone* than always living with them.[12] His [J.J.'s] affection for the *Robinson* novel made me conclude that he would not have thought himself as unhappy as Robinson did, confined to his desert island.[13]

110

So Jean-Jaques, if not Rousseau, the persecuted Rousseau, would have been a happy Robinson, happier than Defoe's real imaginary Robinson. Strange Robinsonian upping of the ante which basically invokes the deep, essential and unique desire of the singular ipseity of someone who at bottom only loves and rediscovers himself in solitude and who, at bottom, *bores himself* in society when he is not *bored*[14] or persecuted *by* that same society.

This Robinsonian upping of the ante takes another turn in the same *Dialogue*—a turn that, as it were, exasperates the Robinsonian and insularoid metaphor, in that—this is why I use the word "exasperation"—Rousseau says both that he is more alone than Robinson and more alone even

11. *Oeuvres completes*, I, p. 644.

12. During the session, Derrida added: "I suppose everyone says a blessing for not having to choose."

13. *Oeuvres completes,* I, p. 812.

14. [Translator's note:] "Ennuyé" here also can mean "bothered" or "annoyed."

in Paris than Robinson on his island. I also speak of exacerbation and exasperation because here we are dealing with the isolation of a persecuted
man in the middle of the city [and the question becomes for us no longer
merely "what is an island?" but "what is a city?" and what is an island in
a city when it is not the Ile de la Cité or the Ile St. Louis, but the island on
which someone is isolated, insularized in the middle of the city, by reason of
an imposed or chosen isolation.[15]] And you will see that the supplementary
turn of the exasperated Robinsonian metaphor is going to be the more singular in that the one who claims to be in, I quote, a "unique position," and
thus alone in being alone in this way, claims to be unique in the sense that
he pushes a certain perversity in favoring the perversion of the others, the
persecutors, to the point of voluntarily cooperating with them and choosing
to isolate himself in the solitude his persecutors want to impose on him. As
for them, they are sadistic, but as for him, he is masochistic, as the other guy
would say. For, subjected thus to a mechanism, a machine, a compulsive
and repetitive automatism of auto-persecutory perversion that turns against
the self the aggression come from enemies with whom he cannot fail to
identify, he helps his persecutors to insularize him in the middle of the city,
he *prefers* this persecution, he gives way to it, he persecutes *himself* as though
he were his own destroyer, he destroys his own protections, as though he
were moved by an auto-immune mechanism. He delivers *himself, in himself, by himself,* to his enemies or his persecutors. He attacks his own *himself,*
his *selfsameness,* his "same," his *ipseity,* by himself cultivating the imposed
insularity. Rousseau appropriates the supposed perversion of the other: he
internalizes it and outflanks it in advance to ensure his sovereign mastery
over it at the very spot where this perversion threatens to destroy his sovereign ipseity.[16] Let me read from the second *Dialogue:*

> I saw him [J.-J.] in a *unique* [I emphasize "unique": he is alone in living
> this solitude and loving it in this way, in electing it when he is elected or
> constrained to it] and almost incredible position, more alone in the middle
> of Paris than Robinson on his Island, and sequestered away from the com-
> merce of men by the very crowd pressing around him to stop him bonding

15. During the session, Derrida added: "Isolation by law: one can be alone on an
island, naturally alone, but when one is alone on an island in a city, when one becomes
an island in a city, this solitude is a solitude of law and not . . ."; the end of this sentence
is inaudible.
16. Sentence added by Derrida at the end of the typescript of this session, with the
indication: "Addition p. 7."

with anyone [unbound bond of social unbinding, etc. Comment.[17]] I have seen him cooperate voluntarily with his persecutors to make himself more and more isolated, and while they were working without respite to keep him separate from other men, to take more and more distance from the others and themselves.[18]

"Take his distance," he says, and if you read what follows (which is, as always, gripping), you will see this distancing (we're going to be talking about this more in a moment, with Heidegger) get complicated and return twice at least, on the same page (826) with the double syntagma of the transitive and the reflexive (distance *them,* distance *oneself* from them: what is the difference (for there is a difference) between distancing the others and distancing oneself from them? "For his part he would like to distance them," says Rousseau, speaking of J.-J., "or rather distance himself from them because their evil nature, their duplicity . . ." etc. And further on: "*'You ask me,'* he would say, '*why I flee men? Ask them themselves, they know even better than I.'"*)[19]

112

What is one fleeing when one distances oneself, flees, takes refuge or goes into exile, like a refugee or one exiled on an island—what is one fleeing when one flees to an island? Or conversely when one flees from the island? And is there not, sometimes, in the same person, in the same desire, a murky concurrence and a strange simultaneity, when it comes to the insularity of the island, between attraction and repulsion, between insularophilia and insularophobia? What must a sort of essence of the island be or signify (if there is an essence) to provoke this double contradictory movement of attraction and allergy?

Of course it has to do with a certain experience of solitude that is often understood as isolating, isolation, insularity. Let us not forget that the Heidegger seminar from which we shall select the part concerning the animal

17. During the session, Derrida added: "The crowd presses in around him, there are too many people and this pressing, this pressure is designed to isolate him, to deprive him of the social bond."

18. Ibid., p. 826. During the session, Derrida added: "They are seeking to isolate him and he is seeking to separate himself, to take his distance. So he competes, he is in competition with his persecutors, he ups the ante: who will isolate him better, 'them' or 'me'?"

19. Ibid., p. 827. During the session, Derrida added: "In other words, knowing who distances whom, who takes distance from whom. When ipseity is at stake, it is hard to say who is *ego, ipse,* the singular one. The difference between 'distancing the others' and 'taking distance from them' is a very precarious and unstable difference."

poor in world is a seminar on the world, of course, but also, at great length, a seminar on finitude and especially what links solitude, *Einsamkeit,* about which he speaks directly rather little, to boredom (*Langeweile*), to getting bored [*s'ennuyer*] (*das Sichlangweilen*) and more precisely to the depth, the becoming-deep of the experience of this getting bored, a word or verb that in German more than in French [or English] implies a temporal dimension, a long interval or duration of time (*Langweile*), therefore a temporalization which is at the heart of the analysis whereby Heidegger refers boredom to the temporalization of Dasein (and more precisely, and this is one of the many interesting things about this analysis which is also, in a sense that is trying to be profound, historical), of Dasein today, the contemporary Dasein. The animal poor in world, in its *Benommenheit* (in its Dasein-less being-captivated) supposedly does not get bored in this deep sense, not even in the sense that, for reason of other preoccupations, Robinson did not get bored either, on his island, and that would be one of our questions.

We won't have time to read together this very rich Heideggerian analysis of boredom (do so yourselves), an analysis that precedes the developments on the question of the world and, in it, of the so-called animal realm. But so as to offer you a concrete image of the style of highly illustrated phenomenological description that Heidegger, rather unusually for him, Heidegger the professor, sometimes goes in for, I'd like — at least to amuse you before I get started — read you a passage. This passage precedes the moment when Heidegger, who wants to distinguish between *becoming bored by* and *being bored with* (which interests him more) proposes to bring out the difference between these two boredoms in order to grasp what he calls "the direction of a deeper becoming" of boredom (and this is indeed again, already, a question of direction and orientation of the philosophical question ("die *Richtung des Tieferwerdens,*" §25; Heidegger's emphasis)). This depth ought to point out the way (it is again, already, this question of the path, of orientation and direction that we were talking about last time) the "path toward originary boredom" (*den Weg zur ursprünglichen Langeweile*). This passage I'm picking, while asking you to read what precedes and follows, is found in the previous paragraph (§24). (Read and comment)

114

We shall attempt to find such a case, and indeed once again, as in the first instance, to find one that is distinctly everyday, accessible to everybody and almost inconspicuous.

We have been invited out somewhere for the evening. We do not need to go along. Still, we have been tense all day, and we have time in the evening. So we go along. There we find the usual food and the usual table conversation, everything is not only very tasty, but tasteful as well. Afterward people sit together having a lively discussion, as they say, perhaps listening to music, having a chat, and things are witty and amusing. And already it is time to leave. The ladies assure us (*Die Damen versichern*), not merely when leaving, but downstairs and outside too as we gather to leave, that it really was very nice, or that it was terribly charming (*Es war furchtbar reizend*). Indeed. There is nothing at all to be found that might have been boring about this evening, neither the conversation, nor the people, nor the rooms. Thus we come home quite satisfied. We cast a quick glance at the work we interrupted that evening, make a rough assessment of things and look ahead to the next day—and then it comes: I was bored after all this evening, on the occasion of this invitation.

Yet how so? With the best will in the world we can find nothing that could have bored us there. And yet I myself was bored. With what, then? I *myself*—did I then bore *myself* [selbst *gelangweilt*]? Was *I what was boring for myself* [*das* Langweilige]? Yet we recall quite clearly that not only was there nothing boring, but I was not at all occupied with myself either, not for a moment. I was not occupied with myself in any kind of pensive reflection that would have been the precondition for such boredom. On the contrary, I was totally involved, involved in and part of the conversation and everything else. Indeed, we do not even say that I was bored with *myself* [*ich habe mich bei* mir *gelangweilt*], but that I was bored with the evening [*sondern bei der Einladung*]. Or is perhaps all this subsequent talk that I was bored after all merely an illusion that arises from an ensuing bad mood over the fact that I have now sacrificed and lost this evening? No: it is quite clear that we were bored, even though it was all so pleasant. Or perhaps it was the pleasantness [*diese Nettigkeit*] of the evening with which we were bored?

Yet when we talk in this way, have we not made an unfair judgment? Is this not ultimately the kind of conduct which only a very blasé person could indulge in, someone who is used to seeing everything in advance in this peculiar light of being fundamentally bored, someone who, due to this peculiar way of being bored in the face of everything, has in advance a dissatisfied, disapproving attitude toward everything everywhere? Yet, we are not now asking whether it was justified or unjustified for us to be bored, nor whether the boredom now at issue can be traced back, in its factical development and whatever provoked it, to a tired, blasé attitude or to something else. We are asking what properly belongs to this *having been bored with the evening* as we have depicted it, and how this form of being bored with . . . is to be *distinguished* from the first form, from becoming bored by . . . in the specific situation of the railway station.[20]

115

20. During the session, Derrida added: "According to many accounts of Heidegger, he was often bored, he seemed bored. The people who report that seem surprised by it!"

[Read what follows: you'll see that it's very funny ... He talks about yawning:]

[...] We even had to hide our yawning; and it was inappropriate to drum our fingers on the tabletop [...].
[...] The yawning and the wanting to drum our fingers were a flaring up, as it were, of the kind of passing the time that we are acquainted with, in which we somehow seek to occupy ourselves. [...] We resort to these attempts from time to time. Just as we are on the verge of playing with our watchchain or a button, cigars are passed around again. We have already let them pass by once, but now we take a cigar. We are not getting sleepy, and yet—we smoke, not to become more sleepy, nor to be stimulated by the nicotine, but because smoking itself is a socially ideal way of passing the time. (H, 165–69/109–12)[21]

The relation is pretty clear between boredom and solitude, between solitude and these premises of an analysis of originary and profound boredom, of what Heidegger will call the abandonment of our own ipseity, our own *Selbst*. Further on (at the end of §<25>), Heidegger will wonder what happens, in boredom, when our own *Selbst* which is known to us (*Unser eigenes Selbst ist uns aber doch bekannt*) is abandoned and finds itself left hanging, indeterminate and unknown in boredom. For after having noted that "Unser eigenes Selbst ist uns aber doch bekannt" (H, 184/122) and that we can unquestionably (*fraglos*) determine it in this way or that, Heidegger resorts to the value of proximity in what is not merely a feigned question, a rhetorical question.[22] He wonders "What could be closer to us than our own *Selbst*? [ourselves, oneself, ipseity: *Was könnte uns näher sein als unser eigenes Selbst?*]." And the question that follows then is, "To what extent is our own *Selbst,* our own self *left behind* and *left standing* in the fact of being bored with something, and, as *standing, indeterminate* and *unfamiliar,* so that it oppresses us as something strange and ungraspable? [*Inwiefern ist unser Selbst im Sichlangweilen-bei* zurück- *und* stehengelassen *und als solches* stehendes unbestimmt *und* unbekannt, *so dass es als dieses merkwürdige Unfassliche*

<hr/>

21. In this whole passage, the German quotations in brackets were written out by hand by Derrida on the photocopied texts of the translation included with the typescript. At the beginning of the quotation, Derrida says that he will not read out the text in German, saying: "It's well enough translated, I think." We transcribe from the recording the few moments where Derrida does however quote the German text.
22. [Translator's note:] "Rhetorical question" is in English in the text.

uns bedrängt?]" And further on he will speak of a state of *"being left empty* ([Leergelassenheit]" (H, 185/122).

This supposed proximity, the supposed proximity of oneself to oneself raises, like every evaluation of the near and the far, the question of orientation. Basically, in the Kant text to which we devoted some reflection last time (*What Is Orientation in Thinking?*), the axiom of subjectivity (sensible then insensible) as zero-point of orientation that prevents me from confusing my right and my left whereas there is no conceptual, objective, and intelligible difference between a right-hand glove and a left-hand glove, this principle of the zero point of subjectivity is not, formally at least, very different, very distant, <from> that proximity to self of the *Selbst* that Heidegger talks about and seems to presuppose.[23]

So one must indeed orient oneself. What is it to orient oneself? What is it to orient oneself in thinking? we were asking ourselves at the turn of last year, and what is the history of this question, some of whose turns and detours, some of whose epochs, we followed in Defoe, Kant, and Heidegger, it being understood that the question of the Orient and of orientation can only arise and be posed, as such, in a place and at a moment of disorientation in the epochal experience of a loss or a suspension of all certainty as to the movement (*Bewegung*) or as to the path (*Weg*) on the ground of an earth, or on the waters of the sea: in other words, when the walker or the geographer, the geologist, the seafarer, have lost their way or, as we also say, *perdu le Nord.*[24] For when one knows where to go, this very knowledge suspends the question and all indecision, even all undecidability. This is good sense itself. This is the very sense of sense, of sense as sense and of sense as direction. The same holds when, in order to orient oneself, one is able to distinguish the near from the far. What is the near? we were asking ourselves at the end of the last session, reading Heidegger when, to break an indecision as to the path to follow for the world, to pose the question of the world, he answered by saying "let's choose the nearest path," the first path, namely, so he said, the closest path for a first elucidation (*Der* nächste *Weg zu einer* ersten Klärung . . .) (H 261/176; Heidegger's emphasis).

23. During the session, Derrida added: "Although he does not speak of subjectivity; but there is a proximity to self as zero-point of orientation that is formally at work."

24. [Translator's note:] "Perdre le nord," literally "to lose the north," is a standard French idiom for "to lose one's bearings."

But beyond the fact that Heidegger subsequently never stopped complicating the approach to proximity, by showing that the proximity of the near was far, and that *Entfernung,* distance, distancing, was also a de-distancing (*Entfernung*) that undid and therefore reduced distance,[25] one can, without going that far today, wonder how these paradoxes work on an island or in a circular movement in which the step that distances us from our starting point is also the step that brings us closer to it: the step that seems farthest from my starting point, on an island where one goes around in circles, like a wheel, like the rotation or rather the wheeling of a wheel, can also be <the one> closest to it. My last footstep always might coincide with my first. That is the law of the island and the law of the wheel, or more precisely of the gearing, the systematic set that holds together the wheels of the machine, of which a clock would be only one example.

Now you have perhaps noticed that on his island, Robinson had some problems with the wheel. I'll go so far as to say that he had crucial problems with the wheel. The wheel was his cross, if one can thus cross or encircle these two figures together.[26] This is as much as to say that Robinson had problems with the circle, with the cycloid, and thus with the return onto itself of the wheel and the road, and not only with the risk of retracing his steps and of taking to be his the footprint [*trace de pas*] that, you remember, plunges him into a terrified meditation or speculation. He risks taking, as he says to himself, the footprint for that of another when it is perhaps his own and he perhaps went that way already himself, like another whose revenant he would be at the moment he is worrying about that footprint.

Why recall the wheel and this compulsive exposure to the return of the re-venant, to the question come [*venue*] from the re-venant?

Before returning to these questions, I am going to look more closely at these allusions to the wheel, to which I suppose that readers of *Robinson Crusoe* tend in general not to pay much attention, as one of the numerous technical details mentioned in passing in the life of a Robinson obsessively busy reinventing technology and forging for himself, like in the beginning, on his island, which is also encircled by seas and oceans, and on which the risks of retracing one's steps are greater than elsewhere, [of a Robinson busy,[27] then] forging for himself, providing for himself as though for the first time in the historical cycle of humanity (I would not even say of hominization,

119

25. During the session, Derrida added: "that it opens, however."
26. During the session, Derrida added: "because it is as a Christian that Robinson thinks, acts and speaks."
27. During the session, Derrida added: "captivated."

for there existed human civilizations without the wheel, Amerindian civilizations for example) [providing for himself] tools and instruments that were already available, as was the wheel, in the world he left behind.

As you know, in the history of mankind the wheel was a dramatic mutation, an extraordinary invention that was extraordinarily difficult to conceive and to bring about, and as soon as this allows one to describe, as one also describes a movement (for it is not enough to describe a circle, to inscribe a circle as a geometer would write one on the sand, in order to invent a wheel as technical prosthesis and material apparatus in the world, a machine capable of describing a movement by carrying it out, here by turning around an axle), as soon, then, as the wheel describes the circular return upon itself around an immobile axis, it becomes a sort of incorporated figural possibility, a *metaphora* (*metaphora* in Greek means vehicle, even automobile, autobus) for all bodily movements as physical movements of return to self, auto-deictics, autonomous but physical and corporeal movements of auto-reference, and therefore more than the mirror and specularity in general, more than theoretical reflection which consists merely in seeing one's own image. This *metaphora* carries or transports the dream of being oneself, in displacement, of displacing oneself while remaining oneself, of being one's own rotation around oneself, of pulling the body and the incorporated relation to oneself, in the world, toward the return to self around a relatively immobile axis of identity—not absolutely immobile, for the axis, the axle, the hub moves too, but immobile with respect to the circle of the wheel itself which turns around it. The wheel is neither the mirror nor simply the circle nor even the turning circle: a fallen tree trunk upon which stones were rolled, for example stones for a pyramid, is not a wheel. It lacks the axis that is both relatively mobile, and relatively immobile. The *metaphora* of this extraordinary apparatus is a figure, the turn of a trope that constructs and instructs in the relation to self, in the auto-nomy of ipseity, the possibility for unheard-of chances and threats, of automobility, but also, by the same token, of that threatening auto-affection that is called autoimmunity in general. What I call iterability, which repeats the same while displacing or altering it, is all at once a resource, a decisive power, and a catastrophe of repetition or reproduction. In this logic of iterability are found the resources both to cast into doubt oppositions of the type *physis/tekhnē* (and therefore also *physis/nomos, physis/thesis*) and to begin to analyze, in a different domain, all the fantasmatics, all the ideologies or metaphysics that today encumber so many discourses on cloning, discourses both for and against cloning. *Klôn* is moreover, in Greek, like *clonos* in Latin, a phenomenon of *physis* like that young sprout or that (primarily vegetable) growth,

120

that parthenogenetic emergence we talked about when we were marking the fact that, before allowing itself to be opposed as nature or natural or biological life to its others, the extension of *physis* included all its others. There again, it appears symptomatic that Heidegger does not speak of the plant, not directly, not actively: for it seems to me that although he mentions it of course, he does not take it as seriously, *qua* life, as he does animality. I always think of the ranunculus [*la renoncule*] (*clonos* in Latin), a marsh or aquatic flower whose name comes from *renonculus,* little frog or froglet.

Little by little, stage by stage—and I do not believe this has often been noticed—Robinson does his apprenticeship in this original rotational technique. Of course, just as he has a certain knowledge of what an island is before being thus insularized on the island of despair, he already knows in principle when he arrives on the island what a wheel is, because he has seen and used wheels in the culture from which he comes. But this is where technology is not to be reduced to a theoretical knowledge or to the efficient use one may make of an instrument. We all have the experience of often knowing how to make efficient use of an instrument (for example an automobile, a telephone, or a computer) without knowing how it works, without even knowing theoretically and in a very general way the law of its functioning, without being technically capable of building or even of repairing the instrument. This is, moreover, where the so-called comparative analysis of the abilities and technical powers of what is called the animal and what is called the human becomes terribly complicated and makes many people say many stupid things [*bêtises*]. This is also one of the problems—that of technology and work—that Heidegger does not address in his treatment of the animal "poor in world," or so it seems to me, and I say so here still under the reserve of a supplementary reading—but we'll come back to this.

So Robinson knows in principle what a wheel is, he has seen wheels, he has used them in Europe, but he does not know, not at all, at the beginning, on his arrival on the island, how to *make* a wheel.[28] He notices that on his island he is wanting a wheeled vehicle, a wheelbarrow, which, in abbreviated English, is called a *barrow* (this word also designates a stretcher, a chariot, a gurney) but more precisely a "Wheel-barrow":

> [A]s to a Wheel-barrow, I fancy'd I could make all but the Wheel, but that I had no Notion of, neither did I know how to go about it; besides I had no possible Way to make the Iron Gudgeons for the Spindle or Axis of the Wheel to run in, so I gave it over. (RC, 69)

28. [Translator's note:] "Comment *faire,* comment faire, si on peut dire, la roue." The idiom "faire la roue" in French means "do a cartwheel" in the gymnastic sense, but also describes what a peacock does when it displays its tail.

But later — and this is the story we would need to follow closely, after
also having encountered difficulties with the hooping, for example of a cask
(RC, 72), after having planned to build himself a wall of stakes and cables
"in a Circle" (RC, 77), but these are not wheels — and it's a big moment, he
manages to provide himself with a wheel: not a wheel for a vehicle of transport, but a wheel like a potter's wheel or a grindstone, a wheel turned by his
foot, to be used to sharpen cutting instruments (axes and hatchets that he
needed just as much to defend himself against the beasts, and to kill them,
as to protect himself against nature by building himself an earthquake safe[29]
dwelling). For the idea of this wheel comes to him after an earthquake that
almost swallows him up. You need to know or remember, as you must have
noticed, that Robinson Crusoe's fundamental fear, *the* fundamental, foundational fear, the basic fear [*peur de fond*] from which all other fears are
derived and around which everything is organized, is the fear of going to
the bottom [*au fond*], precisely, of being "swallow'd up alive," as he has said
just before the invention of the grinder's wheel, the wheel to sharpen axes,
weapons and tools. He is afraid of being swallowed up or "buried alive"
(the expression comes back twice [RC, 75–76)]), thus of sinking alive to the
bottom, of sinking and being dragged down to the depths, as much because
of an earthquake as because of wild or savage beasts, or even because of
human cannibals. He is afraid of dying a living death [*mourir vivant*] by
being swallowed or devoured into the deep belly of the earth or the sea or
some living creature, some living animal. That is the great phantasm,[30] the
fundamental phantasm or the phantasm of the fundamental: he can think
only of being eaten and drunk[31] by the other, he thinks of it as a threat but
with such compulsion that one wonders if the threat is not also nurtured
like a promise, and therefore a desire. Next time — we won't have time
today — we'll look directly at all the phantasmatic resources of this strange
terror, this singular[32] desire: to be swallowed alive, to be buried alive.[33] It is,
moreover, the terror of being buried alive that inspires his first prayer, in
truth a still irreligious prayer, a prayer before prayer, the precursory plain-
tive breath of a distress call which, during the earthquake that threatens
to bury him alive, is not yet truly and religiously addressed to God, to the
Other as God: it is a cry that is almost automatic, irrepressible, machinelike,

29. [Translator's note:] The words "earthquake safe" are in English in the text.
30. Derrida spells this word (in French) both as "fantasme" and "phantasme."
31. During the session, Derrida added: "swallowed."
32. During the session, Derrida added: "terrified."
33. This sentence was added at the end of the typescript of the session with the indication "Addition, p. 16."

mechanical, like a mainspring calling for help from the depths of panic and absolute terror. God is here, apparently, merely that other who would save the life of the child threatened with being carried off, eaten alive in the deepest entrails of the earth. It would be interesting to follow, through the whole book, the apprenticeship of prayer; and to read the whole of *Robinson Crusoe* as a book of prayer, as an experience of "learning how to pray." We would also need to make a parallel, more audaciously (I only point out the premises here), between *on the one hand,* this story of the apprenticeship of prayer, of this invention of prayer reinvented and, *on the other hand,* the invention or the reinvention of the wheel or of gearing as an apparatus we can describe as auto-affective. The wheel turns on its own [*toute seule*]. The machine is what works on its own by turning on itself.[34]

In both cases, the invention would always be a repetition, a reinvention, on the island, a second origin, a second genesis of the world itself, and of technology. But in both cases we would also be dealing with an autonomization, an automatization in which the pure spontaneity of movement[35] can no longer be distinguished from a mechanization, a progress in the mechanization of an apparatus that moves by itself, auto-matically, on its own,[36] toward itself at the moment it travels toward the other,[37] for the other, in the view of the other, elsewhere and far away. We would find again here the problematic of the automat that we unfolded a little last year, and articulated with the problematic of political sovereignty, especially reading Celan's "Meridian" and Valéry's *Monsieur Teste.*[38] For this mechanizing and automatizing autonomization—both auto- and hetero-affective—is not without relation, at least an analogical relation, with what is called sovereignty, or at least with the power of its phantasm, with the phantasm itself, with power as phantasm, with the force of the phantasm that imposes the same on the other, with an unconditional all-powerful self-determination. The nearest and the farthest, the same and the other, touch each other and

---

34. During the session, Derrida added: "and in prayer which, at bottom, is addressed to nobody—one does not know to whom it is addressed—there is also a similar movement that is both mechanical and a movement of auto-affection."

35. During the session, Derrida added, with a clear break: "auto-mobile."

36. During the session, Derrida added: "all alone: what is to be alone [*être seul*]? To work all by itself [*marcher tout seul*]? It works [or walks] all by itself, toward itself."

37. During the session, Derrida added: "that's what the wheel does: it goes [*marche*] toward itself just when it's rolling toward the other." And, at the end of this sentence, he added further: "while remaining close to itself: the wheel leads off into the distance while always remaining close to itself."

38. See *La bête et le souverain, I,* sessions 6, 7, 8, and 10.

come into contact in the circle, on the island, in the return, in the wheel and in the prayer. Everything happens as though, on this fictional island, Robinson Crusoe were reinventing sovereignty, technology, tools, the machine, the becoming-machine of the tool, and prayer, God, true religion. This insular experience, this fiction of the island where everything has to be reinvented, like at the origin of the world, at the origin of the universe itself, and of the universalization of the universe, would seem to answer, while perhaps perverting it, to Bergson's famous formula, at the end of *The Two Sources of Morality and Religion,* which concludes with this definition of the universe, or more precisely, more literally, with the "function of the universe" and the universality of the universal:[39] a "machine to make gods."[40] There is supposedly a "function of the universe," says Bergson who indeed speaks here of a function (and this function, this functioning is never far from a technical or mechanical invention, or even from a fictioning). The universe is a function destined to make something, here "to make gods": "a machine to make gods," says Bergson, gods who are like the machined products of this function.

When the earthquake happens, Robinson, terrorized by the earth [*terre*] itself, terrified by the earth and by the possible interring of his living life, has a presentment of prayer and God and religion, but is not yet there. He even blames himself, in the present of his memory, of not having had at that time, of not yet having had any serious thought about religion. Let's listen to him:

> I had not Heart enough to go over my Wall again, for Fear of being buried alive, but sat still upon the Ground, greatly cast down and disconsolate, not knowing what to do: All this while I had not the least serious religious Thought, nothing but the common, *Lord ha' mercy upon me;* and when it was over, that went away too. (RC, 75)

In other words, this first nonserious reinvention of religion was already a repetition, since, before being cast ashore, he already knew how to pray and he was, like Defoe, a man of religion; and moreover, this repetition or this simulacrum of mechanical reinvention does not last. He had forgotten the

---

39. During the session, Derrida corrected this to "universe."

40. Henri Bergson, "Remarques finales," in *Les deux sources de la morale et de la religion* (1932) (Paris: PUF, 1992), p. 338; trans. R. Ashley Audra and W. Horsfall Carter as *The Two Sources of Morality and Religion* (New York: Doubleday, 1954), p. 317: "It is up to [humanity] to see if wants to continue to live. Up to it to wonder if it merely wants to live, or also furnish the effort needed so that the essential function of the universe, which is a machine to make gods, can be accomplished, even on our reluctant planet."

religion of his childhood on his island and he must reinvent it. He then immediately forgets this beginning of a reinvention as soon as he is reassured. This inchoate, mechanical, and not very serious prayer lasts only the time of fear between two forgettings (RC, 75). The earthquake along with this inauthentic and mechanical prayer — all that happens in April. Well, in June, after having invented a certain wheel (I'm coming to that in a moment), he falls ill, and declares that then he no longer knew what to say ("I knew not what to say"), he cries again *"Lord look upon me, Lord pity me, Lord have Mercy upon me"* (RC, 81), but later, during the same illness, while feverish, his dormant conscience awakens, remorse invades him, he wonders if God is not punishing him for his perversity by inflicting on him cruel and unusual punishments. Then his conscience drags from him words which, he says, *resembled* a prayer addressed to God. After comparing himself to a poor suffering beast, to *"an unfortunate Dog, and born to be always miserable"* (RC, 83), these "reflections" in which fever and remorse combine "extorted some Words from me, *like* praying to God" (RC, 84; Derrida's emphasis). He admits that it was not a real prayer "attended with Desires or with Hopes" (RC, 84), but "rather the Voice of meer Fright and Distress" (RC, 84). This simulacrum of a complaint moves him and makes him weep without however one knowing if the abundant tears are shed on his own account rather than being a true religious deploration. In any case, after another meditation on his sins, especially on the words of his father who had warned him and announced divine justice, as though passing from the words of his father to God the Father himself, he finds the accent of a *true* prayer, the first authentic prayer, worthy of the name: *"Lord be my Help, for I am in great Distress.* / This was the first Prayer, if I may call it so, that I had made for many Years" (RC, 85). He had, then, already prayed in his earlier life, then unlearned and forgotten. He relearns, he reinvents on the basis of a new origin, and even then an "if I may call it so" marks the precariousness or the uncertainty of the experience and its name. Is the prayer of June 28 a true prayer? About one week later, July 4, we finally get the true, the truly true prayer. It is no doubt not insignificant that this coincides with the resolution to read every morning and every evening from the New Testament. After a certain time, Robinson feels profoundly and sincerely contrite about the wickedness of his past life. In this way, all of *Robinson Crusoe* can be read as a confession book, as *Confessions,* in the tradition of Augustine or Rousseau. It is as if Robinson Crusoe retired to an island as an anchorite, an island that would be a human desert, or even a convent or a monastery, a place of retreat, as though he were landing on an island in order to recount his sins, his past failures, his crashes or shipwrecks [*ses échouements ou ses échouages*], his defeats and his failings, and to prepare for pardon, reconciliation and redemption, salvation. To recover an authentic and appropriate relation to himself, Robinson Crusoe confesses his sins by recounting his life.

Dreams confirm him in the movement of repentance, and he finds textual support for them in the Acts of the Apostles, and cries out *"Jesus, thou Son of* David, *Jesus, thou exalted Prince and Saviour, give me Repentance!"* (RC, 90).[41] This is as much a conversion as a more authentic re-conversion to his old faith, a re-birth, a re-surrection whose call, vocation or convocation do not come solely or directly from a universal or ahistorical natural God, but from a Christian incarnate God, from Jesus come to sacrifice himself and save the sinner. And this also passes via the reading of the text of the Bible that he has with him, and that I told you that Defoe, for fear of papist violence, is supposed one day to have learned by heart. But although this re-conversion, this resurrection, is a repetition, it nonetheless presents itself as an absolute first time, the first time in his life, the one and only first time in his life. The text is clear, univocal, and insistent. This is not only the first time on the island, but the first time in his life that Robinson Crusoe has prayed, and as a result this whole story of insular experience, which might look like an ideal or fictive repetition of the origin, in fact presents itself as the true and sole first time, the first act of Christian faith, the first experience of prayer, of addressing God in the person of his son, the first confession of the Christian sinner praying for his salvation and redemption. And not only is he praying for the first time in his life but he discovers for the first time in his life the true meaning of the word "prayer," as if in the Christian religions people did not yet pray or did not yet know the meaning of the word "pray": "This was the first Time that I could say, in the true Sense of the Words, that I pray'd in all my Life; for now I pray'd with a Sense of my Condition [understand that of a sinner], and with a true Scripture View of Hope founded on the Encouragement of the Word of God; and from this Time, I may say, I began to have Hope that God would hear me" (RC, 90). In other words, the true sense of the word "prayer" is the true sense of the word because it is founded on Scripture, i.e. divine words, the Word of God. God gave me his word and by the same token has given me the true sense of the word "prayer," he has given its truth to the word "prayer," and this passes through the text that keeps and attests to this word. The true sense of the word, of the speech of prayer, presupposes the truth of the Divine Word as it is recorded in the New Testament. Elsewhere, before it or

128

41. Acts 5:31.

outside it, there is neither any given word, nor a true sense of the word, nor authentic prayer. That is what the experience of the island teaches Robinson.

In any case, in the interval after an earthquake (RC, 77) that can recall biblical earthquakes (for example in the book of Kings where the point is to hear God's "still small voice"[42]), in the *interval,* after the earthquake *and before* these prayers, Robinson had invented the wheel; he had reinvented a wheel, but this time the sharpening wheel. And the two features to which I draw your attention are that *on the one hand* Robinson is aware in this case of inventing absolutely, of inaugurating without inheriting, because he says he never saw that before in England (which was not the case for the wheelbarrow) and *on the other hand,* he is compulsively driven to compare this invention of the wheel to a major political exploit. And when I say *major,* I mean sovereign, majestic, i.e. *grand* with that *majestas* that in Latin meant sovereignty. I believe there are good reasons to think that this political analogy is neither insignificant nor fortuitous. We are indeed talking about an act of sovereignty and a question of life or death when a living being invents all alone, by himself, a technique, a machine designed to ensure his survival, to decide as to his life and his death, to avoid being swallowed alive.

Listen to Robinson; he has just confided his fear of being swallowed or buried alive, he has just described his project of building a circular wall and noticed that his axes were chipped and dull. He adds:

> . . . and tho' I had a Grindstone, I could not turn it and grind my Tools too, this cost me as much Thought as a Statesman would have bestow'd upon a grand Point of Politicks, or a Judge upon the Life and Death of a Man. At length I contriv'd a Wheel with a String, to turn it with my Foot, that I might have both my Hands at Liberty: *Note,* I had never seen any such thing in *England,* or at least not to take Notice how it was done, tho' since I have observ'd it is very common there. (RC, 77)

There would be much to say, but I will not get into that now, about the invention of a technical apparatus, a machine indeed, that works alone, all alone, and that is not merely a tool, a machine designed to build, to refine, to sharpen tools (axe or knife) but also a machine to deal with tools, an autonomous machine that works on its own and liberates one's hands. The liberation of the hand, a certain freeing of the hand, is considered to be the access to what is proper to man, and an essential moment in the hominization of the living creature. If we had the time, we would treat this question for it-

42. 1 Kings 19:12.

self, and for my part, I would link it not only to techno-anthropological discourses on the liberation of the hand, like those of Leroi-Gourhan (I offered a reading of that in *Of Grammatology*),[43] but also to what Heidegger says about the hand (see "Heidegger's Hand")[44] when he claims precisely that the animal has no hand, but merely prehensile paws, or claws, etc. whereas only *Dasein* supposedly has what can properly be called hands[45] with which it salutes, gives, thinks, and acts (*handelt*). And thought itself, he says, is a *Handeln*. And there is no animal *Handeln*. Allow me also to refer you to my book *On Touching — Jean-Luc Nancy* in which I offer a discourse and a good number of readings on the link between the whole humanist axiomatics of metaphysics and the privilege of the hand [*main*], between humanism and what I call "hu*main*isme."[46]

I would like now (after having brought together—in a mode that I shall speak of again and which is neither that of a causality, of a cause-effect relation, nor an infrastructure-superstructure relation, nor that of a symptomatology, but of another structural concatenation—the technical possibility of the wheel, as a circular, auto-hetero-affective machine, and the possibility of the auto-affective and auto-biographical relation to self in confession, repentance, prayer; between the reinvention of the wheel and the reinvention of prayer as the reinvention of two auto-mobile and auto-affective machines), I would like to draw your attention, then, to another motif that I believe belongs with those two, again in a mode that remains to be thought beyond causality, ground, or symptom. This is the motif of self-destruction that I also call, generalizing and formalizing its use, autoimmune, autoimmunity consisting for a living body in itself destroying, in enigmatic fashion, its own immunitary defenses, in auto-affecting itself, then, in an irrepressibly mechanical and apparently spontaneous, auto-matic, fashion, with an

131

43. Jacques Derrida, *De la grammatologie* (Paris: Minuit, 1967), p. 126; trans. Gayatri Chakravorty Spivak as *Of Grammatology* (Baltimore: Johns Hopkins University Press, 1976), p. 84.

44. "La main de Heidegger (Geschlecht II)," in *Psyché: Inventions de l'autre,* 2:35–68 (especially p. 45); trans. John P. Leavey, Jr., as "Heidegger's Hand (Geschlecht II)," in *Psyche: Inventions of the Other,* ed. Peggy Kamuf and Elizabeth Rottenberg (Stanford, Calif.: Stanford University Press, 2008), 2:27–62 (p. 40).

45. During the session, Derrida added: "and with hands free, not just hands to do things, or to scratch and attack."

46. Jacques Derrida, *Le toucher, Jean-Luc Nancy* (Paris: Galilée, 2000), especially p. 176; trans. Christine Irizarry as *On Touching — Jean-Luc Nancy* (Stanford, Calif.: Stanford University Press, 2005), p. 152.

ill which comes to destroy what is supposed to protect against ill and safe-
guard immunity. Well, Robinson is often invaded by the feeling that a self-
destructive power is mechanically, automatically, of itself, at work within
him. The word "destruction" appears very early in the book, first in the
mouth of his mother who had warned him against his own "Destruction"
(that's the word [RC, 6]); then, destruction as self-destruction, as destruction of the self, is the object, also very early, of a whole paragraph, one of
the points of interest of which is the following: Robinson Crusoe does not
believe that this drive, this self-destructive compulsion and this neurosis of
destiny (this is not a Freudian vocabulary that I am imposing upon him, but
almost his own words) are a thing of consciousness: consciousness, reason
and judgment are here impotent, incapable of resisting this self-destructive
compulsion that works on its own, mechanically, and the vicissitudes of
these drives which are none other than the unfortunate destiny of Robinson
Crusoe ("my ill Fate"). I quote:

132
> But my ill Fate push'd me on now with an Obstinacy that nothing could
> resist; and tho' I had several times loud Calls from my Reason and my more
> composed Judgment to go home, yet I had no Power to do it. I know not
> what to call this, nor will I urge, that it is a secret over-ruling Decree that
> hurries us on to be the Instruments of our own Destruction, even tho' it be
> before us, and that we rush upon it with our Eyes open. Certainly nothing
> but some such decreed unavoidable Misery attending, and which it was im-
> possible for me to escape, could have push'd me forward against the calm
> Reasonings and Perswasions of my most retired Thoughts, and against two
> such visible Instructions as I had met with in my first Attempt. (RC, 13)

So this is indeed a drive to self-destruction, which disobeys reason and
even disobeys what is most intimate inside him, in the inner depths of his
thought. There is here an automatic force that is more intimate to him than
himself and that acts repetitively (to the rhythm of a destiny) and mechanically. Alone, all alone, by itself. Which also explains that this allusion to
the self-destructive drive should multiply itself of itself. It would be easy to
show that this reference to a sort of logic of automatic self-destruction organizes the whole of Robinson's discourse, but to save time I shall mention
only a few passages in which the word "self-destruction" is explicitly and
literally present: for example a little further on, this self-destructive destiny
133 neurosis is described as absolutely originary, innate, congenital: "But I that
was born to be my own Destroyer, could no more resist the Offer than I
could restrain my first rambling Designs, when my Father's good Counsel
was lost upon me" (RC, 37). The offer in question is none other than that of

participating in the slave trade on the coast of Guinea, and you see that giving in here to the self-destructive compulsion, being his "own Destroyer," is also the compulsion to disobey the father or rather to have the father's law founder [*échouer*]. And if there is remorse, repentance, and confession in this whole autobiographical odyssey, this does indeed concern the exposure to failure of the law of the father. And therefore of the sovereign. Which does not happen without the reappropriation of sovereignty on the island, and without the fear of being eaten, swallowed or buried alive by the vengeful anger of the elements, water or earth, or the ferocity of the beasts which, like wolves and other carnivorous beasts, like the cannibals themselves, might reincarnate a paternal figure of anger, of righteous anger and therefore the law, the force of law.

After having spoken of what made him into his "own Destroyer," Robinson Crusoe explains how he played against his own interests, how he played into his own enemies' hands (like Rousseau, you remember, whose autoimmune — some would say suicidal — compulsion we also analyzed). We are dealing here with a subjection or a blind, essentially blind, obedience, in which the subject is constituted by subjecting itself and blindly, irrationally obeying the principle of destruction of its own subjectivity, of its own ipseity, of its own interest or the proper interest of its very reason, scorning even what Kant would call the interest of reason: "But I was hurried on, and obey'd blindly the Dictates of my Fancy rather than my Reason . . ." (RC, 37):[47] and later in the same paragraph: ". . . I went from my Father and Mother at *Hull,* in order to act the Rebel to their Authority, and the Fool to my own Interest."

Finally I should like, in a way that is not too artificial, and still guided by the solidarity or affinity or structural attraction between *on the one hand* this autoimmune automatism that looks like the mechanics of a counter-narcissism that returns to itself only to ruin itself, to ruin the self, and *on the other hand* the production of that strange technical prosthesis, a machine that turns by itself, that turns itself, and is called a wheel, [I should like, then] to note a curious contiguity in the text between a certain moment of auto-appellation that is none other than the mechanical and automatic hetero-appellation come from Poll the parrot — between *on the one hand,* then, this counter-narcissistic and

134

47. [Translator's note:] Derrida has a parenthesis here on Pétrus Borel's French translation of this passage, criticizing its rendering of "I was hurried on" by "j'étais entraîné [I was drawn]," and of "fancy" by "goût [taste]," adding *"fancy,* which I would rather translate as '*mon imagination en cavale* [my imagination on the run],' and perhaps even as '*ma fantaisie fantasque* [my fanciful fantasy],' or even '*mes fantasmes* [my phantasms].'"

uncanny,[48] *unheimlich* psittacism of auto-appellation, and *on the other* a certain return of the wheel. (Read and comment)

135

[. . .] for I was very weary, and fell asleep: But judge you, if you can, that read my Story, what a Surprize I must be in, when I was wak'd out of my Sleep by a Voice calling me by my Name several times, *Robin, Robin, Robin Crusoe, poor Robin Crusoe,* where are you *Robin Crusoe?* Where are you? Where have you been?

I was so dead asleep at first, being fatigu'd with Rowing, or Paddling, as it is call'd, the first Part of the Day, and with walking the latter Part, that I did not wake thoroughly, but dozing between sleeping and waking, thought I dream'd that some Body spoke to me: But as the Voice continu'd to repeat *Robin Crusoe, Robin Crusoe,* at last I began to wake more perfectly, and was at first dreadfully frighted, and started up in the utmost Consternation: But no sooner were my Eyes open, but I saw my *Poll* sitting on the Top of the Hedge; and immediately knew that it was he that spoke to me; for just in such bemoaning Language I had used to talk to him, and teach him; and he had learn'd it so perfectly, that he would sit upon my Finger, and lay his Bill close to my Face, and cry, *Poor* Robin Crusoe, *Where are you? Where have you been? How come you here?* And such things as I had taught him.

However, even though I knew it was the Parrot, and that indeed it could be no Body else, it was a good while before I could compose my self: First, I was amazed how the Creature got thither, and then, how he should just keep about the Place, and no where else: But as I was well satisfied it could be no Body but honest *Poll,* I got it over; and holding out my Hand, and

136

calling him by his Name *Poll,* the sociable Creature came to me, and sat upon my Thumb, as he used to do, and continu'd talking to me, *Poor* Robin Crusoe, and *how did I come here?* and *where had I been?* just as if he had been overjoy'd to see me again; and so I carry'd him Home along with me. (RC, 131–32)

The auto-appellation, the auto-interpellation comes to him from outside, from the world, and thus returns from the outside or from the other toward him. But it remains a circular auto-appellation, because it comes from a sort of living mechanism that he has produced, that he assembled himself, like a *quasi*-technical or prosthetic apparatus, by training the parrot to speak mechanically so as to send his words and his name back to him, repeating them blindly. One could say of every autobiography, every autobiographical fiction, and even every written confession through which the author calls and names himself, that it presents itself through this linguistic and pros-

---

48. [Translator's note:] "Uncanny" is in English in the text.

thetic apparatus—a book—or a piece of writing or a trace in general, for example the book entitled *Robinson Crusoe,* which speaks of him without him, according to a trick that constructs and leaves in the world an artifact that speaks all alone [*tout seul*] and all alone calls the author by his name, renames him in his renown [*le renomme en sa renommée*] without the author himself needing to do anything else, not even be alive. One could imagine that when Poll proffers and calls "Robinson Crusoe," it is referring not only to the character—moreover fictional—called Robinson Crusoe, but also to the title of the book, to which the character intends to be responsible, since he is its signatory, at the very moment that the book, like the parrot and what it calls, no longer needs him.

Now immediately afterward, here is Robinson Crusoe praising the wheel, the wheel that frees the hands, the potter's wheel he has perfected meantime:

> I arriv'd at an unexpected Perfection in my Earthen Ware, and contriv'd well enough to make them with a Wheel, which I found infinitely easyer and better; because I made things round and shapable, which before were filthy things indeed to look on. (RC, 133)

A wheel produces these pots, which are his work (like his journal and his book, in sum), not only better and more easily, but "infinitely" better and more conveniently which means—and it's true—that there is an infinite leap between *on the one hand* any instrument, any tool as an extension of the body, and *on the other hand* the autonomous machine called a wheel, which does without us in finishing and rounding things off perfectly. The leap and rupture in the production of the prosthesis are absolute.

Is it artificial and unwarranted to bring together all these motifs (the machine technology of the wheel, the self-determining autonomy, the self-destructive compulsion and the autoimmune paradoxes which make of Robinson Crusoe his own destroyer and of Defoe, perhaps his own enemy, his own "foe," the parrot and the wheel, etc.)? It would be, incontestably, if the point were to claim to impose bad anachronisms on all these texts, those of Rousseau or those of Defoe. I say bad anachronisms because every reading is not only anachronistic, but consists in bringing out anachrony, non-self-contemporaneity, dislocation in the taking-place of the text. The distinction between the good and the bad anachronism does not have its criteria outside what the reading-writing that busies itself with a given text, with more than one given text, *does, succeeds* or *fails in doing*. I cannot justify in all rigor, I cannot prove that I am right by any argument other than this, which is first of all a question or demand: do you find it interesting to listen

137

to what I'm saying and then to read *Robinson Crusoe* differently? On the other hand, what I say would be artificial and unwarranted if it consisted in doing two things that quite clearly I am not doing and do not wish to do and that, in my view, neither are nor should be done—which supposes a quite different problematic, the very one whose elaboration I am sketching here, or there. I am not claiming to recognize relations of causality, of cause and effect, for example between the techno-scientific, historical or techno-economical conditions of the invention or reinvention of the wheel, and the whole structure of auto-affection, self-determination, automatization or auto-immunity. Beyond these relations of causality or induction, I am thinking, rather, of a structural configuration, both historical and genetic, in which all these possibilities are not separated, and in which everything that can happen to the *autos* is indissociable from what happens *in the world* through the prosthetization of an ipseity which at once divides that ipseity, dislocates it, and inscribes it outside itself *in the world,* the world being precisely what cannot be reduced here, any more than one can reduce *tekhnē* or reduce it to a pure *physis*. The question, then, is indeed that of the world. The wheel is not only a technical machine, it is in the world, it is outside the conscious interiority of the *ipse,* and what I want to say is that there is no ipseity without this prostheticity in the world, with all the chances and all the threats that it constitutes for ipseity, which can in this way be constructed but also, and by the same token, indissociably, be destroyed.

Finally, everything I am placing in relation in these texts would indeed be the effect of an unwarranted artifice, of a bad artifice, of a bad anachronism, if I were claiming, which I am not, that all these compositional artifices (for example, the contiguity of the story of the parrot and the wheel) were deliberately, intentionally calculated by Defoe. I am not sure and I do not claim that they are not, but I'm not sure that they are, and that they would be legible, as such, in his time and by Defoe himself. The possibility of this composition refers to something other than the intentional and conscious decision of an author, but also to something other than pure insignificant chance. So we must try to determine the necessity that imposed neither consciously nor unconsciously, perhaps symptomatically—but then we have to re-elaborate this concept of symptom, along with that of fantasy—[the necessity, then, that imposed] this writing and this composition on such a fiction of an autobiographical fiction. For *Robinson Crusoe* is not so much an autobiographical fiction as the fiction of an autobiography.

Last year, I mean in the last session last December, we had stopped, we had come to a stop and marked a pause, at this strange moment at which, try-

THIRD SESSION ‡ 89

ing to orient himself, and hesitating once more between several paths—in truth, once more between three questions and three paths, Heidegger, it seems, had just decreed that it was best to begin with the first path, namely, he was saying, the nearest path for a first elucidation (*Der* nächste *Weg zu einer ersten Klärung*... [H, 261/176]). This looks, I suggested, like a *coup de théâtre* or a *coup de force*, even though that is not Heidegger's tone, but I maintain that he seemed there, more than once, to take decisions that are so many arbitrary *coups de force* or *coups de théâtre*, unjustifiable decisions. That would be Heidegger's *Walten* to which we shall need to return again, his *Walten*, his force and what he says and thinks and does with the word *walten*.

What does "the nearest" mean in this case? And why begin this way, with the closest to us as Heidegger had already done in *Sein und Zeit*, right at the beginning when he decides to take Dasein as his point of departure and as the exemplary being about which to pose the question of the meaning of Being? We shall see that it is here, in the passage from the 1929 seminar that we have begun to read, a sort of rhetorical or rather pedagogical feint. Heidegger declares that the closest path for a first elucidation would indeed be to limit oneself to the word, and follow the history of the word "world." He recalls that he already did so in *Vom Wesen des Grundes* (1929, the same year or almost).[49] In spite of the declared insufficiency of the exposition that he gives here of the concepts of *cosmos, mundus* and *Welt,* one does find in it, he says, the broad stages of this history of the *world,* of the word and concept "world," a history that can also orient a terminological study. But this history of the word and concept, this philologico-semantic history, is only an exterior (*das Aussenwerk*) of the inner history of the world as a fundamental problem of metaphysics. Heidegger then declares to his students that he does not want to repeat *Vom Wesen des Grundes* (which has just been published), but it would be useful for them to read it. Nevertheless, in qualifying this route—followed in *Vom Wesen des Grundes*—as historiographical, he gives a summary of it that will count in what follows. For in recalling the sense of the word "world" that was dominant throughout a whole history—namely the world is the whole of what is not divine, the whole of non-divine or extra-divine entities, which, in Christianity, will signify creation, being-created, the whole of what is created (*das Geschaffene*) as opposed to the non-created—Heidegger situates man in it, man who then becomes a part, a piece of the world (*Stück der Welt*), but a fragment

140

---

49. [Translator's note:] Translated by William McNeill as "On the Essence of Ground," in Martin Heidegger, *Pathmarks,* ed. William McNeill (Cambridge: Cambridge University Press, 1998), pp. 97–135.

which resembles no other in that he stands opposite or facing this whole of which he is a part; he stands face-to-face with the world (*gegenüber*), which, I would say, in a certain way isolates, insularizes man in the world to which he nonetheless belongs. Now as a piece, opposite and isolated, in his *Gegenüberstehen,* in what makes him stand upright or erect himself facing the world, in view of the world to which he belongs, man *has* the world. This *Gegenüberstehen* is a *Haben,* a having. Having the world, having a world, that's what characterizes the position of man in this classical or Christian determination of the world. And I point out this word, *haben,* in the summary that Heidegger gives of his first historiographical approach in *Vom Wesen des Grundes;* I point out that Heidegger himself emphasizes this *Haben,* for the reference to this enigmatic "having-the-world" is going to be at the center of the analysis of the situation of the animal with respect to the world in the meditation that will follow in this seminar, when he has started this comparative analysis supposed to follow on from the historiographical approach of *Vom Wesen des Grundes,* and—we're coming to this—from the more phenomenological procedure of *Sein und Zeit.* For in our seminar, Heidegger will try to explain in what way the animal poor in world does not have the world, or more precisely—and we will have to dwell on this difficulty, for it concerns as much the sense of the world as the sense of this having—the animal *has* a world in the mode of *not-having.* And if this having without having (the world) looks like a logical contradiction (Heidegger emphasizes the fact: "Somit zeigt sich im Tier ein *Haben von Welt* und *zugleich* ein *Nichthaben von Welt*),[50] he also recalls that metaphysics and the thinking of essence have a logic different from that of common sense or the sound understanding of man. This same logical contradiction, this very contradiction also demands of us that we think or determine otherwise the *poverty in world* of the animal, which consists in having what it has not or not having what it has, and especially that we think otherwise both having and the world, as it is only with respect to the world that this poverty and this having without having are determined. In any case, in the traditional (Greek or Christian) determination of the world according to which man is a fragment of the world facing the world, included in and opposed to what

50. H, 293/199: "The animal thus reveals itself as a being which *both has and does not have world.*" Derrida cites and comments on this sentence of Heidegger's in *De l'esprit: Heidegger et la question* (Paris: Galilée, 1987), pp. 79–81; trans. Geoffrey Bennington and Rachel Bowlby as *Of Spirit: Heidegger and the Question* (Chicago: University of Chicago Press, 1989), pp. 50–52.

includes him, man, as fragment, is both master and servant of the world, sovereign and slave: "Herr und Knecht der Welt [Both master and servant of the world]" (H, 262/177).

In the brief reminder paragraph that follows, Heidegger explains how, in *Sein und Zeit,* he was no longer following this historiographical procedure, this historical path (*Im Unterschied zu diesem* historischen Weg [H, 262]). And he tells us, in a few lines, two or three things of the highest importance for us, and on which I shall conclude provisionally for today.

1. He recalls first that in *Sein und Zeit* he began, in nonhistorical fashion as it were, with the way in which, in everyday life—and he insists on this everydayness (*Alltäglichkeit*)—we move ourselves (*wir uns bewegen*), we are on the way, we walk, we put ourselves on the path in our world (*in unserer Welt*). And we shall see more than once how this *Weg* and this *bewegen* are not simply metaphors, in that they engage Dasein before any distinction between soul and body. Now in this analysis of the way in which we are on the way in our world, Heidegger says that he took his point of departure in what we have every day in our hands or to hand (*Zuhanden*), basically from what the hand of *Dasein* manipulates and maneuvers in its own manner. Thus walking, legs or feet, the body and hands. Now, adds Heidegger, most often we know nothing about any of that, and when we want to describe it, we interpret it wrongly, we misunderstand, we misinterpret (*missdeuten*) everything by importing into it concepts and questions from a domain foreign to it.

2. Heidegger concludes from this that what is the closest to us basically remains already far off and incomprehensible ("Dieses uns ganz Nahe und jeden Tag Verständliche ist uns im Grunde schon fern und unverständlich").[51] This is only one of the many examples of this association, one would be tempted to say this proximity, of the near and the far, of the near as far and the far as near, and already in the figure of the circle that will literally obsess the whole seminar—we'll come to this next time—be it the circle of the hermeneutic approach or of the methodological path that retraces its steps or presupposes what it must seek, or, in a quite different topology, the original encirclement (*Umring, sich umringen*) that characterizes *Benommenheit,* the benumbment or captivation of the animal poor in world. So next time we'll talk about all the different types of circle that this seminar describes, in all senses of the word. I must say from the outset that

51. "That which is so close and intelligible to us in our everyday dealings is actually and fundamentally remote and unintelligible to us" (H, 263/177).

when we get into the real content of this seminar, as minutely as possible, I will do all I can, in spite of my reservations about what Heidegger says here about what he calls, in the general singular, *the* animal, [I will do all I can] to go along with and credit Heidegger as far as possible, and to be his advocate with all requisite loyalty.

3. Finally, we must never forget what this paragraph also tells us, just before the third path chosen, that of comparative examination (*den einer vergleichenden Betrachtung* [H, 263/177]). Heidegger tells us that what was started in *Sein und Zeit,* the "path taken in *Sein und Zeit*" (*der in* Sein und Zeit *genommene Weg* [H, 263/177]) opens onto a perspective that is so broad and far-off, *distant,* that this seminar (which postdates *Sein und Zeit,* in 1929–30) is merely a limited stage and a very partial contribution to the great task opened by *Sein und Zeit.* And here too, Heidegger will use the word "distance" (*Entfernung*) that has been occupying us since the beginning of this session. We are warned that, in spite of all the serious stakes of this seminar, in spite of all the importance I am inclined to give it, it constitutes in Heidegger's eyes only a limited and circumscribed stage on the path opened by *Sein und Zeit,* whose extent, perspective, and horizon reach much further and were never abandoned by Heidegger, who writes this, in which I emphasize again, in conclusion, the literal reference to distancing:

> The path followed in *Being and Time* (*Der in* Sein und Zeit *genommene Weg*) in the attempt to shed light on the phenomenon of world (*zur Aufhellung des Weltphänomens*) really requires (*verlangt aber*) a very broad and wide-ranging perspective (*eine sehr weit- und langgestrecke Perspektive*) which cannot even remotely be made visible here in this lecture (*die hier — in dieser Vorlesung*)—because it is distant from it (*entfernt nicht sichtbar gemacht werden kann*). (H, 263/177) (Reread the translation)

Next time we shall start again from all these circulations that are *described* (in all senses of this word, *describe* the circle), but we shall <not> fail to start again on, and pursue, the path in Heidegger's text of this *walten* we have already talked about. But we shall also come back to everything that is at stake, as to the island, in these terrified desires or desiring terrors of being swallowed alive or buried alive—in their relation to insularity, of course, but also to the maternal womb, and also to the alternative of mournings and phantasms of mourning: between inhumation and cremation.

143

January 29, 2003

Is death merely the end of life? Death as such? Is there ever, moreover,   *145*
death *as such*? If I said "I am going to die living [*mourir vivant*]," what
would you have to understand? That I want to *die* living? Or that I want
above all *not* to die living, not to die in my lifetime? Would that be the last
avowal of an unavowable desire or the panic of an unspeakable terror? To
ask such a question, and for it to have the least meaning, we still need to
know what we mean, we still have to agree on the expression "die living,"[1]
an expression that has a long history, for example an Augustinian history,
which goes much further than the simple signature of a St. Augustine.

Every week, as you've noticed, and every year, we return. We sketch
out a return step in order to start out again. We describe a circle in order to
gain impetus for a new departure, which we believe will allow us to move
forward. Last time we promised to move forward by returning at least to
the crossroads of *three paths:*

1. The first path consisted in returning toward Robinson himself, not
only in this Christian confessional that his journal and his autobiographical discourse, his confessions, were beginning to resemble more and more,
but especially what he avowed as to a properly obsessional terror — and the
configuration of the island is always obsessional, obsidianal: living on an
island is living in a refuge of course, but a besieged refuge, a refuge in which   *146*
the refugee takes refuge as if in a fortification that is besieged, obsessed,
harassed from inside and out — an obsessional terror, then, which we interpreted as the double and single movement of a terrified desire or a panic
fascinated by the desire to be swallowed alive or buried alive (*swallow'd up
alive* or *bury'd alive*), to be called back to life to death in the belly of the earth
during an earthquake, in the belly of the sea during a drowning, or in the
belly of some ferocious animal or starving cannibal; and we wondered what

1. During the session, Derrida added: "Or again that we could die any other way."

could be meant by this double phantasm: be eaten alive by the other, die a living death, so to speak, disappear, leave, decease alive in the unlimited element, in the medium of the other;

2. Then, second path, at the same crossroads, we had promised ourselves to move forward by coming back to the great question of the circle and/or the wheel by treating different types of circles or encirclement in Heidegger's seminar, all the circles—and they are innumerable—that describe first of all the methodological approach of questioning on the way and the manner that Heidegger here justifies and assumes, there rejects, the turns and turnings of this circularity, but also the circle of an animal encirclement (*Umring*), the "self-encircling (*das Sichumringen*)" that characterizes the animal in the benumbment of its captivation (*Benommenheit*) (H, 369/253). The animal encloses itself in a circle, and we shall see what the relations are between the encirclement of the animal *Umring* and what is often called the milieu or the element, the environment, the surrounding world (*Umwelt*) of *Dasein* and/or the animal. We shall see that Heidegger draws from this, as one of its consequences, that the animal reaches the end of its life without dying; the animal does not die;

3. Finally, third path, we promised ourselves to return to the same crossroads to follow and relaunch the trajectory of this peculiar Heideggerian thought of *Walten,* the peculiar use of this word several of whose important occurrences we have already followed, in the 1929–30 seminar, and then, especially, five years later, in 1935, in a political period that is not just any period, in the *Introduction to Metaphysics.* The recourse to this word continues well beyond that, as we shall see, in a very interesting way, and is never without its relation to all the motifs that interest us here. Because *Walten* is a force[2] of which one can say neither that it bears life nor that it bears death.

That is the crossroads of our three promises. They are all questions of the path between life and death, or beyond the opposition of life and death. Now, how are we going to try to keep these promises, and especially keep them together, bind them together in their proper tenor, or recognize their essential liaison or articulation? Let's see.

To do this, I shall try to start again from what was the very first step of this seminar, this year, namely "nostalgia," that "nostalgia" (*Heimweh*),

147

---

2. During the session, Derrida added: "I put the word 'force' in quotation marks because it does not satisfy me, any more than the word 'violence'; in any case, it [*Walten*] is something that is not a thing, not a thing of life or a thing of death."

that home suffering or homesickness,[3] which Heidegger recalled was, for Novalis, what is proper to philosophy. The fragment quoted from Novalis said: *"Die Philosophie ist eigentlich Heimweh, ein Trieb überall zu Hause zu sein* [Philosophy is properly nostalgia, a drive to be everywhere at home]" (quoted in H, 7/5). There is already more than one way to accent this sentence, depending on whether one insists more on suffering, painful desire, lack, or to the contrary on the end of this desire, its purpose, its term, the house, the home, depending on whether one insists more, then, on the desiring desire, thus painfully deprived of what it desires, or, on the contrary, on the desired pole, on the desirable, on the figure of the desirable, the house, the home, the country that announces itself to desire and gives it form. Now the interpretive reading into which Heidegger draws this sentence from Novalis is, in some twenty or thirty lines, of such argumentative complexity and convolution that it could detain us for years.

148

Before saying a few words about this, I note at least, to come back to the insularity of the island, that in any case, nostalgia as homesickness and Odyssean movement, the movement of Ulysses returning, in a circle, to the *nostos* of that Ionian island, Ithaca, the nostalgia for that island, for his home on an island, sketches out that circular return movement[4] around which we have ourselves been turning from the start. You know that thing Levinas says, which I talked about a little in a very old text (already about forty years ago), and to which I permit myself to refer you, at the very end of "Violence and Metaphysics," then. Basically, Levinas declares that the Odyssean traversal that returns toward its point of departure, namely his island and his family, is countered by the departure without return of Abraham. In "The Trace of the Other," aiming precisely at Heidegger and what Levinas intends to criticize in the former's supposed taste for the place, the earth, the sacral paganism of country or Fatherland, Levinas writes: "to the myth of Ulysses returning to Ithaca, we would like to oppose the story of Abraham leaving forever his Fatherland for a land still unknown, and forbidding his servant to take even his son back to this point of departure."[5] To which I had then objected that on the one hand the impossibility of return was

3. [Translator's note:] Derrida adds in parentheses the English word "homesickness" after writing "ce mal du pays [. . .] cette souffrance du chez-soi."

4. During the session, Derrida added: "the turn of return."

5. Emmanuel Levinas, "La trace de l'autre," *Tijdschrift voor Filosofie* 25, no. 3 (September 1963): 605–23 (reprinted in *En découvrant l'existence avec Husserl et Heidegger* [Paris: Vrin, 1967], pp. 187–202), quoted in Jacques Derrida, "Violence et métaphysique," in *L'écriture et la différence* (Paris: Le Seuil, 1967), pp. 117–228 (p. 228, n. 1);

not unknown to the thinker of errancy that Heidegger also is, and that on the other hand it is difficult—this is the least one can say—to ignore the powerful myth of return in Judaism. But let's leave that, in spite of all the political resonances that this drive or this right of return can unleash today, even the right of return, the just return of the Jews and the Palestinians to the same land.

149   After having quoted Novalis, as you remember perhaps, and having described this remark as "romantic," Heidegger nevertheless takes the opportunity to berate modernity, which has supposedly lost the sense of nostalgia. It is as if he were saying: nostalgia is not what it used to be. And the one accused in this indictment of modernity is the city dweller, the man of the city who, an ape of civilization (here it's not the parrot, it's the ape: *Affe der Zivilisation*), who has long divested himself of any *Heimweh,* homesickness. But this is not the point I wished to dwell on. Rather on this: Heidegger wonders why he here appeals to the witness, cites as a witness (*Zeugen*) a poet, Novalis, and not a scientific philosopher, when the point is to define what is proper to philosophy. Pretending to contest his right to appeal to a poet as witness, he quotes for a first time in support Aristotle (this is what interests me, because later we'll be coming to a second quotation from Aristotle). Did not Aristotle precisely denounce in his *Metaphysics* (983a3), asks Heidegger, the lying compositions of the poets, the poet's compulsion to lie? "'Polla pseudontai aoidoi [πολλὰ ψεύδονται ἀοιδοί': Vieles lügen die Dichter zusammen]?" (H, 7/5). Heidegger takes the opportunity to recall, in an interesting and symptomatic social, political and familial configuration, that art, and in it poetry, is the sister (*Schwester*) of philosophy, and that science is perhaps (*vielleicht*) only the intendant, the porter, the servant (*Dienstmann*) of philosophy.[6] After which, according to a movement, a rhetorical step, and an approach that seem to me to merit all the attention we should bring to Heidegger's discursive pragmatics, he leaves things hanging, for the moment he says neither yes nor no to Novalis's assertion, any more than to that of Aristotle, but he draws support from it to pose and formulate his own question, the question that will lead him where he knows he wants to go, namely the question of world. He decides to dwell a few seconds more on Novalis's pronouncement as though on a question, and asks himself:

150   what is that, what can that mean, philosophy as nostalgia (*Philosophie ein*

---

trans. Alan Bass as *Writing and Difference* (Chicago: University of Chicago Press, 1980), pp. 79–153 (p. 320, n. 92).

    6. During the session, Derrida added: "The sister is closer. So we'd have to follow the sister in Heidegger, which would go via Trakl. But I can't get into that this evening."

Heimweh)? He then cites Novalis a second time, or rather takes from him the fragment he needs, namely what comes in apposition to specify what philosophy as nostalgia means, namely a drive, "Ein Trieb überall zu Hause sein," a drive to be everywhere at home: everywhere, you see, a drive that pushes one to find oneself everywhere, in every place, at home, to find oneself in every place. And Heidegger continues, irrefutably,

> Philosophy can only be such a drive [or respond to such a drive] if we who philosophize (*wenn wir, die philosophieren*) [and this passage to the "we" is interesting, Heidegger comes back here to what is closest, he addresses himself to his students, to his listeners, and he includes himself in this supposed community, supposed here to be gathered in an activity or an experience, a search, in truth a community of questioning, of the questioning path, about which there is no doubt that it, this community of the questioning path, consists in philosophizing: right here and now not only are we philosophizing, we have no doubt about that, but we can say "we" only to the extent that we are philosophizing in a philosophizing, in a philosophical progress which gathers us and justifies this "we" that *I am saying*] philosophy can only be such a drive [or respond to such a drive] if we who philosophize are *not* at home everywhere [*wenn wir, die philosophieren, überall* nicht *zu Hause sind:* Heidegger underlines the *nicht*, he puts it in italics, and instead of translating by emphasizing the "not," the French translation says this, which pretty much comes to the same thing: "si nous, qui philosophons, sommes partout *hors de* chez nous [if we, who philosophize, are everywhere *away from* home.]"] (H 7/5)[7]

Rather like Abraham, isn't it?

Little by little, sentence by sentence, Heidegger is going to turn the quotation, and make it rise, as though on a potter's wheel, to bring out what matters to him, namely the link between the "everywhere" (*überall*) and the world as totality of places and therefore beings.[8] To what, he wonders, does the demand of this drive (*das Verlangen dieses Trieb*) rise? Being everywhere at home, what does that mean? (*Überall zu Hause sein—was heisst das?*) Everywhere is not only here or there, in this place or that place, but in every place at every time (*jederzeit und zumal im Ganzen*). Well, this *im Ganzen,*

151

---

7. During the session, Derrida added: "Yes, 'we are *away from* home,' but Heidegger says 'we are *not* at home': it's the same thing, but it isn't the same thing. Especially given that Heidegger emphasizes the *nicht*. It's subtly different." [Translator's note: Here and elsewhere I have modified the English translation of *Trieb* from "urge" to "drive."]

8. During the session, Derrida added: "*überall* is 'everywhere': what is everywhere? It's the world. It is therefore the totality of beings. Our nostalgic drive pushes us toward the totality of beings."

as a whole, and *seine Gänze,* its entirety, its totality, is what we call the world (*nennen wir die* Welt) (H, 8/5). We always refer ourselves to that, to this whole, as such, the world. We always expect something of the world, of the whole, and we are always called (*angerufen*) by something like the whole, as entire. And this *"im Ganzen"* is the world. In saying this: "Dieses 'im Ganzen' ist die Welt," as he had said "seine Gänze nennen wir die *Welt,*" Heidegger for now is only quoting, mentioning, recalling an expression, a speech act, an act of nomination, an appellation, he puts the *im Ganzen* in quotation marks: this whole, this "as a whole," "in totality," that's what we call the world, that's what we're saying or that's what we mean when we say *im Ganzen* or "the world."

But now, starting a new paragraph, he is going to move from this con- statation that is both linguistic and semantic (that's what we call "the world" and toward which we are turned, expectantly, called by what calls to us thus, by which we are thus called (*angerufen*) in calling it: we call "world" what thus calls us) [now, starting a new paragraph, Heidegger is going to move from this constatation that is both linguistic and semantic] to the ontological question: *"Wir fragen:* Was ist das—Welt? [We are asking: *What is that—world?*]" (H, 8/5). It is, as you know, the first of the three questions of the seminar, and the two others will follow closely, since Heidegger is here lay- ing out the map, the route, and the stages of a seminar, and they will always have the same form, which always implies this community of the question- ing "we," the professor and listeners gathered in the immediate proximity[9] of the shared question, in the common proximity that can only bring us close to the closest by the intelligibility, supposed, offered or promised, of the supposedly unavoidable question: *"Wir fragen:* Was ist das—Endlich- keit? [*What is that—finitude?*]" Then "Was ist das—die Vereinzelung?" which is translated [in the French translation] as "What is that—loneli- ness [*esseulement*]" whereas in the title of the seminar *Einsamkeit* is trans- lated as "solitude."[10] And we find again, in this unstable differentiation, the equivocation we were talking about last time, between <on the one hand> being-alone as being solitary, in the trial of desert solitude (*einsame Insel* is a

9. During the session, Derrida added: "of language first of all, for all of this is hap- pening in German."

10. [Translator's note:] In the English translation, "What is that—individuation?" (H, 8/6). The Editor's Epilogue translated in the English edition addresses the apparent hesitation in the subtitle of the seminar between *Einsamkeit* (solitude) and *Vereinzelung* (individuation) (p. 370).

return to this—elsewhere plays the major role you know about in Heidegger: but let's leave that for now).

That, then, is what the world is, namely the whole in so far as we are this path on the way toward it, but toward it insofar as the path traces itself in it, breaks itself in it, opens itself in it, inscribes itself in it. I read or translate or paraphrase:[15] "It is toward this [he has just named the world: what is the world? Reply:], toward this (*Dahin*), toward Being as a whole (*zum Sein im Ganzen*)—it is that toward which we are driven (*getrieben*) in our nostalgia" (H, 8/5). So when he says "toward this (*Dahin*)," and, in apposition, "toward Being in its entirety (*zum Sein im Ganzen*)," it is *that* toward which we are driven in our nostalgia (the world toward which nostalgia drives us, and which is going to define our being), it would be indispensable in order to think this *there* of *Dahin*, the *da* of *Da*-sein, which designates or describes just as much a movement of transcendence as an immobile situation, the *there* or *Da*- of *Dasein* of which Heidegger will say much later that it must be thought of as the *Da*-, the over there of *Sein*, before being thought of in common terms as existence. This *Da*, this *there*,[16] is the dimension of what orients and puts in movement our being as being in the world. Nostalgically. The nostalgic push or drive is what, basically, far from pushing us toward this or that, Ithaca or England, is what pushes us toward everything, toward the world as entirety. Heidegger continues: "our being is this being-pushed [the push or the drive of this being-pushed: *Unser Sein ist diese Getriebenheit*]."[17]

We must stop for a moment on this last sentence: "*Unser Sein ist diese Getriebenheit*," and on the word *getrieben* that announced it in the previous sentence. We must recognize that this *Getriebenheit* that is none other than our very being (*unser Sein*),[18] now determines both the world as that toward which it pushes us, and the nostalgia that pushes us; the nostalgia, this unique nostalgia has no limit, it is our Being inasmuch as it is this urge or this drive, this *Trieb* of *Getriebenheit*. As this *Getriebenheit* also determines the world as that toward which this push of an essential and originary nostalgia pushes us, it is not one drive or urge among others. Everything comes

15. During the session, Derrida added: "or metaphrase, as they say in Greek: *metaphrasis* is translation in Greek."

16. During the session, Derrida added: "remember all this: this is what the animal is going to be deprived of."

17. [Translator's note:] The English translation has "Our very being is this restlessness" (H, 8/5).

18. During the session, Derrida added: "our being is drive [*pulsion*], driving and driven drive, compulsion."

from it, then, all comes back to it, to the push, to the pushing of this *Trieb,*
this drive. It is the one that sets us on the path, if not the road (for the road
that has been broken, opened, beaten, *via rupta,* is merely a species of path,
just as method is merely a species of *hodos*),[19] it is the *Trieb* that sets us on
the path and keeps us on the path. But as it is a movement, a process, a tendency, a force[20] rather than a thing, a process without determinate subject
or object, before any determined subject or object, before any entity, before
any *who* and any *what,* the very word, the nominal or nominalized form of
the vocable (*Trieb, Getriebenheit*) is problematic,[21] and must be read as such.
We can say the same about THE drive or THE push, and even the force.[22] It
pushes [*ça pousse*], but where it pushes there is not yet either drive or push,
or pulse, or being pushed, or a being doing the pushing.

157   *Trieb,* here, does not yet belong to a particular psychoanalytic regime
or code, which is moreover itself very ambiguous and overdeterminable
between the energetic charge as a push whose place is both in the soul, the
psyche, and in the body qua organism. Moreover, Freud also defines the
Trieb, the drive, as a limit concept on the border of the psychic and the somatic, of the soul and the body. In *Three Essays on the Theory of Sexuality,*
more precisely in the chapter on partial drives and erogenous zones, after
having talked about the drive as the "psychic representative" (*die psychische
Repräsentanz*) of a somatic excitation, Freud writes, and this is well known:
"Trieb ist so einer der Begriffe der Abgrenzung des Seelischen vom Kör-
perlichen [The drive (*Trieb*) is therefore one of the concepts on the border

19. During the session, Derrida added: "Heidegger makes clear (in a text I don't
have the reference for here) that the Greeks thought *hodos,* the path, before any method,
any *methodos:* 'method' is a late and more specifically Cartesian interpretation of the
path as repeatable, regulated, etc." See Martin Heidegger, "*Der Fehl heiliger Namen*/Le
défaut de noms sacrés," trans. Roger Munier and Philippe Lacoue-Labarthe, *Contre
toute attente,* nos. 2–3 (Spring–Summer 1981): 39–55; trans. Bernhard Radloff as "The
Want of Holy Names," *Man and World* 18 (1985): 261–67; and session 2 above, note 7.
        20. During the session, Derrida added: "what interests me is the relation between
this *Trieb* and *Walten.*"
        21. During the session, Derrida added: "because this *Trieb* or this *Getriebenheit* is
not something. It is not a being, it is not a thing, it is a movement, a force on the move,
a process before any possible identification of a subject, an object or a being. So already,
using a noun to designate this thing is a problem. What is named *Trieb* or *Getriebenheit*
is thus unnamable in the strict sense of the term: it cannot give rise to a noun."
        22. During the session, Derrida added: "This is why I am hesitant to translate it as
the force; it is not *the* force either, but a forcing, a forcement, an enforcing. It is not a
force in the substantial, subjective, or objective sense of the word."

between the psychic and the corporeal]."[23] On the trembling line of this indecisive border, Freud will determine all sorts of specific drives, but they all bear the trace of this border indecision: partial drive, aggressive drive (*Aggressionstrieb*), drive to destruction (*Destruktionstrieb*), drive to mastery (*Bemächtigungstrieb*), drive to self-preservation (*Selbsterhaltungstrieb* that could be translated, with all the consequences that would bring with it, as "drive to ipseity"), death drive (*Todestrieb*) [which will be called on to play another great role a little later, in our conjoined reading of *both* Robinson *and* Heidegger, and of mourning and the ways of treating our dead body, when we come, after nostalgia, to melancholia and to the death of *Dasein* as opposed to the non-death, if not the immortality, of the animal], life drive (*Lebenstriebe*), ego drive (*Ichtrieb*), sexual drive (*Sexualtrieb*).

You can see that this word (*Trieb*) is everywhere. It pushes up everywhere, it pushes up everywhere there is pushing. But you can also see that even if the push, the total drive that pushes us toward the world, and if the nostalgia that is correlative with it and constitutes our very being, appear to be more originary than the drive that Freud is talking about, this is not so simple, for the very fact that Freud situates the drive on the border between the psychic and the somatic forbids one from circumscribing its domain in a single field, for example in a psychology, a biology, genetics, or a physics (at least in the restricted sense of *physis*), and this *Trieb* is indeed destined to cover the totality of what is, namely the world.

158

Now, let us consider in passing two things, precisely about that totality of beings that Heidegger often defines as *physis,* in the supposedly originary sense of this word, which does not mean what was later understood as nature or physics. Two things, then.

The fact is that on the one hand, *Trieb,* the drive, also designates in German pushing up, in the sense of what grows, of the growing (*phuein*) of *physis,* primarily in the vegetable sense, but also in the sense of the growth of what is born, the offspring, the bud, the child, etc. And so to speak of everything that is, of that totality of entities as *physis* in general, as pushing or pushing up, before any other distinction between nature and its others, between the vegetable and its others, is to speak of what *is* in general, and therefore of the world. The push of this pushing up, this drive or this pulse, is a force, but a force the sense of which remains absolute, and thus inde-

23. Sigmund Freud, *Drei Abhandlungen zur Sexualtheorie,* in *Gesammelte Werke* (Frankfurt am Main: S. Fischer Verlag, 1942), 5:76; trans. James Strachey as *Three Essays on the Theory of Sexuality,* in *The Standard Edition of the Complete Psychological Works of Sigmund Freud,* 24 vols. (London: Hogarth Press, 1953–74), 7:125–243 (p. 168).

terminate, as much a psychic, symbolic, spiritual, etc. force as a physical or corporeal force.

Now, on the other hand, when *Walten* plays the major role that we have begun to analyze, both in this seminar and in a still more glaring way, in 1935, in *Introduction to Metaphysics,* I am tempted to think that such a *Walten* (which also signifies not something or someone, neither man nor God, but the exercise of an archi-originary force, of a power, a violence, before any physical, psychic, theological, political determination, in a moment I shall even say before any ontic or ontological determination), this *Walten* is perhaps indissociable from this *Trieben,* and further on I shall want to follow its track or its destiny much later, in a text of Heidegger's that dates from 1957, which must be reread with the greatest attention. We'll come back to it in a moment.

159   I'm going to leave for a moment the style of commentary or of more or less paraphrastic translation of this paragraph, to mark the fact that if we stopped with this sentence, at this stage of the path, if we stopped or if Heidegger stopped on the path at the moment when he says "towards there (*Dahin*), towards this Being as a whole (*zum Sein im Ganzen*)—it is that toward which we are driven (*getrieben*) in our nostalgia," we would have to conclude that this world, what we also call the entirety, the whole and the everywhere, the everywhere of the world, is where we are not at home (*überall* nicht *zu Hause sind*). Are we not then justified in saying this, namely that we are also *without* this world, or poor in world, like the stone or the animal, or else as Celan says, "Die Welt ist fort" (to which this last line of a poem in *Atemwende* adds, "ich muss dich tragen"). "Die Welt ist fort, ich muss dich tragen." This poem by Celan would moreover call for an infinite reading, which I tried to sketch out elsewhere,[24] but that I leave untouched here, except to recall that this poem can be read as a poem of mourning or of birth (the final "ich muss dich tragen" signaling either toward the dead one that, as one mourning, I carry or must carry in me, or toward the child to be born and still carried by its mother, or even toward the poem and the poet himself who would also be called, familiarly apostrophized by the *dich* of "ich muss dich tragen"), [I leave this poem untouched, then, except to recall] especially that it seems to have as an allegorical, metonymic or theatrical figure, as a central character, a sort of beast, a ram (*Widder*) which can be, all at once or successively, the constellation or the sign of the zodiac nicknamed "the Ram," Aries, the rams of Abraham and of Aaron in well-known so-called sacrificial scenes, or the wooden ram with which one batters down

24. See session 1 above, note 11.

walls (*Mauerbrecher*). What are we to make of the syntagma that gives its title to the seminar "the-beast-and-the-sovereign," when the name of the beast, here the ram (*Widder*) can, figuratively, name so many heterogeneous things and so many characters?

In any case, we should, we could move for a long time, in thought and reading, between *Fort und Da, Da und Fort,* between these two undistancing distancings, these two *Entfernungen,* these two *theres,* between Heidegger and Celan, between on the one hand the *Da* of *Dasein* which is also the *Da* and *Dahin* as world, and on the other hand Celan's *fort* in "Die Welt is fort, ich muss dich tragen": "the world is far, the world has gone, in the absence or distance of the world, I must, I owe it to you, I owe it to myself to carry you, without world, without the foundation or grounding of anything in the world, without any foundational or fundamental mediation, one on one, like wearing mourning or bearing a child, basically where ethics begins."

What is meant by *tragen* ([in French] *porter* [carry, bear, wear]) in this line of Celan's, even before carrying the other in oneself in mourning and the carrying of the child in the mother's womb? The lexical family of *tragen* is very rich, differentiated, and difficult to translate, transport, transfer, *übertragen,* precisely, in Heidegger, where it is not merely a metaphorization (*Übertragen*). When we come back to the *Walten,* in *Identität und Differenz* (1957), we shall see from what thinking of *Austrag* (a word that poses the greatest difficulties of translation: the existing translation by "conciliation" remains very approximate) [from what thinking of *Austrag*] this thinking of *Walten* is indissociable. It's to do with nothing less than the difference between Being and beings.[25]

Meantime, I would be tempted to privilege, so as to make a distant start on this reading and to interpret the long paragraph that follows the unfolding of the three questions (on world, finitude and solitude), I would be tempted to privilege, to emphasize, so as to bring out its relief, two words: the word "force" (*Kraft,* this time) and the word *tragen,* precisely, to bear. *Kraft* and *tragen,* then.

Heidegger has just posed these three questions (world, finitude, solitude), has just brought them together as basically the same question, *in*

160

161

25. During the session, Derrida added: "Because the *Walten* produces nothing less than the difference between Being and beings, i.e. everything that is going to organize more or less indirectly this seminar on the difference between man, between human *Dasein,* and the animal: the animal is unable to accede to the *as such* of beings, i.e. the difference between Being and beings."

Einem, in one and the same—what? In any case, in one and the same one—
and even the solitude or the isolation of loneliness, being *alone* or being *the
only one* in any case is one with the question of the world and of finitude
(*Was ist das in Einem, Welt, Endlichkeit, Vereinzelung?*). And Heidegger adds
a fourth question which, moreover, comes along less as a new question, in
addition, than to open the question of the question (I will explain this) by
responding or corresponding to the three others, a quasi-fourth question
the letter of which matters in that the *Da* is marked in it as the place of
a singular event, of a history. Heidegger has just recalled the *three-in-one*
nature of the questions and he continues: "Was geschieht da mit uns?" not
"what is happening to us? what is befalling us?" but "what is happening
there with us?" "what is this *there* that happens to us and makes of us what
and who we are?" In other words: what is happening *there,* which makes of
us *who* we are or *what* we are, we humans? The question of this event, of
what happens *there* with this question about the *there,* which is neither here
nor there, is the question of what makes a human human, of what makes
us humans, the question of the essence of man in the experience of this *Da.*

Heidegger asks, then: "What is that, *in Einem* [unitarily [*unitairement*],
says the [French] translation], world, finitude, solitude?[26] What takes place
there, with us? ("Was geschieht da mit uns?") What is man, so that with
him some such thing takes place (advenes, *geschieht*) at his foundation (*in
seinem Grunde*)?" (H, 8/6).

And now, to gain access to this foundation, Heidegger is going to cut
through, like so many clouds or shadows (but these are not the shadows
of Plato's Cave, even though sometimes one thinks of them), he is going
to propose to do away with the shadows (*Schatten*) of what in general and
162   commonly defines man, to retain and highlight only his essential definition
as *Da-Sein.* I read and translate:

> Is what we know of man [and here he is going to enumerate the shadows,
> in order to traverse them if not brush them aside, he is going to recall all
> the current definitions of man as living being, animal, *animal rationale,* the
> being of civilization, of culture, person, etc. to keep only *Dasein.* Is what we
> know about man,] the animal, dupe of civilization (*der Narr der Zivilisa-
> tion*), guardian of culture (*der Hüter der Kultur*) and even personality (*ja
> sogar die Persönlichkeit*)—is all this only the shadow in him (*als Schatten an
> ihm*) of something quite other (*eines ganz Anderen was wir das Dasein nen-
> nen*), of that which we name *Dasein?* (H, 9/6)

26. [Translator's note:] The English translation has: "What is all this, taken together:
world, finitude, individuation?" (H, 8/6).

Dasein is therefore something quite different from these shadows, these old humanist definitions of man; it is, as existence, as being-there, the essence of man, the essence that had been and still remains obscured, covered over, hidden by all the shadows. And the first approach that Heidegger makes *here* to *Dasein* (here, for this course, in this sequence, for he had broadly defined it in *Sein und Zeit* which presented itself as an analytic of *Dasein*) is not only nostalgia, but a compulsive nostalgia, a drive (and *Dasein* is thus essentially a drive, *ein Trieb*) that pushes it to be everywhere at home not in a blind and disoriented, directionless way, but directed or rather awakened (the value of wakefulness plays an important role in these pages (*aufwachen, Weckung*)), awakened by or for questions such as those that have just been posed. In other words, *Dasein* is defined by the drive to questioning, and by a questioning that goes to the heart of the whole of beings as such, to the heart of the whole, of the totality of what is, and therefore of the world. This was already the gesture of *Sein und Zeit,* which chose *Dasein* as the exemplary entity and the guiding thread in the question of Being, for the simple reason that the *Dasein* that we are is — we are[27] — a questioning be-ing, as close as can be to the question. But this very questioning, which is not essentially a knowledge or a knowing — one must have its force (*Kraft*) and one must have the force to sustain it, one must have the force to bear (*tragen*) this questioning, one must have the force to support these questions. Force (*Kraft*) is here the force of bearing (*tragen*), of enduring, the force to support and prepare the birth of these questions. A force of bearing is in essence a finite force, otherwise it would have nothing to carry or support, whence the question of finitude, inseparable from the question on the world and on solitude. One is alone as the one who ought to carry, ought to support the question about the world. And it is this finite force that defines existence (*Existenz,* this time). This force of questioning, this force capable of bearing the question of the world, of all that is, this drive-force is the measure of access to what we call — and this is the title of the seminar — *metaphysical concepts*. I'll first read a few lines, slightly modifying here and there the published French translation, which is moreover in general good:

163

> Philosophy, metaphysics, is a homesickness, a drive to be at home every-where (*ein Heimweh, ein Trieb, überall zu Hause sein*), a demand [*ein Ver-langen,* a request, the request of the question, then, the demand of the ques-tion], not blind (*blind*) and without direction (*und richtungslos*) [but in a moment Heidegger will specify that in fact, even if this nostalgic drive is not blind and disoriented, not without direction, nonetheless being awake

27. Thus in the typescript.

consists in searching for paths (*Wege*) and ways to be opened or broken (*die rechte Bahn öffnen,* and then *eine solche Bahn brechen*)]. [Philosophy, metaphysics, is a homesickness, a drive to be at home everywhere (*ein Heimweh, ein Trieb, überall zu Hause sein*), a demand (*ein Verlangen,* a request, the request of the question, then, the demand of the question), not blind (*blind*) and without direction (*und richtungslos*)], but one which awakens us to (*in uns aufwacht*) such questions as those we have just asked and to their unity: what is world, finitude, individuation? Each of these questions inquires into the whole (*Jede dieser Fragen fragt in das Ganze*). It is not sufficient for us to know such questions. What is decisive (*entscheidend*) is whether we really ask such questions [in other words, only if we are really enduring in a questioning manner these very questions, only if we are really questioning, *wirklich,* measuring up to these questions, *ob wir solche Fragen wirklich fragen*], whether we have the strength to sustain them [*tragen,* to *bear* them] right through our whole existence (*ob wir die Kraft haben, sie durch unsere ganze Existenz hindurch zu tragen*). (H, 9/6)

164

So, the reality of questioning, like that of the nostalgic drive, has its condition in a force. And the force is the force to *bear,* to support, to sustain, *Kraft . . . zu tragen.* The *Wirklichkeit,* the effective reality of a question, is the force of the nostalgic drive that pushes us toward the question, and the force of that nostalgic drive should make of that question sustained [*portée*], of the carrying [*port*] and the bearing [*la portée*] of that question, what is at stake in an entire existence. The whole of existence is measured by the whole of the question on the whole, on the world. Otherwise, without that force of bearing, and without the whole of the existence that takes on that force of bearing, it would only be a partial diversion, even if that diversion is called knowledge, knowing, science, even philosophy, or even, as Heidegger will dare to say to his students from his professorial Chair, the philosophy of a professor. I'll read and translate the end of the paragraph in which you will see reappear the driven search for the path and the way to be broken (*bahnen,* the word often used by Freud, moreover, to talk about cerebral, neurological, and psychic facilitations in his early texts. *Bahnen,* it's always the language of an explorer who opens or is seeking to open, by force, a path where there was no path before, to make a space practicable and accessible to comings and goings. Robinson is constantly opening paths for himself):

165

It is not sufficient for us to know such questions. What is decisive is whether we really ask such questions, whether we have the strength to sustain them right through our whole existence. It is not sufficient for us to simply abandon ourselves to such questions in an indeterminate and vacillating manner (*unbestimmt und schwankend*). Rather this urge to be at home everywhere (*sondern dieser Trieb, überall zu Hause sein*) is in itself at the same time a seeking of those ways (*das Suchen der Wege*) which open up the right paths for such questions (*die solchen Fragen die rechte Bahn öffnen*). For this, in turn, we require the hammer of conceptual comprehension [*des Hammers des Begreifens*—and starting here, let's pay attention to Heidegger's work on the language and on the vocabulary of conceptual grasp, *greifen, begreifen, Begriff, ergriffen;* a grasp or a seizing that grasps us, that attacks and takes us, takes us on, takes us by surprise as much as we grasp and take possession of it, where the bearing of a conception, the strength to bear (*tragen*) in conception is the correlative of a grasping force of a *Dasein,* which thus finds itself both grasping and grasped:] [For this, in turn, we require the hammer of conceptual comprehension], we require those concepts which can open up such a path (*derjenigen Begriffe, die eine solche Bahn brechen können*). We are dealing with a conceptual comprehension (*Es ist ein Begreifen*) and with concepts (*und es sind Begriffe*) of a *primordial* kind (*Begriffe ureigener Art* [Heidegger's emphasis: this originary property or this proper originarity defines what Heidegger is calling in this context a metaphysical concept]). *Metaphysical concepts* [he says, emphasizing these words, *Die metaphysischen Begriffe*] remain eternally closed off [*verschlossen,* thus inaccessible] from any inherently indifferent and noncommittal scientific acumen [literally, one that commits to nothing, *unverbindlich,* which in no way obliges, which forces nothing, like a metaphysical concept forces and calls on the existential force it requires]. (H, 9/6)

This point is and will be important for us as to the relation between this metaphysical questioning and scientific knowledge, here visibly devalued and secondarized, especially when we come to the question of the animal. Heidegger, to whom we must grant the merit of having seriously inquired, to the point of citing it extensively, into the scientific, zoological or ethological knowledge of his time as to the animal (von Uexküll, for example, and many others), will nonetheless always judge this scientific knowledge to be incompetent, incapable of measuring up to these metaphysical questions about the essence of animality or the essence of life and death; and this gesture, which is common in Heidegger, this gesture that comes down to discrediting scientific knowledge with respect to certain questions the reply to which is supposedly presupposed by science, precisely—this disqualification of science will be for us a locus of problematization, of course.

Heidegger proceeds by withdrawing, no less, the experience of these metaphysical concepts not only from scientific knowledge, but even from teaching and the professoriate, from the professor's profession of faith, and one must imagine how these paradoxically subversive-seeming anti-

professorial and even anti-university declarations might have resonated in
the public, academic, and more broadly political space at that time (1929–
30), especially when they were taken up *ex cathedra* by a professor who was
already highly famous and even fashionable. I quote and translate before
moving to another stage:

> Metaphysical concepts are not something that we could simply learn (*ler-
> nen*) in this way, nor something that a teacher [or a master, *Lehrer*] or any-
> one calling themselves a philosopher might require to be simply recited
> and applied.
>
> Above all, however, we shall never have comprehended these concepts
> and their conceptual rigor (*Vor allem aber, diese Begriffe und ihre begriffliche
> Strenge werden wir nie begriffen haben*) unless we have first been *gripped* by
> whatever they are supposed to comprehend [and Heidegger emphasizes
> "gripped": *wenn wir nicht zuvor* ergriffen *sind von dem, was sie begreifen
> sollen,* unless we have first been *gripped* by whatever they are supposed to
> comprehend]. (H, 9/6–7)

So we must first be gripped by the very thing (here the world, finitude, or
solitude), grasped by, exposed to, come to grips with, even under the sway
167 or hold of the very thing that these concepts are supposed to grasp. We must
be grasped by what we are grasping. In our existence, the concept must
be grasped before being grasping, or more precisely, our existence must be
grasped, must be in the grasping (which also means astonishment, *thau-
mazein,* being taken aback, being surprised), even before, and so that, the
concepts can grasp. The concept grasps and is grasped, but not in the sense
that I wrote somewhere, in *Glas,* in the course of an interpretative reading
of Hegel rather than Heidegger, "the concept is cooked,"[28] in the culinary
sense, as opposed to being raw, or in the sense of being done for (of having
one's goose cooked).

I find this concept of being grasped (*Ergriffenheit*), the literality of which
is going to insist in the following sentences, all the more troubling for
the fact that in other texts, especially those that I quote in "Heidegger's
Hand,"[29] grasping, the ability to grasp is attributed to the prehensile claw

28. Jacques Derrida, *Glas* (Paris: Galilée, 1974), p. 260: "Dès qu'il est saisi par
l'écriture, le concept est cuit"; trans. John P. Leavey, Jr., and Richard Rand, as *Glas* (Lincoln: University of Nebraska Press, 1986), p. 233; "As soon as it is grasped by writing,
the concept is drunk [*cuit*: or cooked]". [Translator's note: In this context, "saisir" in
French also has the culinary sense of searing or sealing.]

29. "La main de Heidegger (Geschlecht II)" (see session 3 above, note 45), pp. 46–50
[pp. 40–44].

of the animal, the animal's paw, rather than to the hand of man or *Dasein*. It is true that here the point, as much as grasping, is being grasped, being seized (*Ergriffenheit*) as the experience of being-grasped, taken, surprised, astonished, affected by what makes us feel nostalgia, *Heimweh*, and that one might indeed call *unheimlich*, although Heidegger does not here use this word to which he so often appeals elsewhere, in the most serious and decisive moments of all his meditations. We are indeed dealing with an affection, an affect, an affective attunement of questioning thought itself, for what matters to Heidegger at that moment is the affect of a fundamental *Stimmung*. Boredom and nostalgia are among these fundamental attunements of philosophizing. Heidegger writes this, right after what I have just quoted:

> The fundamental concern of philosophizing (*Das Grundbemühen des Philosophierens*) pertains to such being gripped (*Ergriffenheit*), to awakening (*Weckung*) and planting it [to its cultivation, *Pflanzung*]. All such being gripped (*Ergriffenheit*), however, comes from and remains in an *attunement* (*Stimmung*). To the extent that conceptual comprehending (*das Begreifen*) and philosophizing is not some arbitrary enterprise alongside others, but happens in the *ground* of human Dasein [*im* Grunde—emphasized—*des menschlichen Daseins*], the attunements out of which our being gripped (*Ergriffenheit*) philosophically and our philosophical comprehension (*Begrifflichkeit*) arise are always necessarily *fundamental attunements* (*Grundstimmungen*) of Dasein. (H, 9–10/7)

168

All of this was designed, among other things, to justify the word "nostalgia" as one of these fundamental affects and thus to give credit to Novalis's words as poets' words that, this time, and contrary to what Aristotle suggests about poets' words, are not deceitful (*nicht lügenhaft*).

I announced at the outset that Heidegger quoted Aristotle's *Problemata* at least one other time, in a context in which it is again a question of the *Grundstimmungen*, the fundamental attunements of philosophizing. This is much further on in the book, in §44. There it is a matter, I repeat, of the fundamental attunement, but this time not of nostalgia but of melancholy (*Schwermut* or *Melancholie*). Melancholy is not nostalgia, but there is between these two affects an affinity, an analogy, that depends at least on the fact that these two sufferings suffer from a lack, a privation, even a bereavement. Heidegger (about whom many accounts attest to the fact that he was himself of quite a melancholic temperament, some say "depressive," basically like all of us who philosophize, no?) is maintaining that philosophy is melancholic, fundamentally, not in its content, he says, but in its form. And he wants to withdraw this affect, and every fundamental attunement, from all psychology, in which he sees a peril and a tyranny or even an internal corruption (*Verderb*) of our time. He explains this just before recalling those three theses (the stone is without world, the animal is poor in world, man is *Weltbildend,* world-forming, and I quote the German, because the word

169   *bilden* is going to matter to us in moment). So Heidegger explains all that just before beginning what he will call his comparative examination on the basis of the intermediate thesis, "das Tier ist weltarm." Melancholy affects philosophy insofar as it is creative (*schöpferisch*), a word that we often use wrongly, notes Heidegger, whether speaking of art or philosophy. *Creative* should not be understood here as a privilege or a superiority with respect to other activities, such as those of the manual worker or the businessman, but on the contrary as an extra obligation, a duty (*Verpflichtung*) that resides in the very creativity (to create is to be obliged to create), and this is marked in the very attitude that *bears* (bearing again [*la portée*]) this creativity (*tragenden Haltung*). This obligation is, like all duty, the correlative of a freedom. "Creative achievement is a free formative activity [*Schaffen ist eine freies Bilden*]" (H, 270/182). Let us not be astonished to recognize in this freedom, and the *Bilden* it qualifies, something proper to mankind, who is *welt*bildend, as opposed to the animal (*weltarm*)—and which, consequently, is supposedly neither free, nor creative, nor capable of nostalgia, melancholy and mourning (or even, as we shall see in a moment, of death properly speaking). If there is freedom where there is obligation, there is in it a burden, a load, a toiling, something heavy (and thereby *schwer*) that man bears (*trägt* again) in his heavy heart, in his *Gemüt,* in the intimacy of his soul or his heart. *Schwermut,* the heavy heart, melancholy, is the weight of this weight, this heavy burden that one bears in one's heart. Well, all creative action (*alles schöpferische Handeln*) is seized by melancholy, it is in melancholy (*in der Schwermut*) (H, 270/182–83), whether it knows it or not, but the converse is not true: not all melancholy is creative. Now Aristotle, this time quoted without reservation by Heidegger, had clearly understood this alliance between creation and melancholy. In the *Problemata* he asked himself the following question, which clearly bears on humans (*andres*) and not on all living creatures, for example what we call animals:

170   "Διὰ τί πάντες ὅσοι περιττοὶ γεγόνασιν ἄνδρες ἢ χατὰ φιλοσοφίαν ἢ πολιτιχὴν ἢ ποίησιν ἢ τέχνας φαίνονται μελαγχολικοὶ ὄντες (Why are all those men who accomplished eminent things—be it in philosophy, in politics, in poetry or the plastic arts [*bildenden Künsten,* says Heidegger, to translate τέχνας]—clearly melancholics? [*offensichtlich Melancholiker,* as Heidegger translates φαίνονται μελαγχολικοὶ ὄντες]?)."³⁰ Having recalled that Aristotle cites the examples of Empedocles, Plato, Socrates, so many melancholics according to him, and that moreover Aristotle distinguishes between melancholy [*dia physin*] and melancholy [*dia noson*], natural melancholy and sick, pathological melancholy, Heidegger subscribes without delay to this declaration of Aristotle's, which he translates and takes on board: "As a creative and essential activity of human *Dasein,* philosophy stands in the *fundamental attunement of melancholy* (*Schwermut*)" (H, 271/183).

Why have I insisted on the link between nostalgia and melancholy that appear at a distance of almost three hundred pages in Heidegger's [German] text, each time in the vicinity of Aristotle? Why this leap? Because I wanted to situate the question of life and death between the animal and the human *Dasein,* because melancholy is also the affect of irreparable mourning, and because I should like to come back via this route, both toward the question of the circle and toward the phantasm—let's call it the Robinsonian phantasm—of being "bury'd alive" or "swallow'd up alive."

It happens that just before this passage on melancholy, in §43 that I invite you to reread closely yourselves, §43 that concerns a difficulty of content and method concerning the essence of life, Heidegger broaches directly the question of the circle in this philosophical approach. Basically, in order to distinguish between man and animal, we must clarify the essence of the animality of the animal (*das* Wesen der Tierheit *des Tieren*) and the essence of the humanity of man (*das* Wesen der Menschheit *des Menschen*) (H, 265/179). Now we can determine the animality of the animal only if we have already shed light on life, the essence of the life of the living, what makes life life (*Lebendigkeit des Lebenden,* the livingness of the living), as opposed to the inanimate, the lifeless (*Leblosen*), of what cannot even die. For what does not live does not die: the stone does not die, because it does not live. But all that presupposes already that the animal lives and that we have access to what it feels as a living being. In what way does the life of the living become accessible to us? asks Heidegger, again posing the question in the methodical figure of the path ("*Auf welchem Wege* kann und soll die Lebendigkeit des Lebenden in ihrem Wesen zugänglich werden? [*On what path* [Heidegger emphasizes *Auf welchem Wege*] can and must the life of the living become accessible?]" [H, 265–56/179]). Heidegger wonders more than once how life is accessible to us, be it the animality of the animal or the vegetable essence of the plant (*die Pflanzlichkeit der Pflanze*

171

---

30. Aristotle, *Problemata* 953 a 10 ff., quoted by Heidegger (H, 271/183).

(H, 265–66/179): and twice—this is highly interesting in my view—Hei-degger classifies the plant, the plant-being of plants, the vegetable, as they say, among the phenomena of life, like the animality of the animal, but he will never grant to the living being that the plant is the same attention he will grant the living being that the animal is). So, how is life accessible to us, given that the animal, notes Heidegger, cannot observe itself, and that we can only have access to the signs it gives us through interpretation and explicitation? As there is no originary access (*ursprünglichen Zugang*) to the life of animals, we must presuppose,[31] have already presupposed, that the animal lives (*haben wir schon vorausgesetzt*). And at least five or six times in two pages he will call the circular self-moving of philosophy a circle (*im Kreise Sichbewegen der Philosophie, im Kreis gehen, Kreisbewegung*) (H, 266–67/180); twice he will describe as a circle this indispensable and essential movement of philosophical presupposition that common understanding can tolerate no more than it can tolerate dizziness or turbulence. Dizziness (*Schwindel*) is *unheimlich,* worrying, strangely familiar, familiarly disorient-ing, and this is why it is intolerable for common sense which wants to ma-nipulate things, know what the point is, etc. Dizziness is *unheimlich,* like turbulence (*Wirbel*) and the circle (*Zirkel*). But the philosopher must not flee before what is *unheimlich,* dizzying, turbulent; on the contrary he thinks in them the condition to open a path (*Weg bahnen*) in thought. To open a path, one must begin from the circle and accept to go around in circles so as to think presupposition itself. Heidegger concludes his §43 thus:

> We find ourselves moving in a circle (*Wir bewegen uns also in einem Kreis*) when we *presuppose* (*wenn wir* voraussetzen) a *certain fundamental concep-tion concerning* both *the essence of life* and *the way in which it is to be inter-preted* and then proceed on the basis of this presupposition (*aufgrund dieser Voraussetzung*) to open up a path (*gerade den Weg bahnen*) which will lead us to a fundamental conception of life (*zu einer Grundauffassung des Lebens zu kommen*). (H, 267/180)

The paradoxical point to which I now want to draw your attention, as to these vertiginous circles, is the following, and it is a matter of life and death. Heidegger, as you have heard, retains as the first and only sign of life, or even the first criterion of life—of the *Lebendigkeit des Lebens,* the being-in-life of life—the possibility of dying. That is supposedly the differ-

---

31. During the session, Derrida added: "it is this logic of presupposition that interests me here, because this is where we are going to find the circle."

ence between the stone and the animal living being: the stone does not die   *173*
because it does not live. Let me reread the sentence:

> Then again, we can only determine the animality of the animal if we are
> clear about what constitutes the *living character of a living being,* as distinct
> from the non-living being (*Leblosen*) which does not even have the possibil-
> ity of dying. A stone cannot be dead because it was never alive (*Ein Stein
> kann nicht tot sein, weil er nicht lebt*). (H, 265/179)

So it all seems clear and decided: it belongs to the essence of life, and thus
to animality, that the animal lives, that it is alive, because it can die. Now
here, about 120 pages later (H, 388/267), in the middle of the elucidation
of animality poor in world, enclosed as it is in the circle of its *Ringen* and its
Umring, and of its *Benommenheit* (benumbment, captivation), Heidegger
asks again the question of death and comes to the assertion that only man
dies, whereas the animal for its part does not die, but simply ceases to live.
I broached these questions at length and in my turn problematized them in
Aporias,[32] but I shall in the present context hang on only to the paradoxical
sequence that is of interest to us. Having insisted on the fact that death,
the moment of death, is the "touchstone" (*Prüfstein*) of every question on
the essence of life, here is Heidegger affirming that the animal cannot die,
properly speaking, but only come to an end. We shall return again to this
decisive and troubling distinction, along with everything that binds it to the
whole of this discourse. I'll first quote the sentences that count the most, and
ask you to read the whole context, after which I will tell you why and how,
here, I should like to draw from it an argument, one argument at least, and
a link with *Robinson Crusoe* . . . Heidegger writes:

> [. . .] in captivation (*Benommenheit*), as the fundamental structure of life   *174*
> [understand: of the animal], certain *quite determinate possibilities of death*
> [ganz bestimmte Möglichkeiten des Todes], of *approaching death* [des Zum-
> Tode-kommens], are prefigured [*vorzeichnet,* prescribed]. (H, 388/267)

This is all in italics. Heidegger, who for now keeps the word "death" for
the animal, nonetheless goes on, as you will hear, to withdraw the proper
sense of "death" from the animal's "coming to death." He writes, "Is the
death of the animal a *dying* or a way of *coming to an end*? [*Ist der Tod des
Tieres ein* Sterben *oder ein* Verenden?]" (H, 388/267). *Sterben* and *Verenden* are italicized, and their distinction or opposition is thus emphasized.

32. *Apories,* pp. 96ff [pp. 51 ff]; see also session 1 above, note 13.

"Verenden" is not dying, "sterben." And Heidegger confirms this again when
he writes immediately after having recalled *Benommenheit,* captivation, benumbment as the essence of the animal: "the animal cannot die in the sense
in which dying is ascribed to human beings but can only come to an end"
(H, 388/267).

You can see clearly that this link between the inability to die and benumbment depends on this decisive fact, recalled throughout the seminar,
and again just before this passage, namely that benumbment inhibits the
possibility of relating to beings *as such:* the animal as such is incapable of
the *as such.* Therefore, among other things, the animal cannot have, as can
the human *Dasein,* a relation[33] to death *as such.* This is, among other things,
why it cannot speak, nor be nostalgic, or melancholic, nor have a relation to
the whole of beings, to the world as such.

Without getting into this immense problem again, I hang onto this curious non-sequitur that consists in defining animality by life, life by the possibility of death, and yet, and yet, in denying dying properly speaking to the
175   animal. But what seems more problematic still to my eyes is the confidence
with which Heidegger attributes dying properly speaking to human *Dasein,* access or relation to death properly speaking and to dying as such. As
we shall verify more and more precisely and abundantly, what the animal
supposedly lacks is indeed the experience of the *as such,* access to the *as such*
of the entity, to the open, the manifest (*offenbar*), the manifestness (*Offenbarkeit*) of beings *as such,* or even, as Heidegger specifies, *to* the manifestness
of the other, as such, of what is other insofar as it is a being (H, 368/253);
that's what is supposedly lacking in the animal, in *Benommenheit,* the benumbment of captivation that supposedly encloses the animal in its circle
(*Ring, Umring*). What is lacking is not supposedly access to the entity, but access to the entity *as such,* i.e. that slight difference between Being and beings
that, as we shall see, springs from what can only be called a certain *Walten.* A
slight difference, because this difference between Being and beings, this difference that depends on the *as such,* is not a being, by definition; in a certain
sense it is nothing, it is not. But it *waltet.* What does that mean: *walten?* How
are we to translate this word? We'll be wondering about this some more.

For now, and to conclude provisionally today, I wonder if one should
not sharpen up still further this question of the difference between *on the
one hand* dying properly speaking (*sterben*), death itself (*Tod*) and as such,
to which human *Dasein* is supposed (by Heidegger) to be able to be awake
and to have access, and *on the other hand,* the end of living (*verenden*) which

33. During the session, Derrida added: "to its own death."

is supposedly the lot of the natural biological being, i.e. the animal. I am not going to take on this terrible and fascinating question frontally. Of course, one might recall — it would be too easy — so many signs that assure us that it is not enough, in order to have access to death, to one's death as such, to pronounce the word "death," to have this word at one's disposal in one's language, and to see dead people depart, as they say, more and more dead people, see them go away and de-cede at a brisk pace around oneself, see multiply the signs and probabilities of coming death, have the near-- certainty that we are going to die one day or another and that we might die from one moment to the next. This suffices all the less to distinguish clearly between death as such and life as such because all our thoughts of death, our death — even before all the help that religious imagery can bring us — our thoughts of our death are always, structurally, thoughts of survival. To see oneself or to think oneself dead is to see oneself surviving, present at one's death, present or represented *in absentia* at one's death even in all the signs, traces, images, memories, even the body, the corpse or the ashes, literal or metaphorical, that we leave behind, in more or less organized and delib- erate fashion, to the survivors, the other survivors, the others as survivors delegated to our own survival.

All of which is banal and well known: one could go on about it endlessly. But the logic of this banality of survival that begins even before our death is that of a survival of the remainder, the remains, that does not even wait for death to make life and death indissociable, and thus the *unheimlich* and fan- tasmatic experience of the spectrality of the living dead. Life and death as such are not separable as such. Whence Robinson's great organizing fantasy (terror and desire): to be "swallow'd up alive" or "bury'd alive." He knows that one dies a living death anyway, and the only question, the only alterna- tive, is: what is to be done? What will one do, what will the *other,* the other *alone,* do with me as living dead, given that I can only *think* my dead body, or rather *imagine* my corpse, if anything else is to happen to it, as living dead in the hands of the other? The other alone. I have just said *think* my death or rather *imagine* my corpse. Well, perhaps the supposed difference between thinking and imagining finds here its ultimate root, and perhaps thinking death as such, in the sense Heidegger wants to give it, is still only imagination. *Fantasia,* fantastic phantasmatics.

Whence, on the basis of this phantasmatics, the immense variety, among all living beings, human or not, of the cultures of the corpse, the gestures or rites of burial or cremation, etc.

I was hoping, and I had promised you, I had promised myself to talk today about this and in the direction of this phantasmatics of dying alive or

176

177

dying dead, of what happens when people among us, in the West, as they say, still hesitate, more and more, or else decide between burial and cremation, whereas in other cultures they have opted, in massive and stable, still broadly durable fashion, for one or the other. I was hoping, I had promised myself to return too, in the wake of *Walten*, to the origin of the difference of Being and beings, which organizes, as you have seen, this whole problematic.

I did not have time; I hope and promise that I'll do it next time, at the very start of the session.

February 5, 2003

What is a thing?

 What is the other?

 What is the other when it comes to making of me ... what? *Some thing.*
What is the other when he or she employs him or herself in making a thing
of me? Such and such a thing, for example a thing that, like a corpse, is both
a thing and something other than a thing?

 What is a thing?

 What is the other?

 Leaving these questions to wait for a moment, suspended for the time
of a detour, I naturally invite you to read or reread Heidegger's two great
texts on the thing, beginning with *Die Frage nach dem Ding: Zu Kants Lehre
von den Transzendentalen Grundsätzen,* translated into French in 1971 and
published by Gallimard under the title *La Question de la chose,* by Jean Reboul and Jacques Taminiaux.[1] But this work published in 1962 corresponds
to a course given at the University of Freiburg during the winter semester
of 1935–36. So it is pretty much contemporaneous with the *Introduction to
Metaphysics.* And then also read, reread "Das Ding," "The Thing," later
in origin, but published before *What Is a Thing?,* in 1951, then in 1954 in
Vorträge und Aufsätze, translated into French in *Essais et Conférences.*[2] In
"The Thing," the text published earlier, then, but written later than *What Is
a Thing?,* I note in passing, you will come across four or five ... things that
are more directly linked to our current concern. Moreover, since it is death

---

1. Martin Heidegger, *Die Frage nach dem Ding: Zu Kants Lehre von den Transzendentalen Grundsätzen* (Tübingen: Max Niemeyer Verlag, 1962); *Qu'est-ce qu'une chose?,*
trans. Jean Reboul and Jacques Taminiaux (Paris: Gallimard, 1971); trans. W. B. Barton,
Jr., and V. Deutsch as *What Is a Thing?* (Chicago: H. Regnery Co., 1968).

2. "Das Ding," in *Vorträge und Aufsätze* (Pfullingen: Günther Neske Verlag, 1954),
pp. 157–79; trans. Albert Hofstadter as "The Thing," in Martin Heidegger, *Poetry, Language, Thought* (New York: Harper and Row, 1971), pp. 163–80.

and melancholia and mourning that are preoccupying us at the moment, and living death, one can read "Das Ding" as a great text on death, on the mortality of *Dasein,* in opposition to an a-mortality or even an immortality of the beast.

1. On the one hand, the thing (in at least three or four languages: Greek, Latin, German, and English) is not without relation to the possibility of speaking, discussing, debating in public about a matter of litigation: the thing is not merely what one is talking about, but what is not necessarily mute, speechless: the thing chatters and causes to people to chatter [*la chose cause et fait causer*]. And this goes just as well for *Ding, thing, causa, cosa, chose,* etc.

2. Next, in this text resounds the question "What is nearness?" (*Wie steht es mit der Nähe?*),[3] which has occupied us a great deal[4] and will do so again. Heidegger replies to this question with some long developments which could be gathered into a sentence that I quote because the word *walten* again appears in it: "The thing is not 'in' nearness, 'in' proximity, as if nearness were a container. Nearness is at work (*waltet*) in bringing near, as the thing-ing of the thing [the 'thinging' or the 'causing' of the thing, *als das Dingen des Dinges*]."[5] So proximity reigns, dominates, imposes itself, arrives, arises, occurs, prevails (*waltet*) as thing, as the movement of the becoming-thing of the thing, *als das Dingen des Dinges,* as the causation of the thing, if you will hear causation otherwise than as causality, relation of cause to effect. "Das Ding ist nicht 'in' der Nähe, als sei diese ein Behälter. Nähe waltet im Nähern als das Dingen des Dinges."[6] Nearness is not opposed to far-ness: nearness, writes Heidegger in a passage that I leave you to reconsti-tute, "conserves," "keeps" (*wahrt*) farness ("Nähe wahrt die Ferne. Ferne wahrend, west die Nähe in ihrem Nähern": "Nearness preserves farness. Preserving farness, nearness presences [*west,* in the quasi-active, intransi-tively active and energetic sense, a little like *waltet* ('accomplishes its being,' as the [French] translation has it)] nearness in nearing that farness").[7]

3. Next, you would read in it a sublime *sententia* of Meister Eckhart— drawing on the pseudo-Dionysius the Areopagite—a quotation designed to recall that *thing* can mean thing in general, anything or anybody, what-

3. Ibid., p. 158 [p. 163].

4. See sessions 3 and 4 above.

5. Ibid., p. 170 [p. 175]; during the session, Derrida added: "It is the thing that makes nearness possible."

6. Ibid.

7. Ibid.

ever *is,* from the stone to the beast, to man, the soul, and God. This quotation matters to us here, because it is a question of *love,* indeed, but a love that appropriates what it loves to make of it the thing it loves. Meister Eckhart says in Old German: "diu minne ist der natur, daz si den menschen wandelt in die dinc, die er minnet [love is of such a nature that it changes man into the things he loves]."[8] We shall be wondering whether, in death and in mourning, things are not the same as they are in love, and whether loving, then, does not mean loving so as to make it one's lovable thing, to the point of having it at one's disposal, to love eating and drinking it alive, keeping it in oneself, burying or burning it to keep it living-dead in oneself or right up close to oneself, which can also be as far as can be from oneself. Everywhere.

4. Then you would find in it, again with recourse to the vocabulary of *walten* or *durchwalten,* and in a form that is still more firm and trenchant, the assertion from the 1929–30 seminar according to which man alone dies, whereas the animal perishes or finishes. This is in the famous passage on the Fourfold (*Geviert*), earth and sky, divinities and mortals, the earth being— let's recall before we talk about burial—what, remaining, bears (*die bauend Tragende*), while gathering them, water and stone, what grows (the plant), and the animal (*Gewässer und Gestein, Gewächs und Getier*).[9] (Comment on the *Ge-*)[10]

So in this famous passage on the *Geviert,* about the mortals, Heidegger writes:

> The mortals are human beings (*Die Sterblichen sind die Menschen*). They are called mortals because they *can* die [and the important word here is "can [*pouvoir*]," *können,* to be capable of, as much as "die": *weil die sterben können*]. To die means to be capable of death as death [and here too what counts is power [*pouvoir*], *Vermögen,* and power as the power of the "as such," being capable of the "as such," of death as such: a power, faculty or ability that will in a moment be refused the animal: *Sterben heißt; den Tod als Tod vermögen.*] Only man dies (*Nur der Mensch stirbt*). The animal perishes (*Das Tier verdendet*). [This is literally what he said twenty years earlier in the seminar.] It [the animal] has death as death neither ahead of itself nor behind it (*Es hat den Tod als Tod weder vor sich noch hinter sich*).[11]

8. Meister Eckhart, quoted in ibid., p. 169 [p. 174].

9. Ibid., p. 170 [p. 176].

10. During the session, Derrida added: "*Gewässer,* water as a whole; *Gestein,* stone in general, the set of everything that is stony; *Gewächs,* everything that grows, the set of what grows, and *Getier,* the set of animals." On the following line, he added "The important thing is *Ge-,* the gathering."

11. Ibid., p. 171 [p. 176]; Derrida's emphasis.

1 2 2 ‡ FIFTH SESSION

[This sentence counts as more than a mere explicitation, but specifies the fact that the "as such" of death presupposes that one have death *ahead of oneself* and *behind oneself,* that one see it coming by anticipating it in being *zum Tode,* but also that one retain it and recall it in mourning, burial, the memory one keeps, so many possibilities and powers that Heidegger refuses without the slightest nuance to what he calls in a very homogeneous way *Das Tier* in general, the animal in general.] And having said this about death, about death reserved, basically, for man who alone has the power to die, Heidegger calls death the reliquary of nothing, of the nothing (*des Nichts*), the shrine (*Schrein*), he does not say the coffin, but the place where one deposits what is priceless, remains and must remain: (the [French] translation says "the Ark"):

183

> Death is the shrine of Nothing (*Der Tod ist der Schrein des Nichts*), that is [adds Heidegger], of that which in every respect is never something that merely exists [and therefore a mere thing], but which nevertheless presences,[12] even as the mystery of Being itself (*als das Geheimnis des Seins selbst*).[13] As the shrine of Nothing, death harbors within itself the presencing of Being (*das Wesende des Seins*).[14] As the shrine of Nothing, death is the shelter of Being (*das Gebirg des Seins*). We now call mortals mortals — not because their earthly life comes to an end (*endet*), but because they are capable of death as death (*weil sie den Tod als Tod vermögen*) [. . .] They [the mortals] are the presencing relation to Being as Being (*Sie sind das wesende Verhältnis zum Sein als Sein*).[15]

As you see, what here bears the main accent is that death as such, access or relation to death as such is a being-able, a power (*Können, Vermögen*). Such a power or potency defines the mortal, man as mortal, and this power

184

---

12. During the session, Derrida added: "The nothing is without being a being, without being something, and it is this being of the nothing, and so this difference between Being and beings, that passes via the nothing, that is guarded in this Ark that is death. Death is what guards the Being of beings."

13. During the session, Derrida added: "It is in death that lies the secret of Being itself, the difference between Being and beings."

14. During the session, Derrida added: "Presencing, Being, is here too in a sense one cannot call active, because when you say active you are in the opposition of active to passive, *energeia/dunamis*, etc., and you are already off on a different track. But you can see that *west, wesen,* etc., mark a modality of Being that is not simply the static modality of beings. Being happens [*se produit*] as Being."

15. Ibid., p. 171 [p. 176]. During the session, Derrida added: "You see the relation here between the experience of death as such, reserved for man, and the question of Being, the difference between Being and beings. It is the same thing to be mortal and to be able to ask the question 'what is the Being of beings?' or 'what is the thingness of the thing?'"

of as such, of the *as such* [ce pouvoir du *comme tel,* de l'"en tant que tel"] this power to have access to the *as such* of death (i.e. the Nothing as such) is none other than the relation to the ontological difference, and thereby to Being as Being. Without this power,[16] without the force of this power of the "as such," of death as such, there would be no relation to the "as such," and thereby to Being as Being, Being as Being not being one "as such" among others, but the possibility of the "as such" in general: for here it is a matter of Being as Being and not of the being as being. Which passes through the Nothing, not-being and therefore death, as such. And it is this difference of being from Being, this ontological difference that, bearing the "as such," will be, in a text the reading of which I am deferring still, *Identität und Differenz,* [will be] said to *come about* via a *walten:* always the force of this same word that bespeaks a force, a power, a dominance, even a sovereignty unlike any other[17]–whence the difficulty that we have in thinking it, determining it and, of course, translating it.[18]

What is more, in the very passage we are reading, in "Das Ding," and just after what I have been commenting on, the vocabulary of *walten,* in truth of *durchwalten,* comes up, but precisely to say what has prevailed, alas, in metaphysics, namely the definition of man not as the mortal who finds his being in the shelter of Being, the mortal guardian of Being, but as an animal, a rational animal, an animal living being that reason had supposedly merely penetrated, governed, dominated (*durchwaltet*), but without changing anything in the narrow determination of man as animal, as living being, whereas one must define man not as a living being, but as a mortal. *185* This critique of the great metaphysical concept of the *animal rationale* and the *animalitas* of man was already to be found in the *Letter on Humanism.* Here now is this paragraph, which follows immediately from the sentence about mortals being the relation to Being as Being:

> Metaphysics, by contrast, represents [it is only a representation, a *Vorstellung: Die Metaphysik dagegen stellt den Menschen als animal, als Lebewesen vor*] [Metaphysics, by contrast, represents] man as an animal, as a living

16. During the session, Derrida added: "What does *pouvoir* [power, being-able] mean here? Even the word *pouvoir* (*Können, Vermögen*), far from giving us the key to a door that would have access to the Being of beings, this power is itself defined by the Being of beings. Power, here, this singular power here appears as power on the basis of the experience of the difference between Being and beings."

17. During the session, Derrida added: "This is not the sovereignty of God, it is not the sovereignty of a king or a head of state, but a sovereignty more sovereign than all sovereignty."

18. During the session, Derrida added: "and what interests me too is the chain linking *walten, können, vermögen.*"

being. Even when *ratio* pervades [*durchwaltet:* grips with force, by force, traverses as a force] *animalitas,* man's being (*Menschsein*) remains (*bleibt*) defined by life and life experience [*Leben und Erleben:* experience, then, *Erlebnis* as experience but, as the word suggests, lived experience of the living being].[19] Rational living beings must first *become* mortals [and Heidegger emphasizes "werden," *become: Die vernünftigen Lebewesen müssen erst zu Sterblichen* werden].[20] [Insist on the word *Erleben:* implicit critique of Husserl's phenomenology; philosophy — metaphysics — of life: develop.]

In other words, men are doubtless rational animals, but if they are to be worthy of their human essence, of the name of man, and of the being of man as capable of acceding to being as such, they must *become* not only rational living beings, animals endowed with reason and that, *qua* animals, do not die, but they must become mortals, they must, not "learn how to die," as the tradition has been saying since Plato, thus defining the task of philosophy as *epimeleia tou thanatou* (exercise or discipline of preparation for death), but *become* mortal. It is necessary, beyond the rational animal that we are and that, *qua* animal, does not die, it is necessary for us to become mortal. That's the great lesson to be learned, for the deaf, like me, who keep trying to learn how to become immortal, or a-mortal, basically like beasts. Ah! If only we could stay beasts! Unless, contrary to what Heidegger says, we did remain beasts who do not have the power to die, to whom death as such never appears, dying remaining, as Blanchot often complains, impossible, alas. No, insists Heidegger, you have to become mortal. But at bottom, is this not pretty much the same thing? Living death beyond life, live to death, living death, etc. This is perhaps the same circle.

5. What is that — the circle? If now, still in reading "The Thing," you try to follow, gather, collect, link up all the circular turns and returns we had

19. During the session, Derrida added: "And this is what Heidegger would like to, let's say, deconstruct: the determination of man primarily as a living being and not as a mortal. On the basis of life and living, and there it's *Leben und Erleben,* and for my part I read in this sentence an implicit critique or an implicit reservation specifically about Husserl, and phenomenology that determines its phenomenological absolute as *Erlebnis,* as life, transcendental life; *Leben und Erleben;* if he adds *und Erleben,* it's because he has in mind, he's taking critical aim at, the determination of Being as life, the human absolute as living, and thereby phenomenology as a philosophy of life, of transcendental life. Which I had also tried to question long ago." See Jacques Derrida, *La voix et le phénomène: Introduction au problème du signe dans la phénoménologie de Husserl* (Paris: PUF, 1976), p. 9; trans. David Allison as *Speech and Phenomena* (Evanston, Ill.: Northwestern University Press, 1973), p. 10.
20. "Das Ding," p. 171 [p. 176].

begun to analyze (*Zirkel, Kreis, Ring, Umring*), be it the circle as methodological circuit or the encircling of the animal in its *Benommenheit,* you will find here another circle, another series of circles, like rings in the alliance.[21] And this goes via the work or play (but precisely, the play of the world is at stake here), via the work and play of language around *Reigen, Ring,* and *Gering.* We should have to reread closely, with the lens of impossible translations, the last three or four pages of "Das Ding." Broadly speaking, to put it bluntly, Heidegger is meditating on the unity of the Fourfold, *Die Einheit der Vierung* (earth, sky, mortals, and divinities). This being-one of the Four is precisely the world insofar as it worlds or worldifies or worldwides [*se mondialise*] (*weltet*). The world is the four-in-one[22] of the earth, the sky, the mortals, and the gods. And that is the mirror-play of the world, *das Spiegel-Spiel* of the world as the round of the event or of what appears in appropriation (*Reigen des Ereignens*). The world is not what surrounds the four, the Four like a band or a ring (*Reif*). This round (*Reigen*) is the ring (*Ring*) that wraps around itself (*der ringt*) while playing as a mirror (*als das Spiegeln spielt*). This being-gathered of the play of the world, as mirror-play that wraps itself around, is the encircling turn (*das Gering*). The Four (mortals, divinities, sky, and earth) gather, flexibly, by bending to the mirror-play.

187

Now, and here once more we have the praise of the German language, traditional since Hegel: "Nestling, malleable, pliant, compliant, nimble — in Old German these are called *ring* and *gering.*"[23] I leave you to read, in two languages, the three pages that follow and that put to work, to the point of dizziness, all the resources of this idiom. Having given many examples of things that are humble or modest (*Geringen*), among which we find a few beasts such as the heron and the stag, the horse and the bull, Heidegger concludes thus: "Men alone, as mortals, by dwelling attain to the world as world (*die Welt als Welt*)."[24] The last words of "Das Ding" have a proverbial form that Heidegger himself comments on in a note: "Nur was aus Welt gering, wird einmal Ding."[25] Only what humbly, modestly, is born to the world and through it can one day become a thing. Read

---

21. [Translator's note:] "Alliance" is also the standard French word for a wedding ring.

22. In the typescript: "The world is the four." In the recording of the session Derrida says "the four-in-one."

23. Ibid., p. 179 [p. 178].

24. Ibid., p. 181 [p. 180].

25. Ibid. The German text does not have a note [translator's note: and nor does the English]; in the French translation, the translator cites in a note an explanation given by Heidegger.

the note in which Heidegger translates himself and explains his thinking here.

End of the turn or the detour I announced. The initial question was waiting for us: now it comes back.

What is the other—or what are the others—at the moment when it is a matter of responding to the necessity of making *something of me,* of making of me some thing or their thing from the moment I will be, as people say, *departed,* i.e. deceased, passed, passed away, i.e. separated in the distancing of passing or passing on [*du pas ou du trépas*] (*weg, fort, passed away*[26]), when I will no longer be there, *da,* when I will be, to all appearances, absolutely without defense, disarmed, in their hands, i.e., as they say, so to speak, dead?

How and to what will they *proceed* in the time that follows the *deceding?* To decede, to proceed, to retrocede: it is indeed a matter of a procedure, a path, a movement along a path, a path of departure or return; it is indeed a matter of progress or regression or digression, of process and processing, proceeding and procedure, and so already of arrangements that are both technical and juridical, which have themselves left the order of what is called in the current and belated sense *nature.* We are already either in the opposition of *nomos, tekhnē, thesis* to *physis* in the late and derived sense, or else in that differance (with an *a*) of originary *physis,* which takes the forms of law, thesis, technique, right, etc.

Take careful note of the fact that in the question with which we opened this session, in the linking of such a question, in the order or the syntax of such a question, everything about order itself is upset. For in asking, "What is the other? What is the other—or what are the others—going to make of me when, after the distancing step [*pas*] of the passing [*trépas*], after this passage, when I am past, when I have passed, when I am departed, deceased, passed away, gone, absolutely without defense, disarmed, in their hands, i.e., as they say, so to speak, dead?" I have already presupposed, without knowing anything of what "dead" means in the syntagma "when I am, etc. dead," [I have already presupposed] a pre-definition of death, of being dead, namely that being dead, before meaning something quite different, means, for me, to be delivered over, in what remains of me, as in all my remains, to be exposed or delivered over with no possible defense, once totally disarmed, to the other, to the others. And however little I know about what the alterity of the other or the others means, I have to have presupposed that the other, the others, are precisely those who always might

26. [Translator's note:] "Passed away" is in English in the text.

die after me, survive me, and have at their disposal what remains of me, my remains. The others—what is that? Those, masculine and feminine, who might survive me. This is why, deliberately, I formulated my question "What is the other—or what are the others—going to make of me when I am departed, deceased, passed away, gone, absolutely without defense, disarmed, in their hands, i.e., as they say, so to speak, dead?" and I thus began my sentence with "What is the other?" anticipating the response to this very question that I have thus cut in two ("What is the other?" then "What will the others do with me?" for they will do something with me): well, (reply), the other is, the other, it is, the others are those, masculine and feminine, before whom I am disarmed, defenseless, the other is what always might, one day, do something with me and my remains, make me into a thing, his or her thing, whatever the respect or the pomp, funereal by vocation, with which he or she will treat that singular thing they call my remains. The other appears to me as the other as such, *qua* he, she, or they who might survive me, survive my decease and then proceed as they wish, sovereignly, and sovereignly have at their disposal the future of my remains, if there are any.

That's what is meant, has always been meant, by "other."

But having my remains at their disposal can also take place before I am absolutely, clearly and distinctly dead, meaning that the other, the others, is what also might not wait for me to be dead to do it, to dispose of my remains: the other might bury me alive,[27] eat me or swallow me alive, burn me alive, etc. He or she can put me to a living death, and exercise thus his or her sovereignty.

Suppose now, as hypothesis or fiction, that I say the following. If I say "Robinson Crusoe was indeed 'buried alive,' he was indeed 'swallow'd up alive,'" you would not believe me.

"What's he telling us this time?" you would ask: "It's false! What he's telling us is false! This professor is not telling us the truth, he has no respect for the truth. Not only does he put on his philosophy syllabus, side by side, an amusing fiction by an English literary writer of the eighteenth century and the most serious seminar in the world by a great German thinker of this century on the world and on man, not only does he mix everything up, contaminate the one with the other, but here he is now making stuff up when he says out loud, as though he were announcing something on the CNN evening news, reading off a dispatch: '*Robinson Crusoe,* we have just

27. During the session, Derrida added: "literally or figuratively."

learned, really was, in his own words, "buried alive," and really was, as he predicted himself, "swallow'd up alive.""""

"But that's not true," you would object firmly, "this is misinformation again, this is not what the story tells, that's not the narrative we read, that's not what millions of people have read and will read in all languages, that's not the published narrative, *Robinson Crusoe,* the identifiable and self-identical narrative, which is moreover deposited in copyright libraries, which everyone can consult at the British Library, the Bibliothèque nationale de France and the Library of Congress, as millions of readers can attest: that's not what happened, it's not true, Robinson Crusoe was not buried alive, he was not swallowed up alive, he merely spoke of it and was afraid of it. In fact, as we know, he came back from his island alive and well, in fine fettle, more alive as he returned to the English coast than some astronauts re-entering the atmosphere."

To which, without letting myself be intimidated by this consensus, standing up to you, if you haven't killed me already, I would insist in reply: "But it is true, that really is the story, the story itself, not what it tells, no doubt, there you may be right, even though Robinson, in the story, sees himself as though in hallucination — read carefully — he sees himself in advance (that's why he talks about it at such length), he sees the moment coming, he sees himself already buried alive or swallowed up alive."

"No," you would say, "not the moment when he *will be* buried or swallowed up alive, but the moment when he *would be* thus buried or swallowed up alive, the moment when he runs the risk of being buried alive. He is afraid of what might happen to him and which did not happen to him. This is not a future indicative but a conditional, *were* he to be buried or swallowed up alive, he trembles at the thought, for example when there is the earthquake and he does all he can to stop what he sees coming from happening. So that his fantasy, if that's what you want to call it, can remain a phantasm and not become reality."

"Unless," I shall then retort,[28] "unless the difference between the conditional and the indicative, the difference between the conditional, the future, and the present or past indicative are merely temporal modalities, modalizations at the surface of conscious phenomenality or representation that count for little in view of the fantasmatic content that, for its part, happens, really did happen, to Robinson: unless," I would add, "Robinson Crusoe had

---

28. Thus in the typescript. [Translator's note: Derrida writes in the future tense "répliquerai," probably a slip for the conditional "répliquerais."]

done all he could so that, in spite of or through his terror, his desire might speak, and unless what happened to him was the very thing that he wanted not to happen to him. As though the noematic nucleus of the phantasm, as it were (being buried or swallowed up alive), happened to him in any case, irreversibly happened, virtually but irreversibly happened, and the modes in which this noematic nucleus, its modalities or its modifications (present or future, indicative or conditional, perception or hallucination, reality or fiction) as modifications or secondary, relatively secondary, qualities, precisely, remain external and epiphenomenal. He is afraid of dying a living death, and so he already sees it happening, he is buried or swallowed alive, it's what he wanted. Shouldn't have thought of it. Because what's more, and taking another step in provocation, I dare to claim, in the indicative this time, that it really did happen to him."

"Really? How's that?" you would say.

"[29]Well, on another track and according to yet another necessity than that of this pure phantasmatic content, before any temporal modalization, and since you are so keen to talk about the story and take account of the fictional narrative, to take account of the fictional account that this narrative is, this narrative that is simultaneously or successively a journal, a travel journal, a confession, the fiction of an autobiography, an anthropological treatise, an apprenticeship in Christian prayer, and above all, including all else, a literary event in a European national language, I am claiming that dying a living death did happen to 'Robinson Crusoe,' the narrative itself, because when I say, when I pronounce 'Robinson Crusoe,' where you do not see the quotation marks between which I am suspending this proper name or the italics in which I am inclining it, when I say *Robinson Crusoe,* I am naming the narrative, I am referring to the narrative (the narrative is my reference and my referent). Thus naming the narrative, I am calling the narrative by its name, which is our only common referent here (there is no Robinson Crusoe outside the book), and this name-title, this title which is twice over a proper name (like *Hamlet, René, Anna Karenina,* or *Bartleby the Scrivener,* etc.), for every title is a proper name and when a title has the form of a proper name it is twice a proper name, twice the same and another proper name, the proper name as title and the proper name named by the title, all that in one single name with two heads or two referential functions. Here the proper name is the homonym; it's the same as the name of the character in the narrative and the narrator of the narrative,

192

---

29. The quotation marks opened here do not close in the typescript.

of the quasi-autobiographical confession, etc. The narrative entitled *Robin-son Crusoe* and, within it, the character and the narrator, the author of the journal and the character that the author of the autobiographical journal puts on stage are all different, other among themselves, but all are named by the same name 'Robinson Crusoe,' and as such they are all living dead, regularly buried, and swallowed up alive. But of course, as dying a living death, in the present, can never really present itself, as one cannot presently be dead, die, and see oneself die, die alive, as one cannot be both dead and alive, dying a living death can only be a fantasmatic virtuality, a fiction, if you like, but this fictive or fantasmatic virtuality in no way diminishes the real almightiness of what thus presents itself to fantasy, an almightiness that never leaves it again, never leaves it, and organizes and rules over every-thing we call life and death, life death. This power of almightiness belongs to a beyond of the opposition between being or not being, life and death, reality and fiction or fantasmatic virtuality.

193

What does that mean? You have already understood that a book, and, still more acutely, a book the text of which is a fiction in the first person, inserting into the living narrative quotations, inserts, inscriptions from a journal speaking in the first person, etc., that such a book is both alive and dead or, if you prefer, neither dead nor alive; and everything that not only Defoe, but, in *Robinson Crusoe,* Robinson Crusoe himself, both the Robin-son Crusoe who speaks and the one keeping a journal, all that they — there are already a lot of them — might have desired is that the book, and in it the journal, outlive them: that they outlive Defoe, and the character called Rob-inson Crusoe. Now this survival, thanks to which the book bearing this title has come down to us, has been read and will be read, interpreted, taught, saved, translated, reprinted, illustrated, filmed, kept alive by millions of in-heritors — this survival is indeed that of the living dead. As is indeed any trace, in the sense I give this word and concept, a book is living dead, buried alive and swallowed up alive. And the machination of this machine, the origin of all *tekhnē,* and in it of any *turn,* each turn, each re-turn, each wheel, is that each time we trace a trace, each time a trace, however singular, is left behind, and even before we trace it actively or deliberately, a gestural, verbal, written, or other trace, well, this machinality virtually entrusts the trace to the sur-vival in which the opposition of the living and the dead loses and must lose all pertinence, all its edge. The book lives its beautiful death. That's also finitude, the chance and the threat of finitude, this alliance of the dead and the living. I shall say that this finitude is *survivance.* Survivance in a sense of survival that is neither life nor death pure and simple, a sense that is not thinkable on the basis of the opposition between life and death, a survival that is not, in spite of the apparent grammar of the formation of the word (*überleben* or *fortleben,* living on or to survive, survival[30]), [<that> is not] *above* life, like something sovereign (*superanus*) can be above everything, a survival that is not more alive, nor indeed less alive, than life, or more or less dead than death, a sur-vivance that lends itself to neither comparative nor superlative, a survivance or a surviving (but I prefer the middle voice "survivance" to the active voice of the active infinitive "to survive" or the substantializing substantive *survival*), a survivance whose "sur-" is without superiority, without height, altitude or highness, and thus without supremacy or sovereignty. It does not add something extra to life, any more than it cuts something from it, any more than it cuts anything from inevitable death or attenuates its rigor and its necessity, what one could call, without yet thinking of the corpse and its erect rigidity, the *rigor mortis,* if you will. No, the survivance I am speaking of is something other than life death, but a groundless ground from which are detached, identified, and opposed what we think we can identify under the name of death or dying (*Tod, Sterben*), like death properly so-called as opposed to some life properly so-called. *It [Ça]* begins with survival. And that is where there is some other that has me at its disposal; that is where any self is defenseless. That is what the self is, that is what I am, what the *I* is, whether I am there or not. The other, the others, that is the very thing that survives me, that is called to survive me and that I call the other inasmuch as it is called, in advance, to survive me, structurally my survivor. Not my survivor, but the survivor of me, the *there* beyond my life.

Like every trace, a book, the survivance of a book, from its first moment on, is a living-dead machine, sur-viving, the body of a thing buried in a library, a bookstore, in cellars, urns, drowned in the worldwide waves of a Web,[31] etc., but a dead thing that resuscitates each time a breath of living reading, each time the breath of the other or the other breath, each time an intentionality intends it and makes it live again by animating it, like, as the Husserl of the *Origin of Geometry* would say, a *"geistige Leiblichkeit,"*[32] a body, a spiritual corporeality, a body proper (*Leib* and not *Körper*), a body proper animated, activated, traversed, shot through with intentional spirituality.

30. [Translator's note:] The words "living on," "to survive," and "survival" are in English in the text.

31. [Translator's note:] "Web" is in English in the text.

32. Edmund Husserl, *L'origine de la géométrie,* trans. with an introduction by Jacques Derrida (Paris, PUF: 1962), pp. 85–86; trans. John P. Leavey, Jr., as *Edmund Husserl's "Origin of Geometry": An Introduction* (Lincoln: University of Nebraska Press, 1989), pp. 88–89.

195 This survivance is broached from the moment of the first trace that is supposed to engender the writing of a book. From the first breath, this archive as survivance is at work. But once again, this is the case not only for books, or for writing, or for the archive in the current sense, but for everything from which the tissue of living experience is woven, through and through. A weave of survival, like death in life or life in death, a weave that does not come along to clothe a more originary existence, a life or a body or a soul that would be supposed to exist naked under this clothing. For, on the contrary, they are taken, surprised in advance, comprehended, clothed, they live and die, they live to death as the very inextricability of this weave. It is against the groundless ground of this quasi-transcendentality of living to death or of death as sur-vivance that, *on the one hand,* one can say that "Robinson Crusoe," the name of the character and the name of the book, were, according to a first desire or a last terrified will, according to a desire and a will attested to by this book, by all the *Robinson Crusoe*s in their homonymy or their metonymy, [were all] buried or swallowed alive; but also, *on the other hand,* and I'm coming to this now as I had announced I would, one can and must, one must be able, in the wake, the inheritance, i.e. in the reanimating reading and like the experience reanimated, reawakened in the very reading of this psycho-anthropology of cultures and civilizations projected by Defoe and by Robinson Crusoe, one can have to [*on peut devoir*] and one must be able to wonder what is happening today to a culture like ours, I mean in the present modernity of a Greco-Abrahamic Europe, wonder what is happening to us that is very specific, very acute and unique in the procedural organization of death as survivance, as treatment, by the family and/or the State, of the so-called dead body, what we call a corpse, not only in the perspective of religions or philosophies or ideologies that all presuppose, far from making it merely possible, this universal structure of survivance that I have just mentioned, but in the funeral itself, in the organized manner, in the juridical apparatus and the set of technical proce-
196 dures whereby we, as community, family, nation, State, humanity, deliver the corpse over to its future, prepare the future of a corpse and prepare ourselves as one says prepare a corpse.

I was hoping, you remember, I had promised you, I had promised myself that I would speak today — on this subject and in the direction of this fantasmatics of dying alive or dying dead — about what happens when people, among us, in the West, as they say, still hesitate, more and more, or decide more and more between the only two possibilities that are offered to them, and faced with which they remain free (a recent thing, this, rare on the surface and in the history of the human earth) [two possibilities, then]:

inhumation and cremation, whereas in other cultures people have opted massively and in a stable, still largely durable fashion, for one *or* the other, for one to the intransigent exclusion of the other. Today, among us, people hesitate, as you know, there are more and more people, families, and communities that hesitate or cannot decide, whereas the State, which always has the duty and prerogative of the thing, tolerates — this is new — and even goes to the point of making institutionally possible, in the very organization of funeral rites and overcrowded cemeteries, with expensive plots, the operation of two types of funerals, interments, and burial ceremonies.

I ask this question and will try to say a little more about it in the wake or the Wake [*le sillage ou le* Wake] of Robinson Crusoe for at least *two types of reasons*.

First, I repeat rapidly, because in *Robinson Crusoe,* in the book that bears this name, Robinson Crusoe, the character, is obsessed by the perspective of dying a living death, of being buried or swallowed up alive. He sees himself in advance buried or swallowed, taken in or devoured alive.

Next, because *Robinson Crusoe, the book this time,* can and must also be read as a short treatise of anthropology or ethnology. An article communicated to me (and I thank him for it) by our friend Comtesse,[33] rightly insists on this "anthropological treatise" dimension in the style of the eighteenth century. This is an article by Francis Affergan, "Les marqueurs de l'autre dans *Robinson Crusoé,*" published in *Les temps modernes.*[34] One could indeed cite a thousand passages in support of this totally justified remark. For his part, Affergan quotes these few lines that are to be found in the Second Part of *Robinson Crusoe,*[35] which has always been received, as you know, as a sort of long hors-d'œuvre or postscript at the end of his adventures on the island. Everyone agrees that the work entitled *Robinson Crusoe* is essentially constituted by the First Part. Pétrus Borel, for his part, translated both parts which are, in French, bound into a single volume and presented as the "complete text" by the Bibliothèque Marabout, from which edition I quote the passage that is itself quoted by Affergan. This is on page 558 of the complete text in the Bibliothèque Marabout. Robinson Crusoe recalls his trip to China, a long time after the island, and he puts forth on the subject of the Chinese

197

33. Georges Comtesse, participant in Derrida's seminar.

34. Francis Affergan, "Les marqueurs de l'autre dans *Robinson Crusoé*: Contribution à la genèse de l'anthropologie de l'altérité," in *Les temps modernes* 44, no. 507 (October 1988): 22–45.

35. [Translator's note:] Derrida refers to Defoe's *The Farther Adventures of Robinson Crusoe,* published in 1719.

a discourse that no doubt belongs, as Affergan rightly notes, to comparative anthropology (and I emphasize this comparativity because this will also
be the approach deliberately taken up and named as such ("comparative,"
"*vergleichende*" [H, 26off./176ff.]) by Heidegger when he proposes to compare, that will be his word, the relation to the world of the stone (*weltlos*),
the animal (*weltarm*), and, in what then also remains a sort of fundamental anthropology, of the human *Dasein* (*weltbildend*)), a discourse, then, that
of *Robinson Crusoe,* that no doubt belongs to comparative anthropology or
ethnology, but also, as you will hear (but Affergan says nothing about this)
of the most arrogant and grandiloquently colonialist or "British Empire"[36]
ethnocentrism or Eurocentrism, thus announcing the durable and turbulent
relationship between ethnology, as a scientific discipline, ethnocentrism —
sometimes sublimated into concepts that appear to be universalizing — and
the cruelest history of colonialism and imperialisms:

198 But when I come to compare the miserable People of these Countries with
ours, their Fabrics, their Manner of Living, their Government, their Religion, their Wealth, and their Glory as some call it, I must confess, I do not
so much as think it is worth naming, or worth my while to write of, or any
that shall come after me to read.

It is very observable that we wonder at the Grandeur, the Riches, the
Pomp, the Ceremonies, the Government, the Manufactures, the Commerce, and the Conduct of these People; not that is to be wonder'd at, or
indeed in the least to be regarded; but because, having first a true Notion
of the Barbarity of those Countries, the Rudeness and the Ignorance that
prevails there, we do not expect to find any such things so far off.

Otherwise, what are their Buildings to the Pallaces and Royal Buildings
of *Europe*? What their Trade, to the universal Commerce of *England, Hol-
land, France*, and *Spain*? What are their Cities to ours, for Wealth, Strength,
Gaiety of Apparel, rich Furniture, and an infinite Variety? What are their
Ports, supply'd with a few Jonks and Barks, to our Navigation, our Mer-
chant Fleets, our large and powerful Navys? Our city of *London* has more
Trade than all their mighty Empire: one *English*, or *Dutch*, or *French* Man
of War, of 80 Guns would fight and destroy all the Shipping of China: But
the Greatness of their Wealth, their Trade, the Power of their Government,
and Strength of their Armies, is surprising to us, because, as I have said,
considering them as a barbarous Nation of Pagans, little better than Savages, we did not expect such Things among them; and this indeed is the
Advantage with which all our Greatness and Power is represented to us;

36. [Translator's note:] "British Empire" is in English in the text.

otherwise it is in itself nothing at all; for as I have said of their Ships, so may be said of their Armies and Troops; all the Forces of their Empire, tho' they were to bring two Millions of Men into the Field together, would be able to do nothing but ruin the Country, and starve themselves: If they were to besiege a strong Town in *Flanders,* or to fight a disciplin'd Army; one Line of *German* Curiassiers, or of *French* Cavalry, would overthrow all the Horse of *China;* A Million of their Foot could not stand before one embattled Body of our Infantry, posted so as not to be surrounded, tho' they were to be not One to Twenty in Number; nay, I do not boast if I say that 30000 *German* or *English* Foot, and 10000 *French* Horse, would fairly defeat all the Forces of *China.* [. . .] and therefore, I must confess, it seem'd strange to me, when I came home, and heard our People say such fine Things of the Power, Riches, Glory, Magnificence, and Trade of the *Chinese;* because I saw and knew that they were a contemptible Hoord or Crowd of ignorant sordid Slaves; subjected to a Government qualified only to rule such a People; and in a word, for I am now launch'd quite beside my Design, I say, in a word, were not its Distance inconceivably great from *Muscovy,* and was not the *Muscovite* Empire almost as rude, impotent, and ill-govern'd a Crowd of Slaves as they, the Czar of *Muscovy* might with much Ease drive them all out of their Country, and conquer them in one Campaign; and had the Czar, who I since hear is a growing Prince, and begins to appear formidable in the World, fallen this Way, instead of attacking the Warlike *Swedes,* in which Attempt none of the Powers of *Europe* would have env'd or interrupted him; he might by this time have been Emperor of *China,* instead of being beaten by the King of *Sweden* at *Narva,* when the Latter was not One to Six in Number. As their Strength and their Grandeur, so their Navigation, Commerce, and Husbandry is imperfect and impotent, compar'd to the same Things in *Europe*; also in their Knowledge, their Learning, their Skill in the Sciences; they have Globes and Spheres, and a Smatch of the Knowledge of the Mathematicks; but when you come to enquire into their Knowledge, how short-sighted are the wisest of their Students! they know nothing of the Motion of the Heavenly Bodies; and so grosly absurdly ignorant, that when the Sun is eclips'd, they think 'tis a great Dragon has assaulted it, and run away with it, and they fall a clattering with all the Drums and Kettles in the Country, to fright the Monster away, just as we do to hive a Swarm of Bees.[37]

199

37. Daniel Defoe, *Robinson Crusoé,* trans. Pétrus Borel, Illustrations de Grandville (Verviers [Belgique]: Bibliothèque Marabout, 1977), pp. 558–60 [*The Farther Adventures of Robinson Crusoe, being the Second and Last Part of his Life, and of the Strange Surprising Accounts of his Travels Round Three Parts of the Globe, Written by Himself* (London: 1719), pp. 296–99].

200   Before coming to one of my main points today, I want to recall that if
Robinson Crusoe is in this way prey to these phantasms (being buried or
swallowed alive, being afraid of the phantomatic trace of a footprint in the
sand, etc.), he is nonetheless, as a realistic man and as an avowed Christian,
someone who would like to situate himself firmly in good common sense, in
stubborn denial of the spectral and the phantomatic. But also someone who
cannot do this, and who must therefore leave it hanging at the moment of
his confession. He is someone who stands between belief and non-belief, belief in ghosts going against his Christian belief, paradoxically, and his belief
(itself suspended, unbelieving) in phantoms and fantasies (in *phantasmata,* a
word that in Greek means both product of the imagination and fantasy or
revenant), his belief remaining invincible by good sense [Robinson Crusoe
is someone who stands between phantoms and fantasies], and denial [*déné-
gation*], the denial of someone who might not stop saying to you, tugging on
your sleeve, "you know, don't try that with me, I have a lot of good sense,
I do not believe in ghosts, or specters, or revenants, or apparitions—not at
all, anything but, don't go thinking." And we have learned to understand,
we have learned and understood not to be taken in, and when someone says
to you: "Don't go thinking that . . . ," it's exactly the moment to go thinking that . . . , especially if the person in question insists and says: "Don't go
thinking, above all, that *I* believe in . . . ," then you can believe that, very
probably, this person believes and really hopes you will believe that they believe in what they would like not to believe in, but in which they do believe,
at the very moment of suspending judgment in a "really I don't know . . ."
I don't know, he says. What is one doing when one says "I don't know" in
the face of a phantasm or a revenant? It is in this spirit, or as close as can be
to these spirits that I will read and invite you to reread the very beginning
of the *Farther Adventures* of *Robinson Crusoe,* in which he admits that *he does
not know* whether he should believe or not believe in specters, whether he
201   should believe or not believe the people of good sense who say they don't believe in them and that one must above all not believe in them. As though all
these people knew what believing means. Robinson Crusoe does not know,
as he admits, but he has the feeling that his experience, his imagination and
his dreams would in fact push him into believing in them, even if he has to
believe that one must not believe in them. Let me read a passage in which
he is describing the nostalgia and the melancholy that are affecting him like
an illness, and pushing him to imagine he has returned to his island, this
time: not his island in England, but returning from England to his island of
misfortune, his island of despair.

Yet all these Things had no Effect upon me, or at least, not enough to resist the strong Inclination I had to go Abroad again, which hung about me like a chronic Distemper; [so his melancholic nostalgia is *dia noson,* pathological, Aristotle would have said, you remember, as quoted by Heidegger: *dia noson* and not *dia phusin:* pathological, sickly and not natural or normal] particularly the Desire of seeing my new Plantation in the Island, and the Colony I left there, run in my Head continually.[38]

Further on: "I talk'd of it in my Sleep . . ." So this is such a powerful phantasm in its effects that it makes him act and speak in a quasi-somnambulistic way.

For as you have heard, Robinson Crusoe says that nothing had a powerful enough "effect" to contain his desire, his nostalgia, his melancholy, his daydreams, and nighttime dreams. So the fantasy is really [*effectivement*] more effective, more powerful, it is *really* [*en effet*] *more powerful* than what is opposed to it—let's say, good sense and reality, perception of the real, etc. The perception of the real has less power than this quasi-hallucination. Which is thus more real, more effective for him, in his psychic reality, than what is opposed to it by or in the name of a reality principle.

This is the spirit in which he speaks of spirits and mentions the common, good sense discourse about fantasies, specters, and revenants. He ends up saying "I don't know." He does not know, but he is under the sway of the efficacious, powerful phantasm, and he says so. Saying "I don't know" about fantasy and revenants is the only way to take them into account in their very effective power. If I said "I know," "I am sure and certain," clearly and distinctly, not only that I am affected by spectral fantasies, but that there really are such things outside of me, I would immediately dissolve spectrality, I would deny without delay, I would contradict *a priori* the very thing I am saying. I cannot say: "I am sure and I know" that there is some specter there, without saying the contrary and without spiriting the specter away [*conjurer le spectre*]. "I don't know" is thus the very modality of the experience of the spectral, and moreover of the surviving trace in general. Robinson Crusoe will say: "I know not to this Hour, whether there are any such Things as real Apparitions, Spectres, or walking of People after they are dead." I quote:

> I have often heard Persons of good Judgment say, That all the Stir People make in the World about Ghosts and Apparitions, is owing to the Strength

202

38. Ibid., p. 328 [p. 2].

of Imagination, and the powerful Operation of Fancy in their Minds; that
there is no such Thing as a Spirit appearing, or a Ghost walking, *and the
like*; That People's poring affectionately upon the past Conversation of their
deceas'd Friends, so realizes it to them, that they are capable of fancying
upon some extraordinary Circumstances, that they see them; talk to them,
and are answered by them, when, in Truth, there is nothing but Shadow
and Vapour in the Thing; and they really know nothing of the Matter.

For my Part, I know not to this Hour, whether there are any such
Things as real Apparitions, Spectres, or walking of People after they are
dead, or whether there is any Thing in the Stories they tell us of that Kind,
more than the Product of Vapours, sick Minds, and wandering Fancies;
But this I know, that my Imagination work'd up to such a Height, and
brought me into such Extasies of Vapours, or what else I may call it, that
I actually suppos'd my self, often times upon the Spot, at my old Castle
behind the Trees; saw my old *Spaniard, Friday's* Father, and the reprobate
Sailors I left upon the Island; nay, I fancy'd I talk'd with them, and look'd at
them steadily, tho' I was broad awake, as at Persons just before me; and this
I did till I often frighted my self with the Images my Fancy represented to
203 me: One Time in my Sleep I had the Villany of the 3 Pyrate Sailors so lively
related to me by the first *Spaniard* and *Friday's* Father, that it was surpriz-
ing; they told me [. . .][39]

Now, to mark clearly the fact that "dying a living death," being buried
or swallowed up "alive"[40] is indeed, for Robinson, to be delivered over, in
his body, defenseless, to the other, I believe we need to be attentive to the
hierarchized differentiation of these others to whom Robinson is, we have
to say, a "prey," to whom he is prey in the fantasies to which he falls prey.
These others, the element of these others, can be the more other as (they can
be) less other. Now,[41] the more the other is other, the less it is other. Conversely, the less it is other, the more it is other. More other, less other; less
other, more other.

What does this mean?

The earthquake or the storm that buries me or swallows me alive is a
kind of other, isn't it, a kind of external and foreign element; second, the
wild beast that devours me alive is again a species of other, a living being like
me, but very different from me; third and last, the cannibal who devours
me seems to be a third type of other, a living being like me, but also a human
being like me. So that makes three types of other, doesn't it? But the earth

39. Ibid., pp. 328–29 [pp. 3–4].
40. [Translator's note:] In English in the text.
41. During the session, Derrida added: "So, aporia."

and the sea are what is furthest from me and most different from me, most
other; yet they are less others than the living beings, the wild beasts that
threaten to devour me alive and that, closer to me, less different from me
than the sea and the earth, those lifeless elements the sea and the earth, are
nonetheless more other than the sea and the earth. As for savage and can-
nibalistic humans who also threaten to devour me alive, they are still closer
to me, less different from me than the sea, the earth and the beasts, but because of this proximity that almost makes them my fellows [*semblables*] they
are other to a greater extent. Their alterity is the more marked for being
less marked. And the savage cannibals, who are everywhere in the book,
bring to the point of paroxysm the general threat of being put to death and
eaten alive. If there is an other to whom I am delivered over when I die a
living death, it is par excellence, if I may say so, the one I call my fellow, the
other mortal, the cannibal: not just the living carnivore (the beast), but the
anthropophagic man, the cannibal. This is talked about throughout, this
inter-devouring of cannibals. If we had the time we could cite and analyze a
thousand occurrences of this. This is why — and again we'll read this as the
preface, the last, the penultimate preface to what I wanted to say about the
comparison between these two modes of being-delivered-over to the other,
two incomparable modes, that must yet be compared as the only pair of
choices that are given or left to us today, in our countries, i.e. being inhumed
or being cremated, burial or cremation. Robinson calls the hyperbolic point,
the absolute excess of this being-eaten by the other, and thus being buried or
swallowed alive by the other, namely being eaten by cannibals rather than
by wild beasts or by sea or earth — he calls it "the worst kind of Destruction" (RC, 181). I quote the English text to have you hear the consonance
with the self-destruction of the one who presents himself, you remember,
as the "destroyer of himself" ("But I that was born to be my own Destroyer,
could no more resist the Offer than I could restrain [. . .]," etc. (RC, 37)).
For here, what is the worst thing about cannibalism is that these people eat
beings of their own species and thus, in a way, self-destruct, by putting to
death, to living death, their own species, their own lineage. This is literally
"the worst kind of Destruction" because cannibalism consists in devouring
one's own kind, and Defoe will write that very thing, as though without
paying attention, a few lines later, "to devour its own kind" (RC, 182). We
can see at work here, through this extraordinary word "kind," the autoimmune process of self-destruction and autoimmune double bind[42] of which

204

205

42. [Translator's note:] Here and elsewhere, the words "double bind" are in English
in the text.

we shall have a number of examples in a moment when we finally come to
the great and ultimate question of the choice between cremation and inhumation, at the hands of the other, my supposed fellow: *my people [les miens]*,
as they say. You have noticed that, when in French we say "les miens," we
are most often designating those whom one above all does not possess and
who in truth possess you, given that they are the ones who will in a privileged way have the charge, the responsibility, the power to do something
with you, to make of you the thing they want to make of you after your
death, by deciding, after "your lifetime" (as they politely say in English) to
put you in the ground or else to burn you. (When an American archivist
or librarian wants to talk to you about what will happen, on your death,
to your papers and your remains, to your archive, and about the question
of knowing whether your people will be able to decide, he or she does not
say "on your death" or "after your death," he or she says politely, modestly, courteously, like they do in funeral homes,[43] between the fruit and the
cheese [*entre la poire et le fromage*],[44] although there is no cheese, [he or she
says] "after your lifetime.")

In the few lines I am going to read and that I am choosing from the innumerable passages in which Robinson Crusoe talks about cannibalism and
savages, you will recognize *two features*.

1. On the one hand, when Robinson Crusoe speaks of the inhumanity of
these cannibals who might devour him, he speaks of their bestial inhumanity only to the extent that, precisely, they are humans and he recognizes
that fact; they are his fellows, even more other and inhuman insofar as they
are his fellows (you recall what we were saying about this concept of the
fellow [*semblable*] last year).[45] The discourse on cannibalism comes under
the heading of anthropology or ethnology, in *Robinson Crusoe,* whereas the
sentences about the animals that might eat me come under zoology, and
the discourse on the earthquake and the storms come under geography or
geology or physics. Robinson Crusoe would not say of savage beasts that
they are inhuman, inhumanly cruel. At the very moment he talks about the
infinite difference between these cannibals and Europeans, or even between
them and ethnologists, and about their inhumanity, he is recognizing their
humanity, they are others as fellows, more other than the others because fel-

206

43. [Translator's note:] The words "funeral homes," and a little later "after your
lifetime" are in English is the text.

44. [Translator's note:] The French idiom "entre la poire et le fromage" refers to a
moment of polite and inconsequential conversation toward the end of a meal.

45. See the fourth session of *La bête et le souverain, I,* pp. 141–87 [pp. 97–135].

lows. And these fellows are fellows insofar as they are *creatures*. The word "creatures," if one takes it seriously, and if it refers to creatures of the same creator, the same father, is a word that the French translation ought not have let drop when it translates at least once "wretched Creatures" as "sauvages," whereas Defoe writes "these wretched Creatures; I mean, the Savages" (RC, 182).

2. Second, cannibalism itself is inhuman and cruel because it consists (as beasts themselves never do, or so they say) in eating, devouring, taking into themselves, still alive beings of "the same kind" as they. That is the worst cruelty of these others more other than any other because they eat the same. This is a schema whose generality appears to have no exception. Whenever one speaks about the inhumanity of those who commit crimes against humanity, one is speaking of people who still belong enough to the *human race* [*l'espèce humaine*] (to quote the title of Robert Antelme's book)[46] to be guilty of crimes against humanity, to fall, to prove themselves unworthy of the name "human" and of human dignity. To have lost human dignity by being inhuman is reserved for humans alone, and in no way for the sea, the earth, or the beast. Or the gods. One does not say of beasts or of God that they are inhuman. Only humans are said to be inhuman. In principle, neither sea nor earth nor what one calls the animal nor God will be brought before any tribunal to be accused of inhumanity or crime against humanity, even if they have been the occasion or even the agent of the death of millions of human beings. Given that the accusation of crime against humanity cannot be brought against any ahuman living being (beast or God), but only against what is supposed to be human, a crime against humanity is a crime committed by one part of humanity against another part of humanity, or against the essence of humanity or against human dignity, and is thus a crime which has a sui-cidal and auto-immune structure. And as all crime, all guilt presupposes freedom, and thus the sovereignty of the accused criminal, it is at the heart of this sovereignty that the suicidal and autoimmune re-turn is supposed to operate. (Read and comment)

207

> After these Thoughts had for some Time entertain'd me, I came to reflect seriously upon the real Danger I had been in, for so many Years, in this very Island; and how I had walk'd about in the greatest Security, and with all possible Tranquillity; even when perhaps nothing but a Brow of a Hill, a great Tree, or the casual Approach of Night, had been between me and the worst kind of Destruction, *viz.* That of falling into the Hands of Cannibals, and Savages, who would have seiz'd on me with the same View, as I did of

46. Robert Antelme, *L'espèce humaine* (1947) (Paris: Gallimard, 1957).

a Goat, or a Turtle; and have thought it no more a Crime to kill and devour me, than I did of a Pidgeon, or a Curlieu: I would unjustly slander my self, if I should say I was not sincerely thankful to my great Preserver, to whose singular Protection I acknowledg'd, with great Humility, that all these unknown Deliverances were due; and without which, I must inevitably have fallen into their merciless Hands.

When these Thoughts were over, my Head was for some time taken up in considering the Nature of these wretched Creatures; I mean, the Savages; and how it came to pass in the World, that the wise Governour of all Things should give up any of his Creatures to such Inhumanity; nay, to something so much below, even Brutality it self, as to devour its own kind; but as this ended in some (at that Time fruitless) Speculations, it occurr'd to me to enquire, what Part of the World these Wretches liv'd in; how far off the Coast was from whence they came; what they ventur'd over so far from home for; what kind of Boats they had; and why I might not order my self, and my Business so, that I might be as able to go over thither, as they were to come to me.

I never so much as troubl'd myself to consider what I should do with my self, when I came thither; what would become of me, if I fell into the Hands of the Savages . . . (RC, 181–82)

208

Robinson was more afraid than anything, then, of being buried alive or being swallowed, swallowed up, carried off, still alive. But it is not the same thing to be buried or swallowed up alive by the earth or the sea, and to be eaten alive by beasts or cannibals. In the first case, the other, the element of the other, is something non-living, something anonymous and inanimate (earth or sea); in the second case, the other is living, and in each case a single organism, beast or cannibal. But what they have in common, the beast and the cannibal—and this leads us to the same cemetery, where one buries and where one burns, the Père-Lachaise, for example, which also has its crematorium—is that the being-delivered-over to the other is a being-delivered-over to one's fellow, with this one reservation that this situation, the paradigm of this Robinsonade, this fascinated terror or this terrified desire of Robinson's take the form of a hierarchy of fellows. The devouring beast is similar [semblable] to its victim insofar as it is alive (as opposed to the earth and/or the sea): devourer and devoured are both living beings; but the anthropophagic cannibal is *more* similar to his victim than the beast, precisely because he is an anthropoid (only an anthropoid can be anthropophagic). The cannibal is thus more similar to his victim and thus also, paradoxically, more *other,* more of an other than the beast. But he is less similar, precisely because he eats his fellow, and thus becomes inhuman, because he is an anthropophagic human, less human and less my fellow, and thus more other than the non-cannibal Christian Englishman, Robinson's compatriot (two things remain to be proved: first, the purity or supposed innocence of Christianity when it comes to the anthropophagic drive or temptation in the Eucharistic or transubstantial Last Supper, when Christ offers his *corpus* to be eaten and drunk like bread and wine, flesh and blood, in memory of him (*hoc est meum corpus,* etc.), and then, that the English are innocent of all cannibalism (you remember what the vegetarian Rousseau says about this in *Emile,*[47] when he accuses the English of being so cruelly carnivorous that one wonders if he does not suspect them of being secretly and unconsciously anthropophagic: probably like all flesh-eaters. Is not every carnivorous human secretly anthropophagic, with an anthropophagy that is avoided only by the detour of a repression?)).

Good. I say "good" not to lick my chops or to announce the menu, but because I am now finally coming to the two autoimmune double binds that constitute the only two choices left to us today to respond to the fantasy of dying alive: inhumation and cremation.

This is first, and again, a problem of sovereignty. *Habeas corpus,* if one extends a little the idiom and the juridical history that bind this concept and this law to England, *habeas corpus* accords a sort of proprietorial sovereignty over one's own living body. I have the property of my own body proper, that's the *habeas corpus* guaranteed by law: you may have, may you have, your body. I deliberately leave to one side all the immense and formidable problems, both ancient and new, that this supposed sovereignty of *habeas corpus* poses as to birth, conception or birth control, medicine, experimentation, organ transplants, etc., to limit myself to the treatment of death. I shall not even speak of the specific problems of autopsy, DNA research, etc. I shall limit myself to the decision, the choice, the alternative between *bury* and *cremate,* and its relation to the fantasy of the living dead.

It is quite possible in theory, and it is often the case in fact, that the dead man or woman should have sovereignly decided, during his or her lifetime, as to the fate of the corpse to come, by leaving a testament, a last will.[48] But this testament will have force of law only if a third party, the State or a force of institutional coercion, guarantees it and can oblige the inheritors to obey its instructions. It goes without saying that the real sovereignty of the dead person encounters a limit with this third party, and it is even at this limit, which then serves as an ultimate criterion, that one judges what is called

47. Rousseau, *Émile ou de l'éducation,* p. 196–97, cited by Derrida in the first session of *La bête et le souverain, I,* p. 45 [p. 22].

48. [Translator's note:] The words "last will" are in English in the text.

the state of death. A dead person is one who cannot him or herself put into operation any decision concerning the future of his or her corpse. The dead person no longer has the corpse at his or her disposal, there is no longer any *habeas corpus. Habeas corpus,* at least, is not a *habeas corpse,* supposing there ever were such a thing. *Habeas corpus* concerns the living body and not the corpse. Supposing, I repeat, that there ever were a *habeas corpus* for the living body. Because you can guess that I believe that this *habeas corpus* never existed and that its legal emergence, however important it may be, designates merely a way of taking into account or managing the effects of heteronomy and an irreducible *non habeas corpus.* And the *non habeas corpse,* at the moment of death, shows up the truth of this *non habeas corpus* during the lifetime of said corpus.

Now, from the limited and specific point of view that is ours here, namely the fantasy of dying a living death, to sketch out a comparative analysis of the two ways of managing the corpse that are available to us in the West at this precise moment in the history of burial, I shall have once again (I'll explain this) to privilege the autoimmune contradiction or aporia in which this last will[49] is fatally caught, at the moment it is trying to choose sovereignly, and to dictate sovereignly, dictatorially, their conduct to survivors who for their part become the real sovereigns. So that this will, this last will is in fact *a priori* bound by a double bind or a double constraint, a double and contradictory obligation.

What obligation?

Here's where we get started. And in each option we are again going to come across the autoimmune double bind that affects the living or the dying wherever it is acted upon by the fantasy of the living dead. We are starting from the situation or the hypothesis in which there is apparently a choice, isn't there, i.e. a situation that is frequent in our society today, in which neither religion nor State imposes this or that on us, cremation or inhumation, even if they impose on us that we choose between the two. For take careful note of the fact that there still remain many other state constraints: one can be neither buried nor cremated at home (nor even elsewhere, in law), nor bury or cremate our friends the animals, when what we call animals form part of what we call "ours" or "mine."[50] No more can one decide that one is going to bury or submerge or burn the corpse just anywhere, nor that one is going to cut it up to give a little to each of one's own, nor eat it, nor keep it

211

49. [Translator's note:] Here and in the next sentence the word "will" is in English in the text.

50. [Translator's note:] Derrida is referring to French law in this passage.

FIFTH SESSION ‡ 145

at home, embalmed or not, etc. The alternative remains very strict: *inhume* or *cremate,* following procedures that can be monitored by civil society, by the state or its police, by professional corporations registered by the state, etc. One does not have the right to make a corpse disappear, and there is no right to disappearance. The one whom one sometimes calls, in a touching euphemism, the departed [*le disparu ou la disparue*], must on no account disappear without leaving a trace—and it is of these traces, these remains, these mortal remains that we are going to speak now. If someone disappears of their own accord, for example by committing suicide and jumping off the pont Mirabeau, well, the city, the state, and the family have the duty to recover the body and to decide on a so-called normal burial, according to the laws of the city, the constitution of the *polis.* We have long known that the *polis,* the city, the law of the city, politics, are never constituted, in the history of this thing, the *polis* and politics, without a central administration of funerals. Basically, when Robinson is afraid of being buried or swallowed alive, he is less afraid of dying than of dying without being buried, without the social rite whereby we bury or make disappear the departed while keeping them. He is afraid of the pre-social and pre-institutional savagery that would have him die without a funeral, of whatever sort. He is afraid of dying like a beast, basically, if the beast is indeed, as so many people suppose, as Robinson supposes, as Heidegger supposes, a living being that dies without a funeral and without mourning. At bottom, the funeral is what   212 is designed by the survivors, our people, the family, society, the state, to ensure that the dead one really is dead, and will not return, will not have been murdered, i.e. treated as the living dead. Robinson accepts death, but he does not want to be murdered, condemned to death without judgment. And he wants to be sure, like the survivors, that he really is dead dead, with no possible return, dead dead and not living dead. In the Jewish communities of Algeria, where people are buried, of course, with no coffin, straight in the ground in the shroud, which is often, for men, their tallith, well, to make sure one is not burying someone living, one plugs all the orifices and lays out the corpse on cold tiles long enough for stiffening, *rigor mortis,* to confirm beyond all reasonable doubt the legal or medical certification of death that in the end one does not absolutely trust.

What would remain for us to find out, and this will be one of our questions, is whether, at bottom, behind or in the unconscious of funerary culture, whatever the specific rites, the savagery of the unconscious does not continue to operate with the cruelty that Robinson seems to fear when he is afraid of dying a living death like a beast.

Right.

First choice. The first choice that is still the more frequent statistically with us is, as you know, inhumation. If someone intends to decide on this freely, sovereignly for themselves, in other words if, without just going along with things, after having weighed the pros and the cons, and envisaged the only two possibilities that remain for remains, cremation and inhumation, if he or she chooses burial, freely as we say, sovereignly, why would that be? Why burial? With a view to what? To respond to what desire and what motivation? It would be better to say or specify: in view of whom? To reply to the desire and the motivation of whom?

This is where we shall see the first double bind tie itself up. To recall, as a methodological precaution, in the order of the path to follow, a very banal but scarcely contestable axiom, well, it goes without saying that the decision on this matter (inhumation rather than cremation) can only be the decision of a living person and not a dead one (what would the decision of a dead person be? Is this not impossible? Does not the concept of decision imply life at least, the living being with a future at its disposal? Whence the "with a view to what and whom?"), well, this decision will have to be examined either from the point of view of those surviving, living on, the inheritors, or else from the point of view of the one who gives instructions at the moment he or she is going to die, but is not yet "departed" and can therefore only speculate on his or her own death on the basis of the imagination or fantasy of the living dead, at the limit of the dead one who is still alive enough to *see him or herself* die and be buried, and who, to parody the letter of what Robinson Crusoe was saying in a passage I designedly chose to read just now, imagines himself still walking about after his death to see what is going on, still be affected by it, enjoy it or suffer from it ("For my Part, I know not to this Hour, whether there are any such Things as real Apparitions, Spectres, or walking of People after they are dead," said Robinson Crusoe).

From the point of view of the fantasy of the surviving dead, what then can be, for both inhumation and cremation, the calculable advantages or benefits, the enjoyments still counted on? What, on the other hand, are the downsides and the suffering to be feared? In what way are the two contraries indissociably, aporetically affected the one by the other, contaminated, infested the one by the other, the economy of enjoyment in advance rotten, let's say, more soberly, finite and threatened, at its heart, by the economy of suffering—that's the form of the question I would like now to articulate, both for inhumation and for cremation.

There is no point telling you, to our common relief, that these questions are always questions one can keep waiting. As long as possible.

But at least until next week.

February 12, 2003

Courage! Courage, now! You need heart and courage to think, contrary to what many people would be tempted to think. For example, to think the living dead. Whether one is for it or against it, whether one accepts the possibility or the impossibility of it, you need courage to think *that.*

Many people imagine that in order to think, in order to think for example *that,* it is quite enough to think — that is, or so they imagine, to imagine, to *represent* something *to oneself,* to have an idea, to speculate in one's head with words and images, and that not only does one run no danger requiring courage, but that it is even a little cowardly, mere thought, because it looks like a retreat into oneself, a flight to an island, a refuge sought in empty speculation, in representation or in internal images, in a verbal exercise, in words, in hypotheses from the study, while meditating in the warm next to one's stove, as Descartes said, etc.

No, those who tell themselves this story in this way are not thinking *that,* they have not yet begun to think what what is called thinking commits one to, and which demands not only courage, but courage itself, and even allows us to think what the word "heart" or the word "courage" ought to mean. One must think courage itself on the basis of thought, and not the other way around. One needs courage in order to think in general —*if only the courage of one's fear.*

If only the courage of one's fear. How are we to understand that, the courage of one's fear? For just as pardon can only pardon the unpardonable, which seems both impossible and prescribed by the very concept of pardon, so courage can only be the courage of a fear. If I am courageous because I am not afraid, I'm not courageous, it's as simple, as stupid [*bête*], that is, as difficult to think as *that.* Courage is never without fear. If I am courageous without being afraid, I'm not courageous. If I am courageous by nature and because I am insensible, invulnerable to fear, because I ignore fear naturally, because I remain impassive and insensible to fear, invulnerable to fear by reason of a gift of my nature, a chance of my character or of my conscious or unconscious history, if I am immunized in advance against fear by idiosyncrasy, or even by idiocy, by simple stupidity [*bêtise*], if I am protected in advance against fear, against being afraid or scared, against terror, against worry, against anxiety, against anguish, against panic, then it is not possible that I could be courageous, that I would ever have to be courageous, nor even understand what the word "courage" means: the courage to think courage, and therefore fear, to think in general, to say what comes to thought and first of all to tell oneself what one is thinking, to look what one must think straight in the eyes — something or someone — and that scares thought, and heart, the thought of heart and the heart of thought, the thought in the body and as body, i.e. here heart (courage, and the word "courage," comes from the heart, and therefore from thought too). The thought of this fearful courage, of this courageous terror, must be free of any virile, military, athletic, or mystical imagery of heroic exposure, of bravura or martyrdom. It must even be free from any ethical normativity, of any prescription of the type: "the courage (to think) is a virtue, courage is good, the courage (to think) is a duty, one must, it is better to be courageous, better — or so it is implied — than 'fearful'": because obscurely, although courage is not fear, there is no courage without fear, no absolute state of courage, and of heart, without absolute panic.

What would be the affinity, the proximity, the obscure alliance between this courage *of* fear, this fear *of* courage, *and the phantasm?*

217   In previous sessions, more than once, I have had recourse to the word, if not to the concept of phantasm, in particular to figure or configure the contradictory, the inconceivable or the unthinkable, what we are calling, still in the tracks of Robinson Crusoe, "living death," the living death that scared Robinson Crusoe so much, that state in which the dead man is alive enough to see himself die and know that he is dying, to live his own death, to last, perdure, and endure the time of his death, to be present at his death and beyond, without however failing to die, to survive his death while really dying, to survive his death. What I called "phantasm" in this context is indeed the inconceivable, the contradictory, the unthinkable, the impossible. But I insisted on the zone in which the impossible is named, desired, apprehended. Where it affects us. I did this for methodological reasons, namely in order clearly to delimit the field we were going to explore in wondering why *today,* in *our* European cultural area — and thus in its law, its language, its civil and political organization — a decision must be taken by the still living mortal or the still living dying person, or by his or her still living relatives, by the survivors, as to the ritual of burial or cremation. Whatever

this choice be, it implies credit accorded to what, in an obscure way, I have proposed to call a phantasm, i.e. a certain "as if" (an "as if" in which one neither believes nor does not believe, in that dimension of Robinson Crusoe's "I do not know . . ." that we analyzed last time), the "as if," the "perhaps" of an "as if" something could still *happen* to the dead one, as if something could still happen that came to affect the body at the moment of cremation or burial, or even after, beyond that moment; or again "as if," "perhaps," something could still happen to the survivors *on behalf of the dead one,* as cremated or buried body, or on behalf of what remains or does not remain of it, which is sometimes called the Spirit, the specter, or the soul. Under the sign of this "as if," "perhaps," "I do not know," we allow ourselves to have an impression made on us, we allow ourselves to be *affected,* for this is an affect, a feeling, a tonality of pathos, we allow ourselves really to be affected by a possibility of the impossible, by a possibility excluded by sense, excluded by common sense, by the senses and by good sense, excluded by what is often called the reality of the reality principle, i.e. by the impossible possibility that the dead one be still affected or that we could still be affected by the dead one him or herself, by the dead, by the death of the dead one itself, him or herself: just where this affection, this affect, this being-affected, everything seems to tell us—and this is the very sense that we simultaneously give to the word "death," and to the words "sense," "good sense," "reality,"—everything seems to tell us, then, with an invincible authority, that this affection, this being-affected *of* the dead one or *by* the dead one is, precisely, interrupted, radically, irreversibly interrupted, annihilated, excluded by death, by the very sense of the word "death." And indeed just as much by the senses of the words "affect," "to affect," "to happen," etc. There is no affect without life, no event without life, there is neither affect nor event without sensibility, that power to be affected that is called life. It is precisely because this certainty is terrifying and literally intolerable, just as unthinkable, just as unpreventable and unrepresentable as the contradiction of the living dead, that what I call this obscure word "phantasm" imposed itself upon me. I do not know if this usage of the word "phantasm" is congruent or compatible with any philosophical concept of the *phantasma,* of fantasy or fantastic imagination, any more than with the psychoanalytic concept of the phantasm, supposing, which I do not believe, that there is one, that there is only one, that is clear, univocal, localizable.

What is more, Freud himself (as we saw two weeks ago), just as he assigns to such a fundamental, such an indispensable concept as that of drive (*Trieb*) a double belonging, the limit-belonging of a limit-concept between the psychic and the somatic (which means that the psychic and the somatic,

218

the soul and the body become non-concepts, concepts without a rigorous pertinence as soon as one speaks of drive [*pulsion*] or compulsion)—well, similarly, Freud situates the phantasm in this place without <place>, in this place where it has more than one place [*lieu*] and more than one tie [*lien*] at once, thus becoming both ubiquitous and unlocatable: between the conscious and consciousness, between two systems, between the system of the unconscious and the system of conscious perception. If we reread, for example, what Freud wrote in 1915 in "Das Unbewußte" ("The Unconscious"), that chapter of the *Metapsychology,* section 6, "Der Verkehr der beiden Systeme" ("Communication between the Two Systems"),[1] it is clear that this exchange between the two systems, when it comes to the phantasm and also to the drive, means that the concept of each system is inadequate, insufficient to account for, or justify what is called phantasm or drive. It belongs neither to consciousness or the preconscious nor to the unconscious, because it is both at once. But that does not mean that one must, nor that one can, stop talking (moreover, who can ever prove that it is legitimate to talk or not to talk, that one must or must not talk? I defy you to prove the one or the other). (Photocopy all these texts[2])

Freud begins by noting, precisely on the subject of phantasms or phatasmatic formations (or of fantasy, *Phantasiebildungen* — hold onto this word *Bildungen,* it will catch up with us again at the end) that, I quote:

> Among the derivatives of the *Ucs* instinctual impulses (*Unter den Abkömm-lingen der* ubw *Triebregungen*), of the sort we have described, there are some which unite in themselves characters of an opposite kind (*die entgegenge-setzte Bestimmungen in sich vereinigen*). On the one hand, they are highly organized, free from self-contradiction (*widerspruchsfrei*), have made use of every acquisition of the system *Cs* and would hardly be distinguished in our judgment from the formations of that system. On the other hand they are unconscious and are incapable of becoming conscious. Thus *qualita-*

---

1. Sigmund Freud, "Das Unbewußte," in *Gesammelte Werke, Volume X (1913–1917)* (Frankfurt am Main: S. Fischer Verlag, 1946), pp. 288–94; "The Unconscious," *Papers on Metapsychology* (1915), in *The Standard Edition of The Complete Psychological Works of Sigmund Freud,* Volume XIV (1914–1916), trans. and ed. James Strachey, with Anna Freud, Alix Strachey, Alan Tyson, et. al. (London: Hogarth Press, 1957), pp. 190–95. [Translator's note: References to these editions of Freud's collected works will be given hereafter in the forms GW and SE, respectively.]

2. Photocopies of Freud's texts in German, English, and French are inserted in the typescript here.

tively (*qualitativ*) they belong to the system *Pcs*, but factually (*faktisch*) to the *Ucs*.[3]

I break off the quotation for a moment to draw attention to Freud's calm and abyssal audacity when he distinguishes here between the *qualitative* and the *factual*. What does this mean? That's the whole enigma of what he's wanting to talk about, both the enigma of drive excitation, and the enigma of the phantasm, and soon, as you'll hear, the enigma of the symptom. How can the same thing, the same experience, the same affect also, the same phantasm and the same symptom have a quality (and thus a phenomenal sense, the sense of an *Erlebnis*, of a "conscious" or "preconscious" "lived experience," as they say), all the while belonging in fact (and what does "in fact," *faktisch*, mean here?) to the unconscious? This distinction is quite unintelligible, impossible even, it even seems to have no sense, it appears to defy sense and good sense, consciousness, logico-philosophical consciousness *qua* consciousness, precisely. It is not only purely and simply a contradiction, and thus an impossible thought, a thought of the impossible or a conception of the inconceivable. It is a contradiction between a system that excludes contradiction (the Cs system, highly organized and coherent) and the Ucs system which is never hampered by contradiction. The unconscious is what is not affected by contradiction. What is more, in common language and the logic and common sense that organize our lives, it happens every day that one treats as irresponsible and unconscious whoever contradicts him or herself without warning, whoever is not affected by contradiction.

Two pages earlier, moreover, Freud had recalled that the processes of   221
the unconscious system are intemporal (*Zeitlos*) and are not ordered according to the consecutiveness of the temporal order. And this *Zeitlosigkeit*, this intemporality is also an insensitivity to contradiction (*Widerspruchlosigkeit*), an indifference to contradiction: the unconscious knows nothing of contradiction, it doesn't care about it, it contradicts itself all the time without ever contradicting itself, without ever being bothered by contradiction. The unconscious is not ashamed of contradiction. That is why it lies or rather why it always tells the truth even when it contradicts itself from one sentence to the next, it simultaneously lies and tells the truth and never renounces anything. We need to remember all this if we want to continue to dare to think what "phantasm" seems to mean, and *die a living death,* or *die in one's life-*

3. Freud, GW, X:289; SE, XIV:190–91. In the typescript Derrida uses the common [French] abbreviations *Cs, Pcs,* and *Ics* [Ucs] to designate "conscious," "preconscious," and "unconscious" and their German equivalents.

time. So Freud recalls all that, the intemporality and the non-contradiction, the insensitivity to contradiction of the unconscious, before the passage we are now reading, on the "communication between the two systems," in the section entitled "Die besondere Eigenschaften des Systems Ubw."[4]

Freud's gesture here, in "the communication between the two systems," his writing, his manner of writing, his gait, his way of writing, of speaking, of doing things and dividing things up, is *analogous* (I repeat: analogous—comparable, not identical) to what Heidegger does and recommends that we do when he tells us that we should not be discouraged by formal contradictions that scare good sense, for example apparent vicious circles. Thought must have the courage to enter into them, into these circles, to dive into them rather than fleeing and avoiding them. Thought is not afraid of contradiction, which rather belongs to the understanding, the intellect, which worries only the understanding or the intellect. This gesture was also Hegel's: not being afraid of the contradictions of the understanding is the beginning of thought. And one would be tempted, once again from the point of view of courage, to bring together this intrepidity of thought when it affronts and traverses and assumes the circle of contradiction, and what Hegel says about the steadfastness that holds and maintains death in life. You remember this famous passage from the preface to *The Phenomenology of Spirit:*

> Death, if that is what we want to call this non-actuality (*Unwirklichkeit*), is of all things the most dreadful (*das Furchtbarste*), and to hold fast what is dead (*das Tote festzuhalten*) requires the greatest strength [strength [*la force*] again, *was die größte Kraft erfordert*]. Lacking strength, Beauty hates the Understanding (*Verstand*) for asking of her what it cannot do. But the life of Spirit (*das Leben des Geistes*) is not the life that shrinks from death (*das sich vor dem Tode scheut*) and keeps itself untouched by devastation, but rather the life that endures [*erträgt,* again] it and maintains itself in it (*und in ihm sich erhält*).[5]

The life of Spirit begins, then, where death is borne by life, firmly maintained in it, and not denied, even if the understanding wants to distinguish,

4. See Freud, "Die besonderen Eigenschaften des Systems Ubw," in GW, X:285–88; "The Special Characteristics of the System *Ucs*," in SE, XIV:186–89.

5. Georg Wilhelm Friedrich Hegel, *Werke in zwanzig Bänden, III: Phänomenologie des Geistes* (Frankfurt am Main: Suhrkamp, 1970), p. 36; G. W. F. Hegel, "Preface," in *The Phenomenology of Spirit.* trans. A. V. Miller (Oxford and New York: Oxford University Press, 1977), p. 19. [Translator's note: Jean Hippolyte's French translation on occasion construes Hegel's text slightly differently than does Miller's English version. I ignore these differences except where they have a direct bearing on Derrida's reading.]

separate, and oppose life and death, wants not to bear, not take upon itself, not assume, not accept that life bears [*porte*] and comprises [*comporte*] death. At bottom, the true sense of the word "bear" (*tragen, ertragen*) is just as much the sense determined on the basis of bearing life (the mother who bears the child) as the one determined on the basis of the bearing of death by life, of the dead by the living. The life of Spirit is the death of nature or biological death, it bears death, it bears and tolerates [*porte et supporte*] the mourning of death in itself. Spirit attains to its truth only when it finds itself again in this absolute tearing (*in der absoluten Zerrissenheit*), it is torn between the life that it is and the death that it is also, since it bears that death within it like mourning. This spirit (but when one says *Geist,* in German, one indeed says Spirit, but also, spirit defined as a specter or a revenant, a ghost, as I have insisted at length elsewhere[6]), this spirit that has the strength to *bear death,* this spirit is a power (*Macht*), but the power not to turn away from the negative, and therefore the courage, at bottom, not only to look it in the face, but to take the time to look it in the face, to make this gaze last, not to be content with a quick glance, not to look death in the face for a moment and then look away from it the next moment. That's what *bear* means: it is also to bear looking death in the face in an enduring, durable way, taking the time, giving oneself the time that one thus gives to death. Looking death in the face, doing so in the experience of spirit, can also <mean>, think of Hamlet, having the strength, the courage to look the dead one or the specter in the face, to defy it. To be able to bear to bring to bear [*supporter de porter*] on death this mourning gaze that is enduring and durable, to bear the weight of this bearing, of the gaze brought to bear and the mourning borne, the courage to bear death, one needs, I would say, something like a fidelity to death, to what dies and to who dies, as such, as dead: fidelity to death, fiance, confidence, faith, fidelity-to-death to the death, to whom and to what happens to be dead. This fidelity and loyalty not only require time: there would be no time without them, no time as such. But is there ever time as such? Without this spectral spirituality? In any case, we have a sense that

223

6. See Jacques Derrida, *Spectres de Marx: L'état de la dette, le travail de deuil et la nouvelle internationale* (Paris: Galilée, 1993), pp. 175, 185, 201; *Specters of Marx: The State of the Debt, the Work of Mourning, and the New International,* trans. Peggy Kamuf (New York and London: Routledge, 1994), pp. 107, 113, 125–26; *De l'esprit: Heidegger et la question* (Paris: Galilée, 1987), pp. 45, 54, 66; *Of Spirit: Heidegger and the Question,* trans. Geoffrey Bennington and Rachel Bowlby (Chicago: University of Chicago Press, 1989), pp. 24, 31, 40; *La Carte postale: De Socrate à Freud et au-delà* (Paris: Flammarion, 1980), pp. 25, 26; *The Post Card: From Socrates to Freud and Beyond,* trans. Alan Bass (Chicago: University of Chicago Press, 1987), p. 21.

what we have been, for a moment now, obscurely calling courage, which is identified with heart or spirit, has no sense outside this affinity with the faithful endurance of death; it is always the courage (if there is any) not only to speak to death, to have death or the dead one in one's mouth and in one's soul, to talk of it or eat of it, to bite it, but to look death in the face, as such, for more than a second, more than the first second.

224

The power in question (*Macht*) thus consists both in this gaze and in this *insistent,* durable gaze, in the insistence of the gaze, in that power to endure the endurance of that gaze that faces up to the negativity of death. This is what Hegel calls Spirit. Spirit is a power, then, this very power, this sovereignty, basically, a sovereignty that—as with the master in the dialectic of the master and the slave—does not come without the courage to look death in the face. It really is about looking, taking into view, and this way of facing up does not go without sight and image, and image of the face. We shall see the consequence at the end of today's sequence, in the link between phantasm, visual image and imagination.

Such a courage confers sovereign mastery on the master. Spirit is just that, this potency or power, "er ist diese Macht nur, indem er dem Negativen ins Angesicht schaut, bei ihm verwielt," spirit is this power only inasmuch as it faces down the negative, looks it in the face and dwells near it (*indem er dem Negativen ins Angesicht schaut, bei ihm verweilt*).[7] All of this is said in a long passage that I leave you to reread, on the circle, precisely, on what is a circle for the understanding. A few pages earlier, Hegel had given the nickname corpse (*Leichnam*), at least figuratively (but more than figuratively, I think) to the naked result (*das nackte Resultat*) that the tendency leaves behind it when it is mere drive (*das bloße Treiben*) without effective realization, unfinished drive, a drive that does not attain spirit, a drive without effectuation.[8]

I come back to Freud, at the moment when he advances courageously into this contradiction, and not merely this contradiction, but this contradiction between the non-contradictory and the contradictory, between the *Cs* or *Pcs* system and the *Ucs* system. Freud has just relied on this difference between the *qualitative* and the *factual,* on what is qualitatively conscious but in fact unconscious, while being the same thing (it is the same thing, which is not a thing, a something that is called *phantasm* or *symptom* and

225

7. Hegel, *Phänomenologie des Geistes,* p. 36. [Translator's note: Cf. Miller's translation of this passage in *The Phenomenology of Spirit:* "Spirit is this power only by looking the negative in the face, and tarrying with it" (p. 19).]

8. Ibid., p. 13 [pp. 2–3].

which is not a thing), and which is *qualitatively* of the order of phenomenal, phenomenological, conscious quality, but *in fact* of the order of the
unconscious. And on the subject of this undecidable, undecidably both conscious *and* unconscious, he dares to say that its origin, its provenance (*ihre
Herkunft*) remains, as to their destiny, decisive (*Entscheidende*). The origin
of the undecidable is decisive. Decisive for destiny. What is at stake here[9] is
nothing less that *repression*, the original and irreducible, scarcely thinkable
concept of repression. We understand nothing of the concept of repression
if we do not pass through this difficulty, this decisive provenance of the
undecidable, namely of something that is not a thing, is both unconscious
and conscious, unconscious in fact, conscious through the quality of its phenomenological appearing.

The point, then, is to think repression, namely that odd exclusion, that
censorship, which allows only symptoms to pass between the two systems,
symptoms which are also double, in their provenance and their belonging,
doubly inscribed in both systems. I refer you to this text, to what precedes
and follows it, but before quoting it at greater length and then leaving it,
I would like to draw your attention to what appears to be a pedagogical
metaphor, a sort of easy illustration, but which, perhaps, in its social and political dimension is not, I imagine, in its analogical "as if," as metaphorical
as all that, and perhaps refers us to the insular universe of Robinson and his
cannibal savages, whom one imagines to be black, or dark, between white
and black, of color in any case, or already métis, and, conversely, gives us
to think that socio-political exclusions, socio-political conflicts and repressions, and perhaps even all repressions of living beings in general (women,
children, blacks, slaves, savages, animals, etc.) [that all these repressions]
are possible and efficacious only where some psychic repression and symptomatology are at work. With this simple metaphor we might have the
key for at least the principle of a psychoanalytic politics or a political or
even zoo-anthropological psychoanalysis. Freud compares these mixtures
of consciousness and unconscious to métis, to bastards, to hybrids (*Misch-
lingen*) who belong to both races at once. And Freud writes this, to explain
the effects of the provenance, both conscious and unconscious, undecidable,
of these offsprings of drives, of these métis that phantasms and symptoms
supposedly are, in truth of their decisive origin in repression:

226

> We may compare [*vergleichen,* again] them with individuals of mixed race
> (*mit den Mischlingen menschlicher Rassen*) who, taken all around, resemble

9. During the session, Derrida added: "it is here that we need to revive, reawaken
old familiarities."

Whites [*bereits den Weißen gleichen:* thus they are fellows [*semblables*], re-sembling one another in dissemblance[10]], but who betray their coloured descent by some striking feature or other, and on that account remain ex-cluded from society and enjoy none of the privileges of Whites. Of such a nature are those formations of phantasy [*die Phantasiebildungen:* phan-tasms, phantasmatic formations] of normal people as well as of neurotics which we have recognized as preliminary stages in the formation both of dreams and of symptoms and which, in spite of their high degree of orga-nization, remain repressed[11] and therefore cannot become conscious. They draw near to consciousness and remain undisturbed so long as they do not have an intense cathexis,[12] but as soon as they exceed a certain height of cathexis they are thrust back.[13]

227   These offspring are what Freud immediately afterward calls substitute formations (*Ersatzbildungen*), prostheses. And he then notes a supplemen-tary complication which he admits resembles a contradiction (*Widerspruch*) in his exposition, namely that he now has to admit that the censorship that he had placed between the *Ucs* and *Pcs* systems operates also between *Pcs* and *Cs*.[14] The fact is, he says, that every passage from one system to the immediately higher system implies a censorship. And in a somewhat eco-nomic way, by reason of a sort of finitude, because we must exclude the in-finite renewal of inscriptions (*Niederschriften*). The number of inscriptions to be inscribed is finite — that's finitude. For all acts of censorship operate on inscriptions, and substitutes of inscriptions in a system (it is even this concept of inscription which no doubt motivated the choice of the word or metaphor of censorship), and the quantity of inscriptions is finite: so one must censor. It is like a topological economy of the archive in which one has to exclude, censor, erase, destroy or displace, virtualize, condense the archive to gain space in the same place, in the same system, to be able to con-tinue to store, to make space. Finitude is also a sort of law for this economy.

10. In the session, Derrida added this humorous remark: "They are a little white, but not white, not 'white, white, white.'" And, at the end of the sentence: "We know this story, it is 'white, white, white,' but, at bottom, we know that it is black and there-fore terrible, it is worse than if it were 'black, black.' You have seen a lot of American films . . ."

11. In the session, Derrida added: "We do not let them pass, and when they do pass, they do so through symptoms; we know what symptoms are in politics."

12. In the session, Derrida added: "everything near the house, like doormen, ser-vants, nannies."

13. Freud, GW, X:289–90; SE, XIV:191. Translation slightly modified.

14. In the session, Derrida added: "Thus the censorship can operate in more than one place: translate that into the political arena and you will see that it is not insignificant."

To finish for today with this Freudian protocol, you understand easily why I also think it necessary to stress that in *Thoughts for the Times on War and Death* (1915), in the second chapter entitled "Our Relation to Death,"[15] Freud suggests that the relation to our own death is not representable, and that each time we try to represent our own death to ourselves, we continue to be there as spectators, observers, voyeurs, at a distance and subject to   228
imagery, to imagination. We are alive enough to see ourselves and imagine ourselves dead, and therefore, I would add, buried or swallowed up or cremated alive. This is another way of saying, against Heidegger, that we never have any access to our own death *as such,* that we are incapable of it. Our death is impossible. Whence Freud concludes, and I quote: "Hence the psycho-analytic school could venture the assertion that at bottom no one believes in his own death, or, to put the same thing in another way, that in the unconscious every one of us is convinced of his own immortality."[16] Of course—in what would, according to Heidegger's axiomatics, rank us with the animal that does not die, that has no relation to its death as such—we must emphasize, and would have to meditate on, among other words, the word "belief," especially when it is granted to the unconscious. What does *believe* or *not believe* mean for the unconscious? What difference is there between *believing* and *not believing* for the unconscious? This is why I often venture to say that the problem of the meaning of the word "belief" is still today entirely new. And I tried to show not long ago, in this very place,[17] how this concept of belief was strange enough for one always to be able to show that between believing and not believing there is not a radical opposition, such that believing always comes down to believing the unbelievable, believing in what one cannot know, and therefore in what one can only believe, and thus in what one does not believe, in what one does not believe to be believable. (Photocopy both pages (French and English))

It is at the end of the same text that—having recalled that, nonetheless, in primitive man, in original man (*Urmensch*), there coexist in a non-contradictory way two apparently contradictory attitudes with respect to   229
death; the belief in the annihilation of life and the denial of that same belief, the denial of the reality of annihilation—after having recalled, then, that in

15. Freud, "Unser Verhältnis zum Tode," *Zeitgemäßes über Krieg und Tod,* in GW, X:324–55; "Our Attitude Towards Death," *Thoughts for the Times on War and Death,* in SE, XIV:274–300.
16. Freud, SE, XIV:289.
17. Cf. Jacques Derrida, unpublished seminars on Testimony: 1992–93 (sessions 1, 2, 3, 7, and 11); 1993–94 (session 9), and 1994–95 (sessions 3 and 4).

the same primitive man (who moreover survives in us) the dear ones who are an internal possession, a constitutive part of my own ego, or at the same time strangers, or even enemies inspiring in us unconscious death wishes; after having recalled that our understanding and our sensibility have difficulty thus reconciling or coupling love and hate and that it is for this reason, because of this unbearable contradiction, by reason of the unbearable truth of this contradiction love/hate, life/death, mourning and jubilatory triumph, that people cannot tolerate psychoanalysis and that it encounters so many resistances, Freud then sums up: "To sum up: our unconscious is just as inaccessible to the idea of our own death, just as murderously inclined toward strangers, just as divided (that is, ambivalent) towards those we love, as was primaeval man," and he concludes, "But how far we have moved from this primal state in our conventional and cultural attitude towards death!"[18]

And war (because this is a text on war written while war was raging (1915)) would be that destruction of the sediments of culture that makes this primitive or primary man reappear, and these primitive times—still awake and surviving, both dead and alive, beneath culture and civilization. When war speaks, when one speaks of war, when one declares or makes war, one is still speaking this primitive language.

This would be enough to bring us back to Robinson who often describes himself as having returned to the state of nature ("I that was reduced to a meer State of Nature" [RC, 109]) and to our contradictory phantasm of being buried, swallowed up, in short destroyed, killed, living dead. But before moving on, before leaving Freud, I shall not resist—in the name of survival and remains, in the name of what happens after "our lifetime," of Robinson Crusoe, of Defoe, etc., of everything we said about this, last time, of the living death of books and works—I shall not then resist the desire to read with you the only, highly significant, passage in which, to my knowledge, Freud compares himself in turn—like Rousseau—to Robinson Crusoe, to Robinson Crusoe to whom justice would be done only after his death,[19] and the becoming buried alive of his work. In *The History of the Psychoanalytic Movement* (*Zur Geschichte der psychoanalytischen Bewegung* (1914)), Freud writes this:[20]

230

---

18. Freud, SE, 14:299.

19. In the session, Derrida added (in English): "after his lifetime."

20. In the session, before reading the citation, Derrida admitted: "Not having at home the German edition of this text, I have not had the time to consult the German. I translate from the *Standard Edition*."

I pictured the future as follows:—I should probably succeed in maintaining myself by means of the therapeutic success of the new procedure, but science would ignore me entirely during my lifetime;[21] some decades later, someone else would infallibly come upon the same things—for which the time was not now ripe—would achieve recognition for them and bring me honour as a forerunner whose failure had been inevitable. Meanwhile, like Robinson Crusoe, I settled down as comfortably as possible on my desert island. When I look back to those lonely years, away from the pressures and confusions of to-day, it seems like a glorious heroic age. My "splendid isolation" was not without its advantages and charms. I did not have to read any publications, nor listen to any ill-informed opponents; I was not subject to influence from any quarter; there was nothing to hustle me [or pressure me]. I learnt to restrain speculative tendencies and to follow the unforgotten advice of my master, Charcot [. . .][22] (Photocopy the English)

You no doubt have the impression that for a long time now I've been doing all I can to put off the moment at which I shall have to speak about the choice between inhumation and cremation. No: here and now, the moment has come.

I announced last time what I called the "first choice," as one says at the butchers', who are, in our culture, corpse dealers. The first choice, as you know statistically the most frequent among us, is burial. If, we were saying, someone intends to decide freely, for him or herself, in a sovereign manner, i.e. if, without just letting things go, having deliberated about it, having weighed up the pros and cons, and envisaged the only two possibilities that remain for remains, i.e. cremation and inhumation, if he or she opts for burial, freely, as they say, sovereignly, why would this be?

Why, for what, also means in view of what. But it is impossible not also to hear: for whom, oneself or another? To respond to what desire and what motivation, but also the desire and motivation of whom?

That is where we were getting ready to see the first double bind knot itself up. As though, as a first effect of the phantasm of the living dead, we still had to suffer, worry, torment ourselves as to what will happen when we are no longer there to suffer, to worry, to torment ourselves, were it even about the deluge supposed to come after me.

I had taken a methodological precaution, in the order of the path to be followed. It had to do with the trivial axiom, but one that as they say bears

231

---

21. [Translator's note:] Derrida repeats this phrase in English after giving his French translation.

22. Freud, SE, XIV:22.

the stamp of common sense, namely that the decision on this subject (inhumation rather than cremation) can only be the decision of one living and not of the dead. The concept of decision, assuming there is any decision, and if we can speak of a decision on the subject of this funerary modality, [the concept of decision] implies <at> least life, and the life of a living being with a future at its disposal. Whence the "in view of what and to whom?" as though the one dying, as though the mortal could count *on* a future, count *with* the future just where death, according to common sense, would be removing all future from him or her. We shall have, then, to analyze the hypothesis of this decision either from the point of view of the living survivors, the inheritors, or else from the point of view of the one who gives instructions when he or she is going to die but has not yet "departed," and can thus only speculate on his or her own death on the basis of the imagination or the phantasm of the living dead, or, at the limit, of the dead one still alive enough *to see him or herself* die and be buried, and who, to parody the letter of what Robinson Crusoe was saying in a passage I read last time, imagines him or herself still walking around after death to see what's going on, still being affected by it, still enjoying it or suffering from it ("For my Part, I know not to this Hour,whether there are any such Things as real Apparitions, Spectres, or walking of People after they are dead"). And Freud too emphasized the fact that we can live our death only by becoming a spectator of it.

From the point of view of this phantasm of the surviving dead one, what, then, can the calculations be? What can be the ruses, the suppositions, the speculations, in which one might invest, in all the meanings — psychic and fiduciary — of this term? How can the advantages or the calculable benefits, the enjoyments one might still count on, be announced and described for inhumation and for cremation? On the other hand, what are the damages and sufferings to be feared? In what way are the two contraries inseparably and aporetically affected, contaminated, infected the one by the other, the economy of enjoyment rotten in advance, or more soberly let's say finite and threatened, within itself, according to a terrible autoimmune logic, by the economy of suffering — that's the form of the question that I propose to articulate, both for inhumation and for cremation.

Inhumation first. It promises to give time and space, some time and some space. Apparently more humane, less inhumane than cremation, this humane inhumation seems to assure me that I will not be instantaneously annihilated without remainder. In any case, my remains will be more substantial than ashes and my disappearance will require or will take time.

Moreover, since I'm speaking of disappearance, the phantasm we're talking about can rush in, and hurry the desire to persevere in one's being, to   *233*
survive, toward an inhumation that would have me disappear less instantaneously than cremation. There is, with inhumation, a time and a place
for the body, and the body—a concept on which we would have to dwell
for a long time—if it is not the proper living body (*Leib*), is not a simple
thing. Last time, we were associating two questions: "what is a thing?" and
"what is the other?" Well, these two questions are also to be interpreted as
questions about the body, and one of the differences between inhumation
and cremation is that the former allows for the existence of the body, its
duration and its territory, whereas the second avoids the body. Cremation
makes the body disappear. Now the body is something that is not simply
an anonymous and lifeless thing, and we only perceive it, we only have an
experience of it, as the body of the other. Even if we were inclined to follow
Heidegger when he speaks of "being capable" of our own death [*"pouvoir"*
notre propre mort], it is certain that we are "not capable" of our own corpse,
we will never see it and feel it. And yet, if the dead person is one who has
disappeared, the corpse of one disappeared does not disappear, it is not destroyed, *qua* corpse, as it is by cremation. This non-disappearance lends the
phantasm some hope, if you will. Buried, I do not disappear, and I can still
hang on to something, my phantasm can still hold onto my corpse, to the
non-disappearance of my corpse after my own disappearance.

On the other hand, this time to do with space and not only with time
(but here the two are indissociable), a sort of instituted habitat would be
guaranteed me to the measure of my body, my body respected in its integrity, without reduction of dimension, weight, or appearance, in a cemetery
maintained and protected by the state, civil society, family, and all associated institutions, beginning with the possibility of religion or what remains
of it—and if anything remains of it, however little, it's always at the moment of funeral rites that this remainder appears and returns, if only in the
signs of mourning, speeches and funeral orations, however secular they be
(this is not necessarily the case for cremation, for even if, today, a cemetery
might resound with funeral orations at the moment of the cremation, and   *234*
even if it might preserve ashes in urns with proper names, religion no longer plays any role in it, and in the West people do not kneel before urns
as they do before a tomb). And so, as a buried corpse, I would still have a
place reserved to me, I would have a proper place, I could still take place.
Wherever I can take place, there is also time given, and the phantasm of the
daydream can act "as if," tell itself the story of an "as is," precisely as though
the story were not over.

What story? What stories? How can one accord the phantasmatic or the fantastic with the narrative, with narrative fiction, or even with fantastic literature, with stories that accord time and future to the dead person?

Before proceeding and trying to answer these questions, let us note here that the division or the hesitation between inhumation and cremation has no doubt always depended, and today depends more than ever, on the reasonable doubt one might cultivate on the subject of the state of death. We know that the criteria for deciding as to the state of death—in other words, to decide if one is really dealing with a corpse or on the contrary with a moribund living person, a prolonged coma, etc., we know that these criteria are variable and offer no natural, universal, scientific and consensual certainty. They vary from one era of medicine to another, from one state or culture to another. They are not the same, for example, from one state to another in the United States: and we quoted in this very place, two years ago, the remark of an eminent American biologist who said, no less—I'm quoting him—that we should henceforth "deconstruct" death, by which he meant the concept of death.[23] At bottom, we do not have at our disposal an absolute scientific and objective knowledge of the state of death, and so we do not rigorously know what the difference is between a living body and a corpse. And this uncertainty, which always leaves open the possibility that a funeral is being organized for a living person, for a dead person who is still alive—this uncertainty can just as well justify or motivate a phantasmatic preference for inhumation ("as I am not dead, at least take account of that fact, don't be in a rush to destroy me, to annihilate me, don't kill me yet") as it can motivate a preference for cremation ("as I am not as dead as they say or wish or pretend to believe, burn me already so that my death can be irreversible and so that I do not suffer the hell of being buried alive").

Cremation, if it is decided upon by relatives, is a sort of irreversible murder, and if it is decided upon by the dying person, a sort of irreversible suicide supposed to insure against the agonies of a possible awakening and suffocation in a wooden box six feet under, with no one to respond to a cry

23. This is an allusion to session 9 of Derrida's seminar on the death penalty (March 2000), in the course of which Derrida reports some remarks attributed to Dr. Stuart J. Younger: "I think we're in a phase in which death is being deconstructed [. . .] The more we talk, the more we write, the more we find the consensus defining death is superficial and fragile." These remarks are cited in an article by Karen Long, "Oh, Death, Where Is Thy Starting?," *Baptist Standard: Insight for Faithful Living* (November 3, 1999), http://www.baptiststandard.com/1999/11_3/pages/death.html. According to Dr. Stuart J. Younger, consulted via e-mail on June 10, 2009, "[. . .] the citations used by Karen Long come from a conversation and not a published article."

for help. But then it's as if those who protest against cremation in the name of inhumation were also protesting lucidly against what looks like irreversible murder or suicide, rather than looking like a sign of love or mournful respect for the one who has passed or rather who is passing.

Even if they are not always voiced very loudly, one can, then, hear coming from the two cultures or the two parties—inhumers and cremators—a terrible accusation against the other. And it is always an accusation of inhumanity, if not of crime against humanity. The inhumers are more or less explicitly accusing the cremators of being inhuman, since they are committing that murder or suicide that consists in attacking the integrity of a corpse that is perhaps living-dead, and which still has a right to time, to space, and even to hope. The cremators, for their part, are virtually accusing of inhumanity the inhumers who let corpses and perhaps the living dead rot, decompose and perhaps suffer a thousand more deaths down in their hole, their grave, like beasts. Behind these reciprocal accusations, and still more in their modernity[24]—but I said that this choice left open by society between the two modes of funeral was, in the West and only in the West, a highly significant and unprecedented—and thus strictly "modern"—phenomenon of liberation with respect to religious prescriptions, which demand inhumation in European, Greco-Latin or pre-Christian, but also Abrahamic, Judeo-Christian-Islamic religions, and, on the other hand, those that, in India or in Japan, prescribe cremation. If one seeks to identify modernity ("what is it to be modern?" "what is the essential and specific criterion of modernity?" "where is the distinctive sign of modernity?"), well, we have the mark of it first of all here, in the cemeteries (for example in the Père-Lachaise where the two cultures, the culture of inhumation and the culture of cremation, earth and fire, humus and flame, coexist; and many things flow from this, or constitute its premises), behind these reciprocal accusations, I was saying, and still more in our modernity, there are, in the depths of the European scene, on the Western historical and political stage, be it conscious or unconscious, on the stage of memory, crematoria and mass graves.

Whoever professes inhumation, whoever votes in favor of inhumation, for self or for those around him or her, is telling him or herself a story and yielding to the phantasm (and there is phantasm where the place of non-knowledge is left vacant by science itself, in the place where *I do not know,* as Robinson Crusoe says, I have no certain knowledge whether or not there can be spirit, spectral survival in the living dead or after death, what the state of death is, and what a "corpse" means, what the word "corpse"

24. This sentence is incomplete in the typescript.

means, or even what the corpse itself still means [*veut dire:* wants to say], the one that one holds, rightly or wrongly, to be a corpse: the dead person, says Levinas, is not annihilated but is what no longer responds and thus no longer wants to say anything to us)—whoever, as I was saying, professes inhumation, whoever votes in favor of inhumation, for self or for those around him or her, is telling him or herself a story and yielding to the phantasm according to which all is not over and in which moreover so-called death does not consist in an end, does not have the last word, and in which one's story is not over, there is room either for some survival that looks like a secular resurrection or else for some glorious and supernatural resurrection. These two resurrections do better with a body inhumed in its integrity than with a body annihilated and reduced to ashes. What do I mean by secular resurrection, from the point of view of the phantasm? Well, that horrible thing that consists in waking up inside a sealed coffin, a closed grave, a sealed tomb, and having to cry out in the impotence of suffocation in order to call on the other for help. And you know about those maniacs who demand that they be buried with a telephone, a more or less mobile telephone, in order to tolerate the idea that they might thus be buried alive. In *Ulysses Gramophone,* I quoted and re-inscribed in a broader setting this passage from Joyce's *Ulysses* which says "have a gramophone in every grave" and imagines the grandfather waking up in his tomb and beginning to speak . . . (Read *Ulysses Gramophone*)

> Faithful departed. As you are now so once were we.
> Besides how could you remember everybody? Eyes, walk, voice. Well, the voice, yes: gramophone. Have a gramophone in every grave or keep it in the house. After dinner on a Sunday. Put on poor old great-grandfather Kraahraark! Hellohellohello amawfullyglad kraark awfullygladaseeragain hellohello amarawf kopthsth.[25]

As for resurrection in its Christian, Christic form, it most often goes via a scene of inhumation which does not destroy the corpse (how could Christ have been resuscitated if he had been cremated? It's not unthinkable and unimaginable, but much more difficult to imagine and recount. In any case, it's too late now, the story has happened, and it was an inhumation). But it is true that narratives of metamorphosis and of metempsychosis accept and

25. James Joyce, *Ulysses* (Harmondsworth: Penguin Books, 1960), p. 115. Quoted by Derrida in *Ulysse Gramophone* suivi de *Deux mots pour Joyce* (Paris: Galilée, 1987), p. 91; trans. Tina Kendall and Shari Benstock as "Ulysses Gramophone: Hear Say Yes in Joyce," in *Acts of Literature,* ed. Derek Attridge (London: Routledge, 1992), pp. 256–309 (p. 277).

even demand cremation. As for the Christian doctrine of the glorious body, of the body of the blessed chosen after the resurrection, of their body of light ascending to heaven, it also appears to suppose a death that undergoes the trial of earth rather than that of fire, even though one should not exclude (such at least is my hypothesis), among certain Christians who nonetheless have themselves cremated, the imaginary speculation according to which a burned corpse becomes more easily celestial and glorious, light and ascensional, airy, spiritual, than a body buried in its earthly weight; but I believe that, in this case, this goes via a private imagination that the church, unless I'm mistaken, cannot statutorily take on board.

There is another type of benefit counted on in inhumation. It depends on the stability of the place, on the immobile monumentality of the tomb. Whereas an urn, for its part, is mobile and transportable, whereas the ashes themselves, without the urn, are still more dispersed and placeless, I would say without dwelling, without hearth or home, the other recompense, the other economy of inhumation in its immobile taking-place, is that it conditions and facilitates for the survivors (and therefore for the dying person who in advance identifies with them) what is called the normal labor of mourning. Those close to the dead person can come back when they wish, or at regular intervals, to the scene (I won't necessarily say "the scene of the crime," even though the cremators are always ready virtually to accuse the inhumers of crime, namely that of running the risk of burying people alive and over-hastily getting rid of supposed corpses—not to speak of the love-hate and therefore virtually criminal ambivalence that Freud describes so well, precisely in the relation to the dead people one loves and whom one kills just as well, or in any case allows to die (what difference is there between killing and allowing to die, for example on the worldwide scale of famine, of malnutrition and of AIDS, etc.?), criminal ambivalence in the relation to the dead people one loves and whom one kills just as well, or in any case allows to die as much as one regrets their death, with a feeling of criminal culpability that haunts all labor of mourning, and that the labor of morning also has at its function to try to appease, to neutralize, to make innocent). 239

Now the immobile localization of the buried body, its territorialization, allows this labor of mourning to proceed along its path, if I can put it like this, during regular visits and moments of reverence, returns to the tomb that keep the body whole, external or internal procedures, transactions that render one innocent insofar as they are marks of faithful and conservatorial respect maintaining the other alive (in oneself), while maintaining that other in its place outside. The survivor is able to verify each time that the dead one, identified by his or her proper name inscribed on the tomb, really is who he or she is, where he or she is, that he or she rests or reposes (rests in peace) in the right place, in the place of the dead, a place from which he or she will not return.

And this is where the ambiguous or ambivalent, in truth self-contradicting effect of this phantasm, of this phantasmatic preference for inhumation reveals its autoimmunitary character and is carried off into it. Inhumation appears more humane and more immunitary, of course, more protective, more habitable, more hospitable, if I can put it like that—but by the same token it is autoimmunitary and harmful, and thus terrifying for the very phantasm that moves toward it. Not only, as we have just seen, because unlike cremation it leaves open a greater chance and probability to the agonies of the living dead, to the suffocation of being buried alive and awakening in one's tomb before becoming a true corpse again, after indescribable suffering that no one will ever have been able to describe, for good reason. Not only, next, because of the long process of rotting and decomposition that one can only imagine for oneself and for the other, but that one cannot fail to imagine. But also because one sees clearly that the labor of mourning that one appears to facilitate in this way consists, in localizing the dead one, in stabilizing it, in immobilizing it in its place and its static state, in keeping the dead one at a distance, at bay, over there, outside, far off, in a public rather than a private place, ensuring that he or she will not come back home, into one's home or into oneself, neither in fact nor in the form of a revenant. The intervention or interposing of the public, the public space of the cemetery, of the *res publica* or the state, is an insurance apparatus: the dead one will be really dead, an indubitable corpse, but also a public thing, a *res publica,* that will guarantee legally, legitimately, under the sway of that other legal sovereignty, that the dead one will decompose and remain in its place, distant, outside and far from the private or inner space of the survivors, their domicile or their heart, their hearth, the very place where the labor of mourning will ideally have interiorized, memorized, *errinert,* introjected or incorporated him or her. All of that is appeasing, it avoids interminable persecution (the persecution of the corpse by the survivors, the persecution of the survivors by the dead one), only by putting the dead one to death, confirming the dead one in his or her death that one will pretend to approach, symbolically, only at regular and ritualized intervals, during one's visits to the cemetery, on anniversaries, ceremonies, prescribed and formal returns to the scene of inhumation. During the intervals and even on those occasions, the dead one is maintained at a more or less calculable and objective distance, avoided, left, abandoned where he or she is forever under the watch of the cemetery guardians, and thus of the police of state and of law, at least when the tombs are not profaned (an enormous problem I am also leaving to one side).

This intervention, this interposing of the state, the church, or of the *res publica* in general is here all the more decisive and noteworthy (it is this that takes the dead one away from the family and that one asks to take him or her away to keep him or her where he or she is, far off, over there, etc., for as long as necessary), this taking of responsibility by church and/or state is all the more significant for the fact that the very rare cases in which the corpse is both maintained in its integrity, but withdrawn from decomposition and from the agonies of suffocation, are always exceptional cases of dignitaries, sovereigns, or heads of state who are mummified or embalmed, be it the pharaohs and their family, or the heads of totalitarian states (Lenin, Stalin, etc.) whose corpses are not only withdrawn from decomposition but, in the latter cases, kept practically intact, imputrescent and visible in the public space, or in any case always exposed to becoming visible and accessible to view again.   241

It is in order to resist all these negative and autoimmune effects that one goes toward, that one takes refuge in, the phantasm of cremation. Cremation is supposed to avoid the agonies of the living dead, of a cadaverization that has not yet necessarily done its work at the moment of burial. Cremation is also supposed to avoid the horrors of slow decomposition supposed to affect the phantasmatic body of the dead one (which calms both the dead one and the survivors). Finally, it is supposed to suspend the immobile localization of the corpse by depriving it of a place, but also by the same token avoiding holding it at a respectful distance, avoiding distancing it from the life of the survivors.

But the autoimmune or aporetic contradiction also comes back to persecute the phantasm of the cremators. I am deliberately using what is in French a present participle, as you will have understood (the *inhumants* and the *incinérants*), to designate both those who decide for themselves and those who decide for others as to this mode of dealing with the dead, in this exchange without exchange of places that makes everyone crazy with living death, both the dying and the survivors. If on the one hand this phantasm of the cremators, on the side of the surviving family, is consoling, because of the thought that suffocation or decomposition are avoided for the well-beloved dead one (a favor or grace to be done to him or her), in return [*en revanche*] (and I'm deliberately using this word *revanche* [revenge] which promotes war, vengeful resentment and persecution—all that), in return, then, this favor (no suffocation or decomposition) is paid for by absolute annihilation, a more radical way of having the departed depart, a way of going after the flesh, and going after the disappearance of disappearing. To avoid having him or her suffer the suffocation of the living dead and the decomposition of the corpse, one makes the departed depart, one destroys and annihilates him or her in every identifiable trace—I mean in that ashes are no longer remains in human form. To annihilate, to transform death into annihilation (and you know that this is not the same thing, this is the place of a debate or an objection that Levinas addresses to the tradition and notably to Heidegger: death is not, insists Levinas, equivalent to an annihilation, to a reduction to nonbeing, death is not nothingness nor the negative response to the question to be or not to be), to annihilate, to transform death into annihilation, is to deprive the dead one of everything through which he or she can still affect, from the outside, from some exteriority, affect our sensibility in the a priori forms of sensibility, as Kant would say, namely time and space. He or she will not be coming back, the dead one, he or she will disappear in his or her very disappearance in an instant, without even having the time, without the time being left both to the dead one and to the survivors for that cohabitation in mourning that is given rhythm, scansion, and duration by funerals and burial and the earth of cemeteries. Cremation no longer either takes or gives time. Nor space, since, as we were just saying, the immobile tomb is henceforth forbidden, and since the urn is movable and the ashes do not stand in for a body as the corpse would. Ashes do without the body [*font l'économie du corps*]. They do not take place because they do not have place, they are dispersion, and the urn in which they are gathered has no proper place.

One finds in cremation the same aporia, the same autoimmune double bind as in inhumation; *formally,* logically, analogically the same, even if the two ways of dealing with the corpse are seeking, in the sensory *content* of the staging and the phantasm, a quite different modality, another time, another sensory space. This same aporia, this same autoimmune double bind becomes paralyzed, or flaps around while becoming paralyzed, becomes clenched in the contradiction of an unfaithful fidelity, more unfaithful by increase of fidelity, more faithful by a hyperbole of infidelity, a contradiction that simultaneously structures and ruins all labor of mourning, and in truth all relation to others as labor of mourning. I say "relation to others as labor of mourning," for mourning does not wait for death, it is the very essence of the experience of the other as other, of the inaccessible alterity that one can only lose in loving it—or just as much in hating it. One is always in mourning for the other.

For, to come back to cremation, it is because of the fire, and this be-

ing deprived of earth, of territory and an immobile place, that the labor   *243*
of mourning becomes both infinite and null. Infinite because null. And by
the same token showing up the essential impossibility that is and must be
that of the labor of mourning, of the very concept of labor of mourning, a
labor of mourning that can only succeed and achieve its so-called normal-
ity by falling into treachery: one betrays the dead one, one fails in being
successful in the labor of mourning, by interiorizing the dead one who is
thus deprived of his or her very alterity, but one also betrays the dead one
by leaving him or her outside, by respecting her or his infinite alterity and
by above all not taking her or him into the self. When fire has operated,
and in the modernity of its lugubrious theater—i.e. technically infallible,
instantaneously efficacious, invisible, all but inaudible—the corpse of the
deceased will, apparently, have disappeared outside its very disappearance.
But having a place nowhere, having no stable place, no *topos* outside the
survivors, the image or memory of the dead one become ubiquitous, he
or she invades the whole of space and the whole of time, which are purely
interiorized (in the form of an absolutely pure and not empirically determined sensibility). The dead one is both everywhere and nowhere, nowhere
because everywhere, out of the world and everywhere in the world and in
us. Pure interiorization, the pure idealization of the dead one, his or her
absolute idealization, his or her dematerialization in the mournful survivor
who can only let himself be invaded by a dead one who has no longer any
place of his or her own outside—this is both the greatest fidelity and the
utmost betrayal, the best way of keeping the other while getting rid of her
or him. In the same gesture and in the same instant. Carrying [*porter*] the
other in oneself, only in oneself, keeping him or her in one's heart (as one
says on those occasions), where there is no longer any mediation and any
cadaverous or entombed support in the world, grounded in the world. It is
this relation of the survivors and the dead one that <becomes> at once pure,
purified by fire and pure of all body as of all world, it becomes in its way
weltlos or even *weltarm*. Between being *weltlos* and being *weltarm*.

"Die Welt ist fort, ich muss dich tragen," that can also mean, can also
translate (I say also but not only) this duty or promise of fidelity addressed
to the deceased loved one, who has left the world, whom the world has left,   *244*
from whom the world has taken its distance; and especially if fire, for example crematory fire, has deprived the other of an immobile burial place,
of a proper place in the world. I can then, I must then only carry the other
in me, and address myself to him or her in me, promise her or him in me
to carry her or him in me whether he or she hears it or not, and knowing
that if he or she does hear it, it will be only in me, in my heart as one says, as

the other in me, so that the familiar form of address, the *ich muss* dich *tra-gen,* addresses itself as much to the other as — reversing the direction of the apostrophe — to me, to the poet, to the signatory, or even to the poem itself or to the I who, carrying the other in itself, thus becomes the other at the moment that *Die Welt ist fort.* Where there is no longer any world between them and for them, at that end of the world that every death is.

The accessible and inaccessible point of fidelity, of the promise to be faithful in spite of everything, is *affirmed* (and it is of this affirmation that we're speaking, of this affirmation that is invincible to all aporias and to all autoimmune dialectics) — is affirmed, this affirmation, is signed, only in the endurance of this aporia of unfaithful fidelity or of faithful infidelity, as "the more faithful I am the more I am unfaithful," and reciprocally.

All of this reawakens us to a question that has not ceased sleepwalking in our progress today. The question: what is the phantasm? What does phantasm, *phantasma,* revenant, fantasia, imagination, fantastic imagination, mean? If everything we've just sketched out concerned above all the phantasmatic nature of what orients our desire and our terror, our experience (let's call it our Robinsonian experience) of the living dead and the treatment of the corpse, of the essence or the non-essence, of the nothing (*Unwesen:* decomposition) of the corpse, then we're here touching on the simultaneously auto-affective and hetero-affective structure of the phantasm. One cannot think the phantasm without this auto-hetero-affective dimension.

A reflection on the acute specificity of the phantasmatic cannot fail to pass through this experience of living death and of affect, imagination and sensibility (space and time) as auto-hetero-affection.

245   If we had the time and space, I would have proposed a long detour (which I therefore ask you to make on your own) through that book or set of seminars by Heidegger on *Kant and the Problem of Metaphysics,* texts that are pretty much contemporaneous with our seminar of 1929–30, or just a little earlier (1925–28). This too, as you know, is an interpretation of Kant, but the central theme of which is finitude (Heidegger draws a great number of consequences from it) and a reading which, as you also know, is engaged in a profound meditation on time, on the schematism of the transcendental imagination in Kant, precisely around the strange thing that is a pure auto-affection. Now, like others, I was struck by the pedagogical example taken by Heidegger when he is wondering what the image (*Bild*) is and what is the imagination (*Einbildung, Einbildungskraft*), a question that is all the more interesting for us in that human Dasein will be defined in the seminar of 1929–30, as you well know, as *Weltbildend. Bilden, Weltbilden,* is

supposedly what is proper to man, of Dasein in its finitude. The question of knowing how to think *bilden* is no less decisive than that of knowing how to think *Welt*. Now at a given moment, in *Kant and the Problem of Metaphysics*, Heidegger wonders what an "image" is, and he explores all the meanings this word can have in Kant (at least three, three times sight: the immediate sight of an entity, the sight of a reproduction of an entity, the sight of any object). And in order to explore, to explain the second sense, the sight of an image that reproduces, of a reproduction, here is what he writes and in which there suddenly appears the photographic image of a death mask, which is already in its way a reproduction. I read the following to conclude for today: (Read and comment *Kant and the Problem . . .* , translation)

> Now the expression "image" likewise is used frequently in this second sense as likeness. This thing here, this photograph which is at hand, immediately offers a look as this thing. It is image in the first and broad sense. But while it shows itself, it wants to show precisely that from which it has taken its likeness. To obtain an image in this second sense now no longer means merely to intuit a being immediately, but instead means, for example, to buy or to produce a photograph.
>
> It is possible to produce a copy (photograph) again from such a likeness, [a photograph] of a death mask for example. The copy can only directly copy the likeness and thus reveal the "image" (the immediate look) of the deceased himself. The photograph of the death mask, as a copy of a likeness, is itself an image — but this is only because it gives the "image" of the dead person, shows how the dead person appears, or rather how it appeared. According to the expression "image" hitherto delimited, making-sensible means on the one hand the manner of immediate contemplation of a likeness in which the look of a being presents itself.
>
> Now the photograph, however, can also show how something like a death mask appears in general. In turn, the death mask can show in general how something like the face of a dead human being appears. But an individual corpse itself can also show this. And similarly, the mask itself can also show how a death mask in general appears, just as the photograph shows not only how what is photographed, but also how a photograph in general, appears.[26]

246

---

26. Martin Heidegger, "§20: Image and Schema," in *Kant and the Problem of Metaphysics,* 4th ed., trans. Richard Taft (Bloomington and Indianapolis: Indiana University Press, 1990), pp. 63–64.

February 26, 2003

247 {Before beginning, I would like to read some extracts from a letter[1] from my friend Tim Bahti as a supplement, accompaniment, and enrichment of what we said last time on the subject of Veronica, of the shroud and the imprint on the death mask. Tim Bahti writes the following, which I can only quote, as I have nothing to change or add:

> Petrarch played in one of his poems on the sense of "Veronica" as *vera icona*." But the shroud of Veronica — as little as the death mask and Heidegger — is not strictly speaking an icon, but rather what C. S. Peirce calls an indexical. So, as an image (*Bild*), this index-sign — the mask, the shroud — is struck (as when one speaks of "striking a coin") by death or the dying; every other image (the photograph of the mask, for example) is reducible to and reproductive of this virtual point — whence, perhaps, the fascination with the *punctum* of each photograph. Bazin has written some fine pages on the so-called "ontogenetic" link between the object and its photographic image, which he claims is founded on a mimetic relation between art and the corpse.

248 > Let us recall that the *Einbildungskraft* is, in its medieval roots (from German mysticism), the force (*Kraft*) to make enter into the interiority of the soul (*ein*) the image of Christ (*Bild*): *Einbildungskraft* was a mystical exercise. And this Christ is not just anyone! He is the one who is always already struck by death — and promising his survival according to his image. And so, the phantasm of having our death as ours, in us, alive, as an image,

---

1. Derrida improvised this opening to the session by reading an extract from a letter he received from Timothy Bahti, former Professor in the Departments of German and Comparative Literature at the University of Michigan. We found this letter neither in the typescript of the session nor in the Jacques Derrida archives at IMEC. The following extract is reproduced from a copy of the letter, which is dated February 23, 2003 [and written in French], as provided by its author,.

as imaginary. But always oriented toward the index, toward the one who bears, him too, indexes (stigmata).

There. Thank you Tim Bahti . . . is he here? Thank you, this is perfect and a very good introduction, a very good sequel and a very good introduction to today's session.}

As always, always, when I speak or when I write, or when I do *both,* when I teach, as always, always, at each step, with each word I have a sense or presentment, in the future perfect, of the ungraspably spectral figure of an event which could, after the event, put back on stage—a stage as yet invisible and unforeseeable for anyone at all—put back on stage, then, from top to bottom, everything that will have been . . . dictated, whispered to me, I mean by that more or less consciously, or telepathically, or somnambulistically, intimated from within me or enjoined on me from very far outside.

So that I will never say, with the required assurance of indubitable certainty, never will I venture to say: here now, presently, indubitably "I think" (*cogito, sum*) or again, like Heidegger, "we are not yet thinking." I would say, rather: I pre-sense that I do not yet sense, I do not sense it yet but I pre-sense it, I sense that I pre-sense it, I pre-sense that I sense it but I do not yet sense it, and I know still less what will not fail to happen. As though I were forewarned of what I do not see coming.

When I wrote one day, in "Circumfession," if I remember correctly, "I posthume as I breathe,"[2] that's pretty much what I wanted to have felt, rather than thought, or even speculated, or it's pretty much what I wanted to have myself pre-sense. In "I posthume," beyond the obvious sense of the postmortem future perfect, I was playing with breathing and the scent of pre-sensing, of *humer* [to smell, to breathe in] with the sense of having a nose for it, as they say for what, according to me [*d'après moi*], will come after me [*après moi*], even though I do not see it coming, anticipating without anticipating, sensing in the sense that one says that animals sense, and do better with scent and with noses, than we humans, when animals sense catastrophes coming that we do not see coming, for example earthquakes that certain animals register long before we do, even before the earthquake breaks surface, if I can put it like that; I had the feeling, when I said "I post-

249

2. Jacques Derrida, "Circonfession," in *Jacques Derrida,* in collaboration with Geoffrey Bennington (Paris: Le Seuil, 1991), p. 28; trans. Geoffrey Bennington as "Circumfession," in *Jacques Derrida* (Chicago: University of Chicago Press, 1993; 2nd ed. 1999), p. 26.

hume as I breathe," of playing with *humer* rather than playing with earth, *humus,* the earth of burial that a hasty and false etymology thinks it can find in the word "posthumous" to which I shall return in a moment. In saying "I posthume as I breathe," I thought I meant that nothing is, like breathing itself, as natural, spontaneous, habitual, unreflective, reflexive, indispensable to life as being obsessed with the postmortem, fascinated, worried and interpellated, and I thought I was playing in crossing the sense of what comes after death, the flair of breathing, and what comes after burial.

In truth, posthumous, *posthumus* with an *h,* appears to be a faulty spelling, the grammarians tell us, and the spelling error in it is apparently induced by the proximity with *humus,* earth. Littré cites one of these errors in Servius who speaks of a *post humatam matrem.* And Littré adds: "it would be appropriate for the Academy to correct the faulty spelling." It's like for differance, with an *a,* which is another way to posthume by differing or deferring life or, what comes down to the same thing, deferring death. In truth, *postume,* without an *h,* apparently corresponds to the superlative of *posterus. Posterus* qualifies the one who comes after, the one who follows. *Posterus* is the follower or the descendent, the one who is going to come, or even the future itself, posthumous, the superlative here meaning the last follower of all, and above all the one who, being born after the death of the father, child or grandchild, posterity, bears the testamentary future and the fidelity of the inheritance.

250   Well, as you can imagine, this presentment that speculates without knowledge on the posthumous, was a peculiarly premonitory, pressing, pre-sensing presentment last week in all I said — or discreetly avoided saying, with restraint, during the great ratiocinating altercation, the great *argument,* as they say in English to signify dispute, contestation, debate, the great argument between so many living dead in mourning, that I called the *inhumers* and the *cremators.*

It might have looked sometimes like a story about crazy people [*fous*] and crowds [*foules*], in which two waves [*houles*] of demonstrators and counter-demonstrators, at the gates of a cemetery-crematorium, were declaring phantasm-war on each other, with fisticuffs to decide who would win, and if at the end one were going to die alive and burned or alive and buried, although each party must know that at bottom it all made no sense for the dead people they would indeed be one day, because in any case one dies, and one always dies alive and one never dies alive. And that therefore they needed to go home and attempt, in the interval of differance, for as long as possible, attempt to rethink the whole business and to learn again how to talk about it.

I knew that in giving myself over in this way to presentment and premo-
nition, I was running like a daredevil, like a stuntman or like a crazy person
in the crowd of as yet nameless phantoms, my own among many others. I
knew especially that for a long time, for as long as I can remember, and
in a still more threatening way for the last week, so for three weeks back
from today, that Maurice Blanchot was dying, dying a death more immi-
nent than ever. And I already knew that he had opted for cremation. And I
could long have said of Blanchot dying what you can read in *The Last Man:*
"I became convinced that I had first known him when he was dead, then
when he was dying."[3]

The cremation of Maurice Blanchot has just taken place.[4] According to   *251*
his wishes, they say. The cremation took place the day before yesterday, in
conditions, in a landscape, and in a provincial crematorium among the most
unheimlich one could imagine in the twenty-first century, but that I do not
have the heart to talk about here today. The death of Blanchot is for me, as
it is for his friends, his readers, and his admirers, a mournful loss, and, as it
should be for this mourning and no doubt for every mourning, a mourning
without measure, an incommensurable mourning. Of course, you all know
who Maurice Blanchot was, even if you are not French, and I would even
say, alas, with painful irony, *especially* if you are not French (because there
would be so much to say here about the censoring and marginalizing limits
of hexagonality[5] in the worldliness of the cultural world, the world of images and the world of books).

You all know who Maurice Blanchot is in this century, and all the radiat-
ing and abyssal marks that his presence, and his retreat, will have left on it
forever. I wager that they will count more durably in the future, and will remain more discreetly indelible than those of many others, among the most

3. Maurice Blanchot, *Le dernier homme* (Paris: Gallimard, 1957), p. 12; *The Last
Man,* trans. Lydia Davis (New York: Columbia University Press, 1987), p. 4.
4. The cremation of Maurice Blanchot took place Monday, February 24, 2003. Derrida was in attendance, along with Jean-Luc Nancy, among those close to the writer.
The only one to speak at the ceremony, Derrida read the text entitled "To Maurice
Blanchot," which closes the collection *Chaque fois unique, la fin du monde* (Paris: Galilée,
2003), pp. 323–32. The following pages, with some additions by Derrida, were reprised
in the second part of the text entitled "Maurice Blanchot est mort" in the new edition
of *Parages* (Paris: Galilée, 2003), pp. 283–99; they were also published in the conference
proceedings *Maurice Blanchot, Récits critiques,* ed. Christophe Bident and Pierre Vilar
(Tours: Éditions Farrago; Paris: Éditions Léo Scheer, 2003) pp. 608–22.
5. [Translator's note:] French speakers often refer to France as "l'hexagone," because
of its general geometric shape.

visible, the most noisily present in the media and the most popular, who, in society, make the front page and the other pages of written and televised news (I am not only thinking here of politics and war).

Some of you, here, know what and who Maurice Blanchot will have been and remains for me, Blanchot the friend, the thinker and writer whose immense oeuvre has stood watch over and around what matters to me, for a long time behind me and forever still before me. I will never finish paying tribute to Maurice Blanchot. And if the word "gratitude" still has any meaning, more than one meaning, more than just meaning, this is the moment to declare, very soberly, but with a bottomless melancholy, to the memory in me of Maurice Blanchot, my gratitude.

252

Allow me to say no more about this today. "Die Welt is fort, ich muss dich tragen," Celan wrote one day.

The world comes to be lacking. "The world was lacking," is also a quotation. "The world was lacking," four words one can also read in the opening pages of *The One Who Did Not Accompany Me.*[6] On Celan's death, Blanchot wrote the text, a short and dense book, entitled *The Last One to Speak;* and these title words were also words of Celan: "Sprich auch du,/sprich als letzter,/sag deinen Spruch [speak, you too,/speak as the last to speak,/have your say]."[7]

So as to let him speak today, and have the last word (*The Last Word* is one of his titles, an eschatological title by definition—eschatological means the last word, the *logos* or the verb of the end—it was, then, the title of a brief narrative turning around the *il y a,* collected in *Après coup,*[8] and there is also a text entitled "The Very Last Word," which dates from May 1968 and which was collected in *Friendship*[9])—so as to let him have the last word so

---

6. Maurice Blanchot, *Celui qui ne m'accompagnait pas* (Paris: Gallimard, 1953), p. 25. [Translator's note: my translation.] Complete English translation: *The One Who Was Standing Apart From Me,* collected in *The Station Hill Blanchot Reader: Fiction and Literary Essays,* ed. George Quasha, trans. Lydia Davis, Paul Auster, and Robert Lamberton (Barrytown, N.Y.: Station Hill Press, 1999), pp. 263–339.

7. Maurice Blanchot, *Le dernier à parler* (Montpellier: Fata Morgana, 1984), pp. 46–47. [Translator's note: my translation.]

8. Maurice Blanchot, *Après coup,* preceded by *Le rassasement éternel* (Paris: Minuit, 1983).

9. Maurice Blanchot, "Le tout dernier mot," in *L'amitié* (Paris: Gallimard, 1971). Both "The Last Word" and "The Very Last Word" appear in the English translation of *Friendship,* trans. Elizabeth Rottenberg (Stanford, Calif.: Stanford University Press, 1997), pp. 252–64; 265–88.

that he can be at this moment the last one to speak of his death and of the death which has been here our subject for weeks, allow me to quote Blanchot himself—not from *The Instant of My Death,* as one would so rightly be tempted to do, and as I did not long ago,[10] but around the word "companion" or the vocabulary of *friendship* as accompaniment that does not accompany. I shall merely read a few words from *The Last One to Speak* and from *The One Who Did Not Accompany Me.*

In *The Last One to Speak,* again an eschatological title, like *The Last Word,* "The Very Last Word" and *The Last Man,* in *The Last One To Speak,* this great little book that Blanchot sent in 1984 with, among other words of dedication, the following, which I'm taking from a longer letter: "this modest present which takes all its value from the memory of him [Paul Celan, then], so admirable, that we were unable to save from the shipwreck;" in *The Last One to Speak,* then, the first words bespeak both death and the companion lost in advance. I quote:

> Plato: *For of death there is no knowledge,* and Paul Celan: *No-one bears witness for the witness.* [This seems to imply, among so many other things, that on the death of someone, and particularly the death of a friend or a companion, no one has the right to speak in the place of the dead one, for the dead one (in every sense of "for," in his place or to praise him). Blanchot goes on:] And yet, we always choose a companion for ourselves: not for us, but for something in us, outside of us, which needs us to be lacking to ourselves to pass over the line we will not attain. Companion lost in advance, loss itself, which is henceforth in our place.[11]

"[. . .] to be lacking to ourselves to pass over the line we will not attain." We shall see in a moment what is meant here by attaining and awaiting [*atteindre et attendre*], awaiting or attaining, awaiting without attaining or still awaiting at the moment of attaining, still waiting after having attained, and what this impossible death, that was an important motif in Blanchot's thought, means. "[. . .] to be lacking to ourselves to pass over the line we will not attain." This lacking to oneself, like the lack named in the syntagma "the world was lacking" (and so everything, the whole was lacking, we are in a sense *weltlos*), this steadfast lack, this lack without defection, this lack without negativity, hollows things out, i.e. inscribes and signs its affirma-

253

10. J. Derrida, *Demeure — Maurice Blanchot* (Paris: Galilée, 1996); trans. Elizabeth Rottenberg in *The Instant of My Death/Demeure: Fiction and Testimony* (Stanford, Calif.: Stanford University Press, 2000).

11. Blanchot, *Le dernier à parler,* p. 9.

tion also at the end, right near the signature of *The One Who Did Not Accompany Me:* (read *The One Who Did Not Accompany Me* pages 173 to 174 [338 to 339], from "Perhaps everything that dies . . .")

254   Perhaps everything that dies, even the day, comes close to man, asks of man the secret of dying. All this will not last very much longer. Already, I sense in a distant way that I no longer have the right to call out to my companion—and would he still hear me? where is he right now? perhaps very near here? perhaps he is right under my hand? perhaps he is the one my hand is slowly pushing away, distancing once again? No, don't distance him, don't push him away, draw him to you instead, lead him to you, clear the way for him, call him, call him softly by his name. By his name? I mustn't call him, and at this moment I couldn't. You can't? at this moment? But it is the only moment, it is urgently necessary, you haven't said everything to him, the essential part is missing, the description must be completed, "It must be. Now! Now!" What have I forgotten? why doesn't everything disappear? why is it someone else who is entering the sphere? then, who is the one involved here? wasn't it I who took the drink? was it he? was it everyone? that wasn't possible, there was a misunderstanding, it had to be brought to an end. All the force of the day had to strain toward that end, rise toward it, and perhaps he answered immediately, but when the end came, after the scattering of a few seconds, everything had already disappeared, disappeared with the day.[12]

And finally, if I can say that, among so very many other places in an oeuvre that, on the subject of impossible death, still awaits reading and rereading, by you and by us, here almost at random is a passage from *Awaiting Oblivion:* (Read)

❖ He had endured waiting. Waiting made him eternal, and now he has nothing more to do than to wait eternally.

Waiting waits. Through waiting, he who waits dies waiting. He maintains waiting in death and seems to make of death the waiting for that which is still awaited when one dies.

Death, considered as an event that one awaits, is incapable of putting an end to waiting. Waiting transforms the fact of dying into something that one does not merely have to attain in order to cease waiting. Waiting is what allows us to know that death cannot be awaited.

255   He who lives in a state of waiting sees life come to him as the emptiness of waiting and waiting as the emptiness of the beyond of life. The unstable indeterminateness of these two movements is henceforth the space of waiting. At every step, one is here, and yet beyond. But as one attains this beyond without attaining it through death, it is awaited and not attained;

12. *The Blanchot Reader,* pp. 338–39.

without knowing that its essential characteristic is to be able to be attained only in waiting.

When there is waiting, nothing is awaited. In the movement of waiting, death ceases to be able to be awaited. Waiting, in the intimate tranquillity at the heart of which everything that comes to pass is diverted by waiting, does not let come to pass as that which could be adequate to waiting but rather keeps it in suspense, in dissolution, and at every instant surpassed by the empty sameness of waiting.

The strange opposition of waiting and death. He awaits death, in a waiting indifferent to death. And, similarly, death does not let itself be awaited.

❖ The dead came back to life dying.[13]

How to go on? How to leave Blanchot? Blanchot's body, as I was saying, was cremated, really just a few hours ago. It was cremated according to what was reported to have been his wish. Defoe, Robinson Crusoe, Heidegger, for their part, were buried. The posthumous is becoming the very element, mixes in everywhere with the air we are breathing. As for cremation and the ashes that, from now on, in the modern and ineffaceable history of humanity (as we were wondering last time: what is modernity? and one of the answers we suggested was that it was the opening of the alternative and the choice left by the state, in European and Greco-Abrahamic cultures, between cremation and inhumation)—as for cremation, then, and the ashes that, from now on, in the modern and ineffaceable history of humanity, can no longer fail to metonymize, in everyone's consciousness and unconscious, the crematoria of the camps, let us forget nothing, and let us not forget that Blanchot, who will have constantly recalled our thought to this, when he quotes the poem by Celan, "Niemand / zeugt für den / Zeugen [No one / bear witness for the / witness]," is quoting a poem from *Strette,* that precisely begins—this is its title and its opening—with ashes and the path that is occupying us to such an extent here, the path of the hand, the hands of the path, the *che-mains, Aschenglorie* ("*ASCHENGLORIE hinter / deinen erschüttert-verknoteten / Händen am Dreiweg* [ASHGLORY behind your shaken-knotted hands at the threeway"]),[14] the word "glory," *Glorie,* lighting here both the glory that fires up memory and the light, or incendiary or

256

---

13. Maurice Blanchot, *L'attente l'oubli* (Paris: Gallimard, 1962), pp. 55–56; trans. John Gregg as *Awaiting Oblivion* (Lincoln and London: University of Nebraska Press, 1997), pp. 27–28; translation slightly modified for the sake of consistency with Derrida's reading.

14. Paul Celan, "ASCHENGLORIE," in *Atemwende* (Frankfurt-am-Main: Suhrkamp, 1967), p. 68; trans. Pierre Joris as "Ashglory," in *Paul Celan: Selections* (Berkeley and Los Angeles: University of California Press, 2005), p. 104.

crematory incandescence smoldering under its ashes or smoldering ashes themselves; these are the first lines of which the last are, precisely, "No one / bears witness for the / witness."

Last week, during the discussion, I insinuated that there exists an analogy, the analogy of a fiction, perhaps literary fiction, between *Robinson Crusoe* and Heidegger's seminar, in 1929–1930, on world, finitude and solitude, in truth on the animal, and the animal that does not die, on death that is not lived as such by the animal "poor in world." A death that is then for it, for the animal, impossible, in a certain sense—I say in a certain sense because Heidegger also says (these are texts, especially in *Sein und Zeit,* that I have studied and questioned elsewhere, especially in *Aporias,*[15] I do not want to return to them here) that death is, for *Dasein,* the possibility of the impossible.

So we would here need to distinguish between the impossible (dying, for the animal) and the possibility of the impossible (dying, for Dasein). You can sense the fragile consistency, if not the inconsistency of this difference, basically the difference between the impossible and the impossible, between the impossible and the possibility of the impossible as such.[16]

257   Now, Blanchot never ceased dwelling in these places that are uninhabitable for thought, be it this question of the impossible and of the possibility of the impossible, or be it the fictional, even literary space that accepts the living of death, becoming living dead, and even the phantasm of the one buried alive.

First, then, the aporia of the possible impossible. One of the texts in which the impossibility of dying most visibly holds thought in suspense, would be found perhaps, for exemplary example, in *The Writing of the Disaster* (1980), a work that is constantly traversed and travailed by the question of fire and light, but also by "the burn of the Holocaust." Disaster, the word "disaster" is itself determined, situated by the light come from the sky ("If disaster means being separated from the star (if it means the decline which characterizes disorientation when the link with fortune from on high is cut), then it indicates a fall beneath disastrous necessity."[17]). Or again *"Night; white,*

15. See Jacques Derrida, *Apories* (Paris: Galilée, 1996), especially pp. 124–35; trans. Thomas Dutoit as *Aporias* (Stanford, Calif.: Stanford University Press, 1993), pp. 70–77.

16. In the session, Derrida added: "It is a very fragile difference, barely thinkable, barely determinable: it is a difference between the death of the animal and death for Dasein. Death is impossible for the animal, but for man, for Dasein, death is also impossible; it is the possibility of the impossible. Dasein has the power to die its own death, as impossible. Fragile difference."

17. Maurice Blanchot, *L'écriture du désastre* (Paris: Gallimard, 1980), p. 9; trans. Ann Smock as *The Writing of the Disaster* (Lincoln and London: University of Nebraska Press, 1995), p. 2.

sleepless night — such is the disaster: the night is lacking darkness, but brightened by no light."[18] Or again: "The disaster, whose blackness should be attenuated—through emphasis—exposes us to a certain idea of passivity. We are passive with respect to the disaster, but the disaster is perhaps passivity, and thus past, always past, even in the past, out of date."[19] And further on, and I would say consequently, by the consequence of this "always past," he also names, followed by a question mark, "The posthumous disaster?"[20] and especially, lastly, among all these pages I am asking you to reread, *"The calm, the burn of the holocaust, the annihilation of noon — the calm of the disaster."*[21]

I was saying, then, on the subject of the aporia of the possible impossible, that one of the texts in which the impossibility of dying holds thought in suspense, would be found perhaps, for exemplary example, in *The Writing of the Disaster,* when, on the subject of "the glorious, terrifying, tyrannical *infans,* whom one cannot kill,"[22] Blanchot comes on to the question of death, of murder and of suicide. He writes for example: (Read what follows in *The Writing of the Disaster,* pages 113 to 115 [68 to 71], from "But perhaps suicide should be considered differently . . .")

258

> It remains, however, that if death, murder, suicide are *put to work* [I underline, the point here is to know how these deaths can make work, write themselves, *put themselves to work*] and if death loses its sting by becoming powerless power [*puissance impuissante*] [Heidegger: comment[23]] and then negativity, there is, each time one advances with the help of *possible* death, the necessity not to advance any further, not to approach the death without expression, the death without any name, the death outside the concept—*impossibility* itself. [Comment: *against* Heidegger?[24]] [. . .]
>
> But perhaps suicide should be considered differently.
>
> It is possible that suicide is the way in which the unconscious (the wake, the vigilance of what cannot awaken), warns us that something rings false in the dialectic, by reminding us that the child always still to be killed is the

18. Ibid., p. 8 [p. 2] (the italics are Blanchot's).
19. Ibid., p. 9 [p. 3].
20. Ibid., p. 13 [p. 5].
21. Ibid., p. 15 [p. 6] (the italics are Blanchot's).
22. Ibid., p. 112 [p. 68].
23. In the session, Derrida added: "This is a quasi-translation, a quasi-synonym of the 'possibility of the impossible.'" See this passage as modified in "Maurice Blanchot est mort," in *Parages,* p. 289, and *Maurice Blanchot, Récits critiques,* p. 613.
24. In the session, Derrida added: "And that, I imagine, though I cannot prove it, is a critique of Heidegger: impossibility itself, not the possibility of the impossible of which Heidegger speaks, but impossibility pure and simple." See this passage as modified in "Maurice Blanchot est mort," in *Parages,* p. 289, and *Maurice Blanchot, Récits critiques,* p. 613.

child already dead and that thus, in suicide—in what we call suicide—
nothing at all happens. Whence the feeling of incredulity, or fright, which
suicide always provokes in us, at the same time that it incites the desire to
refute it, that is, to make it real, which is to say, impossible. The "nothing
happens" of suicide can perfectly well take on the form of an event in a
story which thereby—by this bold end (the apparent result of purpose-
ful initiative)—displays an individual *bent:* but the enigma is precisely
that in killing myself, "I" do not kill "me," but, giving away the secret as
it were, someone (or something) uses a vanishing me—as a figure for an
Other—the better to reveal to him, and to all, what immediately escapes:
the belatedness of death, the immemorial past of ancient death. There is
no death now or in the future (no death whose present is to come). Suicide
is perhaps—it is no doubt—a fraud, but it has for its stakes to make for
an instant evident—hidden—the other fraud which is the death known
as organic or natural, and which is fraudulent to the extent that it claims
to present itself as distinct, definitively separate and not to be confounded,
able to take place only once, like that banality, the utterly unique, the unthinkable.

But what would the difference be between death by suicide and death
by any other cause (if there is such a thing)? The difference is that the first,
by entrusting itself to the dialectic (entirely founded upon the *possibility* of
death, upon the use of death as power) is the obscure oracle which we do
not decipher, but thanks to which we sense, and ceaselessly forget, that he
who has been all the way to the end of the desire for death, invoking his
right to death and exerting over himself a power of death, he who opens,
as Heidegger said, *the possibility of impossibility*—or again, he who believes
himself to be master of un-mastery—lets himself get caught in a sort of
trap and halts eternally (halts, obviously, just an instant) at the point where,
ceasing to be a subject, losing his stubborn liberty, and becoming other than
himself, he comes up against death as that which doesn't happen or as that
which reverses itself (betraying, as though demented, the mendacity of the
dialectic by bringing it to its conclusion)—reverses the possibility of impossibility into *the impossibility of every possibility.*[25]

Suicide is in a sense a demonstration (whence its arrogant, hurtful, in-
discreet character), and what it demonstrates is the undemonstrable: that
in death nothing comes to pass and that death itself does not pass (whence
the vanity and the necessity of its repetitiveness). But from this aborted
demonstration there remains the following: that we die "naturally," of the
death that requires no fuss and is of no note conceptually (this affirmation
is always to be put into doubt), only if, through a constant, an inapparent
and *preliminary* suicide, accomplished by no one, we encounter (of course,

25. In the session, Derrida added: "There he overturns Heidegger's formula."

it is not "we") the semblance of the end of history, when everything returns
to nature (a nature which is supposed to be denatured), and when death,
ceasing to be an always double death, having apparently exhausted the infinite passivity of dying, reduces itself to the simplicity of something natural,
more insignificant and more uninteresting than the collapse of a little heap   *260*
of sand.[26]

Second, the fiction and the phantasm of the one buried alive. We could
have quoted, last time, on the subject of the terror of being buried alive or
of being walled-in alive, a large number of literary and fantastic texts, for
example by Poe. And no doubt many others. I shall content myself today
with mentioning to you another text by Blanchot, a very old one. It could be
one or other of the two versions of *Thomas the Obscure,* in which this fan-
tastics, this phantasmatics of being buried alive is everywhere. I shall return
to this. But I prefer first to turn to one of the essays gathered in *The Work
of Fire* (precisely) which, in 1945, in a reading of Kafka, a reading which,
like the syntagmas "living death" or "be buried alive," endures and exceeds
the dialectical opposition and the formal contradiction of yes and no, the
contradiction of all contraries.

I quote, and these are the last pages of the chapter or the study which,
precisely, bear the title "The Language of Fiction": (Read *The Work of Fire,*
pages 89 to 91 [83 to 84], from "Where is death's rest? O Death, where is thy
victory?")

> Where is death's rest? O Death, where is thy victory?
> Kafka experienced very deeply the relationships of transcendence and
> death. And that is why, in his work, sometimes it is death that appears
> to beings as that to which they cannot attain, sometimes it is that which
> surpasses beings that appears in the unworking and misery of death. Some-
> times death appears as transcendence, sometimes transcendence appears
> dead. This reversal already shows how dangerous it is to claim to fix, in
> an explicit form, the interpretation of a story in which negation is at work
> and shows itself just as well as the nothing that prevents the absolute from
> being accomplished except as nothingness that measures absolute accom-   *261*
> plishment. The passage from yes to no, from no to yes, is the rule here, and
> all interpretation that avoids this (including that which hypostasizes this
> alternation) contradicts the movement that makes it possible. To see in K.'s
> story the image of the unhappiness of existence that cannot be grasped as
> existence because it cannot be found as the end of existence, remaining un-

26. Blanchot, *L'écriture du désastre,* pp. 112, 113–15 [pp. 68, 69–71] (except for the
first occurrence signaled by Derrida, the italics are Blanchot's).

real, self-negating, insofar as it is not capable of being really nonexistence, profundity of that which is beyond life, assertion of nothingness without memory — it is clear that such interpretation vainly contains the ambiguity of a proposition in which assertion and negation are in continuous threat of reciprocity. As long as it rests in the well-determined form of an abstract thought, it escapes the verdict it renders and it fundamentally disobeys the symbol, losing all its meaning the moment it isolates this meaning and makes it discernable.

So one must plunge the interpretation back into the heart of the story, lose it there and lose it from view, and grasp again the movement of fiction whose details assert only themselves. The inn, the peasants with their stubborn, frustrated faces, the iced light of the snow, Klamm's pince-nez, the pools of beer in which Frieda and K. roll — that is what matters, that is what one must experience to enter into the life of the symbol. There is nothing else to look for, nothing more to understand. And yet, one cannot be content with that either. Bury oneself in the story? But the story itself rejects you. Each episode contains a question about itself, and this question is also the profound life of fiction; it is the story, it shows itself face to face, it asserts itself, it converses. Where is the symbol? Where it appears, where it hides? Where there are only calm, firm appearances, where appearances grate and are torn apart? Where things are present with their natural obscurity, where behind things their emptiness emerges, behind the story the absence of story, behind the profundity of symbol the impossibility that erodes the work and forbids its accomplishment? It is these very questions, and it dies from these questions. In this sense, every symbol that does not ruin the work in which it develops is ruined in the commentaries it provokes, that it cannot prevent itself from provoking. It must, to subsist, be aware of itself in fiction, and those who make it known, make it sterile by declaring it.

Such is the last ambiguity: it vanishes if it awakens; it perishes if it comes to light. Its condition is to be *buried alive,* and in that it is indeed its own symbol, symbolized by what it symbolizes: death that is life, that is death as soon as it survives.[27]

The logic of the phantasm, as we are concerned with it here (be it about living death, the ghost or the revenant, about cremation or the posthumous), [this logic of the phantasm] is not strictly speaking a logic, it resists the *logos,* the *legein* of the *logos,* somewhat in the same way as the eschato-logical is both the thing of the *logos* and what exceeds and comes after the *logos,* the

27. Maurice Blanchot, *La part du feu* (Paris: Gallimard, 1949), pp. 89–91; trans. Charlotte Mandell as *The Work of Fire* (Stanford, Calif.: Stanford University Press, 1995), pp. 83–84 (the italics are Blanchot's).

logic of the *logos*, the extremity of the last, of the last word or the last man, the extremity of the last extremity situated both *in* speech, in *logos* as the last word, still and already out of speech, falling out of it into the posthumous that it is already breathing, precisely, the logic of the phantasm resists, defies and dislocates *logos* and logic in all its figures, be it a question of *logos* as reason and as the logic of non-contradiction and the excluded middle, of yes or no, of the yes and the no, of the decidable either/or, be it a question of *logos* as speech or be it a question of *logos* as gathering and the power of putting together. There is therefore no *logic of the phantasm,* strictly speaking, since, as Freud reminds us, the phantasm, just as much as the drive, is to be found on both sides of the limit between two opposing concepts, like what Blanchot nicknames, especially in *The Step Not Beyond* (we shall come to this in a moment), the neuter. There is therefore no logic or *logos* of the phantasm or of the ghost or of the spectral. Unless the *logos* itself be precisely *the* phantasm, the very element, the origin and the resource of the phantasm itself, the form and the formation of the phantasm, or even of the revenant.

This is why all the things we're dealing with here, sovereignty, the animal, the living dead, the buried alive, etc., the spectral and the posthumous — well, the dream, the oneiric, fiction, so-called literary fiction, so-called fantastic literature will always be less inappropriate, more relevant, if you prefer, than the authority of wakefulness, and the vigilance of the ego, and the consciousness of so-called philosophical discourse.   *263*

Let us take as witnesses to this, so as to remain as long as possible with Blanchot, certain narratives, certain fragments of these narratives that I believe have not yet truly begun to be read.

In order to think (but what does one call thinking? The question is here more acute and more urgent than ever since the point was to think the *logos* beyond the *logos*, to think the phantasm, the *phantasmata,* the phantoms and the revenants beyond the *logos*), well, in order to think the phantasm is what one believes one can oppose *to,* or rigorously distinguish *from,* the effective reality of what happens, and therefore from the undeniable effectivity of the event,[28] it is necessary to think something like a *phantasm of the event* (at bottom, what Freud pointed out about a certain scene of seduction whose very reality, effectivity and eventhood come under the phantasmatic, belong to the phantasmatic, which does not necessarily entail that the phantasm itself was not, as phantasm or as phantom, a real psychic event, with real and *undeniable* consequences), it is necessary, then, to think this thing-

---

28. In the session, Derrida added: "the supposed undeniable effectivity of the event."

less thing that a phantasm of the event would be, but also by the same token, an event of the phantasm, a phantom of the event and an event, a coming or supervening of the phantom.

This phantom of the event is what is explicitly named by the fiction entitled *When the Time Comes.*[29] We're dealing with what the narrator calls "a terrible thing," of which "no one could ever say that it had already taken place," a scene in which it is also a matter of a "decomposed" body, of a "dream body" which had "decomposed," and finally of a "grave," and a "phantom of the event." As often in Blanchot, the terror of this scene never excludes, to the contrary, the affirmation of joy, gaiety, "the jubilant celebration of the future."[30] Nothing less melancholic. I quote: (Read and comment *At the Right Moment,* page 132 [248], start from "A terrible scene," as far as page 135 [249], to the end . . .)

264

> A terrible scene, but one that left me with a feeling of joy, of limitless pleasure. That wonderful head that had been uplifted, what could be more true, and if it had been thrown down lower than the earth, that was just as much part of the exaltation, that was proof of it, the moment when one no longer worshiped the majesty of a piece of debris, but seized it and tore it apart.
>
> I think the vitality of that scene was all the more overwhelming because it was contained in two or three gestures. What had been depicted was inscribed on an infinitely thin film, but behind it rumbled the freedom of pure caprice in which the taste for blood hadn't been awakened. No one could say of such a scene that it had never taken place before; it had occurred a first time and only once and its exuberance was the energy of the origin, from which nothing springs. Even when I went back over it to "think" about it—and it required that: an intense meditation—it didn't take me anywhere; face to face we held each other, not at a distance, but in the intimacy of a mysterious familiarity, because she was "you" for me, and I was "me" for her.
>
> What could I have said about it? She wasn't for one moment unforgettable, she didn't want to be held sacred: even when she was terrifying, there was something extraordinarily cheerful about her. No doubt this could not be relived, the moment of collapse, the dreadful alteration of life, unable to control itself, was a blow to memory—and afterwards? afterwards, chaos and yet I swear the last instant infinitely surpassed all the others, because

29. Maurice Blanchot, *Au moment voulu* (Paris: Gallimard, 1951); *When the Time Comes,* in *The Blanchot Reader,* pp. 203–60. During the session, Derrida specified the genre of the work as a "récit."

30. Ibid., p. 135 [p. 249].

it was on me that this dream body had decomposed, I had held it in my arms, I had experienced its strength, the strength of a dream, of a desperate gentleness, defeated and still persevering, such as only a creature with avid eyes could communicate it to me.

I would like to say this: when a man has lived through something unforgettable, he shuts himself up with it to grieve over it, or he sets off to find it again; he thus becomes the ghost of the event. But this face did not concern itself with memory, it was fixed but unstable. Had it happened once? A first time and yet not the first. It had the strangest relations with time, and this was uplifting too: it did not belong to the past, a face and the promise of that face. In some way it had looked at itself and seized itself in one single instant, after which this terrifying contact had occurred, this mad catastrophe, which could certainly be considered its fall into time, but that fall had also crossed time and carved out an immense emptiness, and this pit appeared to be the jubilant celebration of the future: a future that would never again be new, just as the past refused to have taken place once.[31]

265

As for what literary fiction or the fantastic narrative can stage as to the indecision or undecidability between two living beings, what is called simply the animal, and the human beast, I invite you to read or reread one or other, one and the other, of the two versions of *Thomas the Obscure*. The first version, impossible to get hold of these days,[32] and which I am lucky enough to have, dates from 1941, and is Blanchot's first book. It is in highly enigmatic fashion and—demanding a comparison that I partially tried to do in a seminar about thirty years ago[33]—much longer, at least three times longer than the second version which appeared almost ten years later, in 1950. Reread at least chapter 5 of the second version, the only one now available. For my part, I will read from the first version—since I have it and you will have great difficulty finding it—some passages that correspond to this chapter 5 of the second version, while exceeding it to a great extent. It is in chapter 8 of the first version, at the very beginning, that there unfolds, like an immense phantasm, the apocalyptic, and thus political and metamorphic scene of beasts and beasts, of the "I am dead" and of what Deleuze would perhaps have called the becoming-animal. Here the becoming-animal of

266

31. Ibid., pp. 132–35 [pp. 248–49].

32. This first version was republished in 2005 (Paris: Gallimard), with an introduction by Pierre Madaule entitled "Retour d'épave."

33. This an allusion to an unpublished seminar given by Derrida in 1976–77 at Yale and the École normale supérieure, entitled "Blanchot—*Thomas l'obscur.*" The catalog entry for the collection of Derrida's papers at UC Irvine mentions two copies and eight sessions, "possibly incomplete, given in the spring, transcripts from tape recordings."

the narrator, the becoming-autobiographical-animal of the narrator. I shall read only fragments where, as always, it would be necessary to read and reread everything. Thomas might look like a Robinson since he is initially alone, "in a solitude that weighed upon him," we read on the first page, he is alone on the shore, between the earth and the sea. But if it were an island, it would be one inhabited by foreigners, and Thomas lives there not in his own house, but in a sort of hotel. There are so many hotels in Blanchot. In Blanchot [*chez lui*], people often live in a hotel. The I, the me of the narrator is often at home away from home, the guest of a hotel or a hospital, guest or hostage, at home in the other's home, in the other's home at home. In both versions, the narrative begins "Thomas sat down and looked at the sea." Then Thomas swims, "even though he felt" says the first page, "a sort of unease in going towards the region the boundaries of which were unknown to him." Then, "not far from him, whereas up until now he had been struggling with a solitude that weighed upon him, he noticed a swimmer [. . .]." It is not Friday, but read what follows. Here, much further on, other fragments I wanted to choose: (Read and comment *Thomas the Obscure,* first version, fragments pages 44–48)

> Toward the middle of the night Thomas got up and went downstairs silently. No-one saw him except for an almost blind cat who felt the night change shape and began to run after the new night he could not see. The cat slipped first into a tunnel in which, recognizing no scent and hearing nothing, it stopped, feeling as though it had fallen into a huge hole. Fur on end, it began to meow and made from the back of its throat the hoarse cry with which cats let you know they are sacred animals. It puffed itself up and howled. It drew from the idol it was becoming the incomprehensible voice that addressed the night and spoke to it. Then it brusquely fell silent and, running off as though it had discovered the password to every path, it bounded off after the prey that was fleeing it. This prey looked like a strange kind of dog whose ferocity, strength and ability to make any animal back off was precisely what attracted this eyeless and clawless cat. The image of the dog replaced for the cat the eyes that could accept no image, and this internal dog allowed it to see the being that was escaping it. Horribly mixed up cat-dog, it ran off in pursuit of the one that was a dog only because it was not a visible dog. Having jumped over a bush whose thorns it did not feel but which scratched its inner ancestral enemy, it went down a slope, slowing down, and at the bottom complained. [. . .] Between these two noise-extremities there stretched a kind of articulated language, a lamentation made of the inside of inexpressible words. As it felt this voice of an unknown kind come out of it, it was paralyzed by anxiety. It felt itself to be something other than a cat. It became the unheard-of being whose words

267

were being pronounced in its body. Human feelings that made it more inhuman than any beast were giving it access to an impure fear. Its mouth,
open on the words it was spewing out, was bloody. Its eyes, shining in the
night, were showing the shapes—impossible to see—that were being torn
in it. And it was continuing to expel in a diabolical monologue, like a cory-
phaeus from a tragedy it was reciting, frightening images it was perceiving
with its fur, its ears, its tongue, a beast of fire plunged in an invisible storm.
"What is happening?" it was groaning. "All the spirits I usually communicate with, the spirit that pulls my tail when the bowl is full, the spirit that
takes me away from the morning and puts me to sleep in a comfortable
quilt, and the best spirit of all, the one than meows, purrs and looks so
like me that it is like my own spirit—they have all vanished. Where am I
now? If I feel around gently with my paw, I find nothing. There is nothing
anywhere. [. . .] Already I am darker than this blackness. I am the night of
night. I am going, through shadows I am not because I am their shadow, to
meet the superior cat. Now there is no fear in me, although I am prey to this
void that is rolling and crushing me. My body, which is entirely like that
of a man, blessed body, has kept its dimensions, but my head is huge. [. . .]
But in the state I'm in I don't even have the means of feeling the fear that is
finishing voiding me. I am dead—dead. This head, my head, does not even
see me because I am annihilated. For it is I who am looking at myself and
cannot pick myself out. Oh superior cat that I became for a moment to cer-
tify my own death, like an official doctor, I am now going to disappear for
real. I first stop being a man. I become again a little cold and uninhabitable
cat, stretched out on the earth. I groan once more. I cast a final glance over
this valley that is going to close in again, and in which I see a man: him too
a superior cat. I hear him scratching the ground, probably with his claws.
What is called the beyond is over for me."

On his knees, his back bent, with on each finger a little shovel to replace
the nail, Thomas was trying to dig into the earth. Around him were some
shallow graves on the edge of which the day was held back. [. . .] For the
seventh time he was slowly preparing, leaving his handprints in the earth,
a kind of grave that he was widening to his size. And while he was digging
it, the void—as though it were filled with dozens of hands, then arms, and
finally by the whole body that was moving about in it, was offering to his
work a resistance that soon he could no longer vanquish. The grave was
full of a being whose absence it was absorbing. An immovable corpse was
sinking into it, finding in this absence the perfect form of its presence. It
was a drama the horror of which was felt by the men of the village in their
sleep. As soon as Thomas jumped into the grave he had finished, having
hung a large rock around his neck, he bumped into a body a thousand times
harder than the ground, the very body of the gravedigger who had already
got into the grave in order to dig it. This grave that had exactly his size,

his shape, his thickness, was like his own body, and every time he tried to bury himself in it, he looked like a ridiculous dead man trying to bury his body with his body. So from then on there were all the burial places where he might have taken his place, in all the feelings that are also graves for the dead, in that annihilation whereby he was dying without allowing anyone to think him dead, there was another dead man who had got there before him and who, in his identity with Thomas, was pushing the ambiguity of the death and life of Thomas to the extreme. In this subterrestrial night into which he had gone down with cats and dreams of cats, a double, wound in bandages, his senses closed with seven seals, his spirit absent, was occupying his place, and this double was the only one with whom he could not compromise, because it was the same as he, realized in the absolute void. He leant over that glacial grave. He felt before that abyss that he had opened the most terrible and powerful feeling of absence he had ever known. Like the man who hangs himself, having pushed away the stool on which he was still standing, the last shore, instead of feeling the leap he is making into the void, feels only the rope that holds him, held to the end, more than ever attached, bound as never before to the existence from which he would like to detach himself, he too, at the moment at which he knew himself to be dead, felt absent, quite absent from death. Whatever can be the terror and anguish of the man who awakes alive among the dead is nothing faced with the feeling he was creating for himself seeing himself dead without being able to treat himself as dead. Instead of the horror of Lady Madeline wandering underground, he was up against the worse horror of being faced with death as though he were not dead. Neither his body that left in his depths the cold that comes from contact with a corpse and which is not the cold, but the absence of contact, not the darkness that was oozing from his every pore and which, even when visible, meant that one could not use any sense, any intuition or any thought in order to see him, nor the fact that he could on no account pass for a living person was enough to have him pass for dead. And this was not a misunderstanding. He was really dead and at the same time pushed away from the reality of dead. In death itself he was deprived of death [. . .].³⁴

By way finally of a transition toward Heidegger and the motif of *walten* that still awaits us, I shall recall, then, that the neuter, what Blanchot calls the neuter, is situated (if, that is, one can speak here of place and topology) before and beyond that difference between Being and being, that difference that opens or is found to be open, which is found to open or to be opened by the possibility of manifestation, of the *Offenbarkeit* of the *as such,* namely

34. Maurice Blanchot, *Thomas l'obscur,* 1st version (Paris: Gallimard, 1941), pp. 44–48; new edition (Paris: Gallimard, 2005), pp. 72–78.

what is supposed to distinguish human Dasein from the animal. *Walten pro-duces, bears, brings about, opens* (all these words are not strictly relevant and are all inadequate for *Walten*), [*Walten produces, bears, brings about, opens*] the ontico-ontological difference and thus does not yet belong to either Being or beings. *Not yet* is not a chronological question about time, nor a logical question about order, but it designates a sort of pre-difference, or even   270
an in-difference to ontological difference, a pre-indifference that is nonetheless interested in difference and which prepares or precedes, outside the order of time and logical causality, the difference that it is not yet — or that it is without yet being. If it were a force or a violence, it would be nothing, but a nothing that is not nothing, a nothing that is not a thing, nor a being, nor Being, but which forces or efforces or enforces (as one might say, forcing the English), the difference between Being and beings. The *Walten* resembles this neuter which is neither this not that, neither positive nor negative, nor the dialectic, which neither is nor is not Being nor a being, but beyond or this side of Being and beings.

You imagine the consequences of this when it comes to the criterion of the *as such* which is occupying and will not cease occupying us. Blanchot formulates it literally in many passages in *The Step Not Beyond* (1973). For example this: (Read and comment *The Step Not Beyond,* pages 106–7 [76])

> If being reads itself, writes itself in the neuter, it is not, however, the case that the neuter comes before being, nor only that the neuter would give itself under the veil of difference between being and beings, neither being nor beings (rather the beyond of the two or the hither of the between-the-two), but that the neuter averts it in gently dissuading it from any presence, even a negative one, neutralizing it to the point of preventing it from being called the being of the neuter, even while leading it into the infinite erosion of negative repetition.
>
> The Neuter marks being, effect of every mark: the being marked in the neuter is not remarked and always forgets, in the brilliance of being, this mark of which even the brilliance is only an effect.
>
> The Neuter does not come first, eternal follower that precedes, so that the neuter is nowhere, functioning in language in every place as play of the mark, if that which marks unmarks, and, in the end, neutralizes as far as the line of demarcation that there could be no question, crossing it, of crossing. The transgression that is accomplished as not being accomplished, if it is also affirmed in the neuter, in the neutrality of a never present lure, could not, at least not as a proposition, mark the neuter as that which, always at   271
> play in transgression, would be precisely that which was to be transgressed. As if writing, the incessant movement of writing, freed us from the game of writing.

❖ The Neuter, the gentle prohibition against dying, there where, from threshold to threshold, eye without gaze, silence carries us into the proximity of the distant. Word still to be spoken beyond the living and the dead, *testifying to the absence of testimony.*[35]

Would we be leaving Blanchot if, abandoning here the living dead, the cremators and the inhumers, we were to return to the question "what is life?" at the point where, as we saw, *physis* and *walten* imply each other?

What to say before coming onto one of the most worrying difficulties of Heidegger's seminar, difficulties that will demand from us a reading always as patient as possible, both confident and vigilant, concerned to give credit without indulgence? I'm thinking here especially of that strange concept of *poverty in world* which according to Heidegger constitutes the essence of animality, a poverty which, he will tell us, does not consist in a quantitative relation of degree, of more or less, any more than it signifies an imperfection (the beasts are no less perfect than we are and no one of them is no less perfect than another). For Heidegger begins by suspending all credit given within animality to the hierarchical difference between so-called superior animals and so-called inferior animals. *Poverty in world* does not, supposedly, signify an inferiority. This is difficult to understand, but we must try to follow Heidegger in what he tells us he means by "poverty." The thesis "the animal is poor in world" which seems to concern the animal, might look like a zoological thesis. Is the animal not the object of the science called zoology? What makes us think of a resemblance between the thesis "the animal is poor in world" and the zoological thesis is that it seems analogous to propositions of the type (these are the ones now quoted by Heidegger): "the worker bees in the bee community communicate information about newly discovered feeding places by performing a sort of dance in the hive" (H, 274/186). This is the classic example that we studied, and questioned, and questioned critically last year in Lacan when the latter, speaking of the "dancity"[36] of the bees, wanted to see in it merely a fixed and programmed system of coded signs without language properly speaking, without signifier, without response and without other.

To this example of the zoological proposition, Heidegger adds this other example which is, one must say, just as elementary: "mammals have seven cervical vertebrae" (H, 274/186). To which he has no difficulty replying that the thesis "the animal is poor in world" is not of this order; it is say-

35. Maurice Blanchot, *Le pas au-delà* (Paris: Gallimard, 1973), pp. 106–7; trans. Lycette Nelson as *The Step Not Beyond* (Albany: SUNY Press, 1992), p. 76.
36. See Derrida, *La bête et le souverain, I,* session 4, p. 172 [p. 122].

ing nothing of insects or mammals. As it claims to be valid just as much for animals without limbs, for unicellular animals, amoebae and infusoria, urchins, it has an absolutely general scope, and concerns, as Heidegger says literally and with emphasis, *all* animals, *every* animal (alle *Tiere,* jedes *Tier*) (H, 275/186). Why the animal in general? Why is this thesis more general than the previously cited theses of zoology (*allgemeiner als die genannten Sätze*)? In what is the more general? Because the general thesis is a thesis on animality as such (*über die Tierheit als solche*). It is a thesis on the essence of the animal (*über das Wesen des Tieres*). It is an essential statement as *statement of essence* (*eine* Wesensaussage). And in the reversal that Heidegger then formulates, we can clearly understand his suspicion on the subject of zoological science: we understand the *logic* of the suspicion, but we can also find reason to be wary of the procedure thus engaged by Heidegger and the consequences with which it is heavy.

For Heidegger will say twice, in order to turn things around, "*umgekehrt*": "but conversely." Because he wishes clearly to mark that not only is this generality of the statement of essence not the effect of an empirical induction on the basis of particular examples or of animal species, insects, mammals, so-called inferior or superior animals, animals that zoology would already have taken as an object, but that, to the contrary, conversely, *umgekehrt,* zoology itself, in order to define itself and circumscribe its proper field of objectivity, must presuppose, without saying so and at bottom without thinking it, a general essence of animality, namely the very thesis that Heidegger is seeking to establish when he says "the animal is poor in world." Now this gesture, as I just said, is both strong with a certain philosophical necessity and heavy with many difficulties that we have not finished exploring. I quote:

> Expressed in a rather extrinsic way [*Von außen gesprochen*—and Heidegger goes on to show that this exteriority has to be overtaken, or inverted, because this exteriority leads us to think that the thesis is all the more general because it concerns *all* animals, *every* type or species of animal, *each* individual animal, but in truth, it is the converse: it is general, this thesis, it concerns all animals, each and every one of them, it is general because it bespeaks essence, the essential in essence: generality is founded on essence, on the intuition of essence (as Husserl had said), rather than essence being led astray by the generic multiplicity] [Expressed in a rather extrinsic way (*Von außen gesprochen*)] we could say that our thesis is more universal than these other propositions [the zoological propositions on the dance of the bee or the vertebrae of mammals, etc.]. Yet why is it more universal, and in what respect (*Aber warum und wie allgemeiner*)? Because this thesis is meant

273

to say something about animality as such, something about the essence of the animal: it is a *statement of essence* (*Weil die These etwas über die Tierheit als soche aussagen will, über das Wesen des Tieres—eine* Wesensaussage). It is not a statement of essence simply because it holds true for all animals and not merely for some of them. Rather, it is the other way around: it holds true for all animals because it is a statement of essence. Universal validity [*Allgemeingültigkeit*] can only result from our knowledge insofar as it is essential in each case, and not the other way around. (H, 275/187)

274

This comes down to saying, according to a properly phenomeno-ontological gesture and a procedure familiar to Husserl, that the objective science that zoology wishes to be must count with a presupposition and a predetermination (*Voraussetzung* et *Vorausbestimmung*) of the essence of animality in order to posit itself as zoology, to posit its object and to determine its field. And about this presupposed essence, the zoologist, the zoologist *as such* at least, has nothing to say to us. It is the philosopher (here Heidegger calls him the metaphysician, or in any case calls his thesis "metaphysical"), it is the onto-phenomenologist who can make his own thesis of what is the presupposition, or even the hypothesis, of the zoologist.

Whether one goes along with it or not, what Heidegger says seems thus far quite clear; it indicates unequivocally an order of presuppositions, the order of what comes before and what comes after in statements, an order of what follows, *posterus,* and of what is posterior in the *logical* series of valid statements. And the "*umgekehrt,*" used twice, seems to signify, seal and confirm this irreversible order, this order irreversible *de jure* [*en droit*], if not *de facto.* But the distinction between fact and right is not literally Heideggerian; I'm the one who thinks I need to introduce it here, at least in the interests of clarity. In English, in place of "en droit," one would say "in principle," and here this is exactly what it is about: in principle, the principle comes *first,* it precedes, it has a sovereign precedence, the metaphysical thesis comes first, it goes ahead of the zoological knowledge that follows (*posterus*), even if in fact, empirically, things don't always, apparently, happen this way.

And yet. And yet, this relation between principle and fact is not simple. It is anything but simple and unilateral. Even before we pose our own questions and formulate our own reservations, we should take account of a complication registered by Heidegger himself. For indeed, when he asks himself, given that the thesis of essence, the universal metaphysical thesis ("the animal is poor in world") is first and thus always presupposed, independent of any zoological thesis—when he asks himself, then, if, independent as it is, it need not resemble a verifiable hypothesis, testable for example by a sci-

275

ence of zoology, Heidegger does not reply "no," as one might have expected. One indeed might have expected him to, given what we have just seen: the metaphysical proposition, the statement of essence being primary and thus depending on no zoological authority, on no knowledge of a scientific type, it is not a hypothesis to be verified, to be confirmed or infirmed. Now when Heidegger asks himself whence this thesis is drawn, whether it is arbitrary (*willkürlich*) or if it needs to be verified, tested by some particular research, the reply is surprising, because it is neither yes nor no. It is suspensive, it oscillates in ambiguity between the two. *"Weder das eine noch das andere"*: neither the one nor the other. The proposition of essence does not come forth from zoology but neither can it be independent of it (*Der Satz stammt weder aus der Zoologie, noch kann er unabhängig von der Zoologie erörtet werden*) (H, 275/187). Heidegger admits that this thesis of essence cannot succeed (*auskommen*), it cannot *do without* a certain orientation (*Orientierung*) from zoology and biology, and so it cannot do without this orientation in general, and yet it does not have in the sciences its means of proof, of verification. So the thesis depends on the orientation of the sciences (bio- and zoo-logy), but it has no need to be subjected to their proofs, to their tests, to their properly scientific authority.

Admit that here Heidegger is admitting to a strange situation, not to call it a contradiction. He admits it without embarrassment and declares that for the moment, we do not need to examine this relation (*Verhältnis*) more closely. It is immediately after this that once again, far from retreating when faced with what he identifies as a circle, a circular movement (*Kreisbewegung*), a circular process (*Kreisgang*), a circular character (*zirkelhaft*) of philosophical thinking, of philosophizing (*des philosophierenden Denkens*), by opposition to the understanding (*Verstand*), to vulgar understanding (H, 276/187).[37] This latter (*der vulgäre Verstand*) cannot tolerate the circle and always sees in it a pretext for objection. We, insofar as we are thinking philosophically, ought to assume, take upon ourselves this ambiguity or this equivocation (*Zweideutigkeit*) of philosophical thought as circular thought, even if this particular ambiguity, which is proper to philosophy (*diese eigentümliche Zweideutigkeit*) is worrying, disturbing (*beunruhigende*), even if it leaves us without rest (H, 277/188). One must neither deny it, nor seek to eliminate it, nor again <seek> to eliminate it dialectically. This means that we must work on a clearer determination (*deutlicheren Bestimmung*) of the relations between philosophizing thought and zoology, but also the relations between this philosophizing thought and *all* the sciences.

276

37. [Translator's note:] This sentence is incomplete in the French text.

There now follows a very important subsection that I leave you to read, subsection b of paragraph 45, in which Heidegger draws the consequences of this situation from the point of view of the university institution, of the relation between the sciences and philosophy in general: he does it in the language of the destiny and the Dasein of university communities; he does it in the same tones and with the same force that we will find again, four years later, in the *Rectoral Address*. The internal unity of science and metaphysics is a matter of destiny (*Schicksal*) (H, 279/190). In passing, he mentions the difficulty that the life sciences have in fighting against the tyranny of physics and chemistry, against mechanism (he condemns without appeal mechanism in biology). But he also specifies that it is not recourse to an animal psychology, most often crudely transposed, anthropomorphically, from human psychology, that will answer to this difficulty of thinking the essence of life, i.e. the manner of being of animal and plants (here he does mention plants: *"der Steinart von Tier und Pflanze"*[38] [H, 277/188]), and to the difficulty of articulating a metaphysics of life and biology. When one sees the difficulty encountered by a metaphysical interpretation of life, one sees by the same token, analogically, how great is the difficulty that biology faces in resisting the natural sciences in order to conquer its proper essence.

277

Having thus followed or accompanied Heidegger's argumentation on these difficult relations between the thesis of essence and the sciences, having done all we can to recognize its necessity, to give credit to its force and also its honesty (for after all, Heidegger neither hides nor seeks to hide the difficulty and the worrying circularity), we are in our rights to wonder already—for this will involve all that follows—about the difficulties that one might have more difficulty in taking on than Heidegger seems to think, and that a new organization, or even a new politics of the hierarchy of thinking and the sciences in the university institutions or in research institutions in general, will always have difficulty sorting out.

So I shall attempt to define two malaises that resist Heidegger's diagnosis, and I select them both for their general scope (i.e. the relation between ontology, onto-phenomenological statement of essence and, on the other hand, scientific knowledge) and their consequences for what is to follow, in Heidegger's seminar, as to the animal—and I indeed say, in the general singular, *the* animal in general.

1. The animal in general: that, then, is the first malaise. On the pretext of rendering, in all onto-phenomenological rigor, his statement of essence, his thesis of essence ("the animal is poor in world") independent of zoologi-

---

38. This phrase appears in italics in Heidegger's text.

cal knowledge, Heidegger announces immediately that he is speaking, for his part, as a philosopher, metaphysician and thinker (here he does not, as he does elsewhere, make a distinction between the three), of the *animal in general,* of *every* animal and of *each* animal, under the concept and the common name *animal,* in the singular. Now this gesture (speaking of the animal in general as though it existed, as though this generality of essence corresponded to some ontological unit, and to an ontological unit from which human Dasein stands at a distance), does not such a gesture, far from being here the sign of an independence with respect to positive knowledge, consisting not merely in presupposing a knowledge of the positive type, but more seriously a positive knowledge that is poor, primitive, dated, lacunary, which would reduce knowledge concerning some animal, some species, to the knowledge concerning some other, and would authorize itself to say the same thing on the subject of infusoria and mammals, of the bee and the cat, the dog and the chimpanzee, etc., about which it is naively assumed that they all have in common the same relation to the world (all supposedly "poor in world," and *equally* "poor in world," for Heidegger will <not> delay, as I announced earlier, in saying that poverty in world does not mark a degree and does not admit of a hierarchizable more or less, of superior and inferior), about which it is naively assumed, then, that they all have in common the same relation to the world (they are all supposedly poor in world), but also the same relation to human Dasein in so far as it is *weltbildend,* and even the same relation to the so-called as-structure, the "as such?" We are only beginning to measure this risk.

278

2. Another malaise: although Heidegger is always quick, and rightly so, to be wary of anthropomorphism or anthropocentrism, is not keeping to the essence of the animal in general as it appears in its onto-phenomenological meaning, in its "as such," is this not to be content to say (with the most suspect common sense), to represent, to represent to oneself and to describe the animal as it appears to consciousness or to the common Dasein which indeed tends, in order to think itself, to institute itself or configure itself as consciousness or human Dasein, [tends] to consider that all animals, in spite of their differences, have something in common and a common difference *with respect to human Dasein,* and that at bottom, indeed, between the infusorium and the so-called great ape, there is indeed something common, general, and that these animals appear in the human world as having more in common among themselves than there is between them and human Dasein?

And it is true that for what I would call, aping Heidegger, vulgar Dasein, the amoeba and the so-called great ape or the anthropoid animal have

279

more in common (namely so-called poverty in world) than they have with human and *weltbildend* Dasein. This is indeed how we spontaneously tend to see things. This phenomeno-ontology would then reflect the point of view of common human consciousness, the place of appearing for me or for us, or human Dasein; it would surreptitiously reintroduce the very anthropologism it claims to avoid. Basically, what Heidegger would be describing rigorously, with all the philosophical exigency he can, often against the tradition, often following the tradition, is the animal as it appears to us, and even as it appears to us historically, historially — to us, in our human Dasein. And from this point of view, what he says is perhaps irreproachable, irreproachable in principle, in the principle of its logic, in principle, but then, here's another principle, historiality, by definition, and epocality, is what is neither natural nor eternal — it changes, it can change, sometimes over thousands or millions of years, sometimes furtively, secretly, silently, in one second, for some absolute singularity.

In order to follow more closely the letter and the procedure that are proper to Heidegger, I wonder whether this supposed statement of essence ("the animal is poor in world") does not belong, precisely, and only, to the world, to the limits of the world, or more narrowly to the limits of *this* world that Dasein has formed or configured for itself.

But are not the limits of this world thus configured the very thing that one must try to cross in order to *think*? To cross when setting off to think? To think not only animality in general, the animality of the animal (in other words, the life common to plants, to beasts and to humans, and even to gods), but the differentiated animality *of* animals, in the infinite plural? To think the irreducible multiplicity of these living beings that recall animals, or beasts, nonhuman and non-divine living beings? Not only individuals but the singularity of what are called species and communities, beings-with-one-another proper to each species? And between species?

This limit to be crossed in order to think this, those living beings, this limit from which I was saying we need to set out, looks like the shores, the contour of an island in which a Robinsonian man relates to the animal only for himself, with a view to himself, from his point of view, in his being-for-self. This is how he relates to the animal that he eats, that he domesticates, that he masters, enslaves or exploits as a thing poor in world, that he makes speak like a parrot, whose carnivorous voracity that would devour him alive and without remains he fears, or even the animal he loves, etc. These would be the structural limits of an insular contour, in a word, the limits of a Homo Robinsoniensis who would perceive, who would interpret, who would project everything, the animal in particular, solitarily, solipsistically, in proportion to the insularity of his interest or his need, even his desire, in any case to his anthropocentric and Robinson-centered phantasm.

That is one of the analogies between Robinson Crusoe and the philosophical Robinson, or even the Heideggerian Robinson: their beasts are very similar, and very similar to the animal *in general,* to that human, all too human, projection that is the animal *in general,* for the Cartesian Robinson to start with. In this way you can see all these Robinsons multiplying under our eyes (the Robinson of the Cartesian cogito and his animal-machine, the Robinson of the Kantian and Husserlian "I think," the Robinson of all the transcendental subjectivisms and idealisms (recall the methodological and phenomenological solipsism of Husserl in the fifth of the *Cartesian Meditations*), and Rousseau's Robinson, or Robinsons, and Joyce's, and so very many others, all the others who dream on the basis of Robinson, the figure and destiny of Robinson).

Not that there is only one Robinson, or one Robinsonade in general, but there's a big family there among whom we should recognize common traits, similarities, family resemblances, without hastening to ignore their differential traits and their irreducible singularity. In his way, Blanchot also seems to have been tempted, at least in his growing isolation, in his retrenched retreat, in his discourse on solitude, to be another sort of Robinson, distanced from the city, from the world, from the world of culture, from a certain public space, etc. It would be easy to find Robinsons everywhere, and precisely in the crowd that anachoretic Robinsons seem to flee, because   *281* we know that the crowd, especially the modern city-dwelling crowd, the crowd of industrial age cities, is also peopled with solitary Robinsons. With so many Rousseaus who feel more solitary in Paris than on their island. One must know, then, but I abandon here these facile remarks, that whoever says *I* is Robinson, that the *autos,* the *ipse,* autobiography is Robinsonian, and that each Robinson organizes the economy of his solitude in the company of those, the others, who, as close as can be to him, with him, or even in him (*Mitsein, alter ego,* labor of mourning, etc.), do not accompany him.

But the animal itself, as Heidegger believes he can describe it in his "statement of essence," is also Robinsonian to the extent that its "poverty in world," which deprives it of the *as such,* supposedly also deprives it of the other as other, of that alterity in general. The animal does not let be as such that which, entirely other, as such, is not in his field of programmed interest. So Heidegger says of it what we were just now saying about Robinson himself and his relation to the animal. In paragraph 60 a and b, when he is describing the being-captured or benumbment of the animal, its *Benommenheit,* Heidegger writes this:

> If it is the case that the animal does not comport itself toward beings as such, then behavior involves *no letting-be* of beings as such (kein Seinlassen *des Seienden als solchen*)—none at all and in no way whatsoever (*überhaupt keines, in keinem Modus*), not even any not letting-be. (H, 368/253)

And further down, on the same page:

> Instinctual and subservient capability . . . , the totality of its self-absorbed capability, is a compulsion of the instinctual drives (*eine Zugetriebenheit der Triebe*) which encircles (*umringt*) the animal in such a way that it is precisely this *encirclement* which makes possible the behavior in which the animal is related to what is other. *Related to what is other*—although *this other is not manifest as beings as such* (Auf Anderes bezogen—*dabei ist* das Andere nicht als Seiendes offenbar). (H, 369/253–54; translation modified)

You can refer to remarks that go in the same direction as to what is *"entirely other"* ("*das* ganz Andere") (H, 440/304; Heidegger's emphasis).

A word in conclusion, that of "privation." What does being deprived mean? If "poverty in world," according to Heidegger, translates neither a hierarchy, nor a difference between the higher and the lower (higher or lower animal), nor a quantitative degree, a less as opposed to a more, nor a qualitative imperfection, what then does it mean? Well, according to Heidegger, it signifies a privation, and next time, among other things, we shall have to wonder about the use Heidegger makes of this word, and about the meaning he intends to give it, notably when he writes this, working the German, the *Mute* and *Armut,* as he had worked, you remember, the word "*Schwermut*" in the passage on melancholy we studied together. And in quoting this, I shall stop there for today:

> What is poor (*Das Arme*) here by no means represents merely what is "less" or "lesser" with respect to what is "more" or "greater." Being poor (*Armsein*) does not simply mean possessing nothing, or little, or less than another. Rather being poor means *being deprived* (*sondern Armsein heißt:* Entbehren). Such privation in turn is possible in different ways depending on *how* (wie) whatever is poor is deprived and comports itself in its privation, *how* it responds to the privation, *how* it takes this privation. In short: with regard to *what* such a being is deprived of and above all to *the way* in which it is deprived, namely *the way* in which it is *in a mood—poverty in mood* (*nämlich wie ihm dabei* zu Mute *ist*—Ar-mut. (H, 287/195; translation modified)

282

How could the animal still feel itself to be deprived if it does not have ac-   *283*
cess to beings as such, or to the other, the entirely other as such? How could
it feel itself deprived of the other, for example in mourning, when it ignores
not only death in the proper sense but the other as such? Has it not been
deprived of privation itself? And man, in all that—is he not also deprived
of privation itself? What does it mean to be deprived, if this great canonical
question, from Plato and Aristotle, of lack and privation (*steresis*) returns,
perhaps transformed, I don't know, at the heart of Heidegger's interpretation of poverty as poverty in world, i.e. as *Entbehrung* and *Armut*?

These are some questions that we shall not deprive ourselves of letting
repose, of letting be and re-posing.

March 5, 2003

285   What is it to pray? How to pray? How not to pray? More precisely, if praying consists in doing something, in a gesture of the body or a movement
of the soul, what is one doing when one prays? Is one doing something?
(*Se laisser prier* and *se faire prier,* develop.[1]) Is one doing something with
words, as in a performative that consists in "doing things with words,"[2] doing something with words, without describing, without being constative,
without saying what is as it is? Or else can one pray wordlessly? And in that
case do something that does not presuppose the *logos,* at least the *logos* as
articulated language, or as enunciative proposition? And can a prayer lie?
And if it never lies, does that mean, and if so in what sense, that it is always
true? Finally, can one put the lie to a prayer, or make it lie, in what other
sense? What does *make lie* [*faire mentir*] mean?

     I am not choosing to begin with this question because we have spoken so
much these last weeks of death, of consigning to earth or fire, of cremators
and inhumers, and because it is difficult even when a church does not take
charge of the thing, even in a so-called atheistic milieu, it is a difficult and
rare thing not to give voice, during ritual ceremonies, during one's thoughts
286   or one's experience, to a movement that resembles prayer. And so to some
hymn or oration.

     No, without for the moment linking prayer to death, to the theme of
death and the posthumous, to death and dying, to such and such a death, to
the eve and the day after such and such a death (and in French the day after

---

    1. In the session, Derrida added: "In French, passively one *se laisse prier,* one lets
oneself be asked by oneself, or one lets oneself be asked by another. *Se faire prier* can
mean two different things, to need asking, <inaudible word>, making people wait, *on
se fait prier.*"

    2. [Translator's note:] This phrase is in English in the text.

a death is perhaps its *veille*, its wake[3]), no, I shall give this question, "what is it to pray?" a more general and apparently more neutral scope [*portée*].

What is one doing when one says to someone "I pray you," "*Je vous en prie*,"[4] "I pray you to"? Can one pray without praying *to someone*, i.e. without "addressing" one's prayer to the singularity of a "who"? Can one pray without praying to . . . ? Can one pray without asking or expecting something[5] in return?[6] Is there a link between the quotidian and trivial "je vous en prie" and the orison or chant of religious and sacred prayer that rises and lifts itself above the quotidian, even if it lifts itself every day, at fixed times, or, solemnly, once a year [is there a link and an analogy] between the anemic and mechanical "je vous en prie" and, on the other hand, prayer in the strong sense, with or without active faith, which grips one, and brings with it a sort of ecstasy beyond automatic triviality? Is there a link and an analogy which would in turn be analogous to the link, on which we insisted so much here not long ago, between the most insignificant "pardon" from someone who steps on your toe, or walks in front of you getting on the subway, and on the other hand the guilty and repentant gravity of "I ask your pardon" for the most criminal offense, etc.?

More radically, and we shall measure the stakes of this question later, can one address oneself to someone or indeed to any living being at all — or even something not living — without some implicit prayer coming to bend, to inflect the discourse, or even the simple silent look which, addressing itself to the other, cannot fail to ask of him or her "listen to me, please [*je t'en prie*], listen, I pray you, look at me looking at you, please, turn toward me, turn your attention toward what I'm saying or doing to you, be present to what is coming from me"; and that is the case even if what I'm doing is not simply benevolent and beneficent, generous, giving (one can give love, but one can also give blows): the torturer also prays his victim to receive and to be present, to be aware of the blows he is giving him. One always prays the other to be present to one's own presence. Can, then, this experience of prayer be limited, circumscribed? Or else does it invade the whole field of experience from the moment the other enters into it, i.e. without ever waiting, since the

287

---

3. [Translator's note:] *Veille* means both "eve" and "vigil" or "wake." The word "wake" is in English in the text.

4. [Translator's note:] "Je vous en prie," which can mean "I pray you (for it)," is more often the standard polite response to thanks, as in "you're welcome" or "don't mention it."

5. In the session, Derrida added: "something, this can be something material or something sublime."

6. In the session, Derrida added: "if only to have it heard, hoping that someone hears."

other is what *is* already, whether I'm expecting it or not, whether I want it or not, etc.? And can this experience of prayer be true or false, authentic or inauthentic, as Robinson Crusoe wondered, you remember, when he confessed having only slowly and painfully learned to pray again, and then to pray with a prayer that was authentic and worthy of the name?

So, I pray you not to forget these questions, to which we shall return later. You will have noticed that with the simple phrase "I pray you not to forget, etc.," I have confirmed that every time one speaks to someone else, one asks him or her at least to remember, one prays him or her to remember—at least the beginning of a sentence so as to understand the end and what follows (*posterus* or *posthumus*). I cannot speak to someone without praying him or her, at least implicitly, not only to pay attention, but by that very fact to retain the memory of what I am saying to him or her, be it only from the beginning to the end of the sentence.[7] By praying the other to listen, from the start, I'm praying him or her to retain the memory, to retain in memory; and perhaps every prayer, to whomever addressed, comes down to, or begins by saying or letting be understood: "remember, retain the memory, and first of all remember me, remember what I'm saying to you." As we have spoken a great deal of death by devouring, of living death, of being buried alive, on the basis of Robinson and so many others, including *Thomas the Obscure* and the Kafka of *The Work of Fire* (fire will soon, remember this, be returning again, fire will burn in what we are going to say about another fire and another cremation), [as we have spoken a great deal, then, of death by devouring, of living death, of being buried alive], the "remember" and the "do it in memory of me" is also what is said at the moment when Christ, in the scene of the Eucharist or of transubstantiation, in a sense gives himself to be eaten alive by his disciples in the form and the real presence of bread and wine: "*Hoc est [enim] corpus meum, quod pro vobis datur: Hoc facite in meam commemorationem [Touto estin to sôma mou, to huper humôn didomenon; touto poieite eis tên emên anamnêsin]*" (Luke 22:19).[8] Jesus (who in *Robinson Crusoe* will give the final seal of authentication to prayer, when Robinson Crusoe recognizes that he only really prayed at the moment he addressed himself as a Christian to Jesus), Jesus prays his disciples to eat him, in a sense, to eat him alive, to remember or in order to

288

7. In the session, Derrida added: "However short or long it be. Sometimes, a sentence <lasts?> a lifetime. When one shares one's life with someone, it's a long sentence: 'Remember the subject . . .' [laughter] that's the demand . . ." What follows is inaudible.

8. [Translator's note:] "This is my body which is given for you: this do in remembrance of me".

remember him. And this prayer that he addresses to them while still alive will be the condition of the future prayer of his disciples and their posterity, of their followers, of all Christians, but also the condition of Christianity itself, the condition of the New Testament, named literally at this point in Mark and the condition of resurrection, etc. A little as though, going very fast and skipping all the stages and mediations, we could say that there was something of a call to resurrection, as though there were already some resurrection in every prayer, from the moment it gives while asking to "remember," "remember me, recall, recall me, remember me, recall you me" as one says incorrectly but quite precisely in French: *rappelle-toi de moi,* what an abyssal sentence and what nerve, what a request, what presumption, even if one were Christ![9]

But can one say sincerely to someone "forget me"? Can one say "forget me" other than to mean: do not forget to forget me, remember me, at least enough to forget me, or to get off my back! A bit as though, I was saying, going very fast and skipping all the stages and mediations, we could say that there is in every prayer from the moment it gives while asking to "remember," "remember me, recall, recall me, remember me, recall you me," an appeal as act of faith or of confidence in resurrection, I mean even the resurrection of the glorious bodies or body, the body of fire or light.

So, remember this question about prayer that I abandon here, that I am abandoning to you here — keep it in your memory.

For two different reasons, at least, I will not propose a linear and continuous reading of Heidegger's seminar, any more than I am of *Robinson Crusoe.* This does not mean that such a reading, uninterrupted from start to finish, word for word and irreversibly consecutive and consequential, is not necessary; I even hold it to be indispensable, whether we're dealing with a philosophical-type discourse or, perhaps still more so, of a work composed as a fiction and as narrative, with the unique order and proper temporality of its literality. I am convinced, having also begun by obeying this injunction myself before inviting you to do so in your turn, that one must read and reread these two works in a linear, continuous and repeated way, each of these readings being promised to promise you surprises, changes of accent, a thousand discoveries in moments that are apparently furtive or secondary, etc.

9. [Translator's note:] Remembering is expressed by two main verbs in French: *se souvenir de quelque chose* . . . and *se rappeler quelque chose* . . . ; Derrida is here referring to the very common error of also using the *de* with *se rappeler.*

289

Having recalled this, and having taken this precaution as a matter of principle, I am not doing what one ought to do and cannot do it with you in a seminar. I cannot do all that again with you here for at least two reasons, as I was saying. The one has to do with the obvious lack of time: it would take us years. The other, less obvious, is that I also believe in the necessity, sometimes, in a seminar the work of which is not simple reading, in the necessity, and even the fecundity, when I'm optimistic and confident, of a certain number of leaps, certain new perspectives from a turn in the text, from a stretch of path that gives you another view of the whole, like for example when you're driving a car on a mountain road, a hairpin or a turn, an abrupt and precipitous elevation suddenly gives you in an instant a new perspective on the whole, or a large part of the itinerary or of what orients, designs or destines it. And here there intervene not only each person's reading-idioms, with their history, their way of driving (it goes without saying that each of my choices and my perspectives depends broadly here, as I will never try to hide, on my history, my previous work, and my way of driving, driving on this road, on my drives, desires and phantasms, even if I always try to make them both intelligible, shareable, convincing and open to discussion) [here there intervene, then, not only each person's reading-idioms, with their history, their way of driving] in the mountains or on the flat, on dirt roads or on highways, following this or that map, this or that route, but also the crossing, the decision already taken and imposed on you by fiat as soon as it was proposed to you, to read a given seminar by Heidegger and *Robinson Crusoe,* i.e. two paths, two discourses also on the way and on the path which can multiply the perspectives from which two vehicles can light up, their headlights crossing, the overall cartography and the landscape in which we are traveling and driving together, driving on all these paths interlaced, intercut, overloaded with bridges, fords, no entries or one-way streets, etc.

For example, today, without losing sight of and without forgetting the broad trajectories announced as to the animal said to be "poor in world" and on the putting to work of the German vocabulary of *Walten (Gewalt,* etc.), and on the contrary in order to put them back in perspective, I shall start out again from prayer, from the motif of prayer as a crossing point between Heidegger's seminar or problematic and *Robinson Crusoe.* I shall not go back over what we said about the forgetting and then the rediscovery, and finally the new apprenticeship of prayer by Robinson, of the discipline, the training in view of a prayer the vocation of which — if I can put it this way — is Christian. There is, in the course of Heidegger's seminar, a moment where an allusion to prayer — to this odd type of statement that prayer is, but then evoked in Greek in a context marked rather by Aristotle and from which Christianity appears to be absent—plays a role that I believe to be strategically determining. I shall try to explain why, but before doing so, and to justify still further my point of departure today, with a view to coming back to the difference between Being and being and to *Walten,* I should like to draw your attention to this fact that is not gratuitous: among other places—rarely, I believe—where Heidegger speaks of prayer, there is this passage from *Identity and Difference* (1957),[10] at the very end, where shortly after having used this verb *walten* more than once (and even the expression "Walten der Differenz"), and that we still have to read, Heidegger analyzes what he calls the onto-theological constitution of philosophy, i.e. the way God enters into philosophy as supreme and foundational being, as *causa sui* (and thus, ultimately, as sovereign God). Thanks to a surprising shortcut, but one that I do not think unjustified, I would say that Heidegger says of God that if one wishes to withdraw him from onto-theology, one must learn again to address prayers and sacrifices to him.[11] And perhaps to pray in addressing oneself beyond the sovereignty of God or independently of his supposed sovereignty, of his ontic sovereignty in any case, as fundamental cause, *causa sui* or supreme principle, or as the highest being (*das höchste Seiende*), which is what sovereign (*superanus*) literally means.

Indeed, as soon as metaphysics thinks beings as such in their totality, as a totality (*das Seiende als solches im Ganzen*) and God then becomes the highest being, the most elevated, the supreme foundational being (*das höchste, alles begründende Seiende*) who grounds every thing in reason, then metaphysics becomes a logic as theo-logic or theo-logy. Now the God of this metaphysical onto-theology, this God of the philosophers as *causa sui* or as *Ursache,* as primordial cause, original thing and cause, the God thus named in philosophy, is, says Heidegger (thus rediscovering in his way, with a difference I'll return to in a moment, the vein of a Pascalian discourse against the God of the philosophers, to which Pascal opposes the God of Abraham and Jacob), [the God of this metaphysical onto-theology], is a God to whom man does not pray, and to which he sacrifices nothing. Heidegger writes, I quote and translate:

292

> This is the proper name [*Ursache* or *Causa sui*] for God in philosophy (*So lautet der sachgerechte Name für den Gott in der Philosophie*). [He has just spoken of God as *Ursache,* and now he says that this is the most just and the

10. Martin Heidegger, *Identität und Differenze* (Pfullingen: Verlag Günther Neske, 1957), p. 70; trans. Joan Stambaugh as *Identity and Difference* (New York: Harper & Row, 1969), pp. 71–72.

11. In the session, Derrida added: "For one neither prays nor sacrifices to the God of onto-theology."

most well adjusted name for the thing thus aimed at in philosophy, and he adds:] Man can neither pray nor sacrifice to this God [*Zu diesem Gott kann der Mensch weder beten, noch kann er ihm opfern. Vor der Causa sui kann der Mensch weder aus Scheu ins Knie fallen, noch kann er vor diesem Gott musizieren und tanzen:* Man can neither pray nor sacrifice to this God]. Before the *causa sui,* man can neither fall to his knees in awe nor can he play music and dance before this God.[12]

Of course, Heidegger is not busy enjoining us to pray, to sacrifice or to sing to God. He simply says that the God of the philosophers, the *causa sui,* the supreme Entity, the supreme being (as the revolutionaries of 1789 said), a supreme being who is no more than a supreme Entity, and therefore the sovereign, in the ontic sense of the term—Heidegger simply says that this supreme being is not a God to whom one prays, whom one praises in hymns, or to whom one addresses one's music and one's chants. Heidegger does not refer here, and especially not in the mode of prayer or preaching, to the God of Abraham, the God of Isaac, and the God of Jacob. He simply tells us that if one is to pray to God, and sacrifice for him, in that case it must not be addressed to the God of onto-theology and the philosophers, who moreover has no address and is not listening; if one wishes to address prayers, sacrifices, chance, and dances to God, these must not be discourses and acts destined for the ontic sovereign, the supreme cause, or the most elevated being. The God of the philosophers (Aristotle's *noesis noesos* or pure act, Spinoza's *causa sui,* etc.) is not, in essence, a being who receives prayers and sacrifices and chants and praises and hymns, etc. Does that justify a return to faith or religion? Does that call on us to go beyond all sovereignty, or only onto-theological sovereignty—those are the questions that await us, along with the agency of *Walten,* which I shall attempt to show in a moment is both foreign or heterogeneous, excessive even, with respect to this ontic and therefore theological or theologico-political sovereignty, and that nonetheless, and by that very fact, perhaps constitutes an ontological super-sovereignty, at the source of the ontological difference.

However, I think it is necessary, before going any further, to situate what distinguishes what Heidegger is saying about prayer here from the experience we find in both *Robinson Crusoe* and in Pascal. Heidegger says what he says about prayer in a text the discursivity of which remains theoretical or constative, which in any case is not of the order of performative address, and certainly not of prayer in the strict sense. Heidegger is speaking *of* prayer and *of* God, but he is neither praying to nor addressing a God who would

293

12. Ibid., p. 70 [p. 72; translation slightly modified].

not be the God of the philosophers and onto-theology. Robinson Crusoe, for his part, is writing a book which, in itself, and as an autobiography, is a sort of prayer, a sort of prayer in view of prayer. Robinson Crusoe tells us how he tried to pray, to be reborn to prayer, to allow prayer to be reborn in him, and how he came to pray again. The book itself, the narrative or the journal, does not pray (unless it is implicitly praying the reader to read it with God as his or her witness), but Robinson[13] nevertheless quotes, and several times, which Heidegger never does, insistently quotes prayers, and prayers that are essentially linked to the Christian revelation, as the only prayers worthy of the name. And these are prayers that he learns, that he learns to relearn, and that he quotes as though he were reiterating them in his very writing.

294

As for Pascal himself, we must clearly recall the mode in which the famous remark about "God of Abraham, God of Isaac, God of Jacob" appears. As you well know, it is in a *posthumous* piece of writing (now of course, all writings are posthumous, each in its own way, even those that are known and published during the author's lifetime, but within this generality of the posthumous, within the trace as structurally and essentially and by destinal vocation posthumous or testamentary, there is a stricter enclave of the posthumous, namely what is only discovered and published after the death of the author or the signatory). Pascal's writing on the God of Abraham was strictly posthumous in this latter sense, even though we're not sure that Pascal wanted it to be published. It was posthumous in this very strict sense since it was found written on a piece of paper found in Pascal's clothing after his death. This piece of paper initially takes the form of a journal, of a note to self, dated in Pascal's hand — Pascal, who like Robinson Crusoe, here dates his signature. He inscribes the year, the month, the day, and the hour: "The year of grace 1654. Monday, 23 November," and Pascal thus takes the event in the Christian calendar (not merely Christian as are all calendars hereabouts, but here overloaded with Christianity, with sacred memory and history, since Pascal adds, after "the year of grace 1654. Monday, 23 November," "day of St. Clement, Pope and martyr, and others in the martyrology, / Vigil of St. Chrysogonis, martyr, and others, / from around half past ten in the evening to around half past midnight."[14]

(As I'm mentioning dates, it is perhaps not insignificant to point out that on that date Robinson Crusoe, if we are to believe the first words of his

---

13. In the typescript: "he."

14. Blaise Pascal, "Opuscules — Deuxième partie," in *Pensées et opuscules,* ed. Léon Brunschvicg (Paris: Librairie Hachette, 1946), p. 142. [Translator's note: my translation.]

autobiography, was only twenty-three years old ("I was born in the Year 1632, in the City of *York*" [RC, 3]). He was only nine years younger than Pascal, born in 1623. According to the fiction, it is five years after Pascal's writing that we are reading that Robinson Crusoe lands on his island, and you remember that in order to remind himself of that fact, he says he wrote on a cross-shaped post (which is not insignificant), the date of his arrival on the island. In this way he established a calendar beginning on that date:

295

> I cut it with my Knife upon a large Post, in Capital Letters, and making it into a great Cross I set it up on the Shore where I first landed, viz. *I came on Shore here on the 30th of* Sept. 1659. (RC, 59)

And Pascal was only thirty-one years old when he wrote and put into his clothing the posthumous paper we are deciphering and that he must have kept for around eight years, as he died in 1662, at "39 years and two months,"[15] says his sister. One can wager that a Pascal in our own century would have had a longer life expectancy. But if it is certain that the "remember me" animates the motivation of Robinson's calendar and marks, one might wonder if this is the case with Pascal. To whom did he write this? For whom did he write in general? For there is in Pascal, as moreover—quite differently—in Blanchot, a "do not remember me," a "keep me in oblivion" (we have a thousand examples of this in Blanchot's texts, that I have quoted at length elsewhere, in *Parages* or in *Politics of Friendship*[16]), a "forget me" about which one can always wonder if it is not also praying that one remember to forget and even attach oneself to the one thus praying that one not attach oneself to him. This paradox of the "forget me," "do not love me," is to be found in Pascal, and there again consigned to another "little paper" as his elder sister Gilberte Pascal Périer says in her *Life of Blaise Pascal*. This is how she presents and quotes this "little paper": (Quote and comment on Pascal)

296

> Thus he made it appear, that he had no attachment to those he loved, for had he been capable of having one, it would indisputably have been to my sister; since she was undeniably the person in the world he loved most. But he carried it still farther, for not only he had no attachment to any body, but he was absolutely against any body's having one to him, I do not mean any

15. Ibid., p. 40. [Translator's note: my translation.]
16. See Jacques Derrida, *Parages* (Paris: Galilée, 2003), pp. 72–73, 99–101, and 107–8; *Politiques de l'amitié* (Paris: Galilée, 1994), p. 328; trans. George Collins as *Politics of Friendship* (London: Verso, 1997), p. 296.

criminal or dangerous attachments, for that would be too gross an error to be supposed, as the whole world is convinced of the contrary; but I speak in relation to those friendships, which are of the most innocent nature, and this was one of the things, over which he kept a most regular watch, that he might never give any occasion for it himself, and that he might prevent it in others: as I did not know this, I was quite surprised at the checks he would sometimes give me, and I told my sister of it; complaining to her, that my brother had no affection for me, and that it looked as if I made him uneasy, even at the very time I was the most affectionately employing myself to do him services in his sickness. But my sister told me I was deceived, for she knew to the contrary, that he had as great affection for me, as I myself could wish. By this means, my sister removed my apprehensions, and it was not long before I saw some proofs of what she said: for on the first occasion that presented it self to make me want some assistance from my brother, he embraced that opportunity, with so much assiduity and such tokens of affection, that I had no longer reason to doubt his having a great love for me; so that I imputed the cold reception he gave to my earnest attention how to divert him, to the chagrining circumstances of his distemper. This riddle was never interpreted to me, till just the very day of his death, when one of the most remarkable persons for his great genius and piety, with whom my brother had long conferred about the practice of virtue, told me, he had given him this instruction amongst others, that he ought never to suffer any body whatsoever to love him with any particular attachment: that it was a fault, we do not enough examine ourselves about, because we do not perceive the enormity of it, nor consider, that by cherishing and enduring these attachments, the heart was too much taken up with them, which ought to be entirely devoted to GOD alone: that it was thieving from him, that thing he set the greatest value upon in this world.

We afterwards perceived, that this principle had entered very deep into his heart, for to the end he might always have it presented to his thoughts, he had set it down in his own hand-writing, on a little piece of paper by it self, where were these words.

"It is unjust to make any attachment, though one makes it spontaneously and with pleasure. I should deceive those in whom I should give rise to such a desire, for I am no ultimate end of any body, nor have I what can satisfy that desire. Am I not bordering upon death? If so, the object of their attachment will die too. As I should be blameable to make people believe a falshood, though I contrived it ever so delicately, to persuade them they might with pleasure believe it, and in doing so they gave me a pleasure: just so am I blameable if I make my self to be beloved; and if I draw people into an attachment to me, I ought to warn those who would be ready to assent to this lie, that they ought to give no credit to it, whatever advantage might accrue to me, from their believing it; and it is my duty to warn them too,

297

that they ought not to be attached to me at all: for it is their duty, to employ their lives, and their whole care, to please and after God."[17]

Let's come back now to <this> "Writing Found In Pascal's Clothing after His Death." There can be little doubt that this little piece of paper was destined, if not for someone, then at least to remain, to survive the moment of its inscription, to remain legible in the exteriority of a trace, of a document, even if it were readable only for Pascal himself, later, in the generation of repetitions to come. This is indeed what has been called a *memorial,* to use the word of a witness, Father Guerrier:

> "A few days after the death of Monsieur Pascal," said Father Guerrier, "a servant of the house noticed by chance an area in the lining of the doublet of the illustrious deceased that appeared thicker than the rest, and having removed the stitching at this place to see what it was, he found there a little folded parchment written in the hand of Monsieur Pascal, and in the parchment a paper written in the same hand: the one was a faithful copy of the other. These two pieces were immediately put into the hands of Madame Périer who showed them to several of her particular friends. All agreed there was no doubt that this parchment, written with so much care and with such remarkable characters, was a type of *memorial* that he kept very carefully to preserve the memory of a thing that he wanted to have always present to his eyes and to his mind, since for eight years he had taken care to stitch it and unstitch it from his clothes, as his wardrobe changed." The parchment is lost; but at the beginning of the manuscript in the Bibliothèque Nationale, one can find the paper that reproduced it, written in the hand of Pascal, the authenticity of which was confirmed by a note signed by the Abbé Périer, Pascal's nephew. At the top, there is a cross, surrounded by rays of light.[18]

298   After the date so Christianly specified in the history and calendar of Christianity, a single word, in the middle of the line:

Fire [*feu*]

This word "fire" is, then, isolated, alone, insularized on a single line, and I'm not sure I can interpret it; I'm even sure that I cannot interpret it in a decidable way, between the fire of glory and the fire that reduces to ashes or that still smolders under the ashes of some cremation (*Aschenglorie*). But this

---

17. Gilberte Pascal, "Vie de Blaise Pascal," in Blaise Pascal, *Pensées et opuscules,* pp. 31–32. [*The Life of Mr. Paschal, with his Letters Relating to the Jesuits, translated into English by W. A.* (London, 1744), pp. xliii–xlvi].
    18. Ibid., pp. 141–42. [Translator's note: my translation.]

word "fire" comes before the line that says: "God of Abraham, God of Isaac, God of Jacob,"[19] which is itself a quotation from Exodus and from Matthew.[20]

Now there is no doubt that the general form of this posthumous fragment is both, indissociably, that of a prayer and of a journal for self or for other humans, other brothers in sin, neighbors, a confession basically analogous to Augustine's *Confessions,* confessions designed to avow a sin and to bring the others, neighbors, brothers and sons of God, to a greater love of God (Augustine, as you know, was considered by Jansenius and the Jansenists to be (I'm quoting Jansenius) "the first among doctors, the first among fathers, the first among ecclesiastical writers after the canonic doctors, father of fathers, doctor of doctors, subtle [. . .] angelic, seraphic, most excellent and ineffably admirable"[21] [there is no doubt, then, that the general form of this posthumous fragment by Pascal is both, indissociably, that of the prayer and of a journal for self or for other humans, other neighbors and brothers in sin], and also, primarily, a prayer addressed to God and to Jesus his son, even though often this prayer quotes words from the Bible and thus resembles a mixture of use and mention.[22]

†

299

The year of grace 1654.

Monday, 23 November, day of St. Clement, Pope and martyr, and others
   in the martyrology,
Vigil of St. Chrysogonis, martyr, and others,
From around half past ten in the evening to around half past twelve.

FIRE [feu]

"God of Abraham, God of Isaac, God of Jacob"
not of philosophers and savants.
Certitude. Certitude. Sentiment. Joy. Peace.
God of Jesus Christ.
Deum meum et Deum vestrum.
"Thy God will be my God."
Oblivion of the world and of all, save for God.
He is found only by the ways taught in the Gospel.
Grandeur of the human soul.
"Just Father, the world hath not known Thee, but I have known Thee."

19. Ibid., p. 142
20. Exodus 3:6; Matthew 22:32.
21. Quoted in Pascal, *Pensées et opuscules,* p. 50. [Translator's note: the parenthesis opened four lines earlier should presumably close here.]
22. The words "use" and "mention" are in English in the text.

Joy, joy, joy, tears of joy.
I am separated from him:
Dereliquerunt me fontem aquæ vivæ.
"My God, will you forsake me?"
Oh, may I not be separated from him eternally.
"This is the life eternal, that they know Thee the only true God, and Him whom Thou
hast sent, Jesus Christ."
Jesus Christ.
Jesus Christ.
I am separated from Him; I have fled, renounced, crucified Him.
Oh that I may never be separated from Him.
He is only held fast by the ways taught in the Gospel.
Renunciation total and sweet.
Total submission to Jesus Christ and to my guiding force.
300   Eternally in joy for a day of exercise on earth.
Non obliviscar sermones tuos. Amen.[23]

Heidegger, for his part, is not praying when he speaks, in the third person, of the God of onto-theology and when he notes that one does not pray and does not sacrifice to Him. Heidegger is not praying when he speaks, always in the third person, and not, like when one prays, in the second, he is not praying when he speaks in the third person of the God to whom one would get down on one's knees and pray or for whom one would sacrifice and dance and sing.

Nevertheless, he adds in the following section a very serious remark, namely that thought without God (*das gott-lose Denken*), and thus atheistic or a-theological thinking under the regime of onto-theology, and thus the thinking of those who, as philosophers, declare themselves to be atheists (and this is indeed the case of Heidegger, among others) — well, that they, that their thinking without God is perhaps closer to the divine God, to the divinity of God, more open to it than the thinking of a theism, or of a philosophical belief in the God of the philosophers and of onto-theology. This casts light on what Heidegger often says about his own atheism and about a philosophy which, as such, is incompatible with belief (*Glaube*) in God. Heidegger writes, I quote:

> The god-less thinking (*das gott-lose Denken*) which must abandon the God of philosophy, God as *causa sui,* is thus perhaps [I emphasize the *perhaps,*

---

23. Ibid., pp. 142–43; translation adapted with some modifications from John Tulloch, *Pascal* (Edinburgh and London: William Blackwood and Sons, 1878), pp. 90–91.

vielleicht] closer to the Divine God (*dem göttlichen Gott vielleicht näher*). Here this means only: god-less thinking is more open to Him [*freier:* more free, and "free" is "open" for Heidegger] than onto-theo-logic would like to admit [hold to be true: *wahrhaben möchte*].[24]

So philosophical atheism would be closer to the divinity of God, more re-spectful and more open, better prepared for a God to whom one would pray   *301* and sacrifice, than is onto-theology when it refers to God as supreme Being and *causa sui,* i.e. as sovereign and all-powerful, as origin, cause and ground of all that is, and therefore of the world. Should we conclude from this that the divinity of God that Heidegger seems to be able to say something about—namely that philosophical atheism is perhaps closer to it and more prepared for, open to and welcoming of it—is, as divinity of God, foreign to the attributes of power and of sovereignty, of height and of causal and fundamental principality? Perhaps, but in any case if we must still speak of sovereignty, for this God more divine than the God of onto-theology, it will be another sovereignty, certainly one foreign to ontic power, and therefore foreign to political theology and to creationism, and to fundamentalism, in all senses of the term, in particular the sense that refers to a founding God.

Heidegger is so attached to this last remark that he will immediately suggest that, with its *perhaps,* this thought of a non onto-theo-logical divin-ity casts some light on the path (and I'm insisting on this because of this fig-ure—which is not a figure—of the path and the circle and this time of the "step backward" which has been occupying us from the beginning of the seminar) [thus casts some light on the path] toward which a thought taking a step backward (*Schritt zurück*[25]) is going, the step that goes backward from metaphysics to the essence of metaphysics, the step that brings us back from the forgetting of Difference as such to this destiny that hides from us, that dissimulates (*Verbergung*) the *Austrag* [that we already talked about, that is translated as Conciliation, but it's more difficult to translate than that and we're coming back to it], a dissimulation which, itself, hides itself or with-draws (*der sich entziehenden Verbergung des Austrags*[26]).

This *Austrag* will be precisely—we're coming to this too—what links, in difference, Being to beings and what "*walten.*" So it is toward this *Walten* that the step backward (*Schritt zurück*) directs us through this remark about a God who would no longer be the sovereign God of onto-theology. Can   *302* one pray to *Walten?* That is one of our questions to come.

24. Heidegger, *Identität und Differenz,* p. 71 [p. 72].
25. Ibid., pp. 71–72 [pp. 72–73]; see also p. 65 [p. 67].
26. Ibid., p. 71 [p. 72].

But we have just read all this in a text, *Identität und Differenz* (1957), which is much later than our seminar from 1929–30 toward which, after this long anticipatory detour, we are now returning, precisely on the subject of prayer.

The passage devoted to prayer, in the seminar, is to be found toward the end, in section 72 b. It is dealing with the apophantic (*apophantikos*) *logos* according to Aristotle, i.e. of the *logos* capable of showing (*aufzeigen*), of showing that toward which it is directed as such. You can already see that the question of the "as such" is central to this passage, as we are going to show more precisely. The *logos apophantikos* is a word, or rather a discourse (*Rede*) which, in the mode of giving-to-be-understood, in the semantic mode (*semantikos*), specifically tends to show simply as such that toward which it is directed (*die spezifische Tendenz hat, das, was sie meint, als solches lediglich aufzuzeigen* [H, 448/309]). And Heidegger immediately specifies that only the apophantic *logos*, which shows the thing to which it is directed as such, has the value of an enunciative proposition (*Aussagesatz*). And it is precisely this that is lacking in prayer (*eukhe*) about which Aristotle says — in a passage of the *Peri hermeneias* that Heidegger is clearly thinking of here but that he does not quote — that a prayer can be neither true nor false. Now Heidegger, after a few words of explanation, will brutally exclude from his discussion this prayer, this non-enunciative aspect of *logos* represented by prayer, on the pretext that it belongs to rhetoric or poetics. It seems to me that what is at stake in this exclusion is weighty and serious, for it excludes from *logos* and even from the "as such" everything that is not enunciative speech with a value of truth or falsity. After having, in order to explain what a *logos apophantikos* is (and the whole strategy aims to show that the animal is deprived of it, as we were noting last week — we shall have to return to this), [after having] identified Aristotle's *logos apophantikos* with what he calls enunciative proposition (*Aussagesatz*), Heidegger adds: "An
303   example of a non-apophantic λόγος, εὐκή, prayer [*das Bitten* this time, and not *Beten* as in the text cited above: here it is a question of prayer as request in general and not of religious prayer, of orison, but the nearness of the two remains troubling and equivocal, as the always possible passage from *bitten* to *beten,* and reciprocally. *Eukhe, eukhomai,* in Greek, has the same ambivalence, which can be that of a vow, a wish in general, and a prayer addressed to the gods]" (H, 448/ 309; translation modified). Heidegger is right to specify at this point that when I pray to the other, I do not, essentially, inform him, I do not bring something to his knowledge, I do not say to him: "you know, I'm asking you for something, know that, take note,

as I take note of it myself." No, I am also doing something other than this "making-known," than this gesture of informing. Without using the word "performative," or the opposition constative/performative, Heidegger is indeed analyzing the performativity of prayer, and analyzing it lucidly, when he writes the following:

> If my discourse is a prayer (*Wenn ich bittend rede*), then it is not attempting to inform the other about something in the sense of increasing his or her knowledge. Nor, however, is the prayer (*Die Bitte*) a communication of the fact that I desire something or am animated by a wish. This discourse [*Diese Rede*, this addressed discourse] is not any more a mere desiring, but rather the concrete act (*sondern der konkrete Vollzug*) of a ("*einen anderen Bittens*") "praying another." (H, 448/309; translation modified)

After this important and interesting remark on the specificity of a *logos* that consists in "praying another" ("*einen anderen Bittens*"), about which one might wonder how it can be circumscribed in all rigor, how its domain and its frontiers can be drawn in the *logos* in general (for after all, is there not some implicit prayer in every address to the other? And is there not an implicit address to the other in every statement, however constative it look, even if it be an *Aussagesatz,* an enunciative proposition or proposition destined to make known?[27] We are not a little surprised (and we're not finished with this surprise) to see Heidegger then excluding or suspending any supplementary reflection on prayer (*eukhe, Bitten*) on the pretext, which to me looks scarcely credible, that it has to do merely with poetics or rhetoric and not with the proper task of this seminar. For Heidegger indeed writes: 304

> The examination of these kinds of discourse (*dieser Arten des Redens*) which do not have the character of a pointing out (*des Aufweisens*)—of ascertaining and letting be seen (*des feststellenden Sehenlassens*) what and how something is (*was und wie etwas ist*)—the examination of these λόγοι belongs to rhetoric and poetics (*gehört in die Rhetorik und Poetik*). But the object of the current investigation is the enunciative λόγος (*der aussagende* λόγος). (H, 448/310; translation modified)

27. In the typescript this sentence is incomplete and the parenthesis is not closed. In the session, Derrida resumed the sentence and explained: "I do not know if what I am saying here is clear: at the moment where he withdraws, where he wants to make of prayer something other than an enunciative proposition, Heidegger seems to forget that even the enunciative proposition, insofar as it is addressed to someone, indicates some prayer, a 'listen to me, I say to you.'"

One of the final aims of this Heideggerian strategy is to articulate together what Aristotle in his interpretation of the *logos* says about *sunthesis* (we're coming to this in a moment) and what Heidegger for his part means by "as-structure" (*als-Struktur*) of which in his eyes the animal is deprived. One of the points of departure for this development in Aristotle's wake, is the way the Greeks had characterized man as *zōon logon ekhon* (we talked about this a lot last year)[28] and the animal as *zōon alogon* (*zōon* deprived of *logos*). In its encirclement (*Umring*), in its benumbment (*Benehmen, Benom-menheit*), the animal is *deprived* (*dem Tier fehlt es*), it is lacking, it lacks the possibility of perceiving as a being (*als ein Seiendes*) that to which it is open. "However," Heidegger adds,

305

> to the extent that the λόγος is connected with νοῦς and with νοεῖν, with apprehending something, we may say: There belongs to man a being open for . . . (*ein Offensein für*) of such a kind [derart, underlined] that this being open for . . . has the character of *apprehending something as something* [underlined: *den Charakter* des Vernehmens von etwas als etwas *hat*]. This kind of relating to beings (*Diese Art des Sichbeziehens auf Seiendes*) we call comportment [*Verhalten*], as distinct from the *Benehmen,* the benumbment or the entrapment or the encirclement of the animal (*im Unterschied zum Benehmen des Tieres*). (H, 443/306; translation modified)

So it looks like we have the following system of distinctions: the relation to beings, the relating-oneself to beings (*Sichbeziehens auf Seiendes*), can be of two types: either 1) <the> relation to beings as such, and this is the *Verhalten* of man, or else 2) the relation to beings, yes, but not to beings as such, and this is *Benehmen,* a *Benehmen* which, then, is thereby in turn opposed to the "*Vernehmens von etwas als etwas,*" to the perception of something as something. *Benehmen,* which is one of the two ways (and from this point of view there are not one or three or two + n) of relating to beings (*Sichbeziehens auf Seiendes*), is opposed to or is rigorously distinguished (according to Heidegger) from *Verhalten* and "Vernehmens von etwas als etwas." (Board)

It is thus with reference to the *als-Struktur,* to the ability to perceive beings as such, that Heidegger says that he is interpreting man as *zōon logon ekhon* and the animal as a *zōon alogon.* Even if our interpretation, he says (our *Interpretation*), and our way of posing questions, our problematic, our *Fragestellung* are different from those of Aristotle and antiquity, they say

28. *La bête et le souverain I,* session 12.

nothing new (*nichts Neues*), but they say, as always and everywhere in phi-   *306*
losophy, "*rein dasselbe,*" purely and simply the same thing. As always, Heidegger claims both things at once: that he is seeing and saying what no one
has previously seen and said, but that in doing so he is saying only the same
thing that philosophy, whether it knew it or not, has always been repeating.
Indeed.

And Heidegger believes it is necessary to note this fact, because he had
also noted before that in Aristotle's description of the enunciative proposition, one did not see appear *the phenomenon of the as-* (*als-Phänomen*), any
more than any reference to the whole, the as-a-whole (*im Ganzen*), whereas
for Heidegger the world, the very definition of the world, is the manifestation (*Offenbarkeit*) of beings as such in their entirety, an indispensable definition for understanding both human Dasein, as world-forming, and the
animal as deprived of world, deprived, namely, of the perception of beings
and of the totality of beings as such.

Let's return now to what Heidegger believes he can distinguish from
prayer, namely the *logos apophantikos,* of which the animal is supposedly
deprived. Every *logos* is *semantikos,* says Aristotle: "Ἔστι δὲ λόγος ἅπας μὲν
σημαντικός"[29] Every *logos* gives something to be heard, to be understood, it
has some intelligibility, it signifies, and in this respect prayer too is a *logos
semantikos.*[30] Moreover, in subsection a) of this same section 72, Heidegger
had classified prayer and wish among all the species of intelligibility of the
logos semantikos, which is the most general form of *logos.* This dimension
of intelligibility, of giving-to-be-heard or understood (*Verständlichkeit*) belongs just as much, he was saying, to discursive exchange, to prayer (*Bitten*),
to wish (*Wünschen*), to questioning (*Fragen*), and to recounting (*Erzählen*).   *307*
So Heidegger had clearly classified modes that we would call performative
(questioning, praying, formulating a wish) in the most general category of
logos semantikos. Now a *logos* is semantic, i.e. gives something to be heard or
understood, "*Der* λόγος *gibt zu verstehen*" only by *suntheke,* by conventional
arrangement, by the positing of a conventional law, and not *phusei,* by nature—and Aristotle associates the possibility of *suntheke,* of convention, of

29. Aristotle, *Organon,* vol. 1, *Hermeneutica (De Interpretatione),* ed. Th. Waitz
(Leipzig: Sumtibus Hahnii, 1844), chap. 4, 17a.1, cited in H, 443/306 ("Each discourse,
all discursivity, has in itself the possibility of giving something meaningful, something
that we understand").

30. During the session, Derrida added: "and the animal insofar as it is deprived of
logos does not pray either. Not only does it not have any *logos apophantikos,* it does not
have any *logos semantikos,* any prayer."

conventional arrangement with the possibility of the symbol, of the *sumbolon*. The *sumbolon* is not natural either, and this is why the animal (here considered to be pure nature) does not have access to the *logos semantikos,* nor to the *suntheke,* and so to convention, nor to the *sumbolon,* nor even, as we shall see, to *Bedeutung,* to *signification,* and this is why it is *alogon.* And to explain this, Heidegger specifies that the fact of giving to be heard, to be understood, is not the unfolding of a natural process, like digestion or the circulation of the blood, or like the cry that, in animals, is the result of some physiological state. There is word, beyond the cry, only where there is *suntheke* and *sumbolon.* The inarticulate sounds that animals produce of course indicate (*zeigen*) something; they have a power of indication, animals can even, as people say (but wrongly, because this is inappropriate, underlines Heidegger), understand each other[31] ("*die Tiere können sich sogar — wie wir, obwohl nicht angemessen, zu sagen pflegen — unter sich verständigen*" [H, 444/307]). But none of the voicings (*Verlautbarungen*) produced by animals are words (*Worte*), they are simple *psophoi,* noises. This is moreover what Robinson thought when he heard Poll his parrot emit sounds that sounded like words, but which were not words, according to him, but noises. And what is lacking in these simple noises (*bloße* ψόφοι, *Geräusche*), is signification, *Bedeutung* (*etwas fehlt nämlich die* Bedeutung). What is lacking to the animal, that of which it is deprived, is signification; the animal means nothing and understands nothing through its cry (*Das Tier meint und versteht nicht bei seinem Schrei*) (H, 444/307).

Heidegger, in this way following the Aristotelian *topos* and the most traditional *topos* — which will also be that of Descartes and so many others — also goes further, and this according to a gesture proper to him. He will say, still using his "*umgekehrt,*" his typical gesture with "*umgekehrt*" (conversely) that if indeed *logos* is voice, *phonē,* this is not because signification is a supplement to sound or comes along to add itself to sound, but to the contrary it is only on the basis of configured and self-configuring significations that the character, the imprint of sound, is configured in turn:

> *Die Bedeutung wächst nicht den Lauten zu, sondern umgekehrt, aus schon gebildeten und sich bildenden Bedeutungen bildet sich erst die Prägung des Lautes* [translate and comment]. [Then a second *umgekehrt* comes to confirm the argument:] *Der* λόγος *ist zwar* φονή, *aber nicht primär und dann etwas dazu,*

---

31. During the session, Derrida added "animals, as we often say, inappropriately, can understand each other."

sondern umgekehrt, er ist primär etwas anderes und dabei auch . . . φονή. [Translate and comment.³²] [What in the first place?] *Primär was?* κατὰ συνθήκην.³³
(H, 445/307)

So what comes first, in first place, is not the physical sound, but what   *309*
comes about by convention, conventional agreement. The essential difference between animal phonation, the vocal phonation of the animal (*zwischen der tierischen stimmlichen Verlautbarung*) (*phonē*) and human discourse (*und der menschlichen Rede*) in the broad sense, is what Aristotle indicates when he says that human discourse is *kata suntheken,* which he interprets as "ὅταν γένεται σύμβολον." The "*kata suntheken*" rests in the *genesis* of a *sumbolon.*

Heidegger then gives all the necessary explanations as to what is meant by *sumbolon,* namely the two parts of one and the same thing that two guests or two friends share between them as a sign of engagement or contract or pact, of agreement, so that when they meet up again and join the pieces together they recognize each other, for example from one generation to another, in transgenerational fashion, like two friends bound in friendship by their fathers, etc.—and verbal language is indeed a set of inheritances, of transgenerational pacts. All of which is well known, Heidegger insists, and still in order to show that this is properly human, that animals have access neither to the *logos semantikos,* nor to the *phonē semantikē,* nor to everything that is *kata suntheken,* nor to the *sumbolon.* They are deprived of all that. All of that is what they are deprived of, and on the basis of which there is the *as such* and the *as a whole* as world.

Two remarks of different types at this point:

32. In the session, Derrida translated this passage: "'Die Bedeutung wächst nicht den Lauten zu [signification is not, does not come to be added to sound], sondern umgekehrt [but on the contrary, the reverse], aus schon gebildeten und sich bildenden Bedeutungen bildet sich erst die Prägung des Lautes [signification does not come to be added to sound, but on the contrary it is from already configured (or self-configuring) significations alone that the impression, the <seal [*sceau*]?> of noise, of sound (*die Prägung des Lautes*) is formed].' Then a second *umgekehrt* comes to confirm the argument: 'Der λόγος ist zwar φωνή [*logos* is indeed voice, *phonē,* but not at first, primarily and then by way of a supplement, but on the contrary, *logos* is at first something else and only afterward, thereby, does it become *phonē*].' What comes first in *logos*? '[What in the first place?] *Primär was?*' Response: 'κατὰ συνθήκην.'"

33. "Meaning does not accrue to sounds, but the reverse: the sound is first forged from meanings that are forming and have already formed. The λόγος is indeed φωνή, yet not primarily and then something else besides, but rather the reverse: it is primarily something else and then also . . . φωνή. Primarily what? κατὰ συνθήκην."

1. On the argument whose syntax is organized around the *"umgekehrt"*
(meaning, intelligible signification, does not depend on sound and does not
come along to add itself to it, but conversely, sound signifies by reason of the
meaning, the signification, the symbol which is *kata syntheken,* by convention and pact, by agreement)—this announces and makes intelligible the
assertion that will later so often be repeated by Heidegger, and which might
seem a little surprising, when he says that we do not hear because we have
310 ears, but that on the contrary, *umgekehrt,* we have ears because we hear.

2. The second remark would need to be longer and more complicated. For
one might be surprised to see Heidegger relying on the distinction between
what is natural (*phusei*) and what is conventional or symbolic (*kata suntheken*). One might be surprised, especially, to see Heidegger rely on this
distinction to confirm the fact that the animal has no access to any conventional sign, to anything artificial, etc. One might be surprised for two
reasons at least. First, because the assertion that the animal is a stranger to
learning technical conventions and to any technical artifice in language is
an idea that is quite crude and primitive, not to say stupid. It is not enough
for language not to have words, for it to be pre-verbal or extra-verbal (even
among humans) for it to be *phusei,* and a stranger to all conventionality. A
non-verbal and wordless language can also be *kata syntheke,* among all living beings, human and nonhuman. One does not even need to have domestic animals to know this. And ancient or modern zoological science gives us
a thousand proofs of it. The idea that the animal has only an innate and natural language, although quite widespread in the philosophical tradition and
elsewhere, is nonetheless crude and primitive. Next, one might be surprised
to see Heidegger, who so often warns us against a late interpretation of
physis as *natura,* here give quite a bit of credit to the opposition *physis/thesis,*
physis/nomos, physis versus conventionality or *physis* versus *sumbolon.* We
should have to conclude from this (and I believe one would be right to conclude first) that the *natura* to which Heidegger says *physis* is not to be reduced, is not the *physis* of the Greeks in general, with all the oppositions
physis/tekhnē, physis/nomos, physis/thesis or *physis* versus *kata suntheken.* Heidegger continues to give broad credit to this interpretation of *physis;* but
what he is determined to distinguish from it, as an erroneous and late com-
311 ing interpretation, is modern, post-Galilean or post-Cartesian *natura,* the
one that is spoken in Latin rather than in Greek.

But if we assume all that, at least very schematically, we now have to take
into account an interesting complication. This complication does not over-
turn this schema, but it signals a worry on Heidegger's part. It bespeaks his

desire to bring his own inflection to the reading of Aristotle, by appropriat-
ing, i.e. translating Aristotle's hidden or occulted intended meaning into
his own discourse, or into his own vocabulary, in the syntax proper to his
interpretive arrangement. He does it with two words that he emphasizes,
that he puts in italics: *Übereinkunft* and *Transzendenz*.

What is happening here?

When he asks himself what Aristotle means by the words *sumbolon* or
kata suntheken, Heidegger begins to reply by introducing under the word
suntheke the German word *Übereinkunft*. This is an irreproachable translation. Like *suntheke, Übereinkunft* most often means agreement, arrangement, in the sense of pact or convention. *Suntheke* is indeed the treaty, the
article of a treaty between states or individuals, what is posited by a decision, in sovereign fashion, in the terms of the deliberated convention. *Suntheke* also means, sometimes, arrangement of words or oratorical construction; and there is always the idea, as indicated by the *sun,* but also by *theke,*
of a com-position, a syn-thesis that com-poses, that posits together, that puts
together. It is an arrangement, a jointing of parts or parties (parts of a thing,
all the parties to an agreement). This jointing is also to be found in the *sumbolon.* And the idea of jointing is to be found in a rare but attested usage
of the word *suntheke* for coffin, the wooden box constructed and adjusted,
jointed—which, let it be said in passing, remains for us the obligatory passage or moment of the funeral, be it organized by those we were nicknam-
ing the inhumers or carried out by the cremators. Always, in both cases, you
need some *suntheke,* some coffin, to bury as well as to cremate. You always
need the moment of this wooden box which is indispensable to the organization of any funeral rite, this wooden box that Genet, in *Funeral Rites*   312
(and I made a great deal of this in *Glas* and in "Cartouches"[34]), compares
to a matchbox, and a matchbox, like a reduced coffin, that the narrator has
in his pocket at the burial of his friend, whose "death [. . .] was doubled in
another death."[35] It is also Genet who writes this, in a passage whose interest is that it links the idea or the word "contract," convention, and therefore
suntheke, with that of "funeral rite" (I quote, then):

34. See Jacques Derrida, *Glas* (Paris: Galilée, 1974), p. 18; trans. John P. Leavey, Jr.,
and Richard Rand as *Glas* (Lincoln: University of Nebraska Press, 1986), p. 11; and
"Cartouches," in *La vérité en peinture* (Paris: Flammarion, 1978), pp. 258–62; trans.
Geoffrey Bennington and Ian McLeod as "Cartouches," in *The Truth in Painting* (Chicago: University of Chicago Press, 1987), pp. 225–28.

35. Jean Genet, *Pompes funèbres,* in *Œuvres complètes* (Paris: Gallimard, 1953) 3:23;
trans. Bernard Frechtman as *Funeral Rites* (New York: Grove Press, 1969), p. 29; translation modified.

There is a book entitled *I'll Have a Fine Burial.* [An ideal book, a dream book, a book that I would like to write, but also a book that I am writing, that I have already written and which is every book, which is the hidden meaning of all books, in the work of every book, as the haunting of every book: every book premeditates a fine burial, every book makes arrangements, is in truth a gathering of arrangements for the posthumous which we were speaking about last week, for what follows death, for what comes after, *posterus,* in view of posterity.] We are acting with a view to a fine burial, to formal obsequies. They will be the masterpiece, in the strict sense of the word, the major work, quite rightly the crowning glory of our life. [Thus Jean Genet lets us think that literature itself, literary work or work in general, as glorious testament, is always a sort of contract (*suntheke,* contract or coffin) that one tries to pass on with some institution of funeral rite. Genet goes on:] I must die in apotheosis, and it doesn't matter whether I know glory before or after my death as long as *I know* that I'll have it [and Genet writes, "as long as *I know,*" in italics, clearly marking the important thing, what counts, what "matters"[36] as the very thing: this is not what effectively will happen when I am dead, since I will no longer be there anyway, there will no longer be any world for me, I will no longer be of this world, I will know nothing of it and the glory will not return to me; the important thing, what counts, *in the present,* is that I enjoy *now,* here and now, presently, knowing that I will have it, believing that I know that I will have it, present knowledge of a future glory and not of a present glory that I can easily renounce: enjoyment is present, it presently makes use of something that I do not have at present and which perhaps I never will have, but which I believe I know now that I will have. Genet goes on:] and I shall have it if I sign a contract with a firm of undertakers [*une maison de pompes funèbres*] [the whole of culture, really, society, culture, the State, etc.] that will attend to fulfilling my destiny, to rounding it off.[37]

313

As for the passage on the matchbox, in *Funeral Rites,* here it is (we would need to link it to another text by Genet (published only in Italian in the form of a fictive letter on the *Golden Legend* and the coffin of St. Osmosis, which I also talk about in *Glas*)[38]). I'll read very quickly the passage from *Funeral Rites:* (Read *Funeral Rites,* pages 25–26, matches, burial, fire, cremation[39])

> [. . .] the procession left the church.
> The matchbox in my pocket, the tiny coffin, imposed its presence more and more, obsessed me:
> "Jean's coffin could be just as small."

36. [Translator's note:] This word is in English in the text.
37. Ibid., p. 90 [p. 119; translation slightly modified].
38. *La vérité en peinture*, p. 258 [p. 225], and *Glas*, p. 18 [p. 11].
39. In Derrida's typescript: "inc."

I was carrying his coffin in my pocket. There was no need for the small-scale bier to be a true one. The coffin of the former funeral had imposed its potency on that little object. I was performing in my pocket, on the box that my hand was stroking, a diminutive funeral ceremony as efficacious and reasonable as the Masses that are said for the souls of the departed, behind the altar, in a remote chapel, over a fake coffin draped in black. My box was sacred. It did not contain a particle merely of Jean's body but Jean in his entirety. His bones were the size of matches, of tiny pebbles imprisoned in penny whistles. His body was somewhat like the cloth-wrapped wax dolls with which sorcerers cast their spells. The whole gravity of the ceremony was gathered in my pocket, to which the transfer had just taken place. However, it should be noted that my pocket never had any religious character; as for the sacredness of the box, it never prevented me from treating the object familiarly, from kneading it with my fingers, except that once, as I was talking to Erik, my gaze fastened on his fly, which was resting on the chair with the weightiness of the pouch of Florentine costumes that contained the balls, and my hand let go of the matchbox and left my pocket.

314

Jean's mother had just gone out of the room. I uncrossed my legs and recrossed them in the other direction. I was looking at Erik's torso, which was leaning slightly forward.

"You must miss Berlin," I said.

Very slowly, ponderously, searching for words, he replied:

"Why? I'll go back after the war."

He offered me one of his American cigarettes, which the maid or his mistress must have gone down to buy for him, since he himself never left the small apartment. I gave him a light.[40]

So much for the *suntheke* as contract and as coffin. Let's come back to Heidegger's Aristotle, and the translation of *suntheke* as *Übereinkunft*.

The *synthema,* the *syntheme,* is the convention, the thing agreed upon, the signal of recognition (for example a flag); and *synthemi,* the verb, indeed has the sense of com-position that puts together, that arranges, that joins, that joints, that fits together, for example stones or syllables, but also discourses, poetic works, or even that ensnares and machinates, traps, ruses, lies (I say "lies" because we shall soon rediscover this problem with the *logos apophantikos* that can also lie). So the translation of *suntheke* as *Übereinkunft* is not incorrect. But Heidegger is soon going to pull it in a more determined direction, that he needs in order to justify an interpretation that is, let's say, highly active.

315

After having introduced, apparently innocently, this word *Übereinkunft* which looks just like a correct translation, Heidegger is going to introduce

40. *Pompes funèbres,* pp. 25–26 [pp. 33–34].

another word, more abruptly, and more appropriatingly, that doesn't look at all like a translation this time, but that concentrates everything that is at stake in what Heidegger wants to give us to understand, as to the difference between animal and human, i.e. what the relation to beings as beings signifies. The word that it introduces is the word he has already used a great deal, especially in *Sein und Zeit,* but which in this lexical form appears rarely in this seminar—the word, the noun "transcendence" or the verb "to transcend." Transcendence in the sense of projecting oneself in order to relate to beings as such, as beings. This is the movement of Dasein's *Verhalten* we were speaking about just now, of Dasein relating to beings of such, beyond and transcending what encircles the animal in its drives or its appetites. The animal does not transcend, as does Dasein, and the movement of transcendence is indeed that on the basis of which one has a world as totality of beings as such.

As he is clearly aware that this, the vocabulary of transcendence, is not a translation as was *Übereinkunft,* Heidegger has to take precautions and tell us that it is by an insight of genius, but in confusion, that Aristotle anticipated with the word *sumbolon* what we (we, i.e. Heidegger) today call transcendence. Heidegger is basically going to translate *sumbolon,* or *suntheke,* as transcendence, quite calmly, as though he were making explicit, were content to make explicit and bring to light of day—through what is his own genius—the insight of genius, but unconscious or confused, of an Aristotle who was already doing that, but without quite knowing it clearly. I'll read this magnificent sentence:

> What Aristotle sees quite obscurely under the title σύμβολον, sees only approximately, and without any explication, in looking at it quite ingeniously, is nothing other than what we call today *transcendence.* (*Was Aristoteles ganz dunkel und ganz von ungefähr und ohne jede Explikation mit einem genialen Blick unter dem Titel* σύμβολον *sieht, ist nichts anderes, als was wir heute* Transzendenz *nennen.*) (H, 447/308)

316

And he continues to specify that there is language (*Es gibt Sprache*) only in a being who, essentially, transcends (i.e. relates to beings as beings). Transcendence is at bottom a correlate of the power of the *as such,* of the *als-Struktur* of which the animal is not capable. And Heidegger without more ado adds: "This is the sense of Aristotle's thesis [according to which] a λόγος is κατὰ συνθέκεν," (H, 447/309) and thus *thesei* and not *phusei.*

And while saying that he wishes to abstain from proposing here a history of the interpretations of Aristotle, Heidegger intends nevertheless to explain to us how the classical reading of Aristotle has always gone astray.

It has gone astray by interpreting conventionality, the pact, the idea that language is not *phusei* but *thesei* as though there were *first* natural sounds (animal sounds, in a sense) and as if humans *then, in a second moment,* conventionally, arbitrarily, came to an agreement to fix conventional significations by saying: by such and such a term we shall agree to understand this or that. Of course that can happen, Heidegger concedes, but that says nothing about the very genesis of language, about the origin of language in its inner essence. Aristotle saw this essence much more profoundly (*tiefer*) and he thus supposedly accomplished decisive steps (*entscheidende Schritte* [H, 447/309]) beyond the current theoretical inheritance.

You will understand that these decisive steps are those with which Heidegger himself is making his way, breaking his own path when, claiming to translate Aristotle's intuition of genius (though confused and insufficiently explained), Heidegger explains for his part that words are born of this essen-   *317* tial accord (*jener* wesenhaften Übereinkunft [H, 447/309]) of men among themselves in their *Miteinandersein,* insofar as they are together, in their *Miteinandersein,* in their being-the-one-for-the-other, one-with-another, open to the beings around them, to beings as such. It is this transcendence shared in *Mitsein,* in the common opening to beings, that is the ground (*Grund*) of their original accord which then renders speech, discourse (*Rede*), possible. So it is always *umgekehrt:* it is not the convention that comes to add itself to natural or even animal sound, then to make human language possible, and then human society. On the contrary, conversely, *umgekehrt,* it is transcendence, the opening to beings of such and in their totality (to the world), a transcendence which, originally common, shared in the *Miteinandersein,* permits accord, language, convention, etc., and one cannot separate transcendence from *Miteinandersein.* Transcendence, the movement that bears and relates to [*qui porte, qui rapporteà*] beings as such is from the start a social movement, if you like, a being-one-with-the-other, a *Mitsein.* The *Mitsein* is originary and not derived, and transcendence is a *Mitsein.* There would be no transcendence without this *Miteinandersein.* As soon as solitude itself, which is one of the major themes of this seminar, presupposes transcendence and language, it also presupposes, as solitude as such, as Robinsonophily, Robinsonocracy, Robinsonocentrism, if you will, [solitude presupposes] *Mitsein* and *Miteinandersein.*

It is just after this that Heidegger alludes to the *logos apophantikos* and to this non-apophantic language that is prayer (*eukhe, Bitten*).

But if all *logos semantikos* is not *apophantikos* — monstrative, enunciative — what then does "apophantic" mean and how does one recognize that the *logos* is apophantic? What distinguishes between two *logoi* that are equally *semantikoi,* between two discourses that are both meaningful, one <which> is also apophantic, and one which, like prayer, is not?

318   Here too, Heidegger will quote Aristotle and take his distance from the usual interpretation and even translation; he will take a distance with respect to the dominant tradition and set off in solitude, by virtue of this very distance, along a path that he thinks has not yet been broken. This is the usual Robinsonianism of his solitary and pioneering—conquering, even— way of going about things. This distance (the word is his, he says twice *"man [. . .] abweicht, [. . .] wir müssen davon abweichen"* [H, 449/310]: one steps aside, one deviates, we must step aside, we must diverge, go off, etc.), [this distance] has something venturesome and provocative about it.

Let's see. If every *logos* is *semantikos,* if every *logos* signifies, means something intelligible, but if every *logos semantikos* is not *apophantikos,* i.e. enunciative (we would say constative), if for example prayer is semantic, if it signifies, it is intelligible, but without being apophantic, according to what criterion, then, does one recognize the apophantic *logos*? And the enunciative discourse (*die aussagende Rede*)?

Asking himself this question, Heidegger quotes Aristotle: "λόγος is only ἀποφαντικός, ἐν ᾧ τὸ ἀλεθεύειν ἢ ψεύδεσθαι ὑπάρχει"[41] (*Peri hermeneias, Of Interpretation*), which is usually translated, "apophantic *logos* [enunciative discourse] is the discourse in which we find truth and falsity" (*"in dem Wahr — und Falschsein vorkommt"*) (H, 449/310; translation modified).

That, notes Heidegger, is the usual or natural translation, and when one deviates from it (*wenn man davon abweicht*), one is accused of giving in to arbitrariness or caprice (*Willkür*).

Well, without backing down when faced with this virtual accusation, Heidegger then declares that he will nonetheless deviate from the current translation and that he must do so (*wir müssen davon abweichen*) because this is the price for rediscovering what the Greeks meant, and that the traditional translation does not capture at all. Aristotle says *"en ho [. . .] hyper-*
319   *khei,"* which means the speech is enunciative by virtue of the fact that in it <the ἀλεθεύειν ἢ ψεύδεσθαι> not, as is said and translated, is simply encountered or found but, "in ihr liegt als zugrundeliegend," is found *lying in it as underlying it,* in its grounding sub-soil [and indeed, *hyparkho, hyparkhein* literally means not only to begin, to be at the beginning (*en arkhe*), to be at the principle, but to begin at the bottom, by the base, by what is underneath, to exist before, to be the foundation, and these values are indeed attested

41. Aristotle, *Hermeneutica,* chap. 4, 17a.2, cited in H, 449/310.

by many Greek usages]; so, "in ihr liegt als zugrundeliegend [underlined by Heidegger who adds:] as contributing toward its *ground* and its *essence* (*ihren* Grund *und ihr* Wesen *mitausmachend*)" (H, 449/310).

What is more, Aristotle uses the middle form, *pseudesthai: "sich zur Täuschung machend, in sich täuschend sein"* (H, 449/310), to make oneself into deceit, to be misleading in oneself. Which implies, Heidegger goes on, that the enunciative, apophantic *logos* is a *logos* one of the features of which is that it is able to be deceitful, and thus that the fact of deceit belongs to the essence of *logos*. The *logos* is what can bring about deceit, and therefore lying, the power to have something pass (*vorgeben*) (given as, advance in giving as, in substituting), to pass off something as what that thing is not, the power to make believe, to pretend, to have pass for (*vorgeben*). This *Täuschen* is the power to have a being pass for another, what *is thus,* what is such, for what *is not thus,* for what is not such, and reciprocally, and thus, concludes Heidegger, the power [for elsewhere, we'll come to it next time, Heidegger defines *logos* as a power, here the power] to hide, to withdraw, to *Verbergen, Vorbergen* (to have taken for, to deceive in having taken for) pre-supposes the possibility of *Verbergen* (of hiding).[42] *Verborgenheit,* dissimulation, belongs to the possibility of speaking the truth, to the *aletheuein* which, for its part, is an unveiling that brings out from withdrawal (*Entbergen: aus der Verborgenheit entnehmen:* bring out from dissimulation). The *Vorgeben* (the fact of having pass for, of giving out as, while lying, misleading) presupposes the *Verborgen* (dissimulation, hiding) and the *Entbergen* (and conversely, bringing it out of its hiding place).

Where are we going from here? We shall see that clearly next week, but you already get the picture. The animal is *alogon,* it has neither *logos seman-tikos* nor *logos apophantikos;* it can neither speak, nor pray, nor lie. Because it has no relation to beings as such and therefore could not pass off as such what is not such, or the other way round. The animal neither dissimulates

320

---

42. In the typescript, the following passage has some empty parentheses. We have filled them in on the basis of the recording of the session. For the passage that Derrida is commenting on here, see H 449/310: "Wir müssen sagen: zu dessen *Möglichkeit* es gehört, weil *Aristoteles* betont: ἀλεθεύειν ἤ ψεύδεσθαι, entweder das eine oder das andere, aber eines von beiden, in sich die Möglichkeit zum einen oder anderen, entweder ver-bergen—oder nicht verbergen, sondern gerade aus der Verborgenheit entnehmen, also nicht verbergen, sondern entbergen—ἀ-λεθεύειν [We have to say: which has the *pos-sibility,* because Aristotle emphasizes: ἀλεθεύειν ἤ ψεύδεσθαι, either one or the other, but one of the two, the inherent possibility of one or the other, either concealing—or not concealing, but precisely *taking from concealment,* thus not concealing but *revealing*—ἀ-λεθεύειν]."

nor lies, because it has no relation to truth (Lacan . . .[43]). Prayer, for its part, a human thing, is a *logos semantikos* but not *apophantikos,* it speaks but could neither lie nor tell the truth. A prayer says nothing that could mislead. It cannot and could not be shown to be false (at least in one sense of the term, even if it is not fulfilled: one cannot say that a prayer lies, misleads, attempts to mislead or is mistaken in itself). We shall have to specify why. The *logos apophantikos,* for its part, is also human discourse, but one that can always mislead and lie. The *logos apophantikos* can speak the truth and make the truth only by withdrawing from deceit, lying and retreat, or even from error as such.[44]

Next time, we will put all this into relation with the ontological difference, with the possibility of relating to beings as such in their Being, the ontological difference as it *waltet.* But we shall begin with a semi-confession from Heidegger, who for once recognizes having made a mistake—without however totally making a mistake about this, of course—in *Sein und Zeit.*

43. In the session, Derrida added: "Recall what we said about Lacan last year. It is the fundamental argument for Lacan on the animal: it cannot lie. It has some ruses, but it cannot lie if lying is passing for true what is not true, because it has no relation to the signifier, in Lacan's sense, and thus no relation to the other. Lacan's discourse is totally Heideggerian, which is itself totally Cartesian." See *La bête et le souverain, I,* session 4, p. 171 and passim [pp. 121–22 and passim].

44. In the session, Derrida added: "Heidegger's discourse is very strong in this respect."

March 12, 2003

Last time we started with the immense and undelimitable question of prayer. Can one in fact talk of a "question of prayer?" A prayer, which, precisely, performative though it is, can ask, of course, and ask to be heard, or even received in silence, even if it is asking nothing, but no doubt remains foreign to the question. And thus to science and philosophy. Every question presupposes a prayer, but prayer as such does not ask a question, it remains foreign to the question properly speaking. When one prays, one may ask or desire, but one is not posing a question. Speaking about prayer, especially around Robinson, we said that it was often the movement of a confession and thus of a repentance, and thus of an asked-for pardon.

Well, today, after a long and tortuous detour, we are perhaps going to come back to our old and vertiginous concern for pardon. During the seminar that we devoted to this for years, years ago,[1] the figure of the animal did not fail to preoccupy us. That of the sovereign too, and the so-called sovereign right of grace (mercy[2]). Does the animal have access to this enigmatic thing we call pardon, the only possible pardon, we were saying, namely the impossible pardon, the pardon of the unpardonable?

We will no doubt arrive at this shore or this bank, at the end of the long voyage of this session. I'm speaking the language of water, of sea and ocean, the maritime language of insularity, after having — at risk of being short of air — spoken a great deal about the earth of inhumation and the fire of cremation.

For a few weeks now, I have been wondering, I have been wondering first of all confusedly, and then more and more clearly, more and more thematically, what was pushing me to use — as though to play seriously with

1. Thus in the typescript. Derrida is referring here to his unpublished seminar on perjury and pardon (1997–98): sessions 1, 4, and 8.
2. [Translator's note:] In English in the text.

them—more or less neologizing expressions such as *cremators* and *inhumers*. And taking a certain pleasure in doing so, a secret pleasure, though a definite one, and one indecipherable to me, with a taste that some might share and others judge to be dubious or worrisome, in any case *unheimlich*.

I sensed, I pre-sensed clearly, from afar, that these names invented on the hoof, *cremators* and *inhumers*—these species classifications, basically, the cremators and the inhumers—had a strange resonance, half comic and <half> tragic, as though they designated groups, groupings, gatherings of herds or hunting packs that started looking, in the shadows, not only like animal species (perhaps on the endangered list), but more precisely something like secret societies, orders or sects—religious orders. There are the mendicant orders, the Carmelites, the Benedictines, the Franciscans, the Dominicans, the Augustines, the Trinitarians, the Hieronymites, the Premonstratensians, the brothers of St. John of God, the Teutonics, the silent orders, the Trappists, and now, seemingly, the Cremators and the Inhumers. A little as though these orders, these corporations, these companionships, or these fraternities, these brotherhoods of men uniformly dressed in black, gathered together by obedience to ceremonials and to ritual rules (the one group treats the dead by inhumation, by decomposition in wood and earth, the other group by wood, the modern funeral pyre, or the crematory oven—as for inhumation, reread in *Robinson Crusoe* the passage in which Robinson orders Friday to return to the island "to bury the dead Bodies of the Savages" [RC, 223]), as though, then, these orders or these corporations, these human fraternities, these journeymen of the cemetery tour represented merely an artifact, an organization that is historical,[3] artificial and finally contingent and provisional, sorts of sects which, for a time, would be linked by a vow, and by an activity, an artisanal or industrial labor, a master piece (namely, knowing how to deal with the corpse), but more or less secular and religious orders which in the world were opposed or differentiated only into two groups (neither one more nor one less) during a finite epoch only, an epoch in which I distinguished a sub-epoch or a period that was itself singular and finite, that I nicknamed European modernity, in which, for the first time in the history of humanity, one could choose *freely* (that's the essence of democratic freedom, it can be measured, as free will, when you get close to the cemetery or a crematorium) [one could, then, democratically choose, as they say] the order or sect to which one wished to belong—and even, within the same family, belong to two orders at once—as

---

3. During the session, Derrida added: "political, in the end, for the State is always implicated, in modern Europe, in the organization of cremation or of inhumation."

state and religion, for the first time in history, left to each his or her freedom
to belong simultaneously or successively to the order of inhumers and/or
cremators, and to have oneself treated—as a corpse, one fine day, when
the day came—according to one or the other of these technical and ritual
apparatuses. But the muted question that must in secret have been pushing
me toward these denominations and toward this taxonomy, and toward
this *unheimlich* lugubrious mise-en-scène, must have been (as has only just
become clear as day to me), the following question, the question that will
no longer leave me alone: Why should there only be *two* orders? Why only
two? Why two parties in a democracy? Nothing is less democratic than
limiting the number of parties to two, as is the case in fact, if not by right,
among our bellicose Anglo-Saxon allies. Why not imagine more? So that
the modernity on which I insisted so much (the democratic choice left open
by the union of church and state, in the so-called modern democracies, left
open to the discretion of each and every one between cremators and inhumers) would be merely the penultimate crepuscular phase of a mutation as yet
unheard of. For can one not indeed imagine and see coming another epoch
of humanity in which, tomorrow, one would no longer deal with corpses
either by cremation *or* by inhumation, either by earth or by fire? Would not
the democracy to come gain by opening still wider the spectrum of possible choices? Will one not invent unheard-of techniques, fitted like their
predecessors to the dictatorial power of a phantasm as well as to technical
possibilities and which would then deliver over corpses, if there still are
any, neither to the subsoil of humus, nor to the fire of heaven or hell? In
this future, with these other ways of treating the corpse, today's institutions,
today's orders, would appear as vestiges, anachronistic orders or sects of a
new modern Middle Ages. People would speak of the cremators and the
inhumers (this is no doubt what was obscurely inspiring in me these names
and this dual classification) as oddities that were both *unheimlich* and dated,
as archaic curiosities for historians or anthropologists of death. I'll let you
dream of a death that would no longer leave us in the hands of these itiner-
ant sects of cremators or inhumers, and would definitively put out of a job
these arrogant sects that pass for the religions to which they appeal for their
authority, or the secularizing laity to which they lay claim . . .

You have to be able to dream. [*Faut pouvoir rêver.*]

You have to be able to dream. To think a little, have to be able to dream.

You have to be able, right? But you still have to be able. [*Il faut pouvoir, n'est-ce pas. Encore faut-il pouvoir.*]

Have to be able, *faut pouvoir,* is a sigh familiar to us. It is the transla-

tion into two words, "faut pouvoir," of a sigh we have no difficulty in rec-
327 ognizing. "Faut pouvoir" is also the verbal expression, the discourse of a
sigh that announces a discouragement or even an impotence. It is often
the moment at which one gives up ("listen, *faut pouvoir,* eh . . .").[4] It is in
that case a protestation in the face of an unacceptable request or an excessive demand. "You're asking too much, *faut pouvoir,* you understand." Or
conversely, faced with an exploit that one admires or condemns, one ex-
claims in stupefaction: "Ah! *Faut pouvoir* all the same!" Ah! They dared
to write that, *faut pouvoir,* eh . . . Ah! That idiot dared write and publish
that shameful thing at a given moment, this or that weekly dared to go in
for that abjection, *faut pouvoir,* implying *faut pouvoir le faire,* it takes some
doing to be abject, it's quite something [*faut le faire*]. I shall not give any
examples.

What does *pouvoir* [power, to be able] mean in general? A word on its own
has no meaning, as Austin recalls: only a sentence has meaning, a concatenation.

No one will be able to reply to the question "what does *pouvoir* mean in
general?" no one will have the power to reply to this question, no one will
even have the power to hear it and understand this question, if one leaves
the word "power" in a state of insular isolation, if one does not make a sentence with it. One will never have either the *possibility* or the *power* (hang
on to the association of these two words) to understand what *power* means
if one isolates this word "power" (this verb *pouvoir,* which is also a noun,
which can become the subject or object of a sentence, but also its active
verb), one will never have either the *possibility* or the *power* to understand
what the word *pouvoir* means if one leaves it alone, without a sentence, like
an island with no land bridge linking it to something else in the world.
Which is true of any word. The word has power and can exercise its power,
the power of its supposed meaning only by being caught up and concate-
nated in the chain of a sentence, and thus also in leaving an indetermination
open for other possible sentences.

328   For example, "to be able to pray [*pouvoir prier*]. That was our question
last time. "What is it to pray?" always implies a "what is it to be able to
pray?" Can one pray, is it possible? Can one not pray, is it possible? How
not to pray? How does one have the power to pray or not to pray? These are
questions in which the sense of *pouvoir* begins to be determined by prayer

---

4. In the session, Derrida added: "'to have to be able' [*Faut pouvoir*] when one is not
able."

itself, etc. One could say the same of the question "can one pardon?" Is it possible to pardon the only thing to be pardoned, i.e. the unpardonable, namely what it is impossible to pardon, what one cannot pardon? What is power if all it can do is un-power, if all it can do is what it cannot do [*s'il ne peut que ce qu'il ne peut pas*]—namely the impossible?

If I now say *il faut pouvoir,* a common expression, does that not further complicate things, to the point that the *il faut* indicates both necessity, duty, injunction, but also possibility: one must [*il faut*] have the possibility to be able [*pouvoir*], for example one must be able to do this or that, speak, have access to the ontological difference, to the "as such," etc. But the *il faut* also indicates lack, the failing of failure or default, default of power, impotence, unpower. For if there is duty, necessity, obligation, injunction, required condition of possibility, this is because power is lacking, comes to be lacking, *can* [*peut*] be lacking, precisely. Power *can* be lacking. It is possible that power can be lacking, and that therefore this entire sentence ("It is possible that power might be lacking") comes to collapse in return, in its possibility, like a row of dominos or a house of cards. The *il faut pouvoir* thus also signals toward the "default of power."

What is it that is thus coming to complicate our question? "As we shall shortly show," as La Fontaine would say in the "The Wolf and the Lamb," shortly, after having said something about power, the power of law, of reason or of force: "the reason of the strongest is always the best,/ As we shall shortly show."[5] One must be able to [*il faut pouvoir*] wait. Waiting is what one must be able to do. Wait without attaining [*attendre sans atteindre*], as Blanchot said, you remember. Blanchot also made clear that attaining, attainment never lifts the waiting. One continues to wait, if only in prayer, even when one has attained what one thought one was waiting for. One always has to wait, attain or not. One has to know how to wait, one has to be able to wait, but whether or not one knows it or is able to do it, one waits, one must wait. One must wait and one cannot but wait, that's what "one has to wait [*il faut attendre*]" means. One must, both out of duty and out of necessity. One cannot, one does not have the power to do differently. Robinson is the man who waits, and who—reread it—continues to wait when he has attained what he was claiming, desiring or believing he was waiting for. Let's wait, we must wait, *il faut pouvoir.*

329

5. Jean de La Fontaine, "Le loup et l'agneau," in *Fables,* ed. Marc Fumaroli (Paris: Livre de poche, 1985), p. 51. [Translator's note: my translation.] See Jacques Derrida, *La bête et le souverain, I,* session 1, p. 26, and passim [pp. 6–7, n. 10, and passim].

To move forward and to situate one of the headings of our session, let us now begin with a quotation. You can quickly and easily recognize the author of these sentences:

> A trace is an imprint, not a signifier. [. . .] The imprint of Friday's footprint which Robinson discovers during his walk on the island is not a signifier. On the other hand, supposing that he, Robinson, for whatever reason, effaces this trace, that clearly opens up the dimension of the signifier. From the moment that one effaces it, where there is sense in effacing it, that of which there is a trace is manifestly constituted as signified.
>
> If the signifier is thus a hollow [*un creux*], it is in as much as it bears witness to a past presence. Conversely, in what is a signifier, *in the fully developed signifier that speech is* [I underline], there is always a passage, i.e. something beyond each of the articulated elements, which are by nature fleeting, evanescent.[6]

Why do I quote here these sentences from Lacan? They are taken from
330 *The Seminar, Book 5: The Formations of the Unconscious* (1957–58: oh look, it's the same date as *Identität und Differenz* that we were talking about last time and that we shall talk about again in a moment).

1. I quote these sentences from Lacan in the first place because he mentions Robinson, of course (and I ask myself, although for what matters to us this is only a secondary detail; I ask myself, I ask you if Lacan is justified by the text of *Robinson Crusoe* in saying that the footprint on the sand is indeed Friday's; I'm not sure, and if by rereading you could tell me next week whether or not Lacan is or is not making a first confusion here, that would be good; but once more, that's not the essential thing I want to say).

2. If I quote these sentences from Lacan, this is in the second place because they follow very closely another passage that I shall look at in a moment, a very important passage on the animal, on its inability to have access to the signifier, the *logos* and truth, to the other — a passage that goes in the sense of the conclusions that I put forward last year at the end of the long and patient demonstration I attempted on the basis of numerous texts by Lacan but not this one, which I had not yet located because I was not yet obsessed with Robinson Crusoe. As I don't want to go back over what I said at great length, especially last year, on the argument about *response* and about the

6. Jacques Lacan, *Le séminaire, Livre V: Les formations de l'inconscient (1957–1958)*, ed. Jacques-Alain Miller (Paris: Le Seuil, 1998), pp. 342–43. [Translator's note: my translation.]

erasure of the trace (the animal being classically and dogmatically supposed, by Lacan, to be unable to *respond* and to *erase its tracks* [*traces*]⁷), I will permit myself, so as not to repeat myself, to point out for those who might be interested in these premises a recent publication, though only in English (my text has not yet been published in French), of what is *grosso modo* the equivalent of what I said here last year about Lacan and the animal. This text is to be found in a collective volume edited by Cary Wolfe, with the title *Zoontologies: The Question of the Animal.* My own essay, translated by David *331* Wills, is entitled "And Say the Animal Responded?," an elegant and clever translation of "Et si l'animal répondait?"⁸

3. The third reason, the main one, for my quoting these lines from Lacan, is that once more they are going in the direction of what Heidegger says about the animal and about the *logos semantikos* and then about the *logos apophantikos.* The animal is *zōon alogon,* a living being without *logos*; man, for his part, as *zōon logon ekhon,* has the *power* of *logos*; and Heidegger expressly says — we're coming to this — that the *logos* is a *power,* and he moves easily from *possibility* to *power,* from possibility to faculty and from faculty to power (he says three times in section 73, "*Der* λόγος *is ein Vermögen* [. . .] [The λόγος is an ability [. . .]]" [H, 489/337] (the *logos apophantikos* is "*das Vermögen zu*" and he asks, "*Was liegt diesem Vermögen zu* [. . .]? [The λόγος ἀποφαντικός is able to [. . .], What underlies this ability of the λόγος?]" [H, 489/337] etc.)). Lacan also speaks of power, on the same page as the one I was just quoting, and we also find the same movement, to my mind a problematic one, from possibility, from the possible, to power (immense problem): "[. . .] the signifier *as such* [I underline] is something that *can* [peut] be erased [. . .] one of the fundamental dimensions of the signifier is that it *can* [pouvoir] annul itself. For this there is a *possibility* that we *can* [pouvons] in this event describe as a mode of the signifier itself."⁹ And Lacan recalls on this point the *Aufhebung,* and that this German word is found in Freud to

7. See Derrida, *La bête et le souverain, I,* session 4, pp. 165–74 [pp. 116–74].

8. See Jacques Derrida, "Et si l'animal répondait?," in *Cahiers de L'Herne,* no. 83, *Derrida,* ed. Marie-Louise Mallet and Ginette Michaud (Paris: Éditions de L'Herne, 2004), pp. 117–29; reprinted in the posthumous book by Jacques Derrida, *L'animal que donc je suis,* ed. Marie-Louise Mallet (Paris: Galilée, 2006), pp. 163–91; trans. David Wills as "And Say the Animal Responded?," in *Zoontologies: The Question of the Animal,* ed. Cary Wolfe (Minneapolis: University of Minnesota Press, 2003), pp. 121–46; reprinted in Jacques Derrida, *The Animal That Therefore I Am,* ed. Marie-Louise Mallet (New York: Fordham University Press, 2008).

9. Lacan, *Le séminaire, Livre V,* p. 343; Derrida's emphasis.

say that this signifier is revocable, although Freud's use of the term is not Hegelian, according to Lacan. We shall come back to all this.

332   The point of articulation of what Lacan says, both with *Robinson,* as we have just seen, and with Heidegger, is that precisely, at the point where we stopped last week, Heidegger was also defining the *logos apophantikos* by the possibility of the *pseudesthai,* which was not only the possibility of the false, but also of the dissimulation that hides (*Verborgenheit*), of the deceit that misleads (*Täuschung*), or even of lying, all that flowing from the possibility of withdrawal, of erasure, so that making or speaking the truth (*aletheuein, aletheia*) consists in withdrawing from the withdrawal, bringing out from withdrawal ("entbergen," "aus der Verborgenheit entnehmen" [H, 449/310][10]). Where there is not this possibility of error, of the false, but also of trickery—in short, of dissimulation in general, there is no power or potency of *logos*, and so there is no Dasein as *zōon logon ekhon,* there is only some animal without *logos* (*zōon alogon*). A proposition that was also Lacan's in the numerous texts we read last year:[11] the animal can neither deceive [*tromper*], nor lie, nor even, in the strong sense of the term, deceive itself [*se tromper*].

To deceive oneself, or to have been deceived, as I announced last time, is something that Heidegger admits without admitting happened to him. It happened to him in *Sein und Zeit.* I say "it happened to" rather than saying that he was responsible for or guilty of it, because he exculpates himself by accusing himself, as is always the case, and like everyone else. As we shall see, he admits without admitting, he exculpates himself by accusing himself, precisely on the subject of the *logos apophantikos,* and more precisely still the *pseudesthai.* As though the fault without fault that he admits without admitting, was a fault, a failing, an illusion, a faux pas, that is *both* guilty and innocent.

A faux pas *about* what? About the *pseudesthai* entailed by faux pas, precisely, by deceit or self-deceit [*de tromperie ou de "se tromper"*]. What he then admits without admitting is not simply an "error," as the French translation says for *Täuschung,* in a way that is not faulty or erroneous but insufficiently precise, this word that means, as much as error or illusion, trickery,

333   fraud, ruse, feint—this word, *Täuschung,* that Heidegger used to translate *pseudesthai* (middle voice, he insists) and that he uses again here; not simply an error, then, but also an illusion, a fraud, a ruse, a feint, a deceit, or sometimes a deceiving oneself or better still a "having let oneself be deceived" (all

10. See session 8 above.
11. See *La bête et le souverain, I,* session 4, pp. 141–87 [pp. 97–135].

that at once in a chiaroscuro confusion that, as always, makes the avowal the more uncertain and the responsibility doubtful). Heidegger recognizes having been the victim (*Opfer*) of a *Täuschung* three or four years earlier in *Sein und Zeit,* even though, as he makes clear in a parenthesis that I find very funny (even though . . .), even in *Sein und Zeit* there are exceptions to the effects of this *Täuschung,* and Heidegger goes on to give references to what does *not* fall into the illusion or does not deceive itself already in *Sein und Zeit,* where, however, he seems to have been the victim (*Opfer*) of such a *Täuschung.* It's better that I read and retranslate these striking lines, which are sometimes on the verge of being comical, before reconstituting their context and what is at stake in them. This is in subsection b of section 73.

> The form of the statement taken as positive and true facilitates (*Die Form der Aussage* [thus *logos apophantikos* and not solely *logos semantikos*] *im Sinne der positiven wahren erleichtert*), for reasons we shall not discuss now, the interpretation of the λόγος [in other words, it is easier, more convenient to interpret *logos apophantikos* beginning with the true statement than to do so beginning with the false statement, error, feinting, lying, etc. It is better to go from the true to the false, to the possibility of the false, of deceit and deceiving-oneself, than the reverse. This is a pedagogical convenience, Heidegger seems to say, in a highly classical gesture, the stakes of which are grave [see *Limited Inc*[12]], as he does not fail to remark. And he goes on:] This manner of logically arranging the givens in starting out with the positive true judgment is justified within certain limits (*in gewissen Grenzen berechtigt*), but it is for this very reason it gives rise to the fundamental illusion [thus an approach justified to a certain extent becomes the cause of a fundamental illusion (*Grundtäuschung*)], that it is only a matter of simply relating the other possible forms of statement [implied: faulty, illusory, or deceitful statements/enunciations] to this one in a complementary fashion (*ergänzend*). (H, 488/336; translation modified)

334

So the *Grundtäuschung,* the illusion, the fault, the error, the fundamental deceiving-oneself, if I can put it like that, consists in behaving as though the question of the *Täuschung* were derived and secondary, a supplement to the truth of the true positive statement: in correcting this error or this deceit of the "deceiving oneself," the "self-deceit," of the deceiving of oneself, Heidegger says clearly that one must hold the *Täuschung* or the *pseudesthai* to be a primary, original, originary *possibility* of the truth of the true judgment and that one must therefore start from this possibility rather than seeing in

---

12. See Jacques Derrida, *Limited Inc.* (Paris: Galilée, 1990), pp. 88–89 and 174 [English edition (Evanston, Ill.: Northwestern University Press, 1988), pp. 72 and 150–51.]

it a mere complement or supplement, an *Ergänzung*. Whence the avowal
without avowal that I now quote:

> In *Being and Time,* I myself had fallen victim (*Opfer*) to this *Täuschung* [let's
> never forget that it is not by chance that it is a question, in *Being and Time,*
> of (I emphasize) a *Täuschung;* the *Täuschung,* the "self-deceit" consisted in
> not recognizing that it was necessary to begin with the "self-deceit" and not
> the other way around] [. . .]. (*Ich selbst* [myself, even me, and immediately
> follows the qualification of the avowal] *Ich selbst bin noch* [even me, still,
> etc.]—*wenigstens in der Durchführung der Interpretation des* λόγος—[at least
> (first qualification of the avowal), within limits, and not beyond the inter-
> pretation of the *logos*] *in* Sein und Zeit *ein Opfer dieser Täuschung geworden*
> [. . .]). (H, 488/337; translation modified)

He was, then, a victim—a sacrificial victim, even—a victim supposedly
innocent, like all victims, and a victim of what? Of a *Täuschung?* What
Täuschung? Of a *Täuschung* on the subject of *Täuschung,* a failing as a deceiving oneself, on the subject of failing as deceiving oneself, etc.

335 And the funniest thing, supposing one is of a humor to find this funny, is
that scarcely has he avowed (avowed what? nothing, avowed having been
simply a victim, *Opfer*), scarcely has he avowed without avowing an innocent fault, the faux pas of a victim, than he gives in a parenthesis all the
necessary references to all the places in *Sein und Zeit* already, where he *had
not* been a victim of this fault, he had already virtually corrected all signs
of it (in principle, theoretically, architectonically) and effaced the traces,
for there were already, in *Sein und Zeit,* exceptions to this *Täuschung* about
Täuschung. I quote the parenthesis: "(*vgl. als von dieser Täuschung ausgenom-
men* Sein und Zeit *S. 222 und S. 285f.*) [cf. as exempt from this illusion *Being
and Time,* pp. 222 and 285f.]" (H, 488/337).

Having recognized without recognizing what he has just recognized
without recognizing, he nevertheless promises not to do it again. And precisely in the seminar he is in the process of giving. For let us not forget that
he is speaking to students, and that traces remain of that, of that pedagogical
situation and of what the master avows without avowing to his disciples—
traces remain, then, that he would have wished to be both effaceable and ineffaceable. Could he foresee that in the posterity of the probable improbable
archive, the day would come when a French animal, in turn conducting a
seminar on this seminar and every Wednesday sniffing out the footprints
or the track of an improbable Friday, would come to worry away at these
"*pas d'aveu* [non avowals, steps of avowal]," on these traceless traces of an

avowal without avowal on the subject of a fault without fault, effaced and corrected as soon as committed, denied as soon as confessed, destined to remain as much as to efface itself, to efface its effacement, yesterday, now and tomorrow? Yesterday, now and tomorrow, for Heidegger indeed promises not to do it again and to stay away (this is his word again, *abweichen,* the word we were tracking last time[13]), to stay away, to take his distances by isolating himself forever from this wrong path that he had taken in *Sein und Zeit,* but in truth he had only almost taken [*failli emprunter*], as he makes clear, where he had almost failed [*failli faillir*] by going along it, even if he didn't go along it so very far. I'll quote the last lines of this paragraph. After the avowal without avowal, after the repentance which repents of nothing, here is the promise, the decision and the commitment ([14]Heidegger has just given in a parenthesis the references to the passages from *Sein und Zeit* in which he had already marked exceptions to his own *Täuschung,* and he goes on after having closed the parenthesis:

336

> In the interpretation that follows, while it does not really invalidate what I have said before in *Being and Time,* I must essentially and decisively deviate [stay away] from this. (*Ich muß in der jetzt zu gebenden Interpretation, die freilich das früher in* Sein und Zeit *Dargestellte nicht eigentlich aufhebt, wesentlich und entscheidend davon abweichen.*) (H, 489/387; translation slightly modified)

In no way are we putting Heidegger on trial here, and we do have to recognize, beyond the heroico-comical scene—so significant for us—of the avowal without avowal (which shows perhaps beyond the example of Heidegger that every avowal tends structurally to efface or deny itself in this way, and thus to exculpate the avower *a priori,* to carry off the traces he or she is claiming to leave, while leaving traces of the effacement which is thus ineffaceable, which both distinguishes and brings close to what is imprudently attributed to the animal by both Heidegger and Lacan and so many others)—we do have to recognize, then, to Heidegger's immense credit, that indeed, in the passages from *Sein und Zeit* he references, and which in my view are very important and which I invite you to reread, Heidegger insists strikingly on the co-originarity of truth and untruth for *Dasein.* Non-truth (and thus a certain *pseudesthai*) does not supervene like an accident, after the fact, on a more originary truth, thus requiring

13. See session 8 above, p. 228.
14. The parenthesis opened here is not closed in the typescript.

337 a complementary or supplementary theory. No: non-truth is as originary as truth. The possibility of error and of lying, of dissimulation in general, is required, originarily required, as possibility, by the possibility of truth or of veracity, and also of unveiling. Reread all these pages (pages 222–23), which also concern the structure of the statement (*Aussage*) and of the apophantic *als,* the apophantic *as such,* around propositions of the type: "The full existential and ontological meaning of the proposition: 'Dasein is in the truth [which means here *Entdecktheit, Offenbarkeit*]' (*Dasein ist in der Wahrheit*) also says equiprimordially (*sagt gleichursprünglich mit: 'Dasein ist in der Unwahrheit'*)."[15] This presupposes that truth is dragged away from withdrawal, dissimulation, *Verborgenheit,* and Heidegger insists on the privative character of *a-letheia,* as he does on the necessity of reinterpreting truth otherwise than as adequation.[16]

It is just after this, in the same movement, that Heidegger posits that to Dasein essentially belongs speaking (*Rede*), i.e. that of which the animal will be deprived (the animal that Heidegger does not treat directly here, in *Sein und Zeit*). In the other passage from *Sein und Zeit* to which he refers, we also find attention given to this negativity of non-truth, to this not (*des Nicht und seiner Nichtheit*[17]), in relation to care (for all this belongs to the structure of care (*Sorge*)), *Schuldigsein* and the *Unheimlichkeit* of Dasein, so many things that are refused, as goes without saying, to the animal (explain[18]).

338 I emphasize this value of *Unheimlichkeit*: I have been trying to show for years here that it plays a role that is as essential and decisive, but as little noticed by the most informed readers of Heidegger, as is the value of *walten.* Now this reference to *Unheimlichkeit,* which, for different reasons, is as difficult to translate as *walten* (uncanniness, being out of one's home, but also the quality of what is disturbing, a little frightening, both intimate

15. Martin Heidegger, *Sein und Zeit* (Tübingen: Max Niemeyer Verlag, 1963), p. 222; trans. Joan Stambaugh, revised and with a foreword by Dennis J. Schmidt as *Being and Time* (Albany: SUNY Press, 2010), p. 213. In the session, Derrida reprised this part of the sentence: "the proposition: 'Dasein is in truth' states just as originally, co-originarily: 'Dasein is in non-truth.'"

16. In the session, Derrida added: "Truth as dis-covery, un-veiling, presupposes the possibility of veiling. And *a-letheia,* the *a* showing privately, according to Heidegger, that it must be snatched out of the night, snatched from dissimulation, that truth consists in snatching it from non-truth, which is there from the beginning." The end of the sentence is inaudible.

17. Ibid., p. 286 [p. 274: "the 'not' and its notness"].

18. In the session, Derrida added nothing here.

and terrible, often associated with the Greek *deinon* in *Introduction to Metaphysics,* and always to define Dasein—and you also know the role that this *Unheimlichkeit* <plays> in Freud, in a way that is both different and central), this reference to *Unheimlichkeit* is found in the passage from *Sein und Zeit* being referred to, and in the passage from the seminar we are reading now, on *logos* as power (*Vermögen*) and on possibility (*Möglichkeit*) as power (*Vermögen*). In *Sein und Zeit,* Heidegger writes this:

> The call [*Ruf:* call of conscience (*Gewissen*), the call to responsi-culpability, to being indebted (*Schuldigsein*), which Heidegger had analyzed in the preceding pages, in section 57, and where *Unheimlichkeit* is named at least seven times, the call, he says] is the call of care (*Sorge*). The *Schuldigsein* constitutes the being that we call *Sorge* (care). Dasein stands primordially together with itself in *Unheimlichkeit* ["*étrang(èr)eté*": Emmanuel Martineau's translation]. [. . .] Insofar as Dasein—as care—is concerned about its Being, it calls itself [. . .] from its *Unheimlichkeit* to its potentiality of (*Seinkönnen*). Etc.[19]

Well, this *Unheimlichkeit* is going to reappear in the passage from the seminar that we are reading. For just after the avowal without avowal and the commitment to stay away from the *Täuschung* on the subject of *Täuschung,* Heidegger—this seems to me to be worthy of a particular, micrological attention—is going to make the transition that appears significant and important to me, from possibility to power, from *Möglichkeit* to *Vermögen,* to the *logos apophantikos* as power.

What does this mean and what is at stake in it? As you have no doubt already understood, this question of power is important to me here, and I believe it necessary to give it special attention for two reasons. On the one hand, in the dominant tradition of how the animal is treated by philosophy and culture in general, the difference between animal and human has always been defined according to the criterion of "power" or "faculty," i.e. the "being able to do [*pouvoir faire*]" or the *inability to do* this or that (man can speak, he has that power, the animal does not have the power of speech, man can laugh and die, the animal can neither laugh nor die, it is not capable of its death, as Heidegger literally says: it does not have the power (*können*) of its death and to become mortal, etc.); and, as I said here quite insistently not long ago, Bentham always seemed to me to be on the right track in saying—in opposition to this powerful tradition that restricts

339

19. Ibid., pp. 286–87 [p. 275].

itself to power and non-power—that the question is not, "can the animal do this or that, speak, reason, die, etc.?" but "can the animal suffer?"[20] is it vulnerable? And in the case of vulnerable suffering, of *pashkein*, of patience, passion and passivity, of the affectivity of suffering, power is a non-power; the power to suffer is in that case the first power as non-power, the first possibility as non-power that we share with the animal, whence compassion. It is from this compassion in impotence and not from power that we must start when we want to think the animal and its relation to man.

The second reason for which I am here privileging this determination of the *logos* as *Vermögen*, power or faculty, is that I am looking for a mediating schema with the motif—so hard to translate—of *Walten*, with which we have yet to deal, but about which you know that some possibility of power is necessarily inscribed in it (between force, violence, etc., and associated with the terrible, with terror, with *Unheimlichkeit* and with *deinon* in the *Introduction to Metaphysics* that I hope to talk about again here), *Walten* being the source, the origin, the condition, the force, the violence or the power that make possible and thus capable, the power to accede to the ontological difference, and therefore to the *as such,* and therefore to the *logos,* to the *logos* in general, as *logos semantikos,* and more especially as *logos apophantikos.*

In the section that follows the avowal without avowal, and the commitment to avoid the *Täuschung* about *Täuschung* in *Sein und Zeit,* Heidegger will successively emphasize, by placing them in italics, the words *Möglichkeit* (possibility) and *Vermögen* (power, faculty etc.). The common root, the *Mögen* we talked a lot about recently, authorizes this transition, even if it is a grave one. The essence of *logos*, recalls Heidegger, depends on the fact that in it resides the possibility (*Möglichkeit*) of the "*either* true *or else* false," or the "*not only* positive *but also* negative" (H, 489/337). This possibility is the internal essence of *logos.* It is only if we grasp this that the leap (*Absprung:* the jump or the jumping-off point of the jumper, the high-jumper or parachute jumper), the *Absprung* which will lead us to the *Ursprung,* to the origin, here to the origin of the *logos*, operates. We still have here the figure of the path, even the circular path: with a step backward (*Schritt zürück*) or

---

20. See Jeremy Bentham, *An Introduction to the Principles of Morals and Legislation* (1789) (London: Athlone Press, 1970), p. 44. Jacques Derrida comments on this passage in *L'animal que donc je suis,* pp. 48–50, 115, 142 [*The Animal That Therefore I Am,* pp. 27–29, 81, 103]. See also Jacques Derrida and Élisabeth Roudinesco, *De quoi demain . . . Dialogue* (Paris: Fayard/Galilée, 2001), p. 118; trans. Jeff Fort as *For What Tomorrow . . .* (Stanford, Calif.: Stanford University Press, 2004), p. 70.

a leap, a jumping-off point, we will be able to move backward toward the origin. The step is a leap, always. Every step leaps. The difference between the step and the leap is difficult to grasp. Every step is a leap. Here we're dealing with the backward step of the leap, or the jumping-off point (*Absprung*) of the *logos*, and this jumping-off point, the place for jumping (*Ort des* Absprungs [H, 489/337]), is the internal essence of *logos* as co-originary possibility of the true or false, the positive or the negative. The *logos* is not a formation or a construction that would be found there ready to hand (*ein vorhandenes Gebilde*); no, it is in its essence this possibility (*Möglichkeit*) of this *or* that, the true *or* the false, the positive *or* the negative. And then with a leap—as we can rightly say here—Heidegger moves from possibility to power, as though he were merely translating and making explicit *Möglichkeit*. He says in the very next sentence, emphasizing the word *Vermögen*: "Wir sagen: er ist ein *Vermögen zu* [. . .] (We say that it is a *power for* [. . .])"(H, 489/337; translation modified). And immediately, as you will see, and this is what authorizes me to find here the mediating schema with *Walten,* this power is defined as the power of the relation to beings as such, as they are. Heidegger writes:

> By power (*Vermögen*) we always understand the possibility of a comportment toward [*die Möglichkeit zu einem Verhalten zu:* so *Vermögen* as *Verhalten,* proper to Dasein and not to the animal, you remember this; Heidegger goes on:] i.e., the possibility of a relation to beings as such. The λόγος is a power (*Der* λόγος *ist ein Vermögen*), i.e., it intrinsically entails *having a relation to beings as such at one's disposal* (*d. h. in sich selbst* das Verfügen über ein Sichbeziehen zum Seinden als solchem [emphasized by Heidegger]).[21] In contrast to this, we called *capacity* (Fähigkeit) [and this is the animal] the possibility of behaving, of being related in a captivated and taken manner (*die Möglichkeit zum Benehmen, dem benommen-hingenommen Bezogensein,* Fähigkeit *genannt*). (H, 489/337; translation modified)

And we recognize here the *Benommenheit* of the animal, its beringed benumbment which does not have the *Vermögen* and the *Verhalten,* namely the power to relate to beings as such. I'll quickly read the whole following section that explicates this point clearly, and finishes on the reminder of *Unheimlichkeit:* (Read and comment on the seminar)

> The λόγος ἀποφαντικός is the power to say "either . . . or . . . ," which is the power of the freeing of revealing and concealing (*das Vermögen zum*

341

---

21. In the typescript, this phrase, already emphasized by Heidegger, is further underlined by Derrida.

"entweder-oder" des aufweisenden Entbergens und Verbergens in der Weise des
342 Zuweisens*), which show both in the manner of attribution and of denial,
that is, in a pointing out in which the "is" (being) is expressed in one meaning or another. The character of power (*Vermögenscharakter*), thus oriented,
is the essence of the λόγος ἀποφαντικός; its essential constitution is centered
on this. It is from here that we must pursue the question of whether we can
see anything pointing to the *ground* that *makes this essence possible*. What
underlies this power of the λόγος? What must *necessarily* underlie it if the
λόγος is to be able to be what it manifests to us as, namely *as the possibility*
(Möglichkeit) *of the "either . . . or else" proper to that revealing and concealing*
which show, which pronounce "being"? When we have answered these questions we will see how here too, as everywhere in philosophy, this trivial and
elementary phenomenon of judgment and the statement—a phenomenon
that has already been exhaustively pursued in every possible direction—
returns us at a stroke to a dimension which is none other than that *expanse*
and *uncanniness* to which the interpretation of our *fundamental attunement*
(Grundstimmung) was initially to lead us. (H, 489/337; translation modified)

We find this recourse to power, this discourse on possibility *as* power, on
the becoming-power of a possibility, and therefore of a virtuality and therefore of the emergence of the human beyond the animal, of the *zōon logon*
ekhon beyond the *zōon alogon,* and therefore of the human signifier beyond
the animal code or signal—we find this recourse again in the Lacan we
were mentioning at the beginning, around the reference to Robinson, and I
should like rapidly, briefly returning to the context of this Lacanian excursion to Robinson's island, both to add something, some reference at least, to
what I already said last year about the animal according to Lacan,[22] to spec-
343 ify this language of "power," this transition from the "it can [*il se peut*]" as "it
is possible" to the "it can" as "it has the power to," and also, at the same time,
to welcome into the seminar an animal to which we have not extended the
welcome of our hospitality. We received a visit from thousands of wolves
in what we called our genelycology last year, we welcomed lambs, foxes,
elephants, monkeys, parrots, pigeons, even dogs and cats, but we had never
yet had the honor of a visit from a mink [*vison*]. We had not yet seen a mink
here. Lacan talks "mink" and he has a sort of vision of mink [*vision de vison*]
in the passage that interests me today. Instead of commenting, analyzing or
interpreting Lacan's argument at length, according to a schema and with
aims you already know, I shall here be content to quote from page 343, then
344 of the seminar on *The Formations of the Unconscious,* sentences that use,
as though it were nothing special—but in a way that to my eyes is reveal-

22. See above, note 8 to this session.

ing—the vocabulary of *power,* of the verb *pouvoir* in several grammatical forms (the indicative "peut" and especially the infinitive "pouvoir"). What matters to Lacan is, to quote his own words, what he calls the "emergence" of the "signifier as such" as emergence of the "voice."[23]

What does Lacan do and say after the allusion to Robinson and to "Friday's footprint that Robinson discovers during his walk" and which, according to Lacan, is not a signifier, not yet, but becomes one only at the moment at which, I quote again, "it is erased"? What does Lacan say and do after having noted that the "signifier is thus a hollow" in that it "bears witness to a past presence" and that, "conversely, in what is a signifier, in the fully developed signifier that speech is, there is always a passage," etc. [this is a sentence heavy with unelucidated problems: what does "fully developed" mean here? Is there some not fully-developed signifier, still virtual, merely sketched out, in a sort of teleological scale of living beings on which the animal would indeed have some signifier—contrary to what Lacan stubbornly says elsewhere—but some signifier that is not fully developed, insufficiently developed, poorly developed, without word and without voice, so that the distinction between signifier and non-signifier would no longer be decisive, and there could no longer seriously be a question of an *emergence* of the human signifier, but only of degrees in the *development* of more or less-developed signifiers, with the animal able to have access to some signifier, yes, with all that that presupposes (the other, the unconscious, the truth, etc.), but a feebly developed signifier not "fully developed," to pick up again Lacan's expression when he says that "speech" is "the fully developed signifier"? I leave here unanswered these formidable but essential questions]?

344

What does Lacan do and say, after having also declared that in speech the passage beyond each of the fleeting, evanescent elements in the signifying chain is, I quote, "the very thing that becomes voice," this "passage is voice," says Lacan too, and what then "emerges" as signifier bearing witness to a past presence is, I quote again, "what makes of it a voice"; the passage, Lacan insists again, "takes on consistency as voice."[24] What Lacan does then, immediately afterward, what he says of this passage, can no longer do without the language of possibility and power. I'll read out a single paragraph from Lacan, emphasizing this vocabulary of *power:* (Read and comment on Lacan)

> As for the question of emergence, it is essential to grasp one point, which is that the signifier as such is something that can be effaced, and which leaves

23. See *La bête et le souverain, I,* session 3, p. 140 [p. 96].
24. Lacan, *Le séminaire, Livre V,* p. 343.

only its place—meaning that one cannot find it again. This property is essential, and means that, although one can speak of emergence, one cannot speak of development. In reality, the signifier contains this property in itself. I mean that one of the fundamental dimensions of the signifier is that it can cancel itself out [*s'annuler*]. For this there is a possibility that we can in this event describe as a mode of the signifier itself. It materializes in something very simple, with which we are all familiar, but the originality of which we must not allow to be hidden by its usual triviality—crossing out. Every type of signifier is by its nature something that can be crossed out.

For as long as there have been philosophers who think, there has been a lot of talk about *Aufhebung*, and people have learned to use it in a more or less cunning way. This word essentially means cancellation—for example, I cancel my subscription to a journal, or some reservation I have. It also means, thanks to an ambiguity that makes it precious in the German language, *raise to a power, to a higher situation*. It seems people have not paused enough over this: that properly speaking there is only one kind of thing, crudely speaking, that can be canceled, and that is a signifier. In truth, when we cancel anything else, be it imaginary or real, by that very fact we raise it to the rank, the qualification, of a signifier.[25]

345   This logic and vocabulary of power had imposed themselves earlier, in the same context, when Lacan wanted to identify what, I quote him, "is lacking in animal discourse," namely the signifier, the voice, speech. This demonstration of Lacan's is interesting for more than one reason, especially because Lacan spares no effort to undermine the assurance of those who grant animals a language, or even grant an interest for human-type language to animals—basically a right to speech. And this is where the mink scene supposedly answers the question of so-called domestic animals, of the conversation one has with them, the conversation in which they are supposed to participate when they are domesticated or held captive. I'm going to read and comment on this long passage about domestic animals, about training, conditioned reflexes, animals of luxury and above all animals of lucre ("lucre" is Lacan's word, speaking of the mink. I wonder, without being able to give the reply, what could or could not be made of this Lacan by the "greens" or the "friends of animals" in their combat against the ill-treatment of domestic animals, against Pavlovian experiments, or against hunting mink, or even raising captive mink for the purposes of which you are aware). Perhaps you know—I just discovered it—that the word "vi-

346 son," the signifier "vison," which is an extraordinary word because of all the homonymies and other similar associations it allows for (for example

25. Ibid., pp. 343–44; Lacan's emphasis.

with *la vie* [life] and *vision* [vision], and the vis-à-vis: you may know the expression "vison-visu," now fallen into disuse and which meant face-to-face [*en vis à vis*]. La Fontaine writes: "as they live *vison-visu* [here 'across from each other'], they're always squabbling about their wives," and Mme de Sévigné: "M. de la Trousse had his eyes on the house that is *vison-visu* [the house opposite]"),[26] the signifier "vison," then, if you prefer, which is easily associated with rich clothing, preferably feminine, with the refinements of a scandalous luxury reserved to the French upper classes ("she bought herself a mink coat," is the first example you'll find in the *Robert*), well, the signifier "vison" (a signifier that Lacan curiously does not talk about, *qua* signifier; he talks only about the thing, the animal called "vison"), the signifier *vison* comes from the Latin word (late Latin, I suppose, because it has disappeared from Gaffiot's dictionary), *vissio, vissire* from which descends, as we have every reason to say, the French *vesser,* meaning to fart and spread bad odors, a "vesse" being precisely a fart, the wind that comes out of the body with or without noise, but always stinking. One calls "vesse de loup" (and that's where the mink comes to join our packs of wolves), or "pet de loup [wolf's fart]" a mushroom that gives off bad odors. Raffarin's France of on high[27] ought to be discouraged by the association with stench of the name of this little carnivorous, especially North American mammal sought after by the rich on high and commercialized for its fur. (Read and comment Lacan)

> Here too, a parenthesis to complement what I said last time. Is this to say that the human being is the only one to be taken in with words? Up to a point, it is not out of the question to think that some domestic animals have some satisfactions linked to human speaking. I do not need to invoke specifics here, but we do learn some very strange things if we can have confidence in what is said by those who are more or less appropriately called the specialists, who seem a little credulous. So we have heard it said that mink held captive with lucre in mind, namely to make a profit from their fur, waste away and give only a mediocre product to the furrier if he does not make conversation with them. It appears that this makes the farming of mink very expensive by raising the general cost. What is showing up here, where we do not have the means of taking things further, must be linked to the fact of enclosure, since mink in the wild do not apparently — pending further information — have the possibility of finding this satisfaction.

347

26. See the entry for "vison-visu" in Littré's dictionary.

27. Derrida is alluding here to the expression "La France d'en bas [lowly France, or France seen from below]" employed by Jean-Pierre Raffarin, who was prime minister of the French Republic under President Jacques Chirac, from May 6, 2002, to May 31, 2005.

From there, I'd simply like to move on to show you the direction in which we can refer our problem to Pavlovian studies of conditioned reflexes. In the end, what are conditioned reflexes?

In their most common forms, which have occupied most of the experimentation, the existence of conditioned reflexes rests on the intervention of the signifier in a more or less predetermined, innate, cycle of distinctive behaviors. All those little electric signals, those little bells and ringers they use to deafen the poor animals to get them to secrete to order their various physiological products, their gastric juices, are all the same clearly signifiers and nothing else. They are manufactured by experimenters for whom the world is very clearly constituted by a certain number of objective relations—a world an important part of which is constituted by what one can justifiably set apart as properly signifying. And it is indeed with a view to showing by what sequence of progressive substitution psychic progress is possible that all these things are dreamed up and constructed.

One might wonder why, when all is said and done, this does not come down to teaching these well-trained animals a sort of language. Well, that leap is not made. When Pavlovian theory comes to take an interest in what is happening in humans with language, Pavlov takes the quite correct decision to speak of language not as an extension of meanings as they are in play in conditioned reflexes, but of a second system of meanings. This means recognizing—implicitly, for it is perhaps not fully articulated in the theory—that there is something different in the one and the other. To try to define that difference, we shall say that it depends on what we call the relation to the big Other, insofar as it constitutes the place of a unitary system of the signifier. Or again, we shall say that what is lacking in animal discourse is concatenation.

At the end of the day, we shall state the simplest formula like this: however far these experiments are pushed, what one does not find, and that there is perhaps no question of finding, is the law according to which these signifiers would be ordered. Which comes down to saying that this is the law that these animals would obey. It is absolutely clear that there is no trace of any reference to such a law, i.e. nothing beyond a signal, or a short chain[28] of previously established signals. No kind of legalizing extrapolation is to be seen there, and that's the sense in which one can say that one cannot institute the law. I repeat,[29] this is not to say for all that there is for

348

28. In the session, Derrida added: "'short,' meaning what? Up to what point? Not to mention there are some animals whose chain is very long."

29. In the session, Derrida interrupted the sentence and said: "Well, this concession is extremely important, but Lacan will slide over it here." He resumed the reading and then interrupted it again: "I repeat, this is not to speak as discourse." He continued until the end of the paragraph and commented: "In other words, the idea here is one

the animal no dimension of the Other with a big O, but only that nothing of it is really articulated as discourse.

So where does that take us? If we sum up what we are dealing with in the relation of the subject of the signifier in the Other, namely what happens in the dialectic of demand, it is essentially this: what characterizes the signifier is not to be substituted for the needs of the subject — as is the case with conditioned reflexes — but to be able to be substituted for itself. The nature of the signifier is essentially substitutive with respect to itself.

In this direction, we can see that what is dominant, what matters, is the place it occupies in the Other. What points in this direction, and that I am trying here in various ways to formulate as essential to the signifying structure, is this topological, not to say typographical space, which precisely makes substitution its law. Numbering of places gives the fundamental structure of a signifying structure as such.

It is to the extent that the subject becomes present within a world thus structured in the position of the Other that, as experience brings out, what we call identification takes place. Failing satisfaction, it is with the subject who can accede to demand that the subject identifies.[30]

Of course, Heidegger would have been very wary of the word "signifier" in which, hastily of course, he would have thought he could recognize a borrowing from linguistics, as positive science, incapable of gaining access to the essence of the language it claims to speak about, as the zoologists presuppose the essence of the animal that, qua zoologists, they're incapable of thinking. Nevertheless, putting aside the signifier "signifier," there is, it seems to me, a profound congruence between Lacan and Heidegger. It involves what reserves the *logos* as power to man, and what reserves to the *logos apophantikos* the power to accede to the truth, i.e. to the possibility of the false, of error, of lying, and of *the pseudesthai in general* (of which the animal is supposedly incapable *both* according to Heidegger *and* according to Lacan). And in both cases the difference between man and animal is supposed to be the difference between two "powers."

As the power of the *logos* (*semantikos* and *apophantikos*) is no different in Heidegger's eyes from that of access to beings *as* beings, and to the *als-*

---

of dissociating, which he never does elsewhere, the access to, the experience of the big Other — and he concedes that the animal can have such an experience — and discourse. In other words, what the animal lacks is not the big Other, and therefore the signifier, and therefore truth, in the Lacanian machine, what it lacks is discourse. And here, if we would like to hollow out this concession, we would go quite some way in absolutely undermining the whole machine."

30. Lacan, *Le séminaire, Livre V,* pp. 339–41.

349

Struktur, the structure of the *as such,* of which the animal remains deprived, one might wonder how and from where this *als-Struktur* comes, and therefore the difference between beings and beings as such, and therefore between beings and the Being of beings. One might wonder how it supervenes in what one hesitates to call its history in the usual sense, a *development* and still less a history of life, a life common to man and the animal, both of which are living beings. One hesitates to call this a history, and especially a history of life because these two titles, these two disciplines, these two fields as positive sciences (history and history of life) presuppose that insight has been achieved over what precisely remains to be thought, namely ontological difference, the difference between Being and beings which is comparable to no other difference because it is not the difference between two different X's, between two beings, but a radically altering difference in the same itself [*le même même*]. But of course, one must refer to some historicality, to some event of an other quality in order to think what is happening here, when the power of "as such," when the ontological difference, comes to be possible and to accord a power, to accord itself a power, to accord itself with a power, and a power to relate to it (*Vermögen, Verhalten*).

This is where the word *walten* appears, scarcely noticed by all the readers of Heidegger I think I know, and a word the frequent occurrence of which we had already recognized both in the seminar (1929–30) and in the *Introduction to Metaphysics* (1935) toward which I count on returning from this point of view. Today, as I've been announcing for a long time, I should like to begin by observing its occurrence at the end <of> *Identität und Differenz* (1957), twice at least, just before the passage we were reading last week about the God of onto-theology to whom one could address neither prayer, nor sacrifice, nor music, nor dance. The point is to think how it is, precisely, with beings *as such,* how beings *as such* appear, and the mode of this event, of this arrival as unveiling or non-occultation. Here we must be more attentive than ever to the letter of Heidegger's German. In the eyes of people in a hurry and impatient to find themselves at home with the language they believe they know and with somnolent self-evidences (and that might be the German of many Germans or the French of many French) — in the eyes of those people, Heidegger's writing can sometimes look like an unjustified or annoying game. But here it bears all the weight of what is most seriously at stake at the moment when the most subtle differences are also the most decisive, sometimes even within the same [*au-dedans même du même*] where some people would wish to authorize themselves to mix everything up. At stake here precisely is the difference of the differents, the difference in the same and even as the same [*dans le même et même comme*

le même], and of the far from obvious difference between Being and be-   *351*
ings, between beings and beings as such. One cannot ask the question of
the animal, of language, of man, of what is proper to man (with all the consequences that you imagine) without dealing with these apparently overly
refined and supposedly inconsistent differences. "Being," says Heidegger,
"shows itself as unconcealing Supervening (*Sein zeigt sich als die entbergende
Überkommnis*).³¹ Beings as such appear in the manner of this Arrival which
takes cover in non-occultation (*Seiendes als solches erscheint in der Weise der
in die Unverborgenheit, bergenden Ankunft*)."³² (Comment at length, *Unverborgenheit, bergenden Ankunft*³³)

And this singular event, this coming, this supervening (*Überkommnis*),
this surging up or surprising coming, this coming that falls upon, this coming of what happens thus, is not an event among others. First, because what
advenes in it, what comes and supervenes in this way, is nothing less than
Being, or rather the showing of Being and of beings as such, it is the *as such*
of beings (and so of what distinguishes human from animal and makes possible the *logos*, the *logos semantikos* and the *logos apophantikos*). That is what
distinguishes beings from beings as such, it is in a certain sense *nothing,* it
is not a being, it is not some thing, just as the ontological difference that
supervenes thus is not some thing, some other thing, is not a being differ-   *352*
ent from the being that appears — well, the supervening of this unheard-of
event is not the supervening of some other thing. Or it is like the supervening of nothing and of the nothing that separates Being and beings, beings

31. During the session, Derrida added: "Being shows itself (*Sein zeigt sich*), as the
Supervening (*Überkommnis*) that uncovers (*die entbergende Überkommnis*)."

32. Heidegger, *Identität und Differenz*, p. 62 [pp. 64–65; translation modified].

33. In the session, Derrida added: "Beings as such (*Seiendes als solches*) appear (*erscheint*) in the manner (*in der Weise*) of this Arrival (*Ankunft*) which shelters in non-
occultation (*der in die Unverborgenheit, bergenden Ankunft*). This Arrival which shelters, collects itself (*bergende*) in non-occultation. Thus beings as such appear when
there arrives at the same time as this Arrival (*Ankunft*) which conceals itself, which
shelters in the revealed <revealing?>, the unveiled <unveiling?>, the not-hidden <not-
hiding?>. We have therefore two important words here: *Überkommnis,* Supervening,
and *Ankunft,* which gets translated as Arrival. Supervening/Arrival. Being/Superven-
ing (*Sein/Überkommnis, entbergende Überkommnis*), beings as such (*Seiendes als solches,
bergenden Ankunft, in die Unverborgenheit*). To be/*Überkommnis,* being/*Ankunft.*" These
last two sentences are hard to make out. [Translator's note: The three instances of words
with question marks in angle brackets here reflect the editors' hesitation in transcrib-
ing the recording of the session between in each case the nominalized past participle (*le
décelé, le dévoilé, le non-caché*) and the (homophonous) nominalized infinitive (*le déceler,
le dévoiler, le non-cacher*).]

and beings as such. Or rather,[34] it is the supervening of an absolute alterity, but within the same. This is how we must hear the sentence that follows immediately:

> So Being in the sense of unconcealing Supervening (*im Sinne der entbergen Überkommnis*) and beings as such in the sense of the Arrival that shelters (*und Seiendes als solches im Sinne der sich bergenden Ankunft*), are as different (*so Unterschiedenen*) by virtue of the Same (*aus dem Selben*), the Dimension [it is thus, by the word *"Dimension,"* with a majuscule, that the French translators (more or less justified by a long footnote) translate *Unter-Schied,* in two words hyphenated].[35]

Whatever the translation here, we must clearly see that Heidegger intends to mark the fact that if Being and beings as such *are* (*wesen:* comment: active, quasi-transitive and announcing *walten*) as different, they are (*wesen*) different only as the same, remaining the same, and in the internal splitting of the same of the *Unter-Schied,* where the hyphen thus inscribes this union of the same in difference. Whence the insistence, immediately afterward, on the *between,* the *Zwischen* which slips itself into the same without in a sense dissociating it from itself, without making of it two things or two different beings, where however a certain unique difference, a certain heterogeneity, a certain alterity has precisely been what arrives and supervenes, what happens between the supervening of Being and the arrival of beings as such.

> [Solely this latter Dimension] [let's say the *Unter-Schied,* in two words hyphenated] [. . .] grants and holds apart the between (*vergibt [. . .] und hält auseinander das Zwischen*) where Supervening and Arrival are maintained in relation (*zueinander gehalten*), isolated one from the other and turned one toward the other [in one sole syntagm: *"auseinander-zueinander getragen sind"*].[36]

Here we see again the bearing of *tragen* which has been occupying us from the beginning and which will here play a major role. And this *tragen,* so indispensable here, will in the next sentence find itself re-inscribed in the word *Austrag,* also very difficult to translate, but which is going to play a major role as cornerstone, or if you prefer, keystone in this whole architectonic which is no longer an architectonic in the sense of a philosophical system, but which remains a putting together, an idiomatic jointing—both

353

---

34. In the session, Derrida added: "this comes to the same thing."
35. Ibid., p. 62 [p. 65; translation modified].
36. Ibid., pp. 62–63 [p. 65; translation modified].

powerful and subtle, durable and fragile—of words and concepts, syntagmas and blinding insights. The sentence I am now going to read introduces here the *Austrag*, that *Austrag* which, immediately afterward—this is why I'm insisting on it and dwelling patiently on this passage—will be defined as that *in which* it *walten,* that "in which" the *Walten waltet.* I am not going to translate these words, this verb or this nominalized verb, because we shall have to return to it next time, and give its full scope to the question of translation and interpretation and the stakes of *Walten.*

Here is the sentence that introduces into this context the word *Austrag.* It follows the one we have just read on the *tragen* and the *getragen sind* (I'll quickly reread it: "[The Dimension] [let's say the *Unter-Schied,* in two words hyphenated] which," Heidegger says, "[...] grants and holds apart the between [vergibt (notice this word I underline here) [...] *und hält auseinander das Zwischen*] where Supervening and Arrival are maintained in relation (*zueinander gehalten*), isolated one from the other and turned one toward the other [in one sole syntagm: *auseinander-zueinander getragen sind*]"). Heidegger then continues:

> The difference of Being and beings (*Die Differenz*[37] *von Sein und Seiendem*), as *Unter-Schied* [*Dimension:* and Heidegger speaks difference in Latin, *die Differenz als der Unter-Schied*] of Supervening and Arrival [*von Überkommnis und Ankunft:* recall that the supervening, *Überkommnis,* is that of Being, the arrival, *Ankunft,* that of beings], is the [uncovering and sheltering] *Austrag* of the two (*der entbergend-bergende Austrag beider*).[38] (Comment[39])   *354*

Well, it is in this *Austrag*[40] (that the French translators translate as "Conciliation," and that indeed means in everyday language something like that, something like the ruling, the contractual ruling, the contracted ruling of a conflict or a litigation, the agreement between parties to a dispute, what in a sense brings the dispute or the argument to its end (but we must insist on bearing, remembering what we were saying about Celan's line, "ich muss dich tragen," which was also valid for childbearing: *ein ausgetragenes Kind*

37. In the session, Derrida added: "*Differenz,* this time in Latin."

38. Ibid., p. 63 [p. 65; translation modified].

39. In the session, Derrida reread the citation, modifying it again: "The difference of Being and beings (*Die Differenz von Sein und Seiendem*), as that of *Unter-Schied* [*Dimension:* and Heidegger says difference in Latin, *die Differenz als der Unter-Schied*] of Supervening and Arrival (*von Überkommnis und Ankunft*), is the uncovering and sheltering *Austrag,* is what harbors them and discloses them, uncovers them and re-encloses them (*der* entbergend-bergende *Austrag*)."

40. Derrida resumes this sentence in the following paragraph.

is a child brought to term, borne to birth, to term; so there is in this *Austrag* a reference to difference in dispute, to the term and the contracting party's ruling of this dispute, but also to the bearing that gives birth at term, etc.). The idea of conciliation as reconciliation, that the French translators insist on, is of course not foreign to *Austrag* as the term of a dispute brought [*portée*] before a certain justice. In any case, the word *Austrag,* here and elsewhere, bears all the weight of a thinking of bearing, where it is a question of Being and beings and of the Being of beings).

Well, it is *in* the *Austrag* that it *waltet.* What does "in" mean, and *Austrag* and *waltet,* those are our questions. It is the following sentence:

> Im Austrag waltet Lichtung des sich verhüllend Verschließenden, welches Walten das Aus- und Zuienander von Überkommnis und Ankunft vergibt [again *vergibt*].⁴¹
>
> Within the *Austrag* [<within> the regulation, the conciliation, within the term, in the terminating or determining range of the differend between the differents, between Being and beings, supervening and arrival], within the *Austrag waltet* [which I do not translate for the time being; the French translation says "prevails" [*prédomine*], but we must return to this later] a clearing (*Lichtung*) of what veils and closes itself off, which *Walten vergibt* [an extraordinary verb here that the French translation all but omits in saying simply, in place of "*welches Walten [. . .] vergibt,*" "it is by this prevalence that. . .". But *vergibt* also means here "give" as much as "furnish," "procure," but also to deceive oneself in giving, misgiving, misgive and above all pardon (*vergeben,* "to forgive"⁴²), an important value and a non-negligible connotation here, where *Austrag* can also mean the settlement of a dispute or of a differend, conciliation, reconciliation: so, I resume,] which *Walten vergibt* [gives, misgives, forgives] the being-apart and being-related, the one to the other, of Supervening and Arrival [thus of Being and beings as such], *welches Walten das Aus- und Zuienander von Überkommnis und Ankunft vergibt.*⁴³

What does this *Walten* (verb and noun) mean, *Walten* which is, as if all at once, the event, the origin, the power, the force, the source, the movement, the process, the meaning etc. — whatever you like — of the ontological difference, the becoming-ontological-difference of the ontological difference, of the supervening of Being and of the arrival of beings? Why *walten*? Why this word which so often goes unnoticed? We shall continue asking ourselves this question for a long time.

41. Ibid., p. 63; Derrida's emphasis.
42. [Translator's note:] In English in the text.
43. Ibid., p. 63 [p. 65; translation modified].

A final occurrence of *walten,* in the same text, will detain us next time, when we try to give wider scope to this questioning and to its difficulty, to everything in it that matters to our seminar on "the beast and the sovereign."

The other occurrence says pretty much the same thing: *356*

> Die onto-theologische Verfassung der Metaphysik entstammt dem Walten der Differenz, die Sein als Grund und Seiendes als gegründet-begründendes aus- und zueinanderhält, welches Aushalten der Austrag vollbringt. [The onto-theological constitution of metaphysics proceeds from the *Walten der Differenz* (a very risky French translation, we will see why, but it returns us to our question of sovereignty: "proceeds from the superior power [*puissance*] of Difference"), which holds the one apart from the other and relates the one to the other Being as ground [foundation, *Grund*] and beings as grounded and thus justified in their founding, the *Aushalten* accomplished by the *Austrag*].[44] (Comment at length[45])

44. Ibid., p. 69 [p. 71; translation modified].
45. In the session, Derrida added nothing here.

357   What does "to bear" [*porter*] mean? We have already often wondered, in
more than one language, what *porter, to carry, to bear,*[1] *tragen*—in particular,
last time, to attempt to home in on the sense of *Walten,* around the *Austrag,*
i.e. a kind of contract of the ontological difference.

Die Welt ist fort, ich muss dich tragen.

Among all the imports [*portées*]—and I've already counted a lot, here
and there, in France or Germany—among all the imports comported by
the import of meaning and the musical staff [*portée musicale*] of such an
envoi—*Die Welt is fort, ich muss dich tragen*—which bespeaks both necessity and duty, inflexible injunction, but which nonetheless leaves me free
to look after you where nothing is going OK any more [*là où rien de va
plus*], where nothing is *going* [*là où rien de* va] given that the world is going
away [*s'en va*]—among all the imports that can be sustained by this double
proposition, *Die Welt is fort, ich muss dich tragen,* one of which seems to be
constative (this is how things are, from now on, isn't it, *Die Welt ist fort,*
the world is going to hell), and the other of which, performative rather, *ich
muss dich tragen,* seems to sign a commitment, a promise, an oath, a duty,
like the seal of a love that, at the moment of good-bye, of good-bye to the
world, salutes or swears to work for your safety [*salut*], to save you without
salvation—among all the imports, then, which accord between them a constative proposition and a performative proposition, each held to the other
358   in their radical heterogeneity (for how on earth could you deduce, and by
what right, from the fact that *Die Welt ist fort,* the obligation to carry you?
What demonstrable link between them? Why should I still carry you, if the
world is going away?)—among all the imports which place side by side or
accord between them a performative proposition *and* a constative proposition which is not just any constative proposition (since it concerns nothing

---

1. [Translator's note:] "To carry" and "to bear" are in English in the text.

less than the world itself, the totality of what is and that is called the world), a constatation that, moreover, presupposes at least that the addressee and the signatory[2] of the statement share a language and the comprehension of what "world" means, inhabit the same world enough to be able to hear with one and the same ear and say with one and the same voice *Die Welt ist fort,* so that at the moment at which this phrase is spoken the world is still there, perhaps not here but still there, and the two supposed partners, interlocutors, even lovers in the poem cohabit the same world, precisely this world that is going away, which is getting ever more distant, which is going to go away [*qui va s'éloignant, qui va s'éloigner*], which is going away, this world which has gone away, which is on its way to going away, this world that has just left, which has just, precisely [*qui vient juste, justement*] not come back again, which has just gone away, etc., this world which at bottom comes or advenes only by going away, the world as it goes — well, still beyond all the imports I've already tried to count here or there of this unheard-of double proposition, of this performative lodged like a pearl in the oyster of a constative, like a still unborn child, to be born, to be carried to term in the uterus of the origin of the world as it is, there would be today the import of a declaration of love or of peace at the moment of a declaration of war.

We know today that, for at least a century now, all wars are *world* wars, worldwide and planetary. What is at stake in what we call war is more than ever worldwide, i.e. the institution and the appropriation of the world, the world order, no less. The establishment of a sovereign power and right over the world, of which, still more than the UN, the Security Council would be the emblematic figure, the shadow theater, with all that this collusion of the strongest and the biggest and the winners of this world (i.e. of the last world war) can contain of comedy, of strength and weakness, of phantasm and necessity. There is no longer any local or national war. Supposing there ever was. And in every war, at stake from now on is an end of the world, both in the sense of ends and purposes that some want to impose by force, force without right or the force of right, force of law (*Gewalt,* perhaps) on the interpretation and future of the totality of beings, of the world and the living beings that inhabit it; and at stake is an end of *the* world (*Die Welt ist fort*), in the sense that what is threatened is not only this always infinite death of each and every one (for example of a given soldier or a given singular civilian), that individual death I've often said was each time *the* end of *the* world, *the* end,

359

2. In the session, Derrida said: "le, la destinataire et le, la signataire." [Translator's note: addressee and signatory both masculine and feminine.]

the whole end of *the* world[3] (*Die Welt ist fort*), not a particular end of this or that world, of the world of so and so, of this one or that one, male or female, of this soldier, this civilian, this man, this woman, this child, but the end of the world in general, the absolute end of the world—at stake is the end of the world (*Die Welt ist fort*) in the sense that what is threatened, in this or that world war, is therefore the end of the world, the destruction of the world, of any possible world, or of what is supposed to make of the world a *cosmos,* an arrangement, an order, an order of ends, a juridical, moral, political order, an international order resistant to the non-world of death and barbarity.

Now since the last session—but alas this is no surprise—it is not even a world war as to the appropriation of the world that has broken out after having announced itself for so long, it is the very ruin of the concept of end and of war, the stripping bare of that fact that more than ever *Die Welt is fort,* that the poets, more than ever, more rare than ever, are more touched by the truth than the politicians, priests and soldiers.[4] The armed word of politicians, priests and soldiers is more than ever incompetent, unable to measure up to the very thing it is speaking and deciding about, and that remains to be thought, that trembles in the name "world," or even in saying good-bye to the world. And that what there is to bear, as the responsibility of the other, for the other, must be borne where the world itself is going away by going into the absolute disaster of this armed word that I shall not even call psittacist, so as not to insult Poll, Robinson Crusoe's parrot (*psittakos*), first victim of the humanist arrogance that thought it could give itself the right to speech, and therefore the right to the world as such.

The other day, suffering from the flu and doubtful that I would be able to come here today, I had a nightmare, during which I had been given, by a tribunal, a kind of super-Security Council, assigned an odd mission that I had no desire to take on—the mission of defending eloquently, like a good lawyer, and invoking the authority of Aristotle and Heidegger [of defending, then, and supporting] the thesis that Saddam Hussein, Bush, Rumsfeld, Aznar, Blair, Chirac, Sharon, Arafat, Putin and Paul (I mean the Pope John Paul) and some others massed behind them (it looked a bit like the Nuremberg Tribunal, they all had headphones and my speech was trans-

360

3. See Jacques Derrida, *Béliers: Le dialogue ininterrompu: Entre deux infinis, le poème* (Paris: Galilée, 2003), p. 23; translated as "Rams: Uninterrupted Dialogue—Between Two Infinites, The Poem," in *Sovereignties in Question: The Poetics of Paul Celan,* ed. Thomas Dutoit and Outi Pasanen (New York: Fordham University Press, 2005), p. 140; and *Chaque fois unique, la fin du monde,* p. 11.
4. The Iraq War had begun on March 20, 2003.

lated for them when I was speaking Greek or German), I had then to defend the thesis that all the decision-makers and fancy talkers of this world should all have their right recognized to have access to the *logos*, and not just the *logos semantikos,* but even the *logos apophantikos.* Even Bush. And even Saddam Hussein! And the nightmare, the painful crisis that then agitated my fevered sleep, was due to the fact that, apart from the flu that was making everything a little *unheimlich,* I had no desire, but no desire at all, to demonstrate any such thing: I felt like one of those lawyers assigned by the court to defend against their better judgment a pedophile, matricidal and torturing serial killer,[5] and so I didn't want to defend this cause at any price, but my professional conscience, my well-known sense of deontology, the inflexible intransigence of my philosophical superego insisted and pushed me to say, to say to myself: "Yes, you ought, you nonetheless owe it to truth and justice to recognize and demonstrate, this is your duty, you must still be just with those people, in spite of everything, you must in spite of everything concede that they indeed have access to the *logos semantikos* and even the *logos apophantikos.* Even Bush. They have the power and the right. And they are moreover all the more guilty for that fact. No doubt they will never know, but it would be unjust to deny it to them. Denying it to them would be to behave like Saddam, Bush, Blair and Aznar, and I must never consent to that. If you don't want to be like them, recognize that there is still some *logos apophantikos* when these horrible characters dare to speak to us and to the world while putting their generals and their blind — and moreover so very incompetent — war machines in train. When I awoke, I wondered (but I still had the flu) what would happen if they locked all these Polls up, for example in isolation in that bit of the Island of Cuba called Guantánamo, to teach them how to speak, to have them follow an intensive course of education in *Robinson Crusoe,* a seminar of Heidegger's and Aristotle's *Peri hermeneias.* As soon as my fever went down, I had to recognize that that would change nothing in the current war, of course. And that there is no doubt no possible war, among other things, without *logos apophantikos.*[6] Which makes you think. We'll listen to Kant on this subject in a moment.

We'll be marking here a definite stage of the seminar, before a long halt.

So it seems appropriate to put back into perspective, from quite high up and quite far away, the landscape that has been ours up until now. What have we seen, in sum, from on high and from afar?

5. [Translator's note:] In English in the text.
6. In the session, Derrida added: "This is the tragedy."

We have seen, on the horizon, two textual mountain ranges looming up (*Robinson Crusoe,* and a seminar of Heidegger's on world and animal), two ranges that are themselves inscribed in a long mountain chain of sedimentary formations, all historical through and through (philosophical, theological, political, national, literary, etc.). They are two ranges, both insular and continental, two archipelagos too, which at first sight had very little in common, that's the least one can say: neither their time, with two centuries' interval, nor their country, nor their language, nor their discursive status, nor their genre, nor their belonging to the same regime of speech or writing, the one being the archival transcription of academic speech, a doctrinal teaching of a philosophical or metaphysical type, the other a so-called fictional and literary piece of writing, etc.

But were they not saying, signifying, basically the same? The same as to the sovereign, the beast and as to what *is* between the beast *and* the sovereign, as to that "and" between the beast *and* the sovereign? And if the same, as one of the two, Heidegger, insists, is not the identical, what is *the same* here?

Given that our *parti pris* was indeed to com-prehend, to take together, to take sight of, to take into perspective — not too arbitrarily, however — these two textual mountain ranges, the point is that, from a certain point of view, some correlational correspondence was — by me at least — presupposed, anticipated, suspected, the analysis and explicitation of which ought, in this hypothesis, to give us to think something significant, even revealing, on both sides, as to the double theme which, since last year, has been orienting our seminar, namely the "and" of "the beast *and* the sovereign," the conjunction between what we are calling the beast *and* the sovereign, the beast *with* the sovereign. Our point of view will thus have been chosen with a view to allowing us to see what these two living beings, the beast *and* the sovereign, have to do the one *with* the other, on the subject *of* or *on* the part of the other, in what way — in a certain sense, in their *being-with,* whatever it be — they relate (a question of relation [*rapport*], again, of scope [*portée*], of comportment) to each other, need each other, even the need to exclude each other, ignore each other, subjugate each other, include each other, put each other to death, eat each other, hunt each other, follow and pursue each other, carry, export, deport or support each other, in any case to treat each other in some way or other in a world that is, at least hypothetically, undeniably common to both.

What about this hypothesis? Have they in common something that one can still call "world," *a* world, one and the same world, the "world?" *Was ist Welt?* asks Heidegger.

However little they may have in common, they do indeed inhabit, they

362

363

cohabit, they *live* and live in living together; they are undeniably living beings, whatever that might mean, living beings that die equally or together,
co-diers [*commourans*],[7] as Montaigne might have said, not that they die at
the same moment, but they die together, in any case these ones *and* those
ones, these ones *like* those ones, these ones not far from those ones and in
the same space (water, earth, air, fire) as those ones (even if someone, Heidegger, claims that the beasts cannot—basically do not know how to—die
in the sense that only Dasein *can* sovereignly die its own death)—no one
in the world, not even Heidegger, will deny that both types of living being,
beast *and* sovereign (and moreover, one can always—this was the thesis
and working hypothesis formulated last year as to the resemblance between
them—one can always be both beast [*bête,* stupid] *and* sovereign, sovereignly *bête*)—no one in the world will deny, not even Heidegger, then, that
both types of living being cease living, find death [*trouvent la mort*], as we
say strangely in French to mark clearly the fact that the death one *finds* in
this way is not natural, or foreseeable or essential or necessary; one does
not say in French that someone "finds death" if they die of old age: one
finds death by accident, in a plane or car crash, or at war, and in that case
death surprises me, it finds me as much as I find it at a turn in the road.
No one will say in French, in all conscience, as I just have said out of pure
pedagogical rhetoric, "I find death," I'm trying to "find death," although
the unconscious might think it, and thus begin to say it to itself, although
the unconscious might then think of finding death, for example by driving   *364*
like a crazy person, doing dangerous trapeze stunts, compulsively exposing
oneself to the greatest danger, punishing oneself compulsively by inflicting
on oneself all sorts of ills, some of which might be lethal. One does not find
death by committing suicide, by definition, but immediate or slow and indirect suicides might be unconscious ways of finding death, namely by giving
it to oneself and behaving as though it were befalling one, as it happens, if it
happens [*comme ça se trouve, si ça se trouve*].

But, both animals and men not only die, have a finite life, but they can
find death, both can die before their time and by accident. Heidegger points
out in *Sein und Zeit,* on the basis of I forget which quotation, that from the

7. Derrida adopts this expression from Michel de Montaigne, "De la vanité," in *Essais,*
Book III, chap. 9, ed. Albert Thibaudet (Paris: Gallimard, Bibliothèque de la Pléiade,
1953), p. 1102; trans. Donald M. Frame as "Of Vanity," in *The Complete Essays of Montaigne,* Book III, chap. 9 (Stanford, Calif.: Stanford University Press, 1958), p. 752. Derrida quotes this passage in Derrida and Malabou, *La contre-allée* (Paris: La Quinzaine
littéraire/Louis Vuitton, 1999), p. 15, n. 2; trans. David Wills as *Counterpath: Traveling
with Jacques Derrida* (Stanford, Calif., Stanford University Press, 2004), p. 7, n. 2.

moment of birth one is old enough to die, which means that one can always find death before one's time;[8] and find oneself dead, find oneself faced with death before one's time—well, the beast and the sovereign both turn out to be living beings that find themselves in the situation either of dying of old age, or else of finding death at any moment; and so they live and die together, the one with the other, the one like the other, they coexist, they sympathize, they are con-vivial, they co-habit the world that is the same, even if the one (Heidegger's hypothesis) does not have the world *as such* and as such *nameable,* or is poor in world,[9] even if the other is (Heidegger's hypothesis again), *weltbildend,* the question is indeed that of a community of the world that they share and co-habit. This co- of the cohabitant presupposes a habitat, a place of common habitat, whether one calls it the earth (including sky and sea) or else the world as world of life-death. The common world is the world in which one-lives-one-dies, whether one be a beast or a human sovereign, a world in which both suffer, suffer death, even a thousand deaths. *Was ist Welt?*

For no one will seriously deny the animal the possibility of inhabiting the world (even if Heidegger claims that the animal does not inhabit as man alone inhabits it), no one will deny that these living beings, that we call the beast *and* the sovereign, inhabit a world, what one calls the world, and in a certain sense, the *same* world. There is a habitat of the animal as there is a habitat of plants, as there is a habitat for every living being. The word "world" has at least as a minimal sense the designation of *that within which* all these living beings are carried (in a belly or in an egg), they are born, they live, they inhabit and they die (and "in" does not have here the sense of a

8. Martin Heidegger, *Sein und Zeit,* p. 245 [p. 236: "'As soon as a human being is born, he is old enough to die right away'"]. Heidegger cites *Der Ackermann aus Böhmen,* ed. Alois Bernt and K. Burdach, from the collection *Vom Mittelalter zur Reformation: Forschungen zur Geschichte der deutschen Bildung,* ed. Konrad Burdach, vol. 3, pt. 2, chap. 20 (Berlin: Weidmann, 1917), p. 46. This text, attributed to Johannes von Tepl (also known as Johannes von Saaz), is translated in English by Ernest N. Kirrmann as *Death and the Plowman; or, The Bohemian Plowman* (Chapel Hill: University of North Carolina Press, 1958), p. 19.

9. In the session, Derrida added: "but Heidegger says, in a passage that I do not have time to explicate, that being 'poor in world,' as is the animal, is not to not have any world, rather it is to have one in the mode of 'not having.' In this passage, which I do not have time to read with you (we will look at it next year), Heidegger says that 'poverty in world' for the animal does not mean that the animal has no world, but rather that it has a world in the mode of 'not having.' It has without having, it does not have in having." See H, 293/199.

container, so that all our meditation should be concentrated on the inside of what *in* [*dans*] means—without allowing ourselves to be tempted or put off by the other spelling of the homonym *dents* [teeth], which, in one's mouth and in the toothy aftertaste of the auto-affection of this "self-taste" we were talking about last time[10] between speaking, eating, sucking, biting, licking and tasting, would push us to question what happens between animals with mouth and teeth, the phantasmatic fear of being devoured alive, but also the mournful drive of introjection or incorporation supposing not only an inside of the body, a being "in" the body, an internal surface of the body, of the mouth, etc., but an inside armed with teeth; but I abandon here these more or less tasty homonymies), the word "world," we were saying, that has at least as a minimal sense the designation of *that within which, that in which* the beast and the sovereign co-habit, the very thing that—transitively this time—they cohabit. *On habite dans le monde,* but just as much, as we say in French, *on habite le monde,* one inhabits the world, as inhabitants.[11] And one co-habits the world.

366

Of course, one can always question the supposed unity or identity of the world, not only between animal and human, but already from one living being to another. No one will ever be able to demonstrate, what is called *demonstrate* in all rigor, that two human beings, you and I for example, inhabit the same world, that the world is one and the same thing for both of us. Of course, and this argument, which I hope to be a serious one, could and should be taken very far, in more than dangerous fashion. But in a more current sense, and one that does not contradict this one, there really must be a certain *presumed, anticipated* unity of the world even in order discursively to sustain within it multiplicity, untranslatable and un-gatherable, the dissemination of possible worlds. Not only a multiplicity and an equivocality of the world, of the word "world" (*cosmos, mundus, Welt, world, Mundo*) which would retain a common horizon of univocity, but a dissemination without a common semantic horizon, the noun "world," as a word void of meaning or the meaning without use of the word "world" being merely an artificial effect, a cobbled-together verbal and terminological construction, destined to mask our panic (that of a baby who would be born without com-

10. Derrida is referring to the discussion session that took place March 19, 2003, where he had posed the question of "self-taste" in connection with the poet Gerald Manley Hopkins. This session does not appear in this edition of the seminar. See Editorial Note above, note 8.

11. [Translator's note:] The phrase "one inhabits the world" and the word "inhabitants" appear in English in the text.

ing into the world), destined then to protect us against the infantile but infinite anxiety of the fact that *there is not the world,* that nothing is less certain than the world itself, that there is perhaps no longer a world and no doubt there never was one as totality of anything at all, habitable and co-habitable world, and that radical dissemination, i.e. the absence of a common world, the irremediable solitude without salvation of the living being, depends first on the absence without recourse of any world, i.e. of any common meaning of the word "world," in sum of any common meaning at all.

This can, I admit, look like a lot of apocalyptic statements, but it is also the very tissue, the unwoven tissue [*tissu sans tissage*], the ever unsewn and torn tissue of our most constant and quotidian experience. Perhaps there is too much world in the world, but who can assure us that there is a world? Perhaps there is no world. Not yet and perhaps not since ever and perhaps not ever. I do not say this to roil you up or depress you, but because it is what I must think and say according to the most implacable necessity.

When every day,[12] at every moment of the day and night, we are overcome with the feeling that between a given other, and sometimes the closest of those close to us and of those that we call so imprudently and stupidly, tenderly and violently, *our own,* and ourselves—those with whom we share everything, starting and ending with love, the feeling that the worlds in which we live are different to the point of the monstrosity of the unrecognizable, of the un-similar, of the unbelievable, of the non-similar, the non-resembling or resemblable, the non-assimilable, the untransferable, the incomparable, the absolutely unshareable (we know this with an undeniable and stubborn, i.e. permanently denied, knowledge), the abyssal unshareable—I mean separated, like one island from another by an abyss beyond which no shore [*rive*] is even promised which would allow anything, however little, to happen [*arriver*], anything worthy of the word "happen"—the abyssal un-shareable, then, of the abyss between the islands of the archipelago and the vertiginous untranslatable, to the point that the very solitude we are saying so much about is not even the solitude of several people in the same world, this still shareable solitude in one and the same co-habitable world, but the solitude of worlds, the undeniable fact that there is no world, not even a world, not even one and the same world, no world that is one: *the* world, *a* world, a world that is *one,* is what there is not (and if *"Die Welt ist fort,"* this can also mean that there is the solitude, the isolation, the insularity of islands that are not even in the world, the same world, or on a world map, that there is no common world, be it a life-world,

12. This sentence is incomplete in the typescript.

and that the presumed community of the world is a word, a vocable, a convenient and reassuring bit of chatter, the name of a life insurance policy for living beings losing their world, a life belt on the high seas that we pretend   *368*
to be leaving, long enough to spend a moment during which we pretend to say "we" and to be together together,[13] a moment conventionally called life (which is also death), and even if it is this feeling and this fragile convention that make our loves as much as our hatreds, our so-called ethical or political responsibilities, war and peace, our most quotidian affects no less than our great passions, we should nonetheless recognize for all that that this uncrossable difference is what language and the address to the other cross lightly, I mean with the lightness of unawareness, at least for the time and space of an *as if* of social insurance). For it is not enough that we all of us have—you and me and so many others, here and now or wherever and whenever—the vague comforting feeling of understanding each other, of speaking among ourselves the same language, and sharing an intelligible language, in a consensual communicative action, for example in the use of the words "world" (*Welt, world, mundo*), "our common world," the unity of the world, etc., that does not suffice for it to be true and for anything other to be happening than an agreement inherited over millennia between living beings who are more or less anguished by illness, death and war and murder and eating-each-other-alive, etc., an agreement, then, an always labile, arbitrary, conventional and artificial, historical, non-natural contract, to ensure for oneself the best, and therefore also the longest *survival* by a system of life insurances counting with probabilities and including a clause that one *pretend,* that one make *as if,* signing the insurance policy [*police d'assurance*], basically just the police, out of clearly understood interest— that one pretend, as one says in English ("one pretends")[14] for a lying pretense, for a misleading allegation, that one pretend to give the same meaning, just about the same meaning in the same useful function to similar vocables or signs, etc. For example the word "world" as totality of what is, etc. That no one has ever come across, right? Have you ever come across the world as such? There seems to be in this refined utilitarian nominalism   *369*
nothing more than an animal ruse of life, a life common to the beast and the sovereign (the sovereign being, according to a well-known and scarcely contestable Nietzschean schema, by definition he (one can also call him the poet) who forges language and imposes conventional signification on words

13. Thus in the typescript.

14. [Translator's note:] In English in the text. In French the verb *prétendre* means to make a claim.

in order to survive, to persevere in life, to prevail, to have his values prevail, the word "life" remaining by the same token and simultaneously subject to the same insurance and probabilistic contract and thus as obscure, as little intrinsically guaranteed in its semantic value as the words "carry" [*porter*], "world," etc.).

Yes, don't you agree, it is, it seems to be *as if* we were behaving *as if* we were inhabiting the same world and speaking of the same thing and speaking the same language, when in fact we well know—at the point where the phantasm precisely comes up against its limit—that this is not true at all. And that given this, if *Die Welt ist fort,* if we think we must carry the other, carry you, *ich muss dich tragen,* this can only be one of two things, not a single thing nor three things. Two things, one or the other:

1. Either carry the other out of the world, where we share at least this knowledge without phantasm that there is no longer a world, a common world: I carry you then in the void, the time it takes to fly or swim not from one island to another in the world, but from a non-shore to a non-shore, between two non-arrivals; I carry you, I have to, I ought to, when nothing will happen to us nor welcome us ever on any island or any shore, nor any world, to life to death;

2. Or else, second hypothesis, that where there is no world, where the world is not here or there, but *fort,* infinitely distant over there, that what I must do, with you and carrying you, is make it that there be precisely a world, just a world, if not a just world, or to do things so as to make *as if* there were just a world, and to make the world come to the world, to make as if—for you, to give it to you, to bear it toward you, destined for you, to address it to you—I made the world come into the world,[15] as though there ought to be a world where presently there is none, to make the gift or present of this *as if* come up poetically, which is the only thing that—during the finite time of such an impossible voyage between two non-shores where nothing happens—the only thing that can make it possible that I can live and have or let you live, enjoy or have or let you enjoy, to carry you for a few moments without anything happening and leaving a trace in the world, that belongs to the world, without a trace left or retained in the world that is going away, that will go away—which, before even going to go away, is going going away, leaving no trace, a world that has forever been going to leave and has just left, going away with no trace, the trace becoming trace only by being able to erase itself.

15. In the session, Derrida added: "poetically."

A truth faced with which there would thereafter be no tenable difference <between[16]> the beast *and* the sovereign.

In all this conditional *as if,* what would carry and *tragen* and *Austrag*
still mean? And the world? What is the world? *"Was ist Welt?"* that's Heidegger's question. We're going to come back to it after a little voyage, a
cruise (one often says in English, as I read recently, "cruse-like"[17] to mean
in the style of Robinson Crusoe). A cruse-like cruise, an excursion, a race
around the world before returning circularly, odysseically, like Ulysses, to
the question *"Was ist Welt?"*

For as you know, on the subject of what is the world, this "as if" of the
world has its letters of nobility in philosophy. In a quite different atmosphere and with a quite different pathos than the one I have been indulging
in for the last session of a seminar, Kant said some terribly seismic things
about the "als ob." The *als ob* (as if[18]) is the essential modality in which is
presented the regulative idea of the world, the world as regulative idea of
reason. The world is a regulative idea of reason and it hangs by a mere *als
ob.* And I would be tempted, incapable of doing so here now, to follow very
far and on the most adventurous and dangerous paths the stakes of a serious debate between what Heidegger calls — we've talked about it enough
as the major concept of our seminar — the *als-Struktur* and what for my
part I shall nickname Kant's *Alsobstruktur.* It would suffice to think "regulative" (<as> in "regulative idea") in the somewhat utilitarian and nominal-
ist sense I was just mentioning (a rule in the game in order to come to an
understanding and regulate conflicts and exchanges), and to think what
Kant calls the interest of reason ("Interesse der Vernunft,"[19] unconditional-
ity as its major interest [see *Rogues* and *The University without Condition*[20]]),

371

16. This word is missing from Derrida's typescript but is audible here in the tape
recording of the session.

17. [Translator's note:] Thus in the text, here and in the following sentence: presumably a slip for "Crusoe-like."

18. [Translator's note:] The words "as if" are in English in the text.

19. Immanuel Kant, *Kritik der reinen Vernunft, 2. Auflage 1787,* in *Kants Werke:
Akademie-Textausgabe* (Berlin: Walter de Gruyter & Co., 1968), 3:440; trans. Werner S.
Pluhar as *The Critique of Pure Reason* (Indianapolis: Hackett Publishing Company,
1996), p. 486.

20. See Jacques Derrida, *Voyous: Deux essais sur la raison* (Paris: Galilée, 2003), pp.
124–25, nn. 1–2, 169, 187–88; trans. Pascale-Anne Brault and Michael Naas as *Rogues:
Two Essays on Reason* (Stanford, Calif.: Stanford University Press, 2005), pp. 85, nn.
51–52 [pp. 168–69], 120, 134–35; *L'université sans condition* (Paris: Galilée, 2001), pp.

as the interest of an *animal rationale:* to inscribe a whole Kantian discourse that is apparently so resistant to materialism, to vitalism, to empiricism, to utilitarianism, to relativist nominalism—transcribe it in the service of the Nietzschean-type perspective and perspectivism that we are evoking, at least by analogy, at this moment.

Because for Kant, the world of rational beings, the *mundus intelligibilis* as sovereign reign of ends (*Reich der Zwecke*) that Kant says is "possible"— well, as Kant says himself, it depends twice on an "as if" and on the *logos* of an analogy, i.e. on a *logos* as proportion. *On the one hand,* the formal principle of the maxims for any reasonable being who acts *as if* (*als ob*) he were a legislator is, "Act *as if* (als ob) your maxim were to serve at the same time as a universal law (for all rational beings)."[21] *On the other hand,* the reign of ends, and therefore of incalculable dignity, is possible only by analogy (*nach der Analogie*) with a reign of nature (*Reich der Natur*) at the very point where it is considered as a machine (*als Machine*), i.e. subject to the constraints of calculable laws. And each time one says *Reich (der Zwecke, der Natur)*, it is a question of reigning and therefore of a certain sovereignty.

Whence the decisive and enigmatic role that the *als ob* plays in the whole of Kantian thought, but particularly so around the regulative idea. The point is to consider the way phenomena are linked "*as if* they were the arrangements made by a supreme reason of which our reason is a faint copy (als ob *sie Anordnungen einer höchsten Vernunft wären, von der die unsrige ein schwaches Nachbild ist*)";[22] "*as if* this cause, as supreme intelligence, were the cause of everything, according to the wisest intention (als ob *diese als höchste Intelligenz nach der weisesten Absicht die Ursache von allem sei*)."[23] "For the regulative law of systematic unity wants us to study nature *as if* systematic and purposive unity—amid the greatest possible manifoldness—were everywhere to be found *ad infinitum* (als ob *allenthalben ins Unendliche sys-*

27–32, 67–79, and passim; trans. Peggy Kamuf as *The University without Condition,* in *Without Alibi* (Stanford, Calif.: Stanford University Press, 2002), pp. 209–15, 230–37, and passim.

21. Kant, *Grundlegung zur Metaphysik der Sitten,* in *Kants Werke: Akademie-Textausgabe,* 4:438; Derrida's emphasis; trans. Allen W. Wood as *Groundwork for the Metaphysics of Morals* (New Haven, Conn., and London: Yale University Press, 2002), p. 56; translation slightly modified.

22. Kant, *Kritik der reinen Vernunft,* 3:447; Kant's emphasis [p. 644; translation modified to reflect Kant's emphasis on "als ob"].

23. Ibid., p. 453; Kant's emphasis [p. 651].

tematische und zweckmäßige Einheit bei der großtmöglichen Mannigfaltigkeit angetroffen würde)."[24]

Let's say, as I did in *Rogues,* that I'm sometimes tempted to act "as if" I had no objections to Kant's "as if's." In *The University without Condition,* I addressed the difficult question of the "as if" in Kant and elsewhere, and proposed to think differently such an "as if."[25] I permit myself to refer you to those works.

The question of the world in Kant, and of the "as if" of the world, pushes me to point out to you at least one of the ways in which if we had time we could prolong our conversation with Kant, with a certain Kant. Which Kant? Not only the one who was without any doubt the principal, or one of the principal thinkers of the modern institutions of international law which, like the League of Nations, the UN or its Security Council, were designed to regulate in law the order of war and peace between nations, in the perspective of a treaty of perpetual peace (so much so that the trouble that is today shaking up the structures of this law and these institutions could also be interpreted as the placing in crisis of a certain Kantian spirit, if not a Kantian doctrine). No, the conversation that we would prolong with another Kant, is with the one who, in a particular text, said some very odd—and conjoined—things about war and about Robinson. This text is a short treatise, an opuscule on "The Beginnings of Human History" (*Muthmaßlicher Anfang der Menschengeschichte,* 1786; "Conjectures on the Beginnings of Human History"[26]). Read all of it, of course: there is a translation, at least in the little volume called *La philosophie de l'histoire.* This little text is interesting from our point of view, among a thousand other reasons, because it begins, from its opening lines, by posing the question of literary fiction. And thus of Robinson, for example, and his relation to philosophy. If, given the lacunae in our historical documentation concerning the origins of humanity, says Kant, one were to fill these lacunae by pure and simple conjectures, made up from whole cloth, one would merely be sketching out a fiction, no better than a novel (*nicht viel besser, als den Entwurf zu einem Roman zu machen*[27]). And such a work would not even merit the title of

373

24. Ibid., pp. 459–60 [p. 660]; Derrida's emphasis.

25. See above, note 20 to this session.

26. Kant, *Muthmaßlicher Anfang der Menschengeschichte* (1786), in *Kants Werke: Abhandlungen nach 1781,* vol. 8; trans. H. B. Nisbet as "Conjectures on the Beginnings of Human History," in *Kant's Political Writings,* ed. Hans Reiss (Cambridge: University of Cambridge Press, 1970 [2nd ed., 1991]).

27. Ibid., p. 109 [p. 221].

conjectural or hypothetical fiction, but that of pure novelistic fiction (*einer*
bloßen Erdichtung[28]). So one must make conjectures that are not *erdich-*
tet (poetically fictioned, if you will), but deduced from human experience.
Reread all that, it's gripping, up to the final Remark (*Schluß-Anmerkung*[29])
during which Kant enumerates all the sorrows, ills, sadnesses and regrets
that man can feel. And you will recognize in them all of Robinson's states of
mind. The first sorrow, which can turn to moral perversion, is to lament, to
worry about what in Divine Providence might be bad or threatening. This
was, remember, one of Robinson's temptations. Now to the contrary, says
Kant, one must not accuse divine providence and one must take upon oneself the ills that prevent humanity from improving, without palming them
off on destiny. This is basically the path that Robinson followed when, after
having doubted Divine Providence, he took charge of his destiny and began
to praise Christian Providence.

Second, and here it becomes more interesting, paradoxical and timely:
war. The greatest ills suffered by humanity are due to war, says Kant, or,
more precisely, incessant preparations in view of future war. States waste
their economic and cultural forces in these perpetual preparations, etc.
One could give too many budgeted illustrations today, of this blinding
self-evidence, more massive and determining than ever today. But what is
more original, in Kant, and gives us more to think about, is that he does not
simply condemn this ill, or, in any case, does not condemn it as a simple ill.
To the contrary, he notes that without this pressure toward virtual war (the
war one must prepare for, urgently, even and especially if one wants peace),
without this permanent urgency of war, states, cultures, classes and social
communities, and even their freedom, would suffer as a result. In other
words, it is the constant horizon of war that maintains state and social,
community and cultural cohesion, and it is the same horizon that ensures
a degree of freedom, in spite of restrictive laws. And Kant dares to write
this: "Therefore in the stage of culture that the human species has achieved,
war is still an indispensible means (*ein unentbehrliches Mittel*) of perfecting
it (*diese* [culture] *noch weiter zu bringen*)."[30] So war is indispensable to the
perfectibility of human culture (a pre-Hegelian discourse; cf. scientific and
other progress, etc.). War is thus the condition, the element, the essential
horizon of the state and organized society, of that artificial institution that,
as Kant always repeats, the state is. Without a horizon of war, the state no

374

375

28. Ibid.; Kant's emphasis.
29. Ibid., p. 120 [p. 231].
30. Ibid., p. 121 [p. 232; translation modified].

longer has any reason for being. The end of war is the end of the state. The reason of the state, and even Reason of State, is always what is called war. The state is in essence bellicose, bellicist, even belligerent. It is this relation to the virtual enemy, on which subject, from this point of view at least, Schmitt invented nothing. And Kant adds: "[. . .] and only when culture has reached its full development (*nach eine vollendeten Kultur*)—and only God knows when that will be (*Gott weiß wann*)—will perpetual peace (*ein immerwährender Friede*) become possible and of benefit [*heilsam:* comment[31]: immune, safe, sane] to us."[32]

The second subject of discontent (*Unzufriedenheit*) for humans is the brevity of life (*Kürze des Lebens*).[33] This is what makes this man sigh, "Ah, life will have been so short!" Now Kant, while noting that humans are childish enough to complain about death while being incapable of loving life, asks us to reflect on the number of injustices committed in the hope of future enjoyment (*Genuss*). Each time we look for enjoyment we commit an injustice, he seems to suggest. And so the longer life goes on, the more the desire for enjoyment is unjust, guilty of numerous injustices. And Kant then chooses a figure that sets me dreaming: and here it's no longer a nightmare. Kant wonders what would happen if a man (he says a man, not a woman, not taking any account of the fact that the difference in longevity and average life expectancy would make things worse still) lived, wait for it, to be . . . eight hundred years old and more. What then is Kant's piquant hypothesis? What is his profound hypothesis? Well, that in this case, at eight hundred and over, the father would no longer feel safe from his son (which would lead you to believe that before eight hundred he would feel more at ease; that's the celibate and childless Kant talking), at eight hundred and over, then, the father would no longer feel safe from his son, the brother from his brother, the friend from a friend, etc. They would all become more wicked and vicious, more inclined to vice (*Laster*) as they got older. Vice is a thing of old age, and to get old is to turn vicious. So Kant, that thinker of human perfectibility, was nevertheless convinced that things don't get better with age. One turns bad as one gets older, fathers toward sons, sons toward fathers, brothers and friends among themselves. This view is not so crazy. Not only because, as we can see every day, in so-called developed countries, the lengthening of life is becoming one of the central stakes of the political problem, the political war (the problem of retirement,

376

31. In the session, Derrida added nothing.
32. Ibid., p. 121 [p. 232].
33. Ibid., p. 122 [p. 232].

of how to maintain the funding of pension funds and the problem of generations of workers, is no longer a localizable problem, nor even one that is simply national and circumscribable; this is the central political nexus of all social-democrat capitalist societies in which Social Security and pensions are market indexed, indexed on insurance and savings and investments: that is the problem of the future for our capitalist societies in want of socialism); but also, this Kantian view is not so crazy, because it is possible that one becomes nasty as one gets older, once what is basically the Oedipal war outlined behind this apparently more or less delirious or fictive scene, is a scene that teaches us that it is better to get it all over as soon as possible, that as one gets older the war gets worse, and corrupts hearts and mores. You have to begin with orphanhood, pre-orphanhood and pre-fratricide. Otherwise it gets worse with age and from the earliest ages. Very rapidly and *a fortiori* when you get beyond one hundred. I am more and more convinced that centenarians are not safe from Oedipal crime. Why Kant speaks here only of fathers, sons and brothers, of friends in the masculine, that's a set of questions that I dealt with in *Politics of Friendship*.[34] I permit myself to refer you to it. What does Kant conclude from this hypothesis that has one dreaming, from this eight-hundred-year-old nightmare? Imagine someone experiencing as a nightmare the assurance he had received that he would live for over eight hundred years. Well, Kant tells us that if by some misfortune that happened, if all the men of humanity started to live past eight hundred years, it would be better to destroy the human race and swallow it up, it would be better to have this humanity doggedly pursuing gerontocratic enjoyment disappear, it would be better to make it disappear from the surface of the earth under a universal deluge (*in einer allgemeinen Überschwemmung*).[35] And Kant gives here the reference to Genesis, to the flood and Noah's Ark. This is an indispensable reference for reading this text of Kant's, because in it the question is first of all that of the age that God had in mind for men (120 years), and then of the vices of men that push God to repent for having created them, and especially of the age of Noah the Just at the time of the flood: according to Genesis, Noah was six hundred years old at the time. So Kant has added two little centuries to Noah's age, for good measure, as though six hundred were still OK, but eight hundred

377

---

34. See Jacques Derrida, "En langue d'homme, la fraternité . . . ," in *Politiques de l'amité,* pp. 253–99; also see, on Kant, pp. 302–6; trans. George Collins as "In Human Language, Fraternity . . . ," in *Politics of Friendship* (London: Verso, 1997), pp. 227–70, 273–75.

35. Kant, *Muthmaßlicher Anfang der Menschengeschichte,* p. 122 [p. 233].

too much. But after all, let's not forget, even though Kant takes no interest in this here, that Noah was also the one who sovereignly saved the animals and their descendence, two by two.

Is it surprising that after this allusion to the flood there should crop up in Kant's text the phantom or the silhouette of Robinson on his island? There is a third desire, a third wish (*Wunsch*) of humanity, says Kant. In truth, this desire (*Wunsch*) is merely empty nostalgia (*die leere Sehnsucht*).[36] So it really always has been the question of nostalgia as fundamental tonality of philosophy that has been occupying us from the beginning of this seminar, both in Heidegger and in Robinson, etc.—homesickness. Here nostalgia is empty because despairing in advance, incapable of acceding to its desire, and this is the silhouette or the phantom (*Schattenbild*) cultivated by the poets (so it is always the poetic *as if* that fascinates Kant in this text and elsewhere) of the golden age (*goldenen Zeitalters*) in which all imaginary needs would be satisfied: as natural needs, state of nature, equality and eternal peace among men, enjoyment of a life without concern, ease, reverie, childlike games, etc. Paradise, then . . . Now according to Kant, it is this nostalgia (*Sehnsucht*) that makes us find "Robinsons and voyages to the South Seas so seductive (*eine Sehnsucht, die die Robinson und die Reisen nach den Südseeinseln so reizend macht*)."[37] Kant, who is so Rousseauean in so many other respects, would never have praised Robinson the way Rousseau, as we saw, did so often as much on the level of pedagogy as of literature and philosophy. I will leave you to read the rest of Kant's text.

This year we have done our best to reinterpret all the Western and European interpretations of Robinson Crusoe, from Rousseau to Virginia Woolf, from Marx to Joyce, from Lacan to Deleuze (I'm no doubt forgetting some of those we quoted on Robinson). And since I just recalled that we talked about Marx, I am discovering, thanks to my friend Egidius Berns,[38] that the reference to Robinson Crusoe, before and after Marx, was a classical topos among many economists from the end of the seventeenth [*sic*] century and especially during the whole nineteenth century. This precise and argued reference to Robinson is present in all the manuals of political economy. Robinson is not only a model of education, but is still today an information manual and a novel of education for students of political economy, on the origin of exchange and use value, on labor, on stock raising, etc. As I can-

378

36. Ibid.
37. Ibid. [translation modified].
38. In the session, Derrida added: "who teaches political economy and philosophy at the University of Tilburg."

not dive into this now, I point out to those who might find this interesting
an article in *The New Palgrave: A Dictionary of Economics,* volume 4, which
379   includes in the article on *Robinson Crusoe* two very dense pages full of references to an enormous economic and political economic literature.[39]

But we should also have had to study, in a less European space, and one
not necessarily posterior to Defoe, a whole typology of analogous or ho-
mologous narratives. Noah's Ark is also the story of a sort of island where
a sort of new first man, amid the waters, starts over a sort of genesis, and
for whom the treatment of animality, of the reproduction of animal life, is
the very ordeal itself. I could have mentioned, for example, the story of *Hayy
ibn Yaqzan,* translated into English by Simon Ockley, and written in 1185
or in 581 AH by Abu Bakr ibn Tufayl.[40] This is the story of two islands, one
of which is inhabited and on which there appears a child, whether he was
born by spontaneous generation, or whether he arrived there like Moses
saved from the waters in a basket. This child is Hayy ibn Yaqzan, the living
son of Awake; he is suckled by a gazelle, and at the death of his nurse—the
gazelle, then—he is abandoned to himself, like Robinson, left to his own
devices. His gifts of intelligence, which are at first feeble, develop and allow him to dominate the wild beasts. By increasing his knowledge of the
physical universe and the world, he gains access to metaphysics and ends up
believing in the existence of a sovereign and all-powerful creator. Through
several stages of his ascetic practice, he seeks physical and spiritual union
with the One and the eternal Spirit. Up to the day when, having not yet met
a creature like himself, totally ignorant of the existence of other men in the
world, he is quite astonished to discover, walking toward him on the island,
a creature in his image. This is Asal, a holy man come from a neighboring
380   and civilized island reigned over by the sovereign Salaman, a good and wise
sovereign in a realm where life is ruled by a Koranic system of rewards
and punishments. Asal, who comes from this island, has attained a higher
degree of ascetic discipline than his fellow countrymen, and has decided to
withdraw to the solitude of this small island, which he wrongly believed to
be uninhabited. He teaches Hayy language, and is totally astonished to find
out that the *pure truth* that Hayy has reached is the same as that symbolized

39. See M. V. White, *"Robinson Crusoe,"* in *The New Palgrave: A Dictionary of Economics,* ed. John Eatwell, Murray Milgate, and Peter Newman (New York: Stockton
Press, 1987), 4:217–18.
40. Abu Bakr ibn Tufayl, *The History of Hayy ibn Yaqzan* (1708), translated from the
Arab by Simon Ockley, revised with an introduction by A. S. Fulton (London: Chap-
man and Hall, 1929).

by the religion he himself professes. Learning of the condition of people on the other island, Hayy, seized with compassion, decides to go and meet them — basically to preach. Asal accompanies him so as to introduce him. It's a total and sinister failure. The people understand nothing, remaining idolatrous and attached to the system of sanctions, rewards and punishments. Hayy rapidly understands that the way Mohammed teaches them according to the Koran (namely a crude system of rewards and punishments) was the only efficacious method. (Kant and Christianity as moral religion: develop.[41]) He excuses himself for this intrusion, exhorts them to be faithful to the religion of their fathers and returns with his friend Asal to the uninhabited island. Naturally there would be a very great deal to say about all the possible readings of this fiction, even from the point of view of Koranic exegesis. And above all about this concept of pure truth which is to be found at the middle of the narrative. It seems that there are on this subject very fine exegeses by Ibn Arabi, the Andalusian philosopher and mystic, who was somewhat trained and informed in Hellenism, via Plato, Aristotle and Averroes, especially about a thinking of the unconditioned (*anhupotheton*) in this narrative.

Was ist Welt? Here we are back again.

So Heidegger's gesture, which consists in inscribing all these questions about the animal in a problematic of the world, in the horizon of the question *Was ist Welt?* seems to be highly sensible, lucid, necessary and indispensable.

I'm not going to pass again along all the paths that we have followed, opened, or broken in the previous sessions. I shall merely content myself, for this quasi-final session, with emphasizing that these two texts that undeniably deal with solitude (*Einsamkeit*), of the isolation of man in a situation said, at least by way of fiction, to be originary — that these two texts have in common the presupposition of an absolute difference between beast and man, of a transcendence or of an emergence of the power of man (speech, technics, knowledge of beings as such, etc.). All of this goes without saying. Things get complicated however, when it comes to interpreting this power as *sovereignty*.

We have read, and I won't go back over it, more than one passage in *Robinson Crusoe* in which he expressly used theological and political language and rhetoric. Sometimes, and more than once, he compared himself jubi-

381

---

41. In the session, Derrida added nothing here.

lantly to a sovereign surrounded by his subjects of different religions on his island, on an island that was his kingdom; sometimes in his apprenticeship of Christian prayer, he spoke *of* God or *to* God as a sovereign or an absolute sovereign, all-powerful Providence, his own human and Robinsonian sovereignty being at one and the same time subject to divine sovereignty, and to its image. And the relation to savages as well as to women and beasts was the condescending, descending, vertical relation of a superior master to his slaves, other sovereign to his submissive subjects—submissive or submissible, mastered or to be mastered, by violence if need be—subjected.

Now in Heidegger, the undeniable eminence of Dasein compared to the animal poor in world, deprived of the power of speech, of the power to die, of the power of relating to beings as such, deprived both of *als-Struktur* and, I shall now say, of *Alsobstruktur* (this is basically what Lacan says with the stubbornness you're familiar with: the animal does not know how to feign feigning, nor how to lie or deceive, it does not have a true *Alsobstruktur*), this power of the *Weltbildend* man, capable of the *logos apophantikos* was not explicitly defined, by Heidegger, in the theological political figure of sovereignty, even if this value of *Vermögen,* of *Verhalten* as *Vermögen,* of power and power to configure the world and the totality of beings as such could make one think, without a word, of some sovereignty, and even if basically the glance cast by man on the animal resembles in many ways, like an invariant in sum, that of Robinson and so many others, from Descartes to Kant and to Lacan. At bottom, all these people, from Defoe to Lacan via Heidegger, belong to the same world in which the animal is cut from man by a multiple defect of power (speech, dying, signifier, truth and lie, etc.). What Robinson thinks of his parrot Poll is pretty much what Descartes, Kant, Heidegger, Lacan, and so very many others, think of all animals incapable of a true responsible and responding speech, of a *logos semantikos* and a *logos apophantikos.*

Now, having recalled this more than summarily, if I am insisting so much on the word *Walten,* and on all the striking occurrences of this verb (sometimes nominalized), throughout Heidegger's corpus after *Sein und Zeit,* this is because, appearing, as we have seen, in our seminar of 1929–30, these occurrences seem without doubt to appeal to a sovereignty of last instance, to a superpower that decides everything in the first or the last instance, and in particular when it comes to the *as such,* the difference between Being and beings, the *Austrag* we were talking about last week, but which appeals to a sovereignty so sovereign that it exceeds the theological and political—and especially onto-theological—figures or determinations of sovereignty.

Walten seems to be so sovereign, ultra-sovereign, in sum, that it would further be stripped of all the anthropological, theological and political, and thus ontic and onto-theological dimensions of sovereignty.

It is the point of this excess that matters to me: that of a sovereignty so sovereign that it overruns any historical configuration of an onto-theological and therefore also theologico-political type. This is why these last weeks I rather rushed toward the end, to this text from 1957, *Identität und Differenz,* which both put to work in a decisive place the word and motif of *Walten,* and precisely concerned the limits of onto-theology, of the constitution of the onto-theological (*Die onto-theo-logische Verfassung der Metaphysik,* as the title of this essay states), and thus the constitution of what is called the theologico-political which can only be *ontic,* by reference to the all-powerful God, cause and ground of beings, *causa sui.* Moreover, that would explain why Heidegger uses so infrequently, if indeed he uses it at all, the word and the political concept of *sovereignty*—his relation with Schmitt having remained, as I tried to show elsewhere,[42] extremely obscure and ambiguous. So the language of sovereignty, in the strictly political or theologico-political sense, would no longer suit him. No longer quite adequately, perhaps, because it would suit him all too well. *Walten* would be too sovereign still to be sovereign, in a sense, within the limits of the theologico-political. And the excess of sovereignty would nullify the meaning of sovereignty.

But what does "excess of sovereignty" mean, if sovereignty, in essence and by vocation, by its structure, signals and signifies itself primarily as excess itself, as normal abuse, surplus and transcendence beyond or compared with any determinable measure? Is there any possible excess of sovereignty or else is this hypothesis absurd? Absurd like sovereignty itself, which exceeds all responsibility of meaning, before meaning, before the law of language and meaning. Meaning and the law are summoned to appear before the sovereign rather than the other way round. This in any case is the hypothesis that orients the reading I began last time and that I would like, that I would have liked, to pursue more minutely today. As you see, late in my life of reading Heidegger, I have just discovered a word that seems to oblige me to put everything in a new perspective. And that is what happens and ought to be meditated on endlessly. If I had not conjoined in one problematic the beast *and* the sovereign, I wager that the force and organizing power of this German word that is so difficult to translate, but that informs,

383

42. See Derrida, *Politiques de l'amité,* pp. 102, n. 1, 143–48, 173, 189, n. 2, 274–79, 391–401 [pp. 107–8, n. 4, 122–25, 150, 170, n. 39, 245–49].

gives form to the whole Heideggerian text, would never have appeared to me as such. Any more than it has appeared, to my knowledge, to others.

I note in a way that is still preliminary that in *Introduction to Metaphysics* (1935), a course that was completely written out and that follows five years later the seminar we are reading this year, a superabundant use is made of the vocabulary of *Walten* (*durchwalten, Mitwalten, umwalten, verwalten, Verwaltung, Übergewalt, vorwaltend, bewältigen, unbewältigt, Gewalt,* and of course, *Allgewalt, Gewalt-tat* and *Gewalt-tätigkeit,* etc.). Now, I invite you to read a note by the translator Gilbert Kahn, who, in the translation published by PUF, made moving, heroic and desperate efforts, both clairvoyant and blind but always respectable, to translate this untranslatable. His translation of the *walten* family is dominated, one would be right to say, by the vocabulary and semantics <of> *domination,* precisely, of *dominium* ("perdominate" (neologism), "predominate," "circumdominate") and dominated too by the vocabulary of power ("potent," "prepotent," "prepotency"). The vocabulary of violence often imposes itself as an appropriate vocabulary to translate the same family of words in *walten,* and these words ("domination" and "potency," "power") indeed seem to signify what is understood in general by sovereignty (*superanus:* that which is above, hierarchically transcendent; and which dominates by force, violence, power). What is more, and here is the note I just announced, in the "index of German terms grouped by family" that is to be found at the end of *Introduction to Metaphysics,* one reads the following, even before the lexicology and taxonomy of meanings: "*Walten:* perdominate [which is obviously a neologism, basically meaning *dominate through and through, absolutely*] [. . .]"; and Kahn then opens a parenthesis which I'll read because, not fortuitously, the word "sovereignty" appears in it: "[. . .] (approximate signification: to hold sway sovereignly), to reign."[43] And Kahn refers to an example on page 34 of the translation which uses the words "reign" and "superiority," for *Waltet* and *Überlegenheit.*

I'll first quote the sentence, and then I'll say why the example appears to me to merit that one start with it and dwell on it a little. The translation says the following; I'm isolating this proposition:

> [. . .] in poetry (*in der Dichtung*) (the poetry that is authentic and great [*gemeint ist nur die echte und große;* which we understand to mean *only* the poetry authentic and great]) there reigns (*waltet*) an essential superiority of the

43. Gilbert Kahn, "Index des terms allemands groupés par families [index of German terms grouped by family]," in Martin Heidegger, *Introduction à la métaphysique,* trans. Gilbert Kahn (Paris: PUF, 1958), p. 237. [Translator's note: my translation.]

spirit with respect to all that is purely science (*eine wesenhafte Überlegenheit des Geistes gegenüber aller bloßen Wissenschaft waltet*).[44]

Let's mark a pause: what reigns (*waltet*), what imposes itself, what im-   *385* poses its power and its force and its potency (three words, "force," "power," "potency," that I use prudently, like the word "violence," for *walten* does not necessarily literally mean to reign, as Kahn translates it, if reign implies a royalty, nor to dominate, if to dominate implies a sovereign lord and master, nor force, power and potency and violence, although all these words (to reign — used by Kahn — to dominate, force, power, potency, violently impose oneself, etc.) are so many virtual connotations, potential, precisely, potentially potent, in every use of *walten*, even if these connotations are only connotations, confused contagions, but are neither centrally determining, nor essential, nor exhaustive — whence the need for prudence, whence the extreme difficulty of speaking and translating as close as can be to what here is trying to be thought in a language which is not just a national language, German, but the language of a discourse articulated once only by someone (Heidegger) who, with this language, makes a given sentence and not another, to say this and not that.

So, let us paraphrase with prudence and restraint: what in poetry rules and affirms its superiority, and thus its sovereignty, is *spirit;* and the sovereignty of spirit *waltet,* imposes itself, prevails, affirms itself above science, any simple science.

I choose to begin with this example for two reasons. First, because it is the first use of *walten* translated as "to reign in sovereign fashion" in Gilbert Kahn's glossary; but especially because the superiority, eminence or excellence of poetry, the spiritual sovereignty of poetry (a sovereignty already determined as spiritual, a concept one might judge still to be caught up in metaphysical or onto-theological oppositions (allow me to refer you here to what I said about it in 1987 in *Of Spirit*[45])), this spiritual sovereignty in any case marks the fact that the *Gewalt* of what *waltet* here is not a material, physical, biological or natural force, it is not a real potency, a potency of the thing. If there is sovereignty, superiority, excellence (*Überlegenheit*   *386* which *waltet*) in the poetic, it is of the order of spirit. And this defines spirit as much as it lets itself be defined by spirit. What is spirit? one will ask.

44. Martin Heidegger, *Einführung in die Metaphysik* (Tübingen: Max Niemeyer Verlag, 1976), p. 20 [*Introduction à la métaphysique,* p. 34]. [Translator's note: my translation.]

45. See Derrida, *De l'esprit,* pp. 131–56 [pp. 83–96].

Well, spirit is what prevails, what is superior, what rises and situates itself above (*Überlegenheit:* spirit is what in poetry *waltet* and whose *Überlegenheit waltet*). Sovereignty is spiritual. And all knowledge (that of the sciences but also that of philosophy) will be hierarchically subordinate to it.

The fold that must be re-marked here is that this poetic and spiritual sovereignty of language, as Heidegger will make clear immediately afterward, itself signs, in a sense, the untranslatable and idiomatic use of the word *walten* itself. It is a word and above all a writing gesture, a singular pragmatic use, signed by Heidegger who, presenting himself as a faithful thinking inheritor of the German language, is going ceaselessly to affirm and refine the vocabulary and syntax of *walten,* in defiance of all translatability, to designate what is most difficult and necessary to think, to know, namely, what? [*à savoir, à savoir quoi?*] Well, to know Being, the Being of beings, the difference (without difference), the *Unter-Schied* between Being and beings, and thus the *as such,* the apophantic, the *als-Struktur,* etc.

So as to mark clearly the continuity that interests me and before returning to the narrow context of this passage, let me recall very rapidly what we said at the end of the last session about the word *Austrag,* a word that itself is very poetic and singular in the use Heidegger makes of it, a word that is so difficult to translate and that bears all the weight of the thinking of bearing [*portée*], where it is a matter of Being and beings, and the Being of beings.

For, as you remember, it is *in* the *Austrag* that it *waltet:* "Im Austrag waltet Lichtung des sich verhüllend Verschließenden, welches Walten das Aus- und Zuienander von Überkommnis und Ankunft *vergibt.*"[46] In the *Austrag* (*in* the regulation, the conciliation, within the term, the terminating or determining bearing of the dispute among the different, between Being and beings, supervening and arrival), in the *Austrag* there *waltet* (the French translation says *prédomine* [predominates]) the lighting (*Lichtung*) of what closes itself off and veils itself: "which *Walten vergibt* (an extraordinary verb, I noted, here, which the French translation all but omits in saying simply, in place of '*welches Walten [. . .] vergibt,*' 'it is by this predominance that . . .')." Now *vergibt* means here as much *gives* as *provides, procures,* but also to make a mistake in giving, giving badly, misdeal and especially pardon (*vergeben,* to forgive[47]), an important value and non-negligible connotation where *Austrag* can also mean resolution of a conflict or a dispute, conciliation, reconciliation), and so, I pick up the quote again, "which *Walten vergibt* [gives, gives badly, pardons] the being apart and related, the one to the other, of

387

46. Heidegger, *Identität und Differenz,* p. 63; Derrida's emphasis.
47. [Translator's note:] This phrase appears in English in the text.

Supervening and Arrival [thus of Being and beings as such] (*welches Walten das Aus- und Zuienander von Überkommnis und Ankunft vergibt*)."[48]

We were asking what this *Walten* (verb and noun) means, naming as it does at once the event, the origin, the power, the force, the potency, the source, the movement, the process, the meaning, etc.—whatever one likes—of the ontological difference, the becoming-ontological-difference of the ontological difference, of the supervening of Being and the arrival of beings?

> *Die onto-theologische Verfassung der Metaphysik entstammt dem Walten der Differenz, die Sein als Grund und Seiendes als gegründet-begründendes aus- und zueinanderhält, welches Aushalten der Austrag vollbringt.* [The onto-theological constitution of metaphysics proceeds from the *Walten der Differenz* (a very risky French translation, we will see why, but it returns us to our question of sovereignty: "proceeds from the superior power of Difference"), which holds the one apart from the other and relates the one to the other Being as ground [foundation, *Grund*] and beings as grounded and thus justified in their founding, the *Aushalten* accomplished by the *Austrag*].[49]

388

After this reminder that has confirmed for us the heading of this Heideggerian thinking of *walten,* I return to the passage from *Introduction to Metaphysics* from which we set out. As always, I invite you to reread all of it, well beyond the passage that, for lack of time, I must extract. The word *walten,* as the *walten* of poetry that thus marks its spiritual superiority, appears here in the course of a meditation on nothingness (and this is not insignificant), and more precisely around the question that is the very origin of metaphysics: "why is there something rather than nothing?" Or more precisely, and here there already appears the difference between Being and beings that passes through the nothingness of nonbeing: "*Warum ist überhaupt Seiendes und nicht vielmehr Nichts?* [Why are there beings and not rather nothing?]."[50] After having insisted on the fact that this allusion to the nothing ("and not rather nothing") is not a redundant and useless adjunction to the question "why are they beings?"; after having shown that the naming of nothingness matters here, contrary to what is thought by the logic of logicians and the logician's interpretation of *logos* for which naming

48. Ibid., p. 63 [p. 65; translation modified].
49. Ibid., p. 69 [p. 71; translation modified].
50. Heidegger, *Einführung in die Metaphysik*, p. 1; trans. Gregory Fried and Richard Polt as *Introduction to Metaphysics* (New Haven, Conn., and London: Yale University Press, 2000), p. 1; translation modified.

the nothing is saying nothing, naming nothing; after having shown that this logician's or scientific interpretation of the *logos* corresponds to a hardened forgetting of Being (*Seinsvergessenheit*), Heidegger appeals to philosophy and poetry that belong to another domain, reign or rank than science; to the reign and rank of spiritual Dasein (*einem ganz anderen Bereich und Rang geistigen Dasein*).[51] To speak of the nothing, and therefore of nonbeing, and therefore already of Being as different from beings, although not other than beings—this the scientist cannot do, but the poet and the philosopher can. For the true discourse on the nothing, the true way of speaking about non-being (*das wahre Reden vom Nichts*)[52] always remains "strange," inhabitual. Here Heidegger does not say *unheimlich* but *ungewöhnlich*. And to give an example of this strange, inhabitual, poetic, sovereign and authentic saying of the nothing, Heidegger here refers to a literary work to which I would be tempted to give here rather special attention for several reasons. Four or five reasons at least.

1. First because the question is that of poetically saying the nothing, of course. And the nothing that encounters the nothing, in not being there, non Da-sein. (Naturally, Heidegger had abundantly spoken of all this in *Was ist Metaphysik?* (1929), around anxiety and the origin of negation.[53])

2. Next, because in this poetic or literary quotation that says the nothing, well, the landscape that gives its tonality, the world on the horizon, is not an island, the sea or the ocean, but the mountain, a landscape or horizon closer to Heidegger than to Robinson.

3. Next, because the predicate of sovereignty or superiority (*Überlegenheit*) is granted not to potency but to a certain impotence (*Ohnmacht*).

4. Because Heidegger quotes a contemporary and non-German writer, which is extremely rare for him and therefore all the more symptomatic.

5. Because the contemporary, non-German writer, quoted and admired in 1935 by Heidegger, the one who speaks so well and has such a true discourse on the nothing, is none other than the great Norwegian Knut Hamsun—whose genius we are not denying if we recall his pro-Nazi commitments and his proximity to Quisling which have meant that he has become a painful heritage for his country, something that is clear

389

390

51. Ibid., p. 20 [p. 28].
52. Ibid.
53. Heidegger, *Was ist Metaphysik?*, in *Wegmarken* (Frankfurt am Main: Vittorio Klostermann, 1967); trans. David Farrell Krell as "What Is Metaphysics?," in Martin Heidegger, *Basic Writings: From* Being and Time (1927) *to* The Task of Thinking (1964), ed. David Farrell Krell (New York: Harper & Row, 1977).

to anyone approaching Norway still today, its culture, its literature and its politico-literary memory. (Read and comment *Introduction to Metaphysics*)

> True talk of Nothing (*Das wahre Reden vom Nichts*) always remains unfamiliar (*bleibt immer ungewöhnlich*). It dissolves, to be sure, if one places it in the cheap acid of a merely logical cleverness. This is why we cannot begin to speak about Nothing immediately, as we can in describing a picture, for example. But the possibility of such speech about Nothing can be indicated. Consider a passage from one of the latest works of the poet Knut Hamsun, *The Road Leads On* (*Nach Jahr und Tag* (1934)). The work belongs together with *The Wayfarer* (*Der Landstreicher*) and *August* (*August Weltumsegler*). *The Road Leads On* depicts the last years and the end of this man August, who embodies the uprooted, universal know-how of today's humanity, but in the form of a Dasein that cannot lose its ties to the unfamiliar, because in its despairing powerlessness (*in seiner verzweifelten Ohnmacht*) it remains genuine and superior (*echt und überlegen bleibt*). In his last days, this August is alone in the high mountains. The poet says, "He sits here between his ears and hears true emptiness (*Er sitzt hier mitten zwischen seinen Ohren und hört die wahre Leere*). Quite amusing, a fancy (*Ganz komisch, ein Hirngespinst*). On the ocean (earlier, August often went to sea) something stirred (at least), and there, there was a sound, something audible, a water chorus. Here — nothing meets nothing and is not there (*Hier — trifft Nichts auf Nichts und ist nicht da*), there is not even a hole (*ist nicht einmal ein Loch*). One can only shake one's head in resignation (*Mann kann nur ergebungsvoll den Kopf schütteln*)."[54]

As I have to conclude as quickly as possible, I will not be able to undertake with the required precision and proximity the work of reading and interpretation of the semantic, syntactic and lexical network of *Walten,* at least in *Introduction to Metaphysics,* in which this network is peculiarly rich and plentiful. I am sure that if you want to, you can do it without me. I shall be content, from a point of view that is rather taxonomic or topographical, to situate, to classify too schematically (promising myself to come back to this next year), some of the most strategic places. 391

I shall begin, as we were just speaking of the poetical, with what is said about the chorus in Sophocles's *Antigone* and its opening lines which are usually translated thus: "Manifold is the uncanny, yet nothing / uncannier than man bestirs itself, rising up beyond him [after which are named the sea, the earth, the beasts, etc.: *polla ta deina, Vielfältig das Unheimliche, nichts*

---

54. Heidegger, *Einführung in die Metaphysik,* pp. 20–21 [pp. 28–29]. The German quotations inserted in this passage have been transcribed from the recording of the session.

doch / über den Menschen hinaus Unheimlicheres ragend sich regt [. . .]]."⁵⁵ On the basis of the translation of *deinon* (terrible, worrying, strange) by *unheimlich,* and before replying to the question of knowing why one would translate *deinon* as *unheimlich,* Heidegger declares that *deinon* designates the frightening, the terrible (all of this can also be read as a discourse on terror, terrorism, and even state terrorism), but conceived in the sense of "überwältigende Waltens," the "prepotent predominance," as Kahn translates it, which provokes panic, anguish, respectful fear (shock and awe,⁵⁶ as Bush would say). *"Das Gewaltige, das Überwältigende ist der Wesenscharakter des Waltens selbst":*⁵⁷ an apparently redundant but not tautological formula to say that the *über* forms part of the *Walten,* to say that, pretty much following Kahn's translation, the violent, the prepotent, and thus what is superlatively more violent, predominant in violence, is the constitutive essential character of the dominance that is itself predominant potency. In its eruption, *Walten* can retain in itself *(an sich halten)* its prepotent potency (kann [underlined] *es seine überwältigende Macht an sich halten*),⁵⁸ but by holding it back it is all the more terrible and distant, and anything but harmless [*inoffensif*] *(harmlos)*.

But on the other hand, *deinon* signifies the *Gewaltige,* the violent, in the sense of the one who uses violence, who not only has it at his disposal but is himself *gewalt-tätig,* so that this violence characterizes not only his acts, his action, but his existence, his Da-sein, the there of his being-there. At that moment, Heidegger explains to us that he is giving to *Gewalt-tätigkeit,* to violent activity, no longer the usual sense of arbitrary brutality or violation, but a sense that goes beyond this usual interpretation. There is a *Gewalt* of Dasein which is not this violence of brutal violation.

For beings as a whole are, as *Walten,* "das Überwältigende," *deinon* in the first sense. Beings are violent, per-dominant and pre-potent. Thus there is

55. Ibid., p. 112 [p. 156].
56. [Translator's note:] This phrase appears in English in the typescript.
57. Ibid., p. 115 [pp. 159–60]. In the session, Derrida translated this passage as follows: "The *Gewalt,* the violent, the more than violent, *Überwältigende,* the prepotent, more than powerful, overpowering is the character of the essence of *Walten* itself. In other words, the 'more' is the essential character of *Walten."* [Translator's note: The English translation reads: "The violent, the overwhelming is the essential character of the sway itself."]
58. Ibid., p. 115 [p. 160]. In the session, Derrida translated this passage as follows: *"Walten* can retain in itself its overpowering power." [Translator's note: The English translation reads: "When the sway breaks in, it *can* keep its overwhelming power to itself."]

no longer any limit to this definition of *Walten* as *Überwältigende*. It is as if *to be beings* and *Walten* were the same thing, with this overdetermination of the "over," precisely, this overbidding of the *Über*, of the extra, the excess of trans-potency, the pre-potency in the sense of the prevailing that wins out in a combat. If there is no longer any limit and if the whole of beings is, as *Walten, das Überwältigende*, one will not be surprised to find this *Walten* and this *Überwältigende* everywhere (and as I believe I shall not have time, let me point out at least that you can see it extend as much to the *logos*, precisely, as to *physis*).

Well, man also is *deinon* (*unheimlich*) inasmuch as, belonging in his essence to Being, he remains exposed (*ausgesetzt*) to this *Überwältigende*. He is thus doubly *deinon* (this is why he is the most *unheimlich*): he is violent inasmuch as he is exposed to the violence of *Walten*, of beings, and in as much as he is in a position to exercise this violence himself, to do violence. I leave you to read all these pages that deploy these semantics with great lexical wealth; you'll find many things in them, still in the reading of Sophocles (it is both a literal reading of Sophocles and a powerful, super-powerful Heideggerian appropriation-translation), on the elements, animals, states, this value of the state to which I would have liked to have time to give special attention here. Etc.

And I jump too rapidly to this passage in which, analyzing Sophocles's text as a speaking of the beginning (compare it with the text from Kant, as different as can be, on the nonscientific, conjectural, but nonfictional beginnings of history)—a speaking of the beginning that is not a science of nature, but, says Heidegger, a "mythology" in the least pejorative and least primitive sense of the term—Heidegger recalls that the first strophe and its antistrophe name the sea, the earth, and the animal in so far as they constitute the *Überwältigende*, what the *Gewalt-tätige*, in all its *Übergewalt*, makes burst open into the *Offenbarkeit* (translate and comment).[59] Then in the second strophe, the question is that of the characterization of man; but what in man comes down to nomination, language (*Nennen, Sprache*), to comprehension (*Verstehen*), to *Stimmung*, to passion or to building (*Bauen*), so many things denied to the animal, all that belongs to the *überwältigenden Gewaltigen*, no less than do the sea, the earth and the animal. The difference—and here two new verbs from the same family appear—is that *this* (*dieses*, namely the sea, the earth, the beasts, everything that is not human

393

59. In the session, Derrida added: "makes burst open in the Open. It is a super-violence which makes all these things appear in the Open, *Offenbarkeit*, in the openness [*l'apérité*]."

in the world) *umwaltet* man, "circum-dominates" him, as Kahn translates it, surrounds him with its power or besieges him with its violence or with power, *den Menschen umwaltet und trägt, bedrängt und befeuert,*[60] surrounds him with its power, carries him, oppresses him, inflames him, whereas *that*
394 (*Jenes*, speech, nomination, *Stimmung,* passion, what he does not share with the elements — earth, sea, fire, and animals), *durchwaltet als solches,*[61] grips him with its violent predominance, and grips him with this *Walten* as such, as the very thing that man, *als das Seiende, das er selbst ist,* as the being that he is himself, *eigens zu übernehmen hat,* must properly assume. The violence that grips man is indeed that of the *as such* of beings that Dasein is and that he must take upon himself, in its *Walten,* as such. This *Durchwaltende* loses nothing of its *Überwältigende* because of the fact that man takes it on and takes it directly into his power (*Gewalt*). This only hides the uncanniness, the *Unheimliche* of language (*das Unheimliche der Sprache*).[62] And Heidegger adds that *die Unheimlichkeit dieser Mächte,* the familiar worry, the worrying familiarity of these powers, of these potencies, resides in the fact that these powers and these potencies appear precisely to be reliable, domesticated in familiarity. But what one forgets in that case is that man is seized, gripped, *durchwalten* by the *Gewalt* of this *Walten,* and it is because one forgets this and attributes to this man, as to a subject, the initiative or the invention of language, of comprehension etc. — this is why man has paradoxically become a stranger (*uneinheimisch* this time)[63] to his own essence. Because he believes he is the author, the master and possessor, and the inventor of these powers, he ignores the fact that he is first of all gripped, seized, that he must take them on, and he then becomes basically a foreigner — this is the whole story — to his own *Unheimlichkeit.*

The definition that Heidegger then gives of the ipseity of the self-same (*das "sich selbst"*) is linked to this effractive departure from self in order violently to break open, to capture, to tame (*Ausbrechen, Umbrechen, Einfangen, Niederzwingen*). It is through this violence that breaks open ground or path, captures, tames, that beings are discovered or revealed or unveiled, and ap-
395 pear *as* sea, *as* earth, *as* animal — the *as* is three times emphasized (als *Mer,* als *Erde,* als *Tier*).[64] The *als,* the *als-Struktur* that distinguishes man from the animal is thus indeed what the violence of *Walten* makes possible. And one

60. Ibid., p. 119 [p. 166].
61. Ibid. [p. 166: "pervades [man] in its sway"].
62. Ibid., p. 120 [p. 166].
63. In the typescript: "unheimisch".
64. Ibid., p. 120 [p. 167].

will not be surprised to recognize this same violence in the *Gewalttätigkeit des dichterischen Sagens,* in the violence of poetic saying, *des denkerischen Entwurfs,* the project of thinking, the thinking project, *des bauenden Bildens,* the edifying image (and the *Weltbilden* of the world for man, as man himself, unlike for the animal, is also a *Bilden*), and finally, what I would have liked to analyze more closely here of *des staatschaffenden Handelns,* the action that creates states.[65]

All of this does not depend on a *Vermögen,* on a power, on a faculty that man has at his disposal, but consists in taming and joining (*Bändigen und Fügen*) forces or violences (*Gewalten*) that come to grip man and thanks to which beings are discovered *as such.* This *Erschlossenheit* of beings, this patency of beings as such, is a *Gewalt* that man must master (*bewältigen*) so that in this *Gewält-tätigkeit,* he may be himself, among beings, historical (*geschichtlich*). For all of this concerns the historicality reserved to Dasein and to Being, denied to the animal and to the other forms of life. There is historicality of man (and not of the animal) only where the *Gewalt* of this *Walten* irrupts to make beings as such appear, in the middle of which man is gripped by violence.

Now, during the vacation (to which you are aspiring more and more with each passing second), you can reread, beyond what I can do here with you, the whole of *Introduction to Metaphysics,* and re-inscribe a passage such as this in a network of texts that are different, rich, but consistent with this one on the subject of *Walten* as *physis,* as *logos* ("the λόγος" says Heidegger "has the character of *Durchwalten,* of the φύσις"[66] [he also says that δικέ, justice is *überwältigend*];[67] "and even, in the end, *Walten* as *eidos* or *idea,* when Being, to know *physis,* after the dehision of *logos* and of *physis,* receives the predominant name of *idea* or of *eidos* (*Für das Sein* (φύσις) *drängt sich* [imposes itself] *am Ende als maßgebender und* vorwaltender *Name das Wort* ἰδέα, εἶδος, "*Idee,*" *vor*)"[68] (translate)).[69] How does one impose names, that is one of our great questions. From then on, says Heidegger, the interpretation of Being as idea dominates (*beherrscht*) the whole of Western thought, up to Hegel and beyond.[70] And the idealism that then dominates Western meta-

396

65. Ibid.
66. Ibid., p. 102 [p. 142].
67. Ibid., p. 123 [p. 171].
68. Ibid., p. 137 [p. 192]; Derrida's emphasis.
69. In the session, Derrida translated the passage as follows: "For Being (φύσις), Being is φύσις, imposes on itself an end, as a name which gives the measure, which is *vorwaltender,* predominant, hegemonic, the word ἰδέα, εἶδος, idea."
70. Ibid.

physics through and through is a determination of violence. Ideology (*eidos* plus *logos*) and idealism are not innocent, one must recognize their violence. It is through war that idealism too imposed its interpretation of Being, a war for the victory of an idea, of the idea of idea, of the intelligible as *eidos*, i.e. as visible object. It would suffice that you give me a few more hours for us to be able to deduce from all that both the superarmament of ideology and idealism, and its inseparability from the televisual image relayed by satellite. Think about it when you're watching television.

I would like to end, if you'll give me one more second, on a single final quotation from Heidegger that could be given many readings and that I leave you to appropriate as you wish as you watch the war on television, in Iraq, but also closer to us. Heidegger writes this, which seems to mark the absolute limit of *Gewalt* or of *Gewalt-tätigkeit*. It's about what will basically have been besieging this seminar, behind the cohort of cremators and in-humers of every order, and other guardians of the mourning to come: death itself, if there be any, was our theme. Heidegger writes this, but I'm not sure that I will read it as he writes it or interpret it as he auto-interprets it — we would have to reconstitute the whole passage: "*Nur an* einem [underlined] *scheitert alle Gewalt-tätigkeit unmittelbar* (There is only *one* thing against which all violence-doing, violent action, violent activity, immediately shatters)." Notice that, as much as the failure and limit of violence, of the out-bidding of *Walten,* of *Gewalt,* what seems to count here is immediacy, what is immediate in this limit that imposes failure on *Gewalt* and *Walten* (*unmittelbar* is the last word). (Repeat German and French) "*Das ist der Tod* (it is death)."[71]

The question, that was the question of the seminar, remains entire: namely that of knowing who can die. To whom is this power given or denied? Who is capable of death, and, through death, of imposing failure on the super- or hyper-sovereignty of *Walten?*

397

71. Ibid., p. 121 [p. 168].

INDEX OF NAMES

[Translator's note:] The index is based on that provided in the French edition, and is restricted to the main body of the text. I have attempted to aerate the entries for Heidegger and Defoe by removing references to incidental occurrences of their names and by providing subentries.

Ricardo, David, 25
Rousseau, Jean-Jacques, 18, 20–25,
    31, 64–69, 80, 85, 87, 143, 158, 199,
    275
Rumsfeld, Donald, 260

Schmitt, Carl, 7, 21, 24, 45, 273, 279
Selkirk, Alexander, 14
Sévigné, marquise de, 249
Shakespeare, William, 15, 17, 129, 153
Sharon, Ariel, 260
Smith, Adam, 25
Socrates, 113, 153
Sophocles, 285, 287
Spinoza, Baruch, 208
Stalin, Joseph, 167

Taminiaux, Jacques, 119
Tournier, Michel, 26
Trakl, Georg, 96

Uexküll, Jakob von, 109

Valéry, Paul, 78
Veronica, Saint, 172

Williams, John, 14
Wills, David, 10, 237
Wolfe, Cary, 237
Woolf, Virginia, 4, 14, 17, 24, 31, 33,
    158, 275

Younger, Stuart J., 162

MICHEL LISSE

is a researcher at the Fonds national de la recherche scientifique in Belgium and professor at the Université catholique de Louvain.

MARIE-LOUISE MALLET

holds the agrégation in philosophy and has been a program director at the Collège international de philosophie.

GINETTE MICHAUD

is professor in the Département des littératures de langue française at the Université de Montréal.

GEOFFREY BENNINGTON

is Asa G. Candler Professor of Modern French Thought at Emory University.